Coaching Basketball's Zone Attack

Using Blocker-Mover Motion Offense

Kevin Sivils

KCS Basketball Enterprises, LLC

KATY, TEXAS

Copyright © 2015 by **Kevin Sivils**

All rights reserved. No part of this publication may be reproduced, distributed or transmitted in any form or by any means, without prior written permission.

Sivils, Kevin/KCS Basketball Enterprises, LLC.
21211 Park Willow DriveStreet Address
Katy, Texas 77450
www.kcsbasketball.com

All photographs by Jeremy Yutzy of Yutzy Photography unless otherwise noted.

Book Layout © 2014 BookDesignTemplates.com

Coaching Basketball's Zone Attack: Using Blocker-Mover Motion Offense/ Kevin Sivils. -- 1st ed.
ISBN-13: 978-1519197917
ISBN-10: 1519197918

The information provided in this book is on an "as is basis." The author and publisher shall have neither the liability nor the responsibility to any person or entity with respect to loss, damages or injury arising form the information contained in this book.

Contents

Using This Book	1
Why Attack Zone Defense With Blocker-Mover Motion Offense?	3
The Father of Blocker-Mover Offense – Coach Dick Bennett	9
The TEAM Concept and Zone Attack Offense	11
You Get What You Emphasize	13
What is Good Offense?	15
Key Offensive Fundamentals	19
Common Types of Zone Defenses	21
Strengths and Weaknesses of Common Zone Defenses	25
Why Does the Opponent Play a Zone Defense?	31
All Zones Become a 2-3 Zone	33
The Mental Approach to Attacking a Zone Defense	43
Zone Attack Principles – Offensive Building Blocks	45
Spacing and Gaps	47
Move the Ball and Move People	55
Penetration	59
Use of the Dribble to Attack	61
Screen the Zone	67
The Inside Game Against the Zone	77
Planning to Rebound and Floor Balance	81
Principles of Attacking – Strategy and Attacking a Zone Defense	85
Adapting Blocker-Mover Motion for Zone Attack Offense	89
Alignments Versus Zone Defense	125
Attacking the Gaps of Zone Defense With Blocker-Mover	133

Distort the Zone Defense	**141**
Take the Defender Away (Use of Dribble to Attack)	**147**
Overload the Zone Defense	**153**
Blocker-Mover Zone Attack Motion Using Screening Concepts	**157**
Use Fakes to Freeze and Shift the Zone Defense	**181**
Putting It All Together	**183**
Applying Zone Attack Principles to an Existing Zone Attack Offense	**215**
Thoughts on Teaching and Practicing Zone Attack Offense	**221**
Thoughts on Teaching and Practicing Blocker-Mover Zone Attack	**223**
Drills to Teach Key Offensive Fundamentals	**233**
Drills to Teach Zone Attack Principles and Concepts	**269**
Lagniappe	**295**
About the Author	**299**
Contact the Author	**301**

Using This Book

At every coaching clinic I have ever attended the coaches present have wanted information about attacking zone defenses. It is a topic both veteran and new coaches are interested in.

As a young coach I struggled to help my teams effectively attack zone defenses. The information in this book is a result of years of effort on my part to learn effective principles of offense for use against attacking those pesky zone defenses.

A significant portion of this book is about adapting the Blocker-Mover Motion Offense to attacking a zone defense. ***The rest of the book is really about taking the zone offense you run and making it more effective by adding the zone attack principles and tactics that will best fit your particular zone attack offense, your personality as a coach and the personnel available for your team.***

Some coaches are leery of changing the offense they have learned and had some success with. I am not asking you to throw the baby out with the bathwater. Take what ideas you think will work and add them to what you already teach.

One of the chapters in this book is dedicated to providing ideas on how to go about taking a simple zone attack offense and adding some of the principles described in this book. Also included are drills designed to teach some of the essential fundamentals for sound offensive play.

If you have any questions about attacking zone offense and would like more information, just check the page with information for contacting me, the author, and I will do my best to answer any question you might have.

Much of the content of this book has appeared in my previous book ***Fine Tuning Your Zone Attack Offense.*** I strongly believe in using sound offensive principles to attack any defense. This book is full of sound zone attack concepts, any of which can be used to run Blocker-Mover Motion Offense as a zone attack offense or to improve any other zone attack offense you as a coach may already use and feel more comfortable with.

1
Why Run Blocker-Mover Offense to Attack a Zone?

Set plays, continuity based offense or rules based free-lance offense? The argument has been raging among basketball coaches since Dr. Naismith invented the game of basketball. Both approaches to the game have their advantages and disadvantages.

The inventor of Blocker-Mover offense, Coach Dick Bennett, has long been an advocate of Motion Offense and all the benefits of running this type of offensive system. The creation of Blocker-Mover hails back to Coach Bennett's days as the head coach at University of Wisconsin-Green Bay.

Every offense is more efficient with better players. Coach Bennett's challenge while at UW-Green Bay was how to win with only a few good players. Many of his athletes were of a D-II caliber or were converts from other sports. His son, Tony, was the lone exceptional player.

The answer for Coach Bennett was the creation of the **Blocker-Mover offense**, an offense he claims is rooted in his love for and fascination with the Green Bay Packers.

The offense is based on the idea of running as simple a version of motion as possible with specific responsibilities for positions while at the same time providing as much flexibility as possible. Bennett decided to use only two positions, blockers and movers.

Other well-known coaches liked the **Blocker-Mover** enough to create their own hybrid versions. The Blocker-Mover is believed to have influenced Coach Knight's thinking in regards to his "pairs" version of motion offense. Coach Don Meyer developed what he called Screeners-Cutters and openly attributed a great deal of the conceptual ideas behind this as coming from Bennett's Blocker-Mover.

I first used the Blocker-Mover out of necessity, for the same reasons Coach Bennett first created the offense. I had a good point guard and one good offensive player with a lot of hard working role players. The Blocker-Mover gave us a way to create shots for our best player and yet be very adaptable. Since we already ran Motion Offense, it was a logical adaptation.

Why Coaches Like Blocker-Mover Motion Offense

The Best of Both Worlds

Coach Bennett's creation is a mild compromise between the certainty and control of set plays or continuity offenses while retaining the random and free-lance nature of rules based offense. Bennett accomplished this through the use of alignments and Blocker areas.

One Offense for Everything

Well, sort of. Blocker-Mover can attack any variation of man-to-man defense, hybrid defenses such as a box and one or a triangle and two and with some alteration in tactics, a fair number of zone defenses.

This leaves more practice time to work on fundamentals, fast break, shooting or defense. It increases player confidence due to familiarity. They do not have to learn a new offense just to face a particular defense for one game.

Efficient Use of Practice Time

Fundamentals are critical to the success of Blocker-Mover offense, particularly the fundamentals of screening and cutting. The same is true for every other effective offensive system but, sadly, most coaches don't pay attention to the details of cutting and screening, thereby reducing the effectiveness of the offense they teach.

With careful planning and drill selection, all drills used to work on Blocker-Mover offense and the fundamentals of cutting and screening can be used to work on both half court offense and fundamentals at the same time, making more efficient use of practice time.

Difficult for Opponents to Scout

Every time the offense runs Blocker-Mover in a single half court offensive possession, it is unique. Less knowledgeable opponents present to scout leave with little to go on or believing they have to prepare for 40-50 well executed set plays.

Teaching Game Instead of Teaching Plays

For Motion Offense in general and Blocker-Mover in particular to work, the coach must teach players how to play the game of basketball instead of how to run set plays.

High Degree of Carryover

Installing Blocker-Mover offense takes time. Once players learn how to run the offense, the level of retention is high. Without realizing it, players will run the offense when playing pick-up games, games during open gym or other unstructured situations. Why? They have learned how to play basketball instead of running set plays.

This absorption of the concepts of offensive basketball means when it is time to begin the next pre-season, the returning players have a much higher degree of offensive readiness than most players. Your team will be further along in preparation for early season games due to the high degree of carryover from one season to the next.

Player Coaches on the Court

Smart players are essential for high-level success in the game of basketball. Running an offense like Blocker-Mover forces players to become students of the game, to think like coaches on the court. It also forces coaches to do a great job of teaching the game of basketball, not just how to run set plays.

Adaptability During Games

Things always come up during games. They just do. With Blocker-Mover offense it is not necessary to invent a new play during the game. Simply communicate with players what offensive building blocks to use or change alignments to attack the opportunities the defense is presenting.

On the surface, it may appear like major adjustments have been made. The reality is a shift in focus on how to attack has been made. Since the players have developed an understanding of offense, a change in alignment or restriction on offense helps them focus on how to attack the opportunities the defensive pressure is creating (All defensive pressure is vulnerable. If the defense takes something away, it must give something up.).

Why Players Like Blocker-Mover Offense

Blocker-Mover Maximizes a Player's Abilities

Players with limited skills but good basketball IQ can be significant contributors in the Blocker-Mover system. Blockers must be intelligent players but do not necessarily have to have a complete basketball skill set, just a willingness to put the team first and recognize limits

Movers are freed up to attack and best take advantage of their offensive skills. They are not limited to the confines of a set play or a continuity offense.

Skilled offensive players can be either Blockers or Movers, depending on how their skills can be best put to use for the benefit of the team.

Blocker-Mover Gives Players Freedom

Once players have learned to run Blocker-Mover, they are free, within the rules of the offense, to be as creative as they desire, so long as it is for the benefit of the team.

Blocker-Mover Provides Structure

While many players love the freedom a Motion Offense provides, they struggle with the lack of structure set plays and continuity offense provides. These players prefer the rigid nature of set offense.

Blocker-Mover is a compromise between the two approaches. The use of alignments that assign areas to Blockers provide enough structure that these players can adapt and flourish will not losing the random nature of a pure Motion Offense.

Players Can Play Every Position

Within limits, any type of Motion Offense allows players to play every position. Granted, the best ball handler will still bring the ball up and the best shooter will take most of the shots, etc, players can play a variety of positions and move to different areas on the court. Even though the Blockers are confined to their areas, they have the freedom to move about as necessary within the assigned area.

Players Must Learn Every Skill

There will always be position specific skills in the game of basketball, regardless of the offense used. Blocker-Mover requires every player to be able to dribble the ball twice, pass and catch, shot lay-ups, set and receive screens and to cut correctly. Every player must master these skills and the underlying movement skills to execute the skills correctly. As players improve their skill level, they experience an increase in confidence through demonstrated ability as well as more fun playing the game of basketball.

The Cons of Running Blocker-Mover Offense

Thinking Player's Offense – Do You Have High Basketball IQ Players?

This is a thinking player's offense, and for that matter a thinking coach's offense. Players have to be able to see what opportunities and challenges the defense is presenting and then act accordingly. This means you as the coach must be a great teacher and you have to learn to trust your players.

One Selfish Player Can Destroy the System

This is true of any type of offensive system, but in a rules based offense, one selfish player who refuses to operate within the boundaries of the offense and instead does as that player pleases, chaos will soon follow. If you have a player, or players, who are not willing to put the team first at all times, this is not the offense for your program at this time.

Players Must Master and Use Fundamentals

Every offensive system is at the mercy of the quality of the execution of basic fundamentals, but this fact is multiplied in effect with rules based offenses. A missed screen in a continuity offense can be covered up as the players continue to execute the continuity. Over dribbling in a set play means the offense will have to reset and attack again. Neither is a desirable outcome, but nor are they the end of the game. In a motion-based offense, failure to execute fundamentals correctly at game speed for the welfare of the team means the offense will quickly bog down and fail.

Are You a Great Teaching Coach?

This is an offensive system that requires constant teaching and re-teaching. Are you as the coach up to the challenge? There are coaches who are great motivators, game managers or good at the promoting a program and attracting quality players yet are not great at teaching the game of basketball. Be honest with yourself about your ability to teach the game.

You Have to Let Go

Running Blocker-Mover effectively means no steady diet of calling set plays from the sideline. You have to let your players run the offense and make the decisions of how to attack the defense. Can you give up the bulk of control over the offense during games to your players? Your control is during practice when you are teaching and able to apply restrictions.

Blocker-Mover Offense Against Zone Defense

Mention motion offense and most coaches think in terms of attacking a man-to-man defense. Motion offense is an effective offense to attack any zone with so long as some simple adjustments are made. In the case of Blocker-Mover offense, there are many advantages in making the needed adjustments. Alignments can be used to distort the zone or line up in the gaps. The basics of movement, hunting for opportunities (gaps and screens), balancing the floor and maintaining spacing are very similar. The carry over from attacking man-to-man defense to attacking a zone defense is considerable, maximizing teaching and practice time.

Pros of Using Blocker-Mover Against a Zone Defense

Alignments are the Same for Attacking Every Defense

Players use the same alignments and start from the same positions, regardless of the defense being attacked. The less the offense has to remember, the more freedom players have to play.

The Rules Are Almost Identical

The players learn one set of rules to attack any defense, requiring only a few adjustments to be made to attack any given type of defense, zone, hybrid or man-to-man defense.

Blocker-Mover Alignments Allow for Immediate Attack of Gaps

The basic alignments of Lane-Lane, Top-Bottom and Lane-Wide allow the offense to immediately line up in gaps of a zone defense. The freedom to attack from a familiar alignment based on assigned areas of the Blocker-Mover offense makes adjusting to any zone defense to start the offense easy.

Blocker-Mover Alignments Allow for Immediate Distortion of Zone Defenses

The nature of the alignments used in Blocker-Mover allow for easy distortion of any zone defense before the offense starts attacking.

Blocker-Mover Rules Encourage Screening a Zone Defense

Too few zone attacks take advantage of the benefits of screening a zone defense. The hardest defensive tactic for man-to-man defense to defend is the combination of a correctly executed cut combined with a correctly set screen. The same is true when attacking a zone defense, a tactic seldom used in most zone attack offenses.

The constant "hunting" for Blockers by Movers and "hunting" for Movers against man-to-man defense to set screens and cut carries over in attacking a zone. Both types of players have built the habit of looking for opportunities to team up to set a screen and cut for an advantage.

2

The Father of Blocker-Mover Offense – Coach Dick Bennett

This coaching legend has had an enormous impact on the game of basketball as the creator of not just the Blocker-Mover Offense but what is know popularly known as the Pack Line Man-to-Man defense, played by countless teams across the United States. Bennett's defensive innovation started with the famed on-the-line-up-the-line man-to-man defense his UW-Stevens Point teams made famous and Coach Bennett now refers to as Push Man-to-Man defense.

Arguably, having met and talked to Coach Bennett extensively on several occasions, his greatest contribution to the game would be his Five Biblical Principles: Humility, Passion, Unity, Servanthood and Thankfulness, principles Coach Bennett lived his life by and based much of his coaching philosophy on.

Coach Bennett played football and basketball at Ripon College and began his storied career as a high school coach in Wisconsin, winning 168 games at Wisconsin Eau Claire High School, leading the team to a state runner-up finish in the 1975-76 season.

His college coaching career began the following season as he moved on to University of Wisconsin-Stevens Point, building the Pointers into a nationally ranked power in the NAIA, coaching future NBA player Terry Porter.

Bennett became a nationally noted figure, although his Push defense had already made him a well-known figure in the coaching profession, when he took on the challenge of rebuilding the University of Wisconsin-Green Bay program. Bennett's efforts coaching the Phoenix resulted in the creation of the Blocker-Mover offense and the Pack defense, all the while building the Phoenix into an excellent mid-major basketball power. Coach Bennett coached his son Tony while at UW-Green Bay.

Coach Bennett finally landed his dream job when he was named the head coach of the University of Wisconsin Badgers. Bennett would lead the Badgers to the NCAA Division I Final Four in his fifth season at the helm of the Badgers.

Citing exhaustion, Bennett retired the following season but after a two-year absence from the sidelines, Bennett returned to the bench to take on the challenge of rebuilding the Washington State Huskies. After three years at the helm of the Huskies, Coach Bennett retired for good, leaving the program in the capable hands of his son Tony Bennett, now the head coach of the University of Virginia.

The Bennett family seems to having coaching in the genes as Coach Bennett's brother, Jack Bennett, would lead the UW-Stevens Point program to back-to-back NCAA Division III titles. In addition to his son Tony, Bennett's daughter, Kathi Bennett is the head coach of the University of Northern Illinois women's team.

Bennett is known for his innovations in the game of basketball, his contributions to offensive and to an even greater extent, defensive thinking in the game. Having had the opportunity to meet and talk with Coach Bennett, I would argue his greatest contribution was his philosophical approach to coaching, how he worked his way through problems to find solutions.

For Bennett, a devout Christian who coached and taught at public institutions his entire coaching career, finding a way to share his faith when the law prohibited it became a cornerstone of his thinking as a coach. The result was an approach Coach Bennett referred to as his Five Biblical Principles. These five principles were how he lived his life, how he made his faith real on a day-to-day basis. These principles were also how the solved problems as a coach.

It sounds strange coming from me, but when you hear Coach Bennett explain how helping on a screen or setting a screen as a Blocker are examples of a player demonstrating both humility and servanthood at the same time, you get a sense of the profound faith and belief Coach Bennett had in what he was teaching. When you saw his teams play, you saw his five principles carried out in very real ways on the court. His teams truly became greater than the sum of their parts.

As a young head coach when I first met Coach Bennett, his influence had a profound effect on me while I was devising my own ideas about coaching and what core values I should teach.

For coaches who want to learn more about Coach Bennett, please check the chapter at the end of this book titled Additional Resources where you will find a list books and DVDs about Coach Bennett and his systems of play. You may also visit my coaching website (CoachSivils.com) where you will find a large number of clinic lecture notes from Coach Bennett in my Clinic Notes page.

3
The TEAM Concept and Zone Attack Offense

If you only take one principle away from this book I hope it is this. The single most important thing in the game of basketball is being a TEAM! Nothing is more important.

You can have great individual players, a sound approach to offense and defense, a great rebounding scheme and be fundamentally sound, but if those players are not a TEAM in the true sense of the word, they will never achieve their full potential nor will the group ever have the best possible experience.

Great individual offensive players can at times effectively attack a man-to-man defense without a coordinated effort from their teammates. This simply is not true when attacking a zone defense.

Zone defenses were designed to stop the gifted individual offensive player. Zone defenses by design decide where the defense will defend, which defender will defend each area and how each defender will support his or her teammates.

The weakness of a zone defense is the offense decides who will attack which individual defender, where the attack will take place and how the attack will be executed. For the attack to be success though, it must be a coordinated TEAM effort, not a mindless uncoordinated effort by a collection of a individuals.

The principles and tactics in this book are not complicated. They do require a coordinated effort, the kind that only happens consistently when the players understand and have bought into the TEAM concept.

4

You Get What You Emphasize

Players seldom do what their coach teaches. Yet, players always do what their coach emphasizes. Paying lip service to concepts as important as team attitude, mastery and execution of basic fundamentals, work ethic, sound offensive and defensive play will not produce players or teams who demonstrate these traits.

A coach must emphasize the concepts important to the program, the success of the team and the development of the players. Playing a self-centered, selfish player while verbally stressing the team concept teaches players raw ability is more important than demonstrating a team first attitude.

The same is true when if comes to executing a sound zone attack offense and taking advantage of the opportunities the offense can present. Teaching players offensive concepts will not produce positive result unless those concepts are emphasized.

Playing time is one of the best ways to emphasize what is important. Sitting down a self-centered, selfish player for lack of team play sends a message to every player on the team. If you want playing time, you must demonstrate a team attitude.

Sitting players down for failure to execute team offensive concepts sends a powerful message. Attaching both positive and negative consequences to concepts taught and practiced in daily practice sessions is another way to emphasize essential concepts of any kind.

Coaches do not need to go overboard setting extreme consequences for the concepts being emphasized. Two push-ups for failure to execute will effectively communicate the desired message. A drink of sports drink instead of water during a hydration break is a simple but effective reward.

Consistency is essential. Players watch their coach like a child watches their parents. Players, like children, learn almost as much by observing their coach's attitude, actions and choices as they learn from direct instruction from their coach.

Always be aware, players will do what you emphasize, not what you teach!

5
What is Good Offense?

Good offense starts with the mastery of basic fundamentals. Players must be able to cut, pass, catch, dribble, face-up in triple threat, make lay-up and free throws, pivot and dribble. If these basics are not mastered, it almost does not matter if the team has a sound offensive system or not.

After mastery of basic fundamentals, spacing is the first team concept that makes up good offense. When players are spaced properly on offense, the defense will be placed at a disadvantage, creating opportunities for the offense. Poor spacing allows one defender to guard two or more offensive players or to not have to guard an offensive player at all.

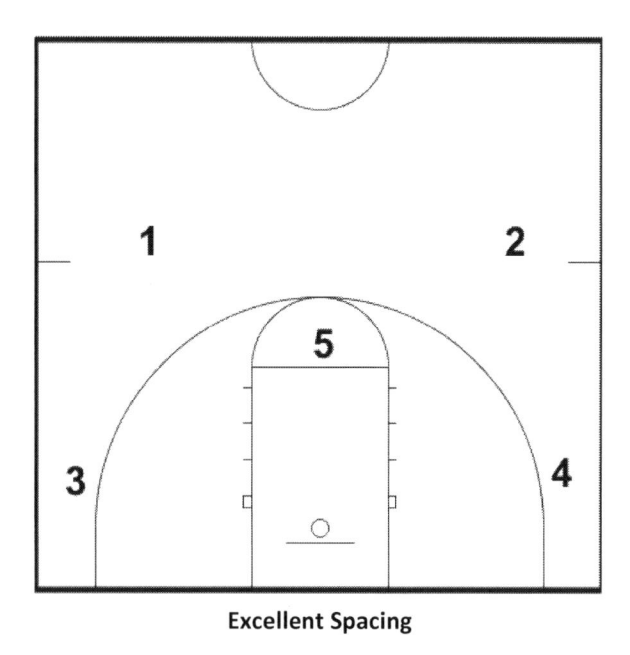

Excellent Spacing

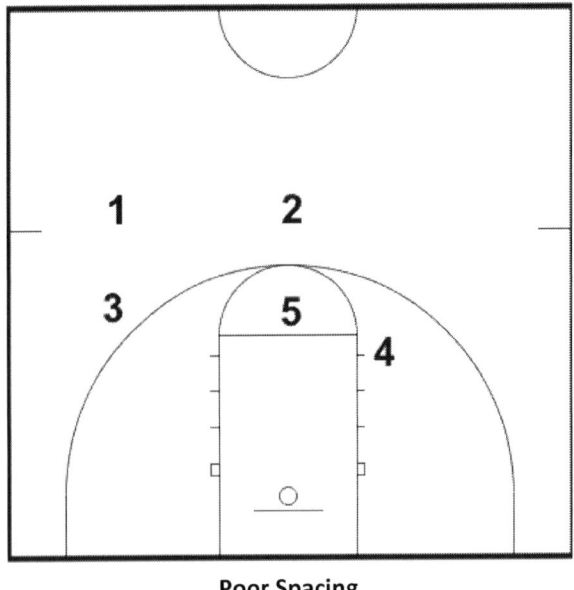

Poor Spacing

Good offensive basketball moves the ball forcing the defense to readjust its basic positioning as all defenses are geared to defend the ball. An offense with little ball movement allows the defense to position defenders to create a numerical advantage for the defense. Players must be 15-18 feet apart, far enough to space the defense out but close enough to pass effectively.

All attacking offenses look to penetrate the defense, either by the dribble, pass or cutting. Good zone attack offenses all have this trait.

Offensive players who simply stand are easy to defend. Good offense moves players, forcing the defense to react, adjust position and constantly reposition.

The most difficult offensive play to defend is the screen. At best, a screen requires two defensive players to defend successfully. Screening creates help and recovery situations with recovery being the aspect of defense most likely to cause a mistake the offense can take advantage of.

Great post players require a minimum of two defensive players to reduce their effectiveness. Any time the defense is required to use two defenders on one offensive player, one offensive player must be left undefended. In addition, the low post game produces high percentage shots and numerous opportunities to draw fouls.

High percentage shots are the goal of every offense. Some of the highest percentage shots to be obtained in basketball are a result of offensive rebounds. Sound offensive schemes have a plan for obtaining good offensive rebounding position and balancing the floor in order to have one or two offensive players in position to begin making defensive transition to prevent easy fast break scoring opportunities.

Finally, effective offensive attacks are assertive in their mental approach. Passivity leads to playing tentatively, allowing the defense to be the aggressor. Over time a passive approach will lead to turnovers, particularly at key moments in fiercely contested games.

6
Key Offensive Fundamentals

After the triple threat position, the most important basic skill needed against any zone defense is the fake, either the shot fake or a pass fake. Zone defenses are designed to position and defend based the location of the ball.

Watch an aggressive and effective zone defense. All five defenders move as one when the ball is passed and arrive in the correct defensive position when the ball arrives at its intended target. An effective shot fake or pass fake will cause the same well-coached zone defense to either freeze momentarily or to shift itself out of position. The use of the fake against a good zone defense allows the individual offensive player to use the aggressiveness and unity of the defense against it to attack it.

The ability to pass away from the defense, dribble the ball to relocate 15-18 feet away with two dribbles, make lay-ups, execute pivots without traveling, v-cut and catch the ball are essential fundamentals.

Other necessary habits include always facing the basket in triple threat position upon catching the ball, looking under the net and the ability to make free throws.

Position specific skills for a point guard include the ability to see all four teammates, handle the ball under pressure and be an effective communicator. Post players must be able to seal a defender, establish position, catch the ball in traffic and execute a post move and score with contact from the defense.

Perimeter players need to be able to drive from the three-point line to the goal in one dribble and make a lay-up or power shot. The ability to shoot the mid-range jump shot and the three-point shot are also important.

Regardless of the position played, when attacking a zone defense, all offensive players must understand how a zone defense works, how it should be attacked and how each individual player's role contributes to the success attack and score against a zone defense.

7

Common Types of Zone Defenses

Zone defenses, when the offense initially attacks, fall into one of two categories, an even front zone or an odd front zone. Once the offense has made one pass, dribble the ball to relocate it or in some way started the offensive attack, zone defenses can morph into something else.

An even front zone defense is a zone that has to defenders in the front of its initial alignment such as the most common zone defense, the 2-3 zone. The 2-1-2 zone is another even front defense.

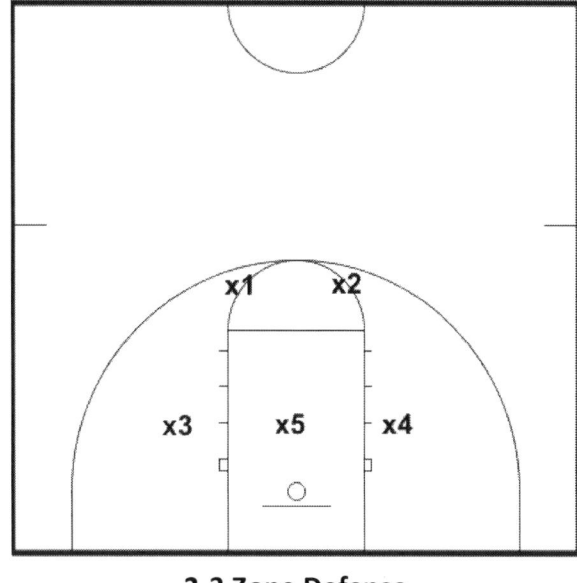

2-3 Zone Defense

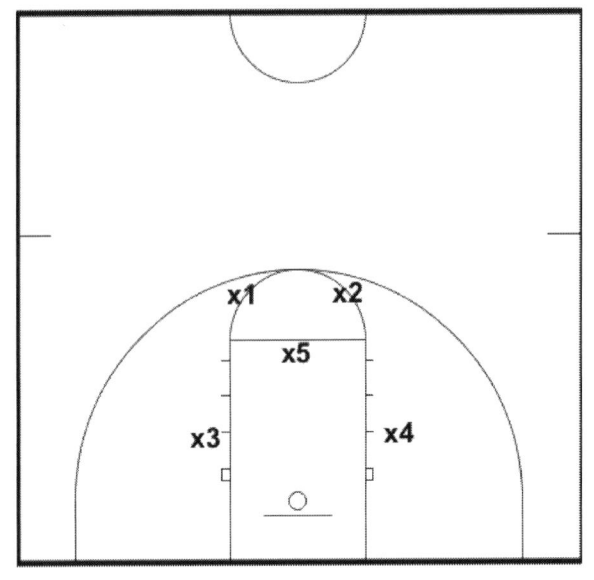

2-1-2 Zone Defense

The 1-2-2 zone defense is an example of an odd front zone defense. These zone defenses present the offense with an odd number of defensive players in their initial alignment. Additional common odd front zone defenses are the 3-2, the 1-3-1 and the so-called match-up hybrid zone, the 1-1-3.

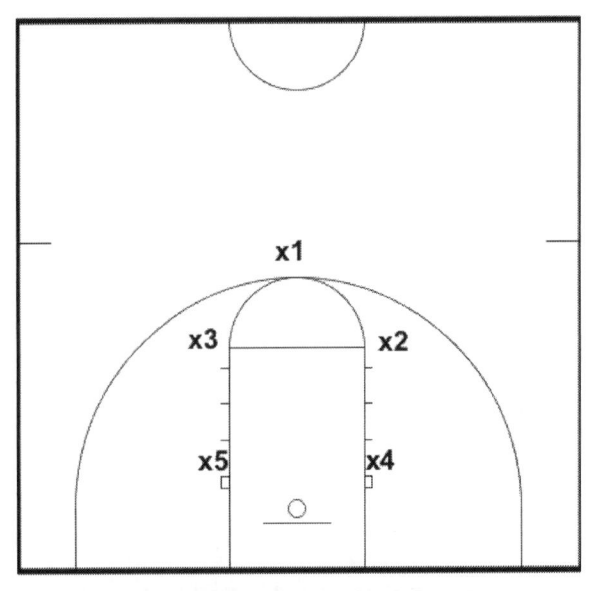

1-2-2 Zone Defense

3-2 Zone Defense

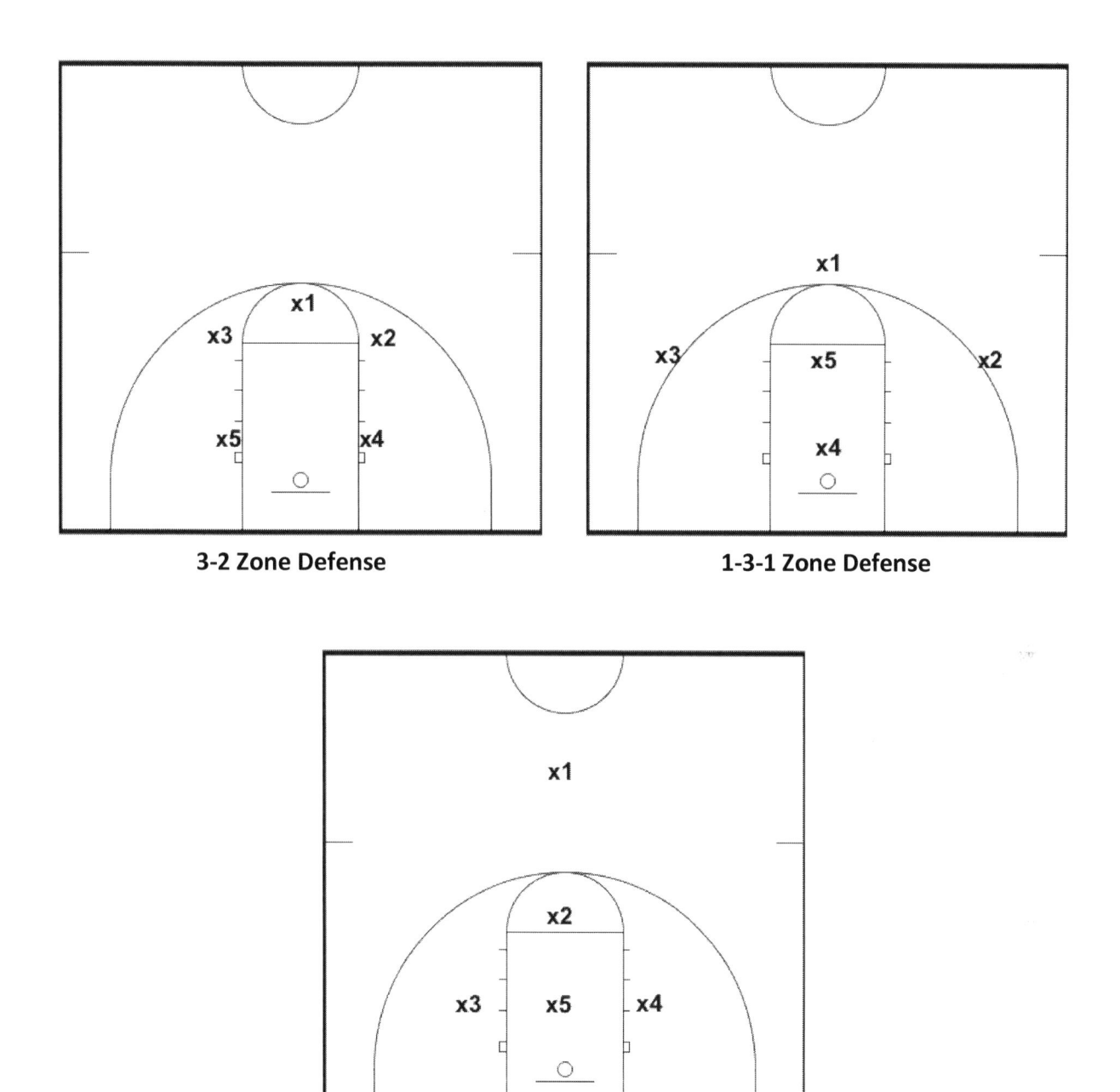

1-3-1 Zone Defense

1-1-3 Hybrid Zone Defense

Zone defenses can utilize many defensive tactics to give the offense a different look or take advantage of how the offense attacks. Trapping the wings or corners is just one such defensive tactic.

The type of zone defense, odd or even front, often determines the initial alignment the zone attack will utilize. For this reason it is important for all offensive players to be able to recognize the type of zone defense, the specific zone defense being used and the strengths and weaknesses of that particular zone defense.

8

Strengths and Weaknesses of Common Zone Defenses

Each common zone defense was designed with a specific purpose in mind, either to utilize the talents of specific players or to defend a specific offensive tactic or area of the court. Each zone defense by virtue of its initial alignment has made the "decision" of the areas of the court most important for that defense to defend.

It is not possible to defend the entire court. By choosing to defend some areas with a greater advantage due to positioning, other areas of the zone defense become vulnerable.

Knowing the strengths and weaknesses, as well as the vulnerable areas, of a zone defense, allows players to have a better understanding of how to adjust to attack a zone defense. Strong areas should be avoided and weaknesses and vulnerable areas must be exploited.

The most commonly used of all zone defenses is the 2-3 zone. This defense is strongest along the baseline and is an excellent defense for initiating a fast break attack from. The 2-3 zone provides a rebounding triangle by virtue of its initial alignment and allows for easy coverage of the low post and the corners of the court. The two-guard front allows for pressure to be applied to the ball quickly after defensive transition has been finished as well as pressure the wings.

The 2-3 zone, as effective as its initial alignment is, has weaknesses. The zone has three distinct "gaps," areas where the offense can penetrate via a pass, a cut or by dribble penetration. The 2-3 is vulnerable in the high post area via a pass to a high post player or by penetration from the point guard. If the 2-3 moves its back line defenders up, or away from the goal, the zone becomes vulnerable on the baseline behind the zone, particularly in the "short post" area.

2-3 Zone Defense

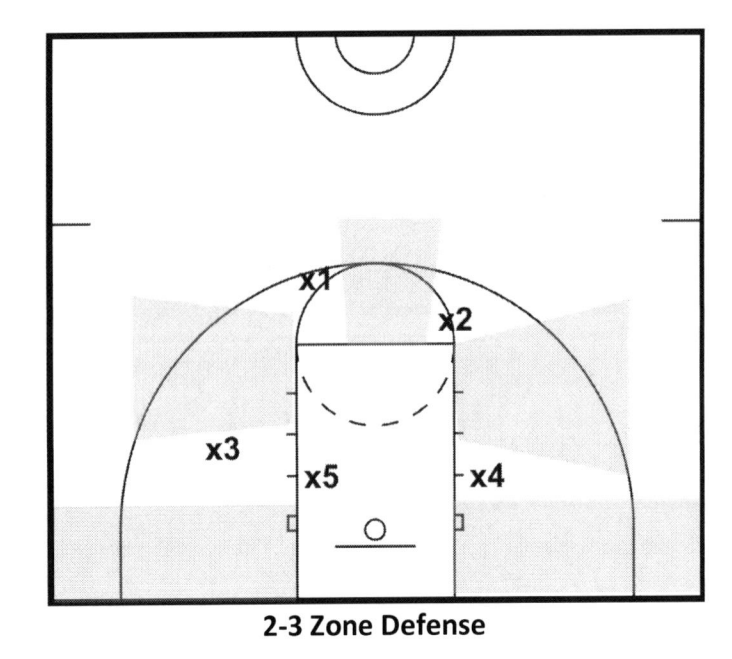

The 2-1-2 zone defense is very similar to the 2-3 zone with the main difference being in the middle defender having responsibility to defend the high post area. This adjustment makes the lane area immediately in front of the goal vulnerable to high low passes and an excellent low post defender who is skilled in sealing a defender when posting.

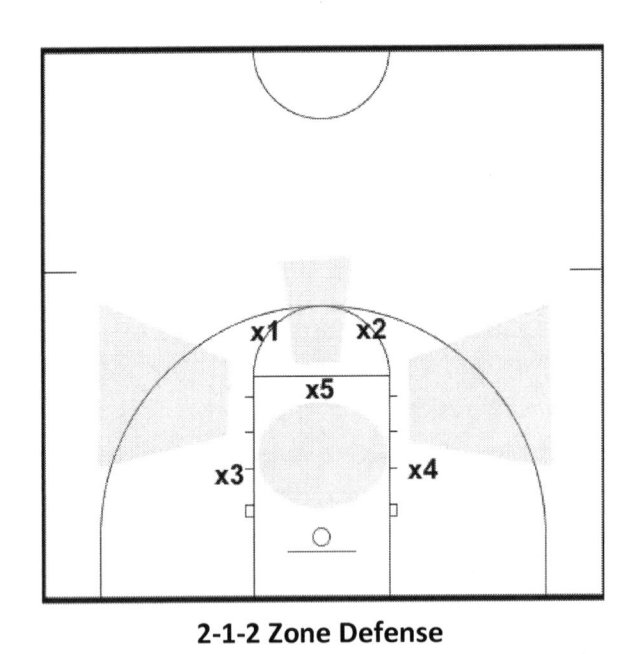

2-1-2 Zone Defense

The 3-2 zone defense and 1-2-2 zone defense are both strong against preventing dribble penetration down the middle of the zone. Keeping two tall, effective rebounders close to the goal as well as low post defense are strengths of these two defenses. Offenses designed to shoot three-point shots from the wings and the top may struggle against these two defenses. Both are good springboards for fast break offense.

Both zones are vulnerable to back screening, diagonal skip passes from the corners, shot attempts, both two-point and three-point, on the baseline, flash cutters in the gaps from behind the zone and the high low post game if the ball can be entered into the high post area. The most vulnerable area of these two zones is the lane area.

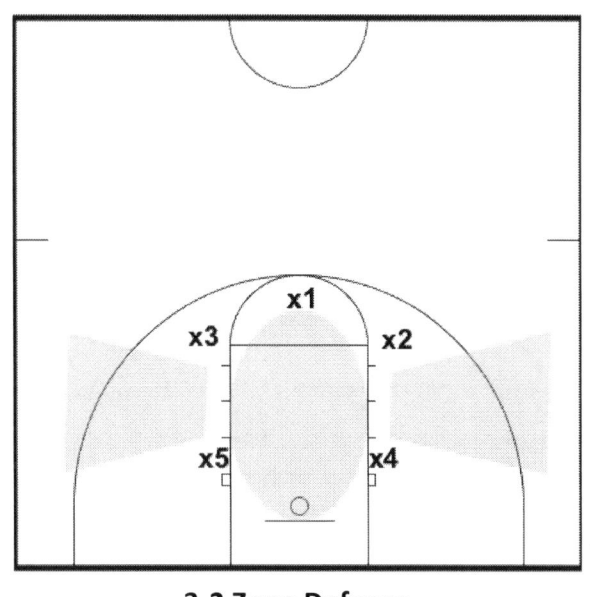

3-2 Zone Defense

The 1-2-2 defense can be vulnerable to penetration, by pass or dribble, in the gaps if the point defender of the zone extends too far to pressure the ball. Quick ball reversal combined with shot fakes can exploit these gaps to pass the ball into the high post area, allowing the offense to take advantage of the open area in the lane to shoot, drive or pass.

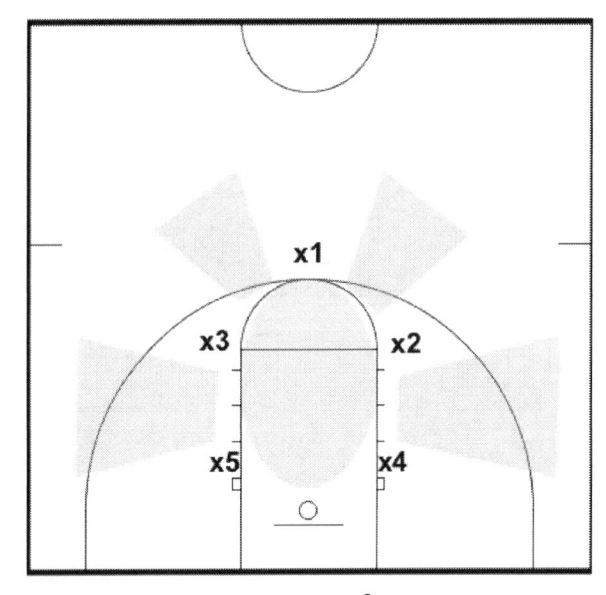

1-2-2 Zone Defense

The 1-3-1 zone defense is very strong down the middle of the court, can cause considerable disruption of rhythm for teams who rely on passing alone for rapid ball movement, pressure three-point shooters on the wings and top and is strong against the low post.

The 1-3-1 is vulnerable to diagonal skip passes from the corner, two-point and three-point shots on the baseline and corner and penetration in the gaps of the zone by dribble, pass or flash cutter from behind the zone.

Smart zone attack offenses can effectively screen the 1-3-1 zone defense, but this particular zone is more difficult than most to effectively screen.

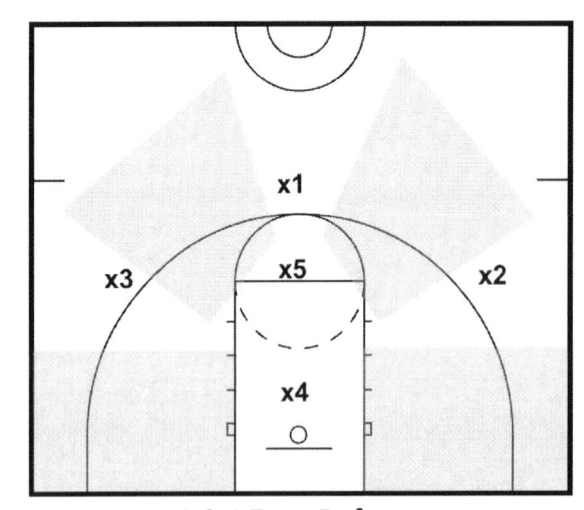

1-3-1 Zone Defense

The 1-1-3 hybrid zone defense can present challenges to many zone attack offenses during the initial stage of attacking the defense due to the match-up man-to-man nature of the two tandem defenders at the front of the zone.

Once the ball has been moved to the corner or wings, the 1-1-3 becomes an aggressive 2-3 zone defense designed to eliminate ball reversal. Once the 1-1-3 has morphed into the 2-3 zone, it has all of the vulnerabilities of the 2-3 zone and is extremely vulnerable to the diagonal skip pass from the baseline corner with the pass receiver attacking with the dribble. The screen-in tactic is also very effective when combined with a skip pass from the opposite wing.

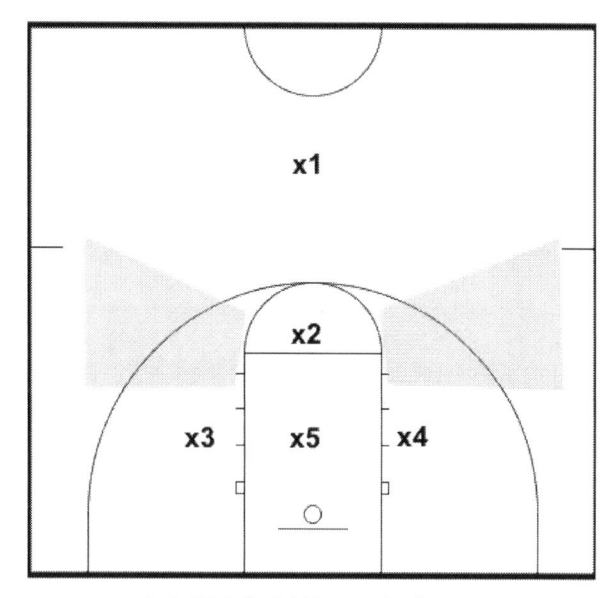

1-1-3 Hybrid Zone Defense

9

Why Does the Opponent Play a Zone Defense?

When strategically planning for an upcoming opponent who plays zone defense it is wise to ask the question "why does the opponent play a zone defense?"

Other strategic questions include, "is playing a zone defense a strength for the opponent? Does the opponent have a weakness requiring the use of a zone defense to cover up?"

If zone defense is a strength, why is the use of the zone a strength? How can this be negated?

If the opponent is hiding a weakness, what is that weakness? How can it be exploited?

Reasons zone defense can be a strength for an opponent include:

- It allows the opponent to be aggressive.
- The zone defense utilized fits the personnel of the opponent.
- Zone defense allows the opponent to initiate the opponent's preferred offense with greater ease, particularly the fast break.
- Zone defense compliments the full court defense the opponent utilizes.
- Weaknesses the opponent may be hiding with a zone defense can include:

- Poor man-to-man defense skills or coaching.
- The need to hide a particular player on defense, either because of foul trouble, lack of size or athleticism or lack of defensive skills.
- The need to protect a gifted offensive player if the opponent lacks balanced offensive skills.
- Lack of depth requiring a limited number of players to play the bulk of the minutes.

It is important to understand why the opponent is playing zone defense in general and a specific zone defense in particular. This information allows the specific principles best suited to attack the zone defense utilized by the opponent to be practiced in preparation for the playing the opponent.

10

All Zones Become a 2-3 Zone

All zone defenses morph into some form of a 2-3 zone when the ball is moved to the corner, if the zone defense pressures the ball. This is worth being aware of for a variety of reasons. Care must be taken to teach players about the strengths and weaknesses of the 2-3 when the ball is in the corner, particularly odd front zones.

Odd front zones are vulnerable to the diagonal skip pass from the corner once in the 2-3 zone alignment. Even front zones are vulnerable to a skip pass on top followed by a direct dribble attack.

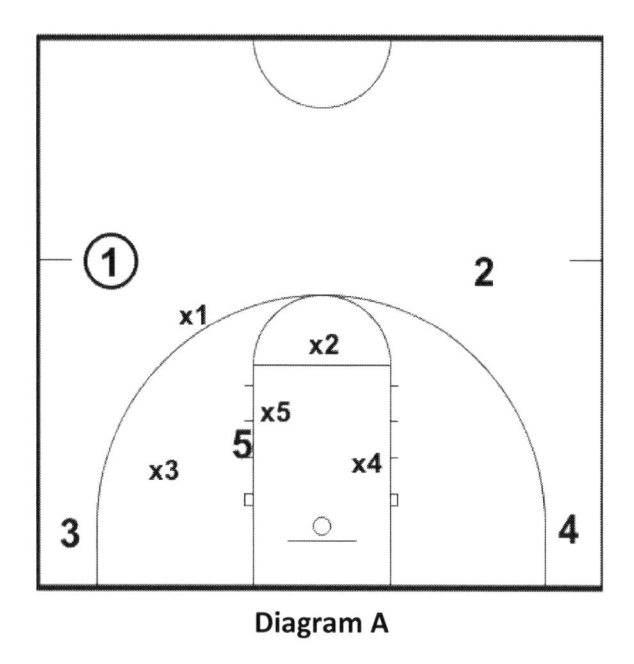

Diagram A

Diagrams A and **B** depict the normal slides of an aggressive 2-3 zone defense that both pressures the ball and wants to eliminate ball reversal.

Diagram B

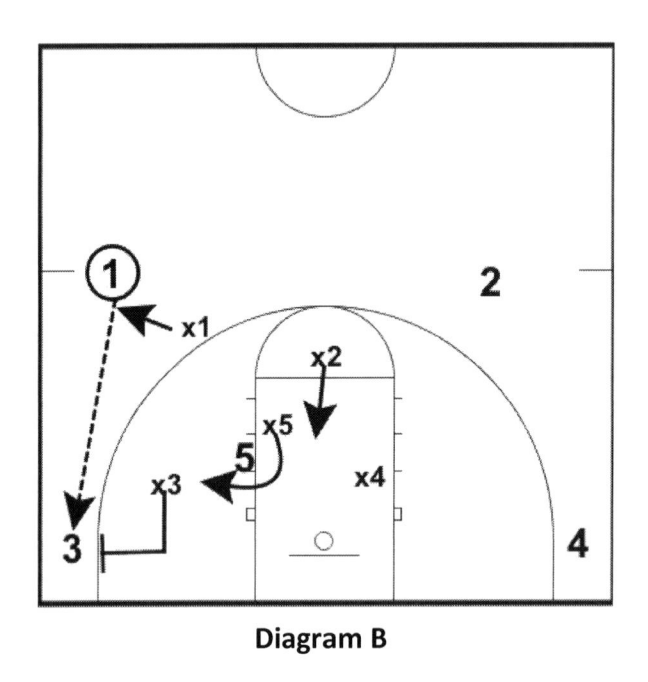

Diagram C depicts an aggressive 2-3 zone positioned to pressure the ball and eliminate ball reversal. X3 is applying pressure to the ball and X1 is denying the direct pass back to #1. This aggressive attitude and positioning creates pressure while disrupting easy movement of the ball on the perimeter.

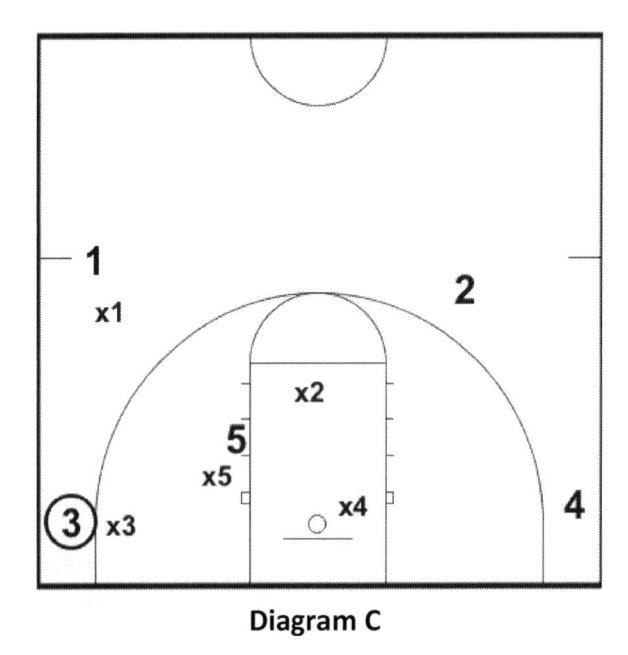

Diagram C

All Zones Become a 2-3 Zone

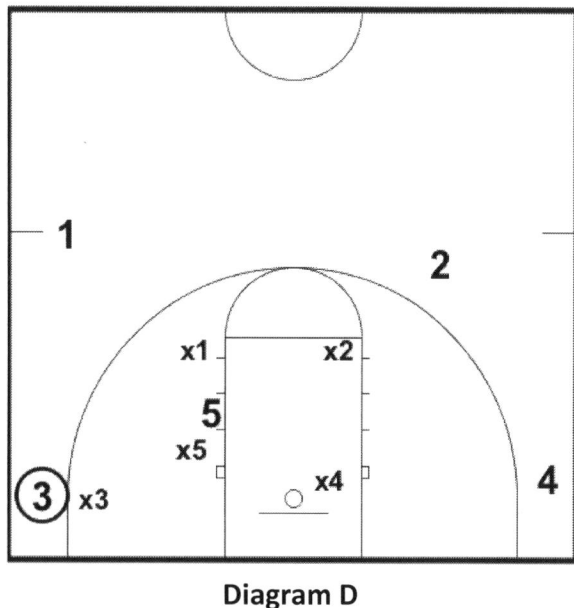

Diagram D

Diagram D depicts a more passive 2-3 zone. The ball is being pressured but more emphasis is being placed on protecting the high post. The defense is willing to allow the offense to reverse the ball with a pass.

So what is the big deal? Why is this piece of information important? Forcing zones to alter their basic shifts and slides, making the defense do something it does not want to is a key principle in attacking any zone defense.

Assertive defenses do not want ball reversal and all defenses are vulnerable if the ball penetrates the defense, either by pass or dribble. Passive defenses protect the post and lane areas and are specifically designed to prevent penetration by pass or dribble.

Having the knowledge and ability to immediately hurt either of these types of defenses forces the opponent to be reactive from the start of the game, giving the offense a distinct advantage. The defense will have to reveal its adjustments to these tactics immediately and abandon its normal defensive style of play early in the game.

Diagram 9 depicts the diagonal skip pass attack against an assertive 2-3 zone alignment. The attack should begin with a pass fake to #1 to freeze the defense momentarily. #2 adjusts to the open gap the defense presents with its positioning.

Upon catching the ball #2 may either shoot a three-point shot or shot fake the defender X2 and drive the lane line, forcing X4 to help, creating either a baseline jump shot or a three-point attempt for #4. #5 seals X5 out of the lane and is available for a pass as well from either #2 or #4 if X4 is able to react to the pass to #4 (**Diagrams E** through **H**). Note in **Diagram 9** #1 and #3 are moving to floor balance.

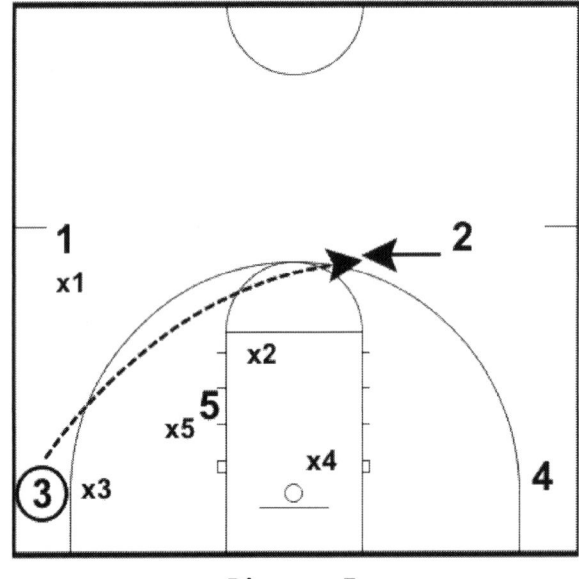

Coaching Basketball's Zone Attack Offense Using Blocker-Mover Motion Offense

Diagram E

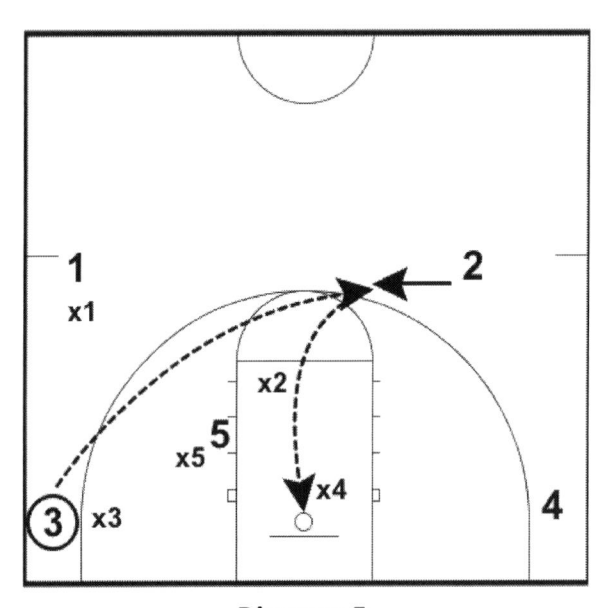

Diagram F

All Zones Become a 2-3 Zone

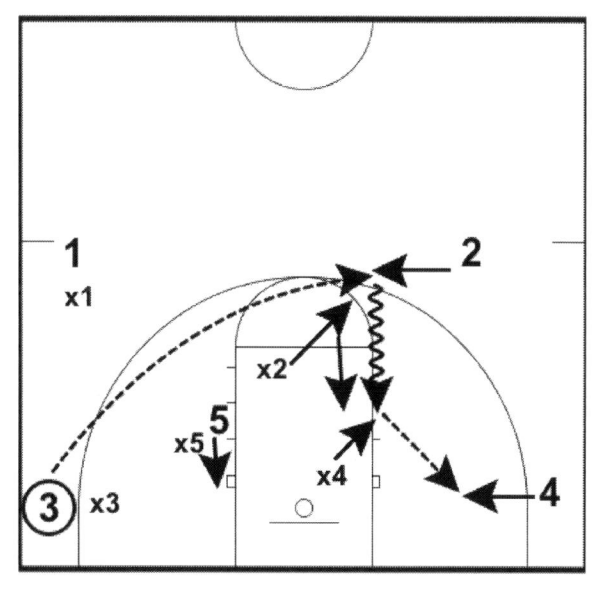

Diagram G

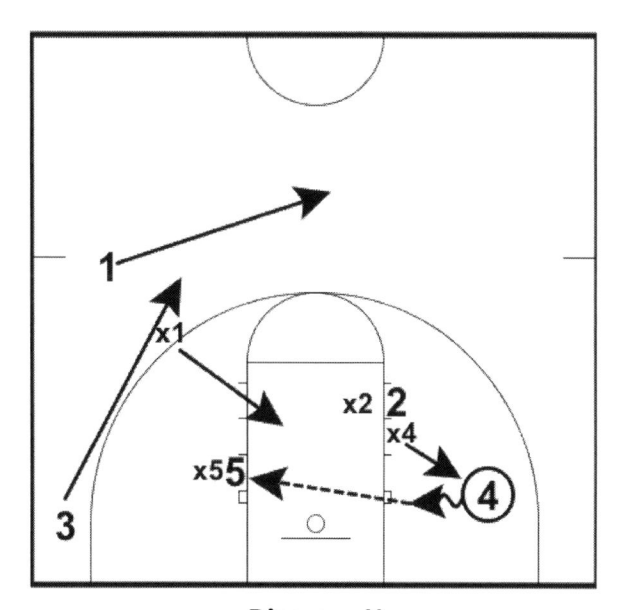

Diagram H

Diagram I

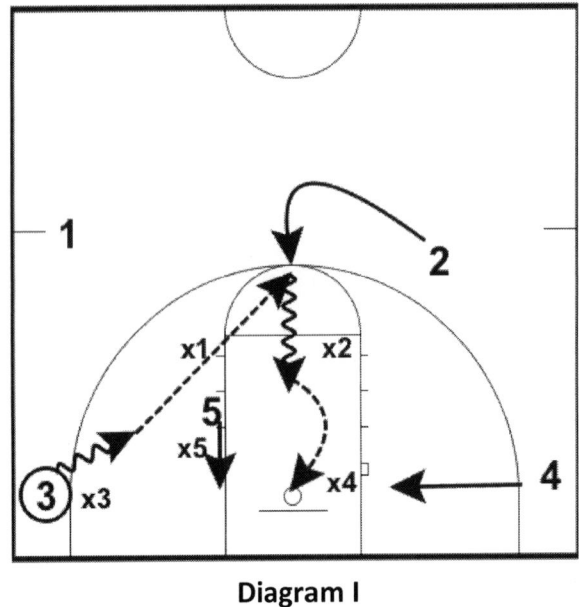

Attacking a more passive zone defense is shown in **Diagram I**. #2 has slipped right into the gap in the zone defense. #3 freezes the defense with a short dribble penetration and passes to #2.

#2 has the option of shooting the three-point shot, shot faking and driving for a score or a pass to either #4 or #5 (**Diagrams I** through **L**). Note in **Diagram L** #1 and #3 are moving to floor balance.

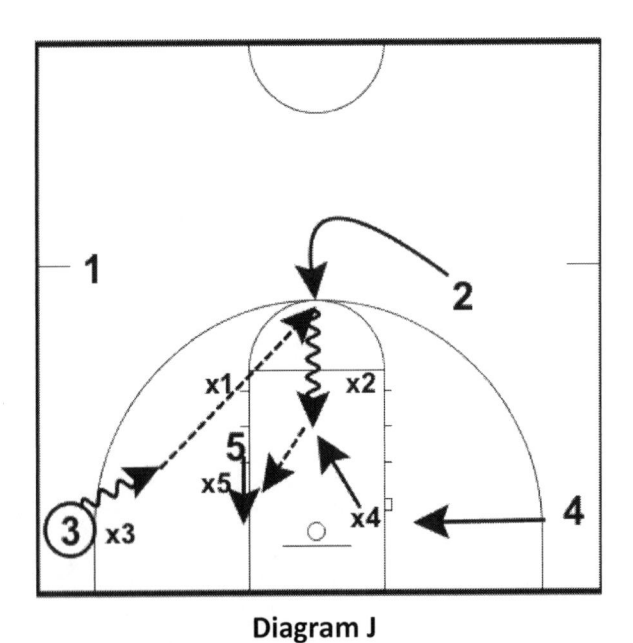

Diagram J

All Zones Become a 2-3 Zone

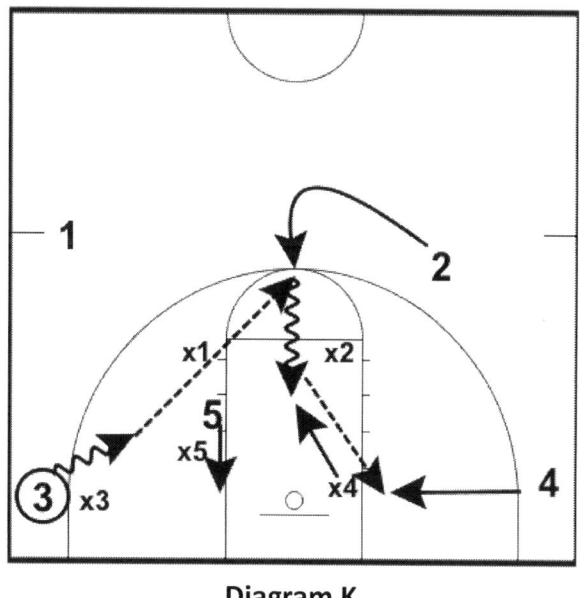

Diagram K

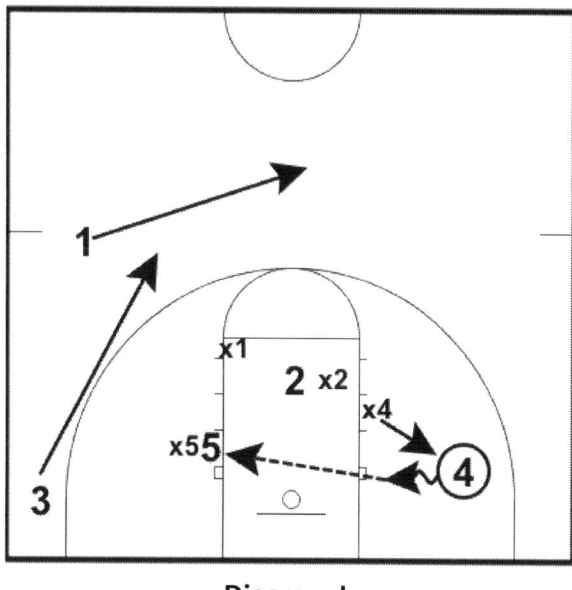

Diagram L

Knowing all zone defenses morph into a 2-3 zone when the ball is moved to the corner allows a zone offense to be ready to attack and place the defense at a disadvantage the first offensive possession of the game the opponent deploys a zone defense, regardless of the type of zone defense.

How do the common zone defenses morph into a 2-3 zone? **Diagrams M** through **N** depict the shifts and are labeled to identify the type of zone defense deployed as well.

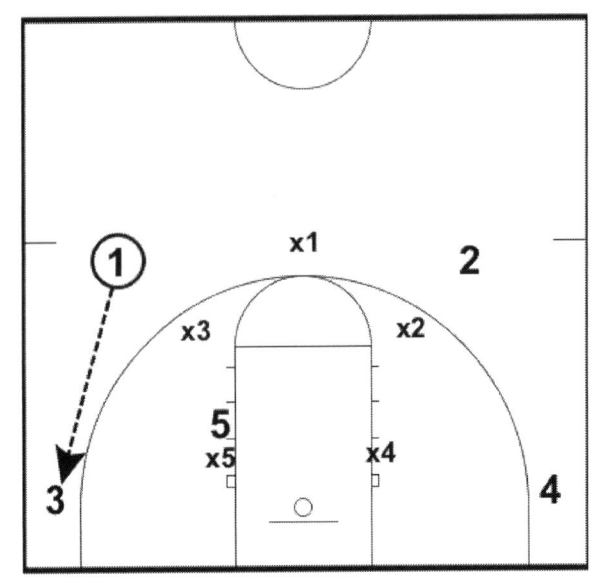

Coaching Basketball's Zone Attack Offense Using Blocker-Mover Motion Offense

Diagram M – Aggressive 1-2-2 Zone

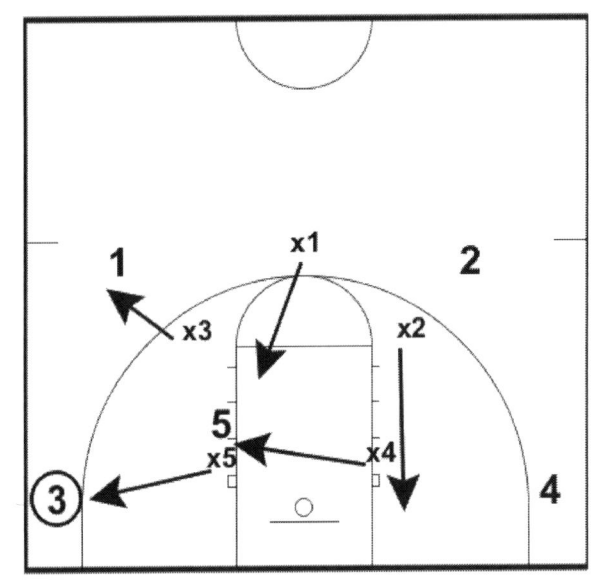

Diagram N – Aggressive 1-2-2 Zone

All Zones Become a 2-3 Zone

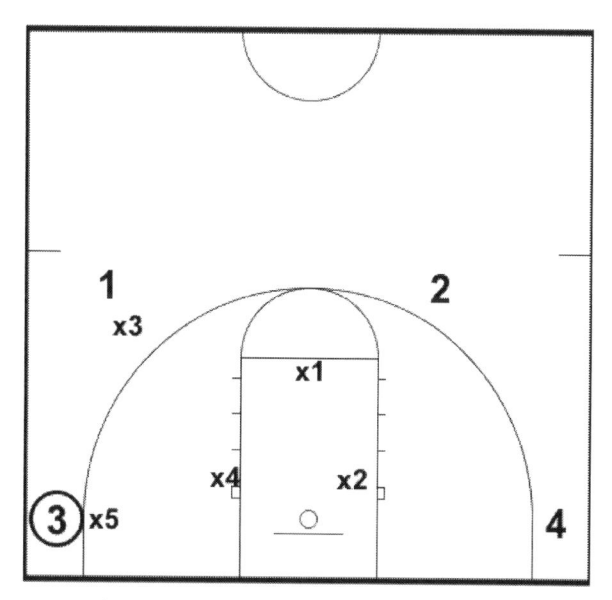

Diagram O – Aggressive 1-2-2 Zone

Examine **Diagram O** and **Diagram C**. There is no difference in the areas being defended, only a difference in the players responsible to defend a specific area. The aggressive 1-2-2 zone morphed into a 2-3 when the ball was passed to the corner.

Examine **Diagram 9-Q** and **Diagram 9-D**. The passive 1-2-2 zone morphed into a passive 2-3 zone. Again, the same areas of the court are defended with only the players defending the area changing.

Diagram R through **Diagram T** depicts a 1-3-1 zone. Compare **Diagram T** and **Diagram C**. The assertive nature of the 1-3-1 zone causes it to morph into a 2-3 when the ball is moved to the corner. The 3-2 zone and 1-1-3 are not depicted due to their similarity to the 1-2-2 and 2-3.

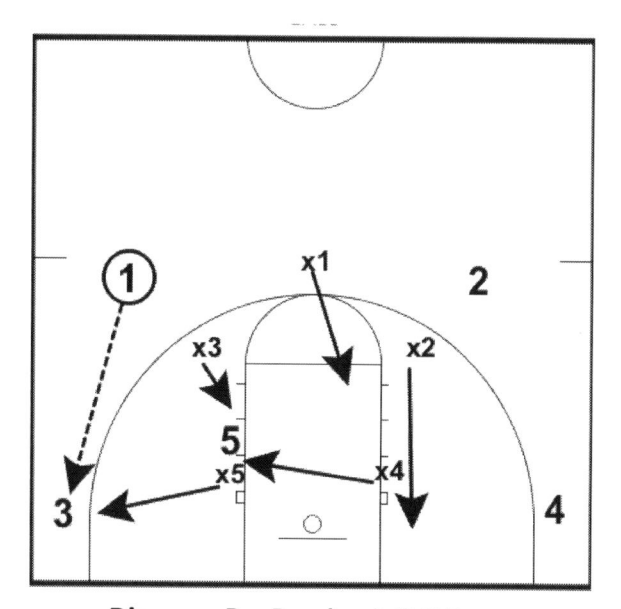

Diagram P – Passive 1-2-2 Zone

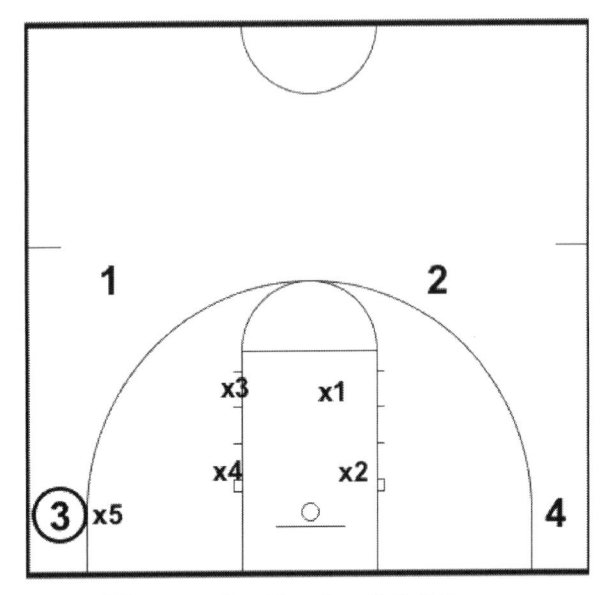

Diagram Q – Passive 1-2-2 Zone

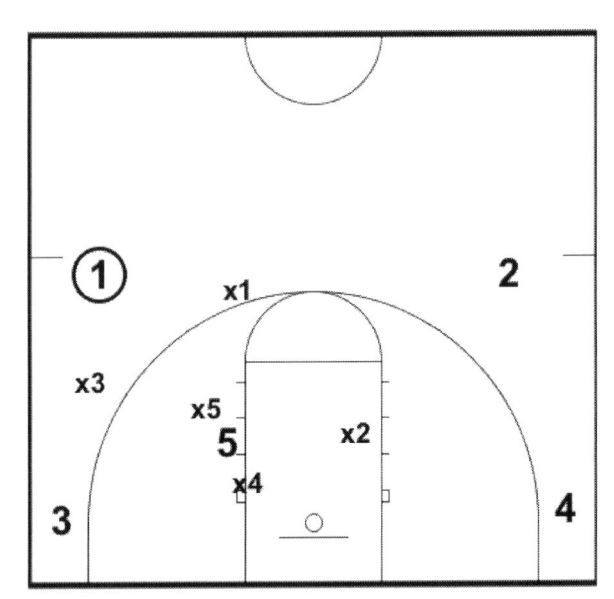

Diagram R - 1-3-1 Zone

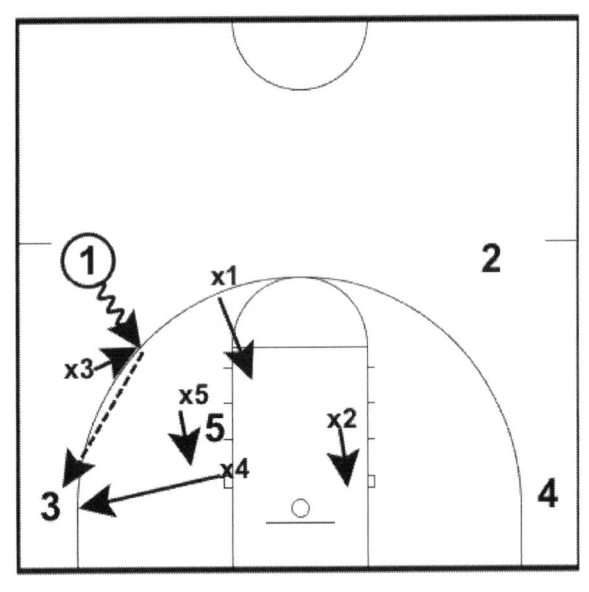

Diagram S – 1-3-1 Zone

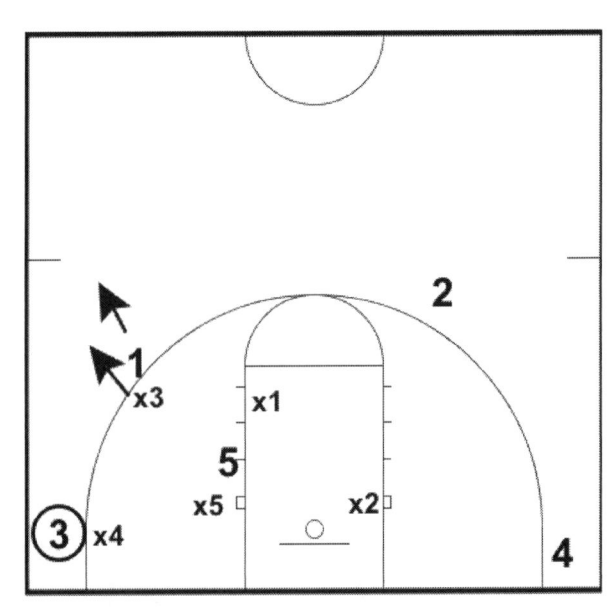

Diagram T – 1-3-1 Zone

42

11

The Mental Approach to Attacking a Zone Defense

Number 1
Be Assertive and Confident

Zone defense, even when a strength for the opponent, has weaknesses capable of being exploited. An offensive unit should view every zone defense as an opportunity to be exploited and taken advantage of.

Zone defenses by their very nature want to cause the opponent to become passive on offense. Zone defense, even aggressive zones, should be attacked! Refer to zone offense as zone attack!

Knowing how to identify the weak points of a zone and how to exploit these weaknesses will breed confidence in offensive play. Teaching players to be assertive against a zone and to attack will prevent a passive approach to zone offense.

Number 2
Identify the Zone as Quickly as Possible

In order to be confident and assertive in attacking any zone defense, the offense must identify the form of zone defense being played. This is essential in order for the appropriate tactics and concepts to be used to attack the zone at its weak points.

Number 3
Identify the Weakness of the
Zone and Attack

Identify the weak points of the zone and attack. All zones have weak points. There is some variation in these weak points due to slight variations in how a defensive unit plays the zone or the personnel being utilized.

Teams must have a plan to test the normal weak points of the specific zone being played and have an idea of how to identify and recognize the weak points.

Number 4
Identify the Weakest Defender in the
Zone and Attack

In addition to identifying the weak points in a zone defense, it is essential to determine if a weak defender and what position the weak defender is playing in the zone.

Upon identifying the weak link defender, this defender should be attacked in as many different ways as possible by the offense. The goal should be to not only score as many times as possible but to force the opponent to change defenses or move the weak defender to another spot in the zone allowing other parts of the zone to be attacked.

Number 5
Think in Terms of Principles of Attack

Zone offenses are pre-determined patterns or continuities while other zone offenses are motion oriented. Regardless of the type of zone offense, all need to be flexible enough to allow adaptation to attack the differences and variations in zone defenses.

This flexibility allows specific principles to be applied in attacking the weak points of a zone defense. The offense should think in terms of how every zone defense it faces can be attacked, which principles and tactics should be used to attack and how to apply the principles in attacking the defense.

12

Zone Attack Principles – Offensive Building Blocks

Principles of attacking a zone defense can be categorized in order to organize the concepts, making the information easier for both coaches and players to utilize. The seven categories of zone attack principles are:

- Spacing and gaps
- Move the ball and move people
- Penetration
- Use of the dribble to attack
- Screen the zone
- The inside game against the zone
- Planning to rebound and floor balance

Spacing and gaps are concepts having to do with taking advantage of natural gaps in the zone defense through the use of proper spacing of offensive players and using alignments to place offensive players in the gaps of the zone defense.

Move the ball and move people are concepts concerning how the offense flows, the ball is moved to advantage for the offense and moving offensive players to attack the zone defense. Often these two seemingly different movements are interconnected and considerable time and effort must be spent to coordinate the two successfully.

All defensive systems are vulnerable to penetration and the zone defense is no different. Concepts in this category concern penetration by a variety of means, not all of which involve the use of the dribble to penetrate.

The use of the dribble as an offensive weapon is one of the must misunderstood and misused of all offensive weapons. Players and coaches tend to think of the dribble as a means to attack for a score. Against a zone, the dribble is a tool to attack the zone to set up the score.

One of the most effective weapons against man-to-man defense is the screen. This excellent offensive tool, when combined with ball movement and player movement is one of the most difficult offensive weapons for man-to-man defense to defend. Yet this same concept is seldom applied against a zone defense. The screen, when combined with ball and player movement, is one of the most effective concepts available to attack a zone defense.

Zone defenses were often created to defend against great inside offensive players and are still effective in that role. Many teams when confronted with a zone defense abandon any serious attempt to enter the ball into the post, either high or low, and resort to utilizing only mid-range jump shots or the three-point shot as a means of attacking the zone. Sadly, with simple concepts and principles, it
can be easier to enter the ball into the post against a zone than against a good man-to-man defense.

One of the arguments against zone defenses is zones are weak against the offensive rebound due to the fact the defenders do not have individual block out assignments. This is true for poorly coached zone defenses but well coached zone defenses have specified rebounding schemes and are quite effective in limiting offensive rebound opportunities.

One of the best ways to obtain high percentage shots and draw fouls is by obtaining offensive rebounds. Many zone offenses are weak in the area of planning to position for offensive rebound opportunities.

During this phase of the offense, when neither team is in possession of the ball, it is essential the offense prepare for the likelihood of having to make defensive transition. The zone offense must have a scheme for balancing the floor on a shot attempt to prevent the opponent from fast breaking and to begin the transition to defense.

13

Spacing and Gaps

Number 6
Proper Spacing is Essential

Spacing is offense and offense is spacing. All players must be 15 to 18 feet apart. Correct spacing prevents the zone from being able to utilize one defensive player to defend two offensive players in one area.

Number 7
Constantly Readjust Spacing

As the offense attacks the zone and players move spacing must be maintained and players must be aware of the need to maintain, and if necessary, adjust spacing in order to prevent the defense from being able to use one defender to guard two offensive players.

Number 8
Stretch the Zone From Behind

Zone defenses want to defend as little area of the court as possible. The further from the goal the zone offense initiates its attack, the less area the zone has to defend (**Diagram A**).

Diagram A

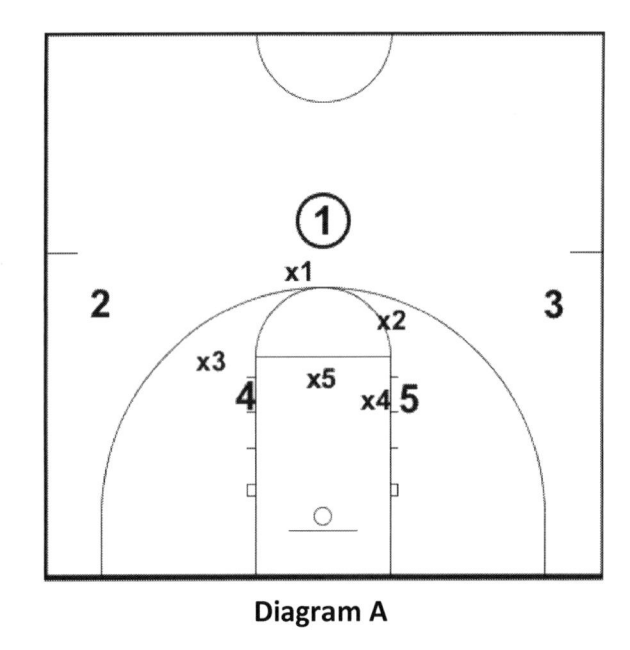

Moving the post players deep behind the zone defense forces the zone to defend a greater area of the court, creating larger gaps in the zone for the offense to exploit (**Diagram B**).

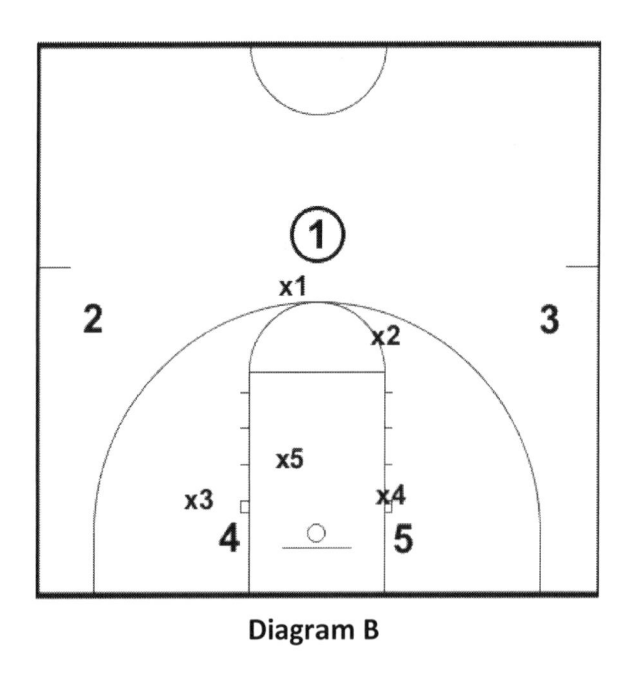

Diagram B

Number 9
Flash Into Gaps

Zone defenses by their very nature have "gaps" in the defense. A gap is the space between two defenders in the zone. Cutters can exploit gaps by flashing into the gaps, particularly from behind the zone.

Spacing and Gaps

This tactic is effective due to the space between the defenders and the fact all five zone defenders will usually be focused on the ball by design (**Diagram A and B**).

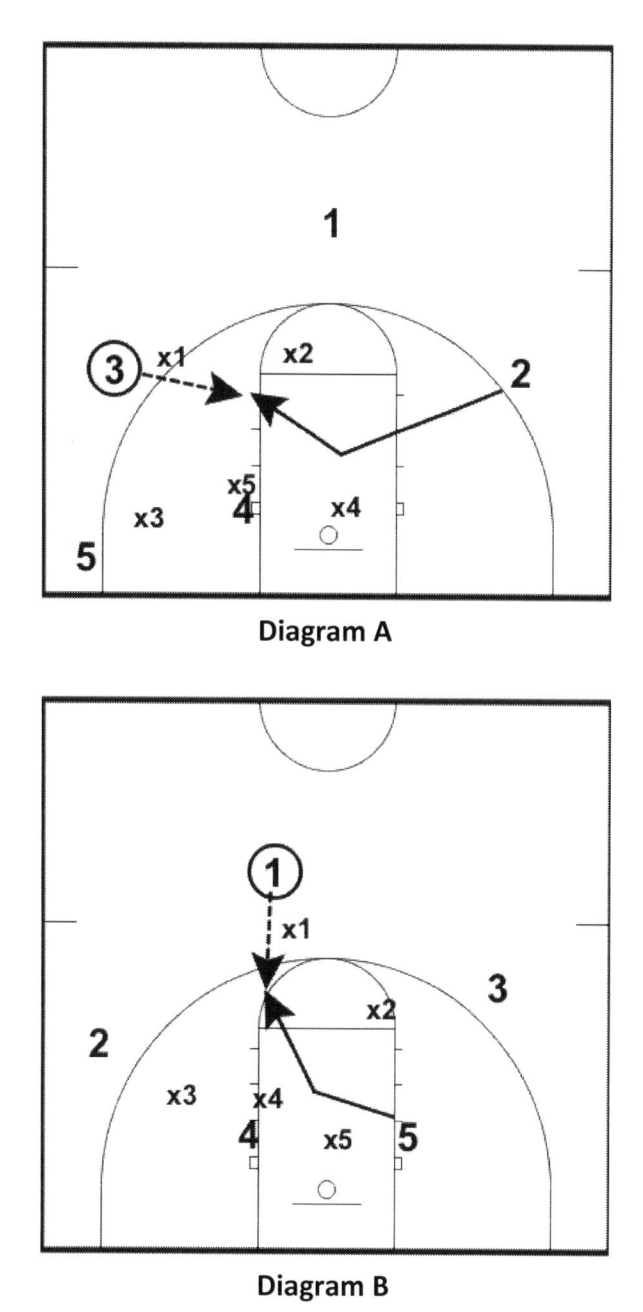

Diagram A

Diagram B

Number 10
Line Up in the Gaps

There is no reason to ever give the opponent a break, particularly on defense. Initiate offensive play as frequently as possible with the upper hand. One of the best ways to do this is to line up in the gaps of a zone defense, forcing the defense to begin adjusting its' positioning immediately.

Even front zones such as a 2-3 or 2-1-2 are best attacked by zone attack offenses starting from an odd front alignment (**Diagram A).** Odd front zones such as a 1-3-1, 1-2-2 or 3-2 are best attacked with an even front zone attack offensive alignment (**Diagram B** through **Diagram D**). Exceptions to these guidelines exist but only in the initial alignment and usually only with teams who play extreme up-tempo fast break offense whose attack quickly morphs into a zone attack offense with players in the gaps of the zone.

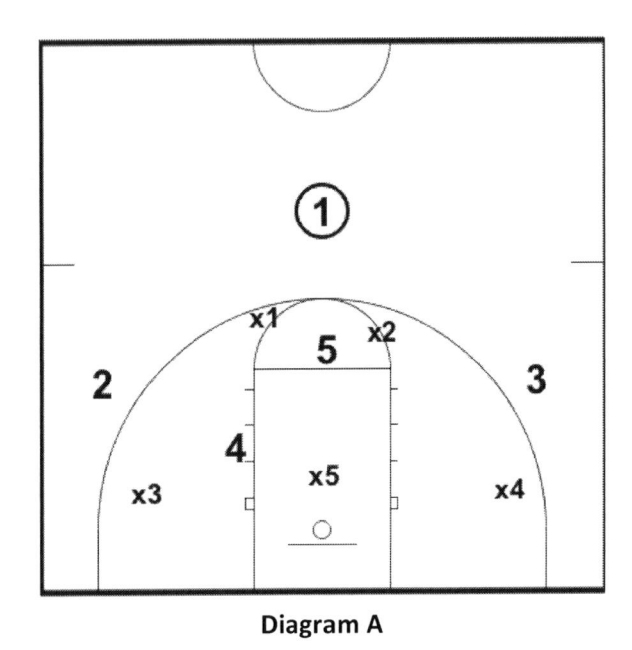

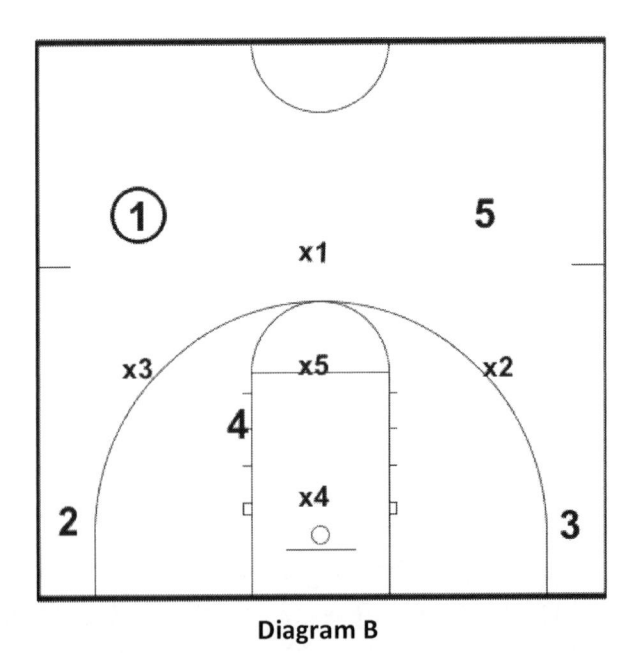

Diagram A

Diagram B

Spacing and Gaps

Diagram C

Diagram D

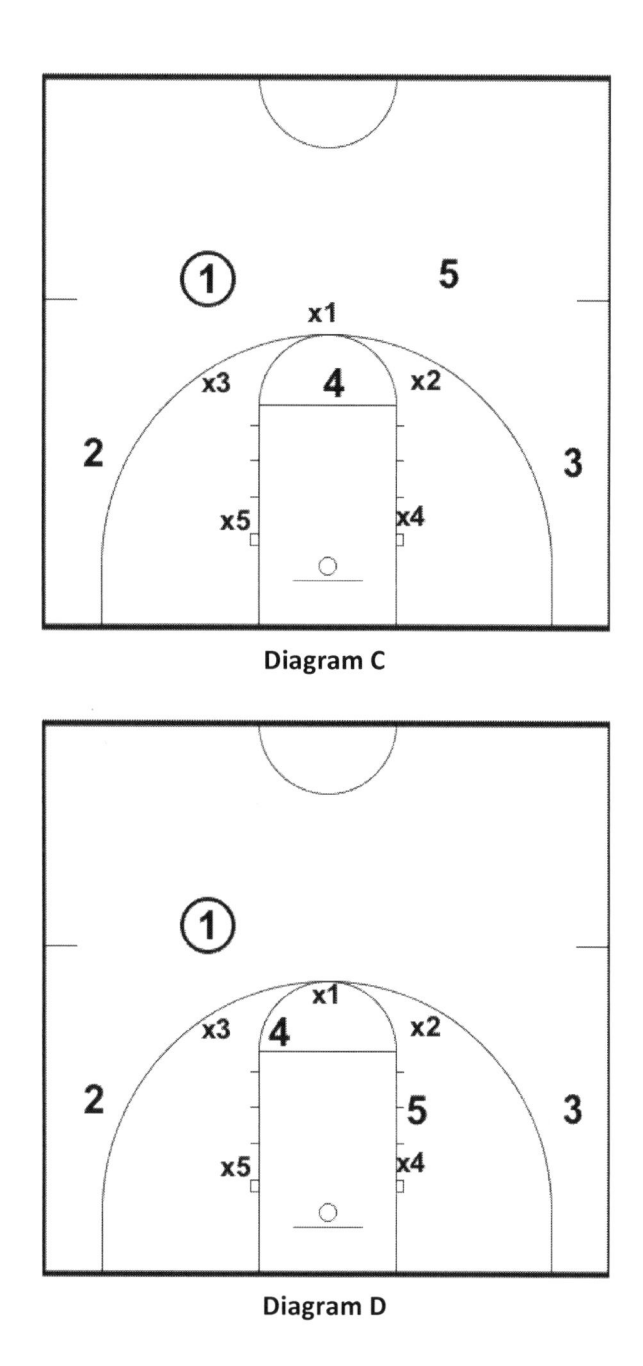

Number 11
Use Alignments to Distort the Zone

One of the primary advantages of utilizing zone defense is the defense chooses where it will defend. Distorting the zone through the use of alignments when entering the offense forces the zone to defend in areas and ways it would prefer not to.

The alignment depicted in **Diagram A** is a personal favorite to distort a zone defense and cause problems for the zone in terms of who and how the zone defends the alignment. The alignment is shown in **Diagram A** without a zone defense for clarity. The offensive player #1 has made a basket cut to the "short post" or "short corner" and received a pass. #1's back is facing the baseline, allowing #1 to have complete vision of the other four offensive teammates and all five defensive players. **Diagram B** shows the alignment with a 2-3 zone defense shortly after #1 has received the ball.

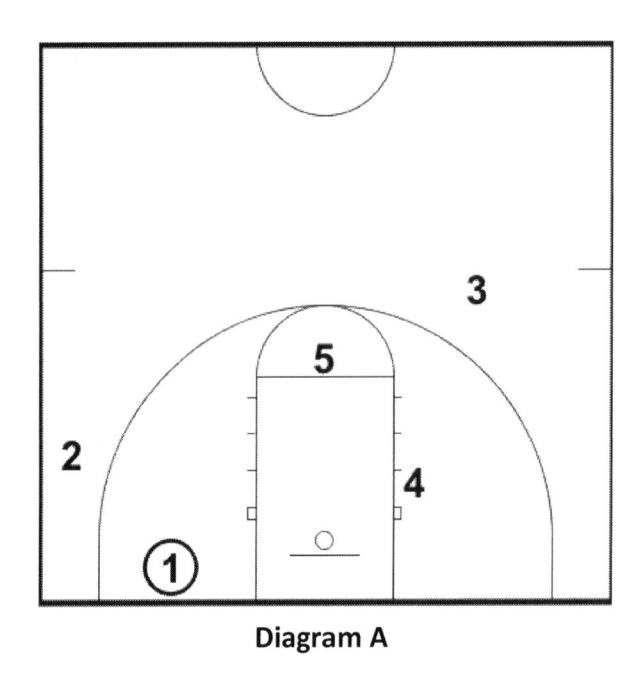

Diagram A

Spacing and Gaps

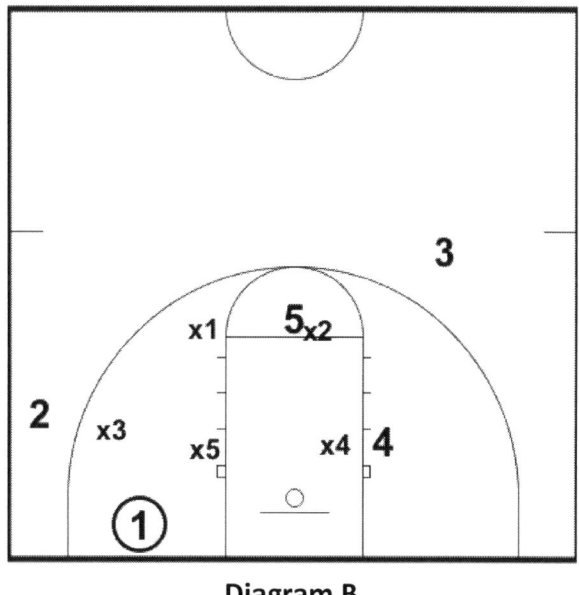

Diagram B

As shown in **Diagram C** the defense has decided to use X5 to cover the player with the ball. X3 must remain in position near #2. If X3 covered the ball then #2 would be wide open for an easy three-point shot on a pass from #1. The defender X5 seems to be the logical choice to defend #1 since there is not an offensive player in X5's zone defense area.

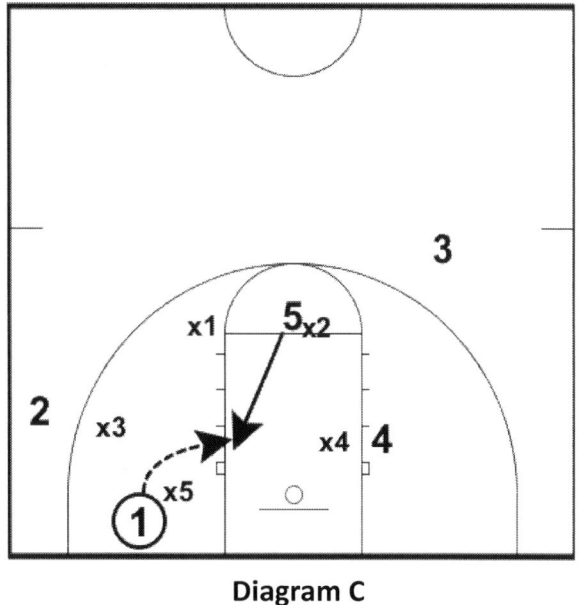

Diagram C

When X5 moves to cover #1, it opens a gap in the ball side low post allowing #5 to roll down the lane for a lay-up.

The next time the ball is entered into the short post and X5 covers, X4 will react to #5's cut and move to prevent the lay-up (**Diagram D**). This leaves #4 open for a bounce pass for a power shot.

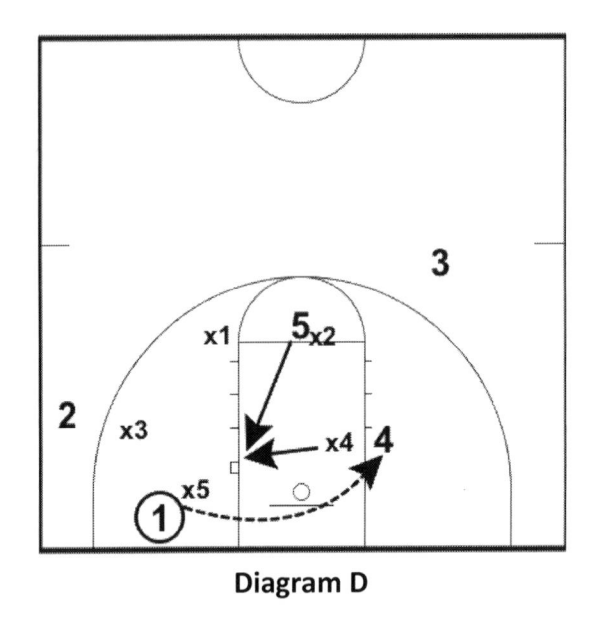

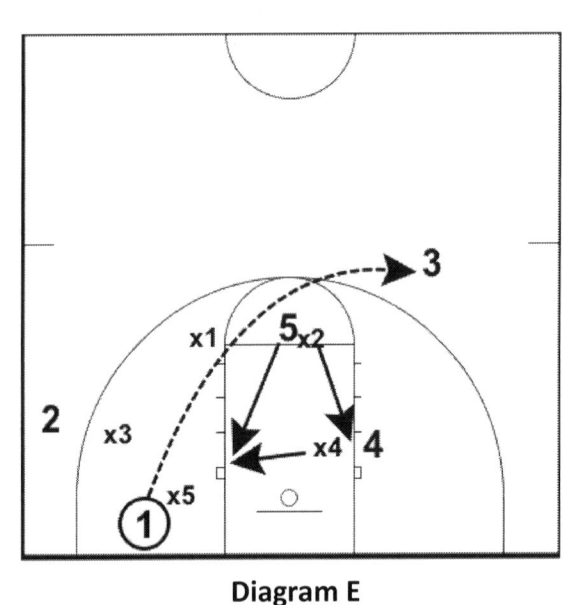

Diagram D

Diagram E

The scoring pass to #4 forces X2 to cover down on #4 the next time the ball is entered into #1 in the short post (**Diagram E**). This creates a diagonal skip pass to #3 for an uncontested three-point shot or an attacking drive into the lane area.

Granted, #1 must be a skilled passer to make these passes and have the ability to read the defense to determine which shot option is available, but all of these opportunities were created by putting a good passer in an area that is unnatural for a 2-3 zone to defend (the 1-3-1 zone defense is the zone best suited to handle this alignment).

14

Move the Ball and Move People

Number 12
Always Assertively Face-up and Look Under the Net

With the possible exception of a low post offensive player, every single time an offensive player receives the ball, the player must without fail face-up and look under the net. This habit allows the offensive player to see all four teammates as well as all five defensive players.

This habit allows the offensive player to take advantage of open teammates, potential defensive mistakes and scoring opportunities. Failure to assertively face-up allows the defense to pressure the ball into possible turnovers and the offensive player is not able to attack the defense by pass, drive or shot.

Number 13
All Zone Defenses Key Off the Ball

Man-to-man defense can be described as one defender guarding the ball and four defenders helping. Zone defense is five defenders guarding the ball and a specified area of the court. For a zone defense to be effective, it must work this way. In fact, this is a strength of zone defense.

Like most things though, a strength can also be a weakness. Because the zone keys on the ball, the offense can set up attacking tactics behind the zone or use fakes to freeze or shift the zone.

Number 14
Move the Ball With a Purpose

One of the worst habits players can develop on offense is to move the ball with no specific purpose in mind. This is particularly true in regard to the use of the dribble.

The ball should only be moved with a specific purpose in mind. The following are six acceptable reasons to move the ball in a zone offense by pass or dribble:

- To score.
- To improve passing angle.
- To feed the post.
- To distort the zone defense.
- To take advantage of a potential scoring opportunity two passes away.
- To escape trouble

Number 15
Move the Ball to Distort the Zone

Regardless of the zone defense, all want to defend specific areas of the court and to do so in specific ways. Distorting the zone by moving defenders out of their assigned areas creates gaps and rotational problems for zones.

Dribbling the ball off the baseline when pressured by a backline defender of a 2-3 zone will create a gap on the baseline for a shooter to slip into. Passing the ball into the short post area will force the defense to change its zone slides to cover the ball.

Number 16
Move People to Distort the Zone

Just as moving the ball can cause a zone defense to distort, so can moving people. Initial alignments are one way to distort a zone. Lining up post players deep in the court near the offensive team's goal will force all zone defenses to either back up from the initial desired defensive areas or to spread the zone out vertically, creating larger than normal gaps in the zone defense.

Number 17
Move People Into the Gaps

All offensive systems want open players to receive the ball, either for open shots or the ability to face-up and pass the ball without defensive pressure on the ball. Placing players in gaps or moving players into gaps in zone defenses make this goal more easily achievable for zone offenses. It has the further benefit of possibly distorting the zone defense from its desired positions.

Number 18
Flash Cutters From Behind the Zone Into the Gaps

Take advantage of the zone defense's need to maintain constant visual contact with the ball and its location. Timed flash cuts into gaps from behind the line of vision of the zone defenders gives the offense the added advantage of the element of surprise.

This is one of the key reasons why all offensive players must assertively face-up and look under the net after receiving the ball. Failure to do so will rob the offense of the brief opportunity available to pass the ball to a cutter moving into a gap from behind the zone.

As the cutter moves into the open area of the zone defense, the cutter also moves into the visual line of sight of the defenders, allowing the defenders to adjust their position accordingly. The flash cutter will usually be open briefly, requiring a well-timed pass to the flash cutter.

Number 19
Use Shot Fakes to Freeze the Zone

One of the most effective weapons against any zone defense, and one of the least used, is the ball fake. A two-inch shot fake will momentarily freeze the zone defense due to the zone's fixation with the ball. This one second may be all that is required to give a cutter time to move into an open area, allow a screen to be set or for an offensive player to move into position to score.

Note, if the offensive player with the ball is not facing the basket, the shot fake will not be believable and will not achieve the desired effect of freezing the zone.

Number 20
Use Pass Fakes to Shift the Zone

Just as a shot fake will freeze a zone, an excellent pass fake that is believable capable of shifting all five zone defenders in the direction of the pass fake.

This can create openings in the zone, relieve pressure on the ball or force the defense into poor position to recover. For a pass fake to be believable there must be an offensive player in the general area of the pass fake.

Number 21
Change Direction

Combining a pass fake or shot fake with a change of direction of the movement of the ball can force the zone defense into poor position and create problems when the defense recovers. This is a particularly useful concept against zone defenses that are well coaches and aggressive in moving as a unit.

An example of effective use of this tactic would be for an excellent three-point shooter located on a wing to pass the ball to a teammate on the top of the key area. This teammate takes one hard dribble away from the three-point shooter towards the other wing, pass fakes to the wing and passes back to the three-point shooter.

While the ball was being dribbled off the top, the former ball side low post offensive player moved up the lane and set a flare screen on the back of the zone.

The extra few feet created by shifting the zone and the one or two seconds obtained by the pass fake and one dribble is often all that is needed to obtain an excellent shot for the three-point shooter (**Diagram A**).

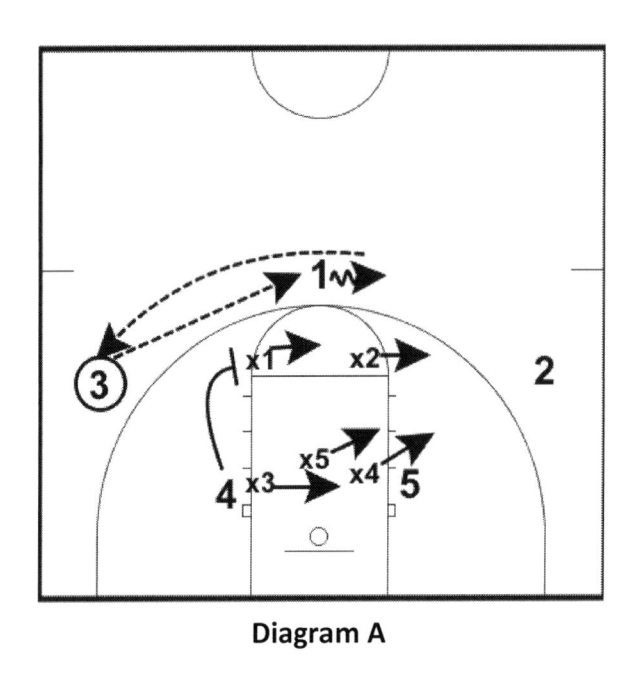

Diagram A

Number 22
Use Skip Passes

Most well coached defenses are good at providing help. This is not where the defense is usually beaten by the offense, recovery from providing help is.

Skip passes are an excellent way to force the defense to cover long distances in recovery. Mistakes in closing out or positioning can be taken advantage of by forcing the defense to cover long distances. If the defense is forced to move twelve feet at maximum speed in recovery, the offense can use the defense's momentum against individual defenders This is done by driving in the direction opposite of where the defender came from, usually towards the goal.

15

Penetration

Number 23
Penetrate With the Dribble

All defenses are designed to prevent penetration towards the goal. One of the best ways to create help and recovery situations leading to defensive breakdowns and mistakes is to penetrate the zone with the dribble.

Dribble penetration forces defenders to leave their designated area to provide help or to prevent an uncontested shot. This forced movement creates gaps for other players to slide into for scoring opportunities (**Diagram A**).

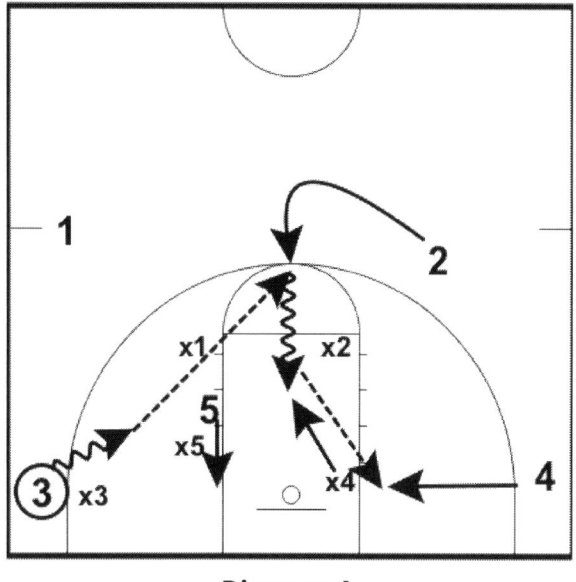

Diagram A

Number 24
Penetrate With the Pass

The dribble is the most commonly thought of method of penetrating a zone but it is not always the most practical. Passing the ball into an open area of a zone defense inside the high post, low post, short corner or lane areas is equally effective and often easier and safer than penetrating the zone with the dribble.

Number 25
Penetrate With Cutters

Cutters moving through key areas of a zone can have the same effect as penetrating a zone with the dribble or a pass. The cutter passing through a vulnerable area of the zone defense can "drag" a defender with the cutter, creating a gap or open area by moving the defender out of his or her designated area (**Diagram A**).

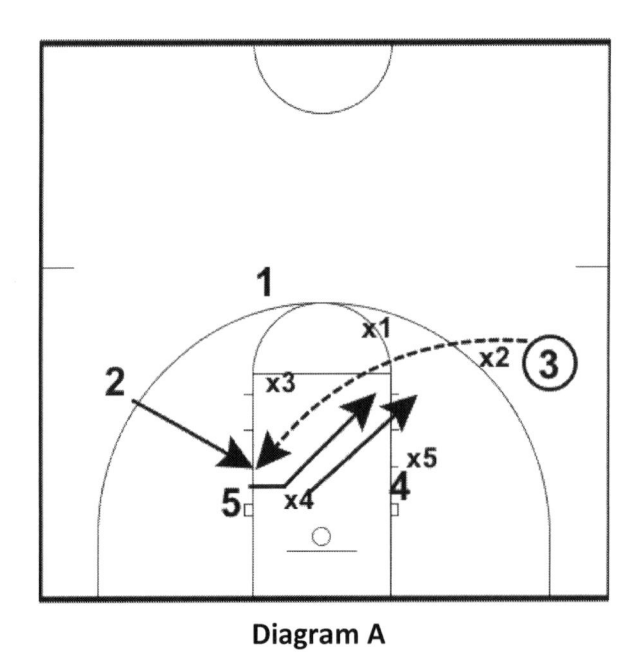

Diagram A

16

Use of the Dribble to Attack

Number 26
Freeze and Slide

The first priority of all defensive systems is to stop the ball. Dribbling directly at a defender in a zone defense will force the defensive player to guard the ball in an effort to stop the ball from penetrating. The drive directly at the defensive player requires the defender to "freeze" in place in order to block the direct path of the attacking ball handler in the attempt of dribble penetrating directly to the goal.

Once the defensive player has been "frozen," the natural tendency of all defensive players is to now defend the ball so long as the ball handler continues to dribble the ball. This tendency should be taken advantage of by dribbling the zone defender away from his or her designated area of zone defense, either creating a gap, distorting the zone or forcing another defender to cover the newly opened gap in the zone, creating yet another distortion of the zone (**Diagram 26-A**). This concept is referred to as freeze and slide.

Diagram A

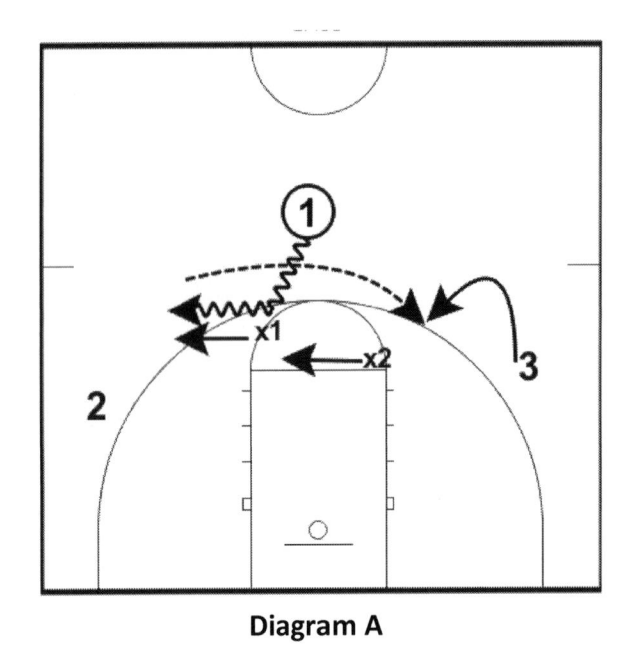

Number 27
Dribble Off the Baseline

Baseline zone defenders are vulnerable to the dribble off tactic when the ball handler in possession of the ball is an excellent three-point shooter. The nearest baseline defender must go out and pressure the ball or concede an easy three-point attempt.

The shooter dribbles the ball assertively off the baseline using two dribbles, faces-up to the basket and pass fakes towards the next perimeter offensive player in the direction the ball handler was dribbling or a teammate in the high post. This freezes the baseline defender for a second.

While the dribble off has been taking place a cutter from behind the zone has been moving towards the now unoccupied ball side corner (**Diagram A**).

The ball handler rips the ball across his or her chest and passes the ball away from the on ball defender to the cutter now occupying the corner (**Diagram B**).

Often a single dribble off can create enough space and time for a good three-point shot. If X4 is a hard working defender X4 might be able to recover to the shooter who has just occupied the corner. If this is the case, immediately repeat the dribble off. Seldom is a defense able to defend this tactic twice in a row without making an adjustment to the basic zone defense's coverage.

Use of the Dribble to Attack

Diagram A

Diagram B

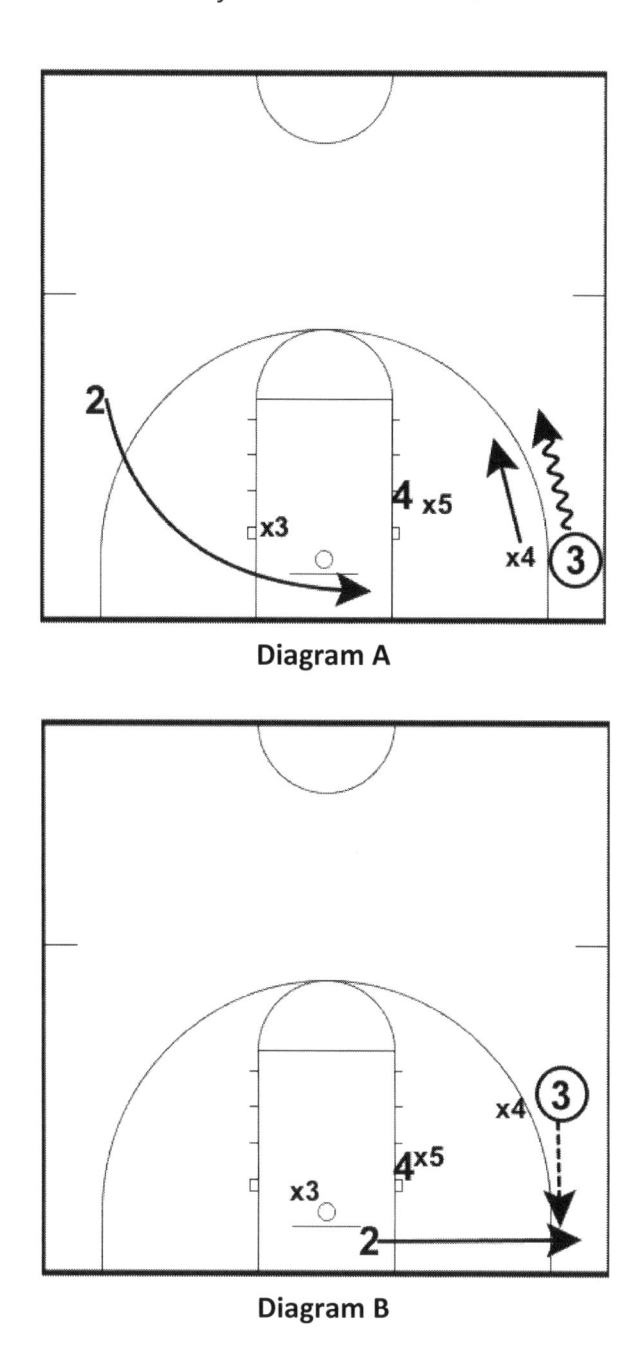

Number 28
Dribble Off the Top

Dribbling the ball off the top of the three-point circle when combined with an effective pass fake can draw the top defenders of the zone in the direction the ball handler was dribbling. If the defense has shifted enough a three-point shot is possible. This tactic can also create gaps or seams for a pass from the perimeter player who received the initial pass to a flash cutter or post player (**Diagram A**).

Coaching Basketball's Zone Attack Offense Using Blocker-Mover Motion Offense

Diagram A

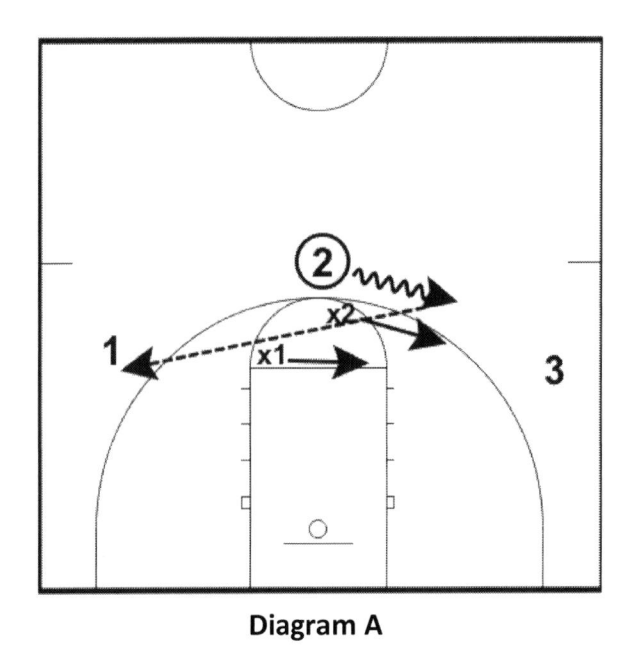

Number 29
Penetrate and Skip

Penetrate and skip is a concept that combines penetration via the dribble with a skip pass. This combined tactic takes advantage of a gap in the zone and the fact a penetrating drive will draw or freeze zone defenders in place. The skip pass creates a long recovery situation for the zone and creates the possibility of a three-point shot attempt, further penetration on the dribble or a pass in a gap created by the long recovery of the help side zone defenders (**Diagram A**).

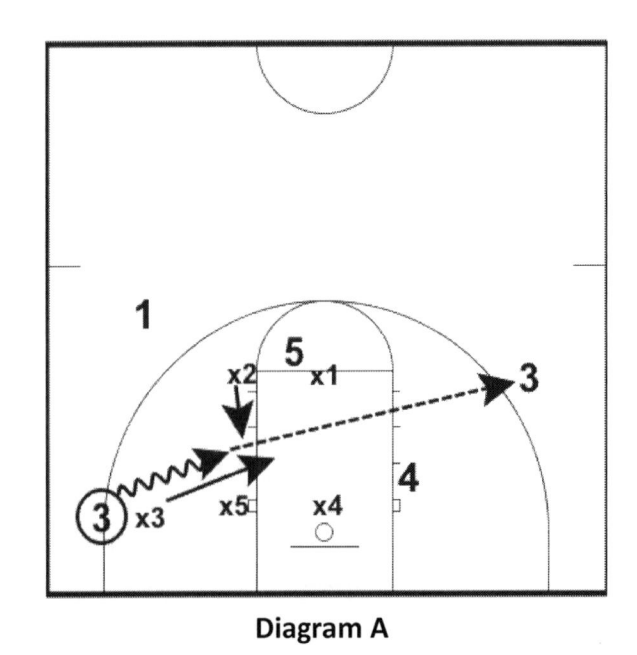

Diagram A

Number 30
Loop

The dribble loop can be used to create a variety of opening as well as to move the ball to the wing if the zone defense is making a point to wing pass difficult. **Diagram A** depicts a dribble loop without any defenders for the purpose of clarity.

The ball handler dribbles directly at the player intended to make the loop cut. The cutter makes a curved cut underneath the ball handler being careful to create sufficient space as depicted and always facing the ball and maintaining eye contact with the ball handler. The ball handler, upon reaching the wing, faces-up and rips the ball across his or her chest and passes with the outside hand away from the defense to the loop cutter on top.

Diagram A

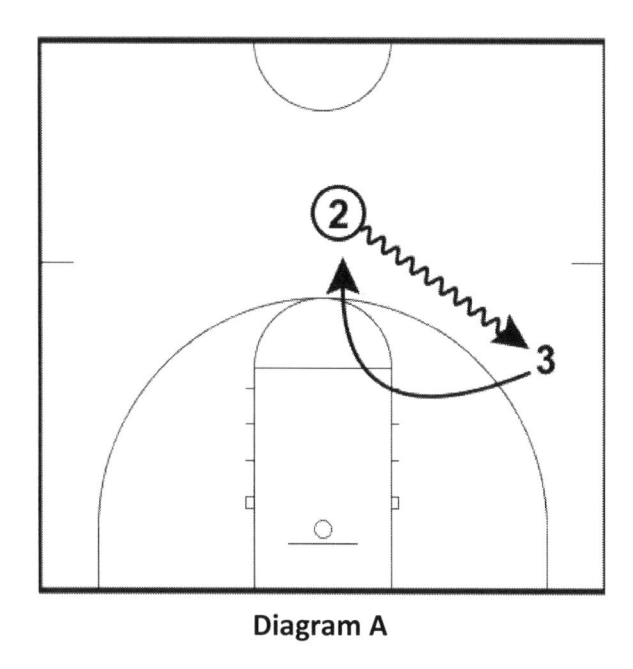

Diagram B shows the defensive action of a 2-3 zone against a loop cut. The backline defenders have been omitted for clarity. X2 maintains pressure on the ball as #s drives towards the wing initiating the dribble loop.

X1 shifts over to cover the ball side high post area while #3 loop cuts underneath the dribble and immediately faces-up upon arrival at the top of the three-point circle. The simple dribble loop alone may be enough to obtain a three-point shot. If a seam in the zone is available a high low ball side low post feed can be made as well.

Coaching Basketball's Zone Attack Offense Using Blocker-Mover Motion Offense

Diagram B

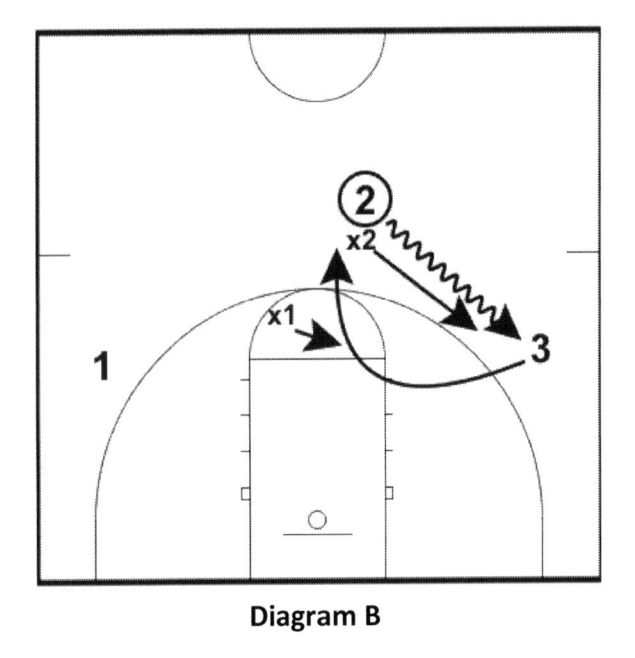

A hard dribble at X1 will freeze the defender allowing a pass to the open shooter on the wing. Often this will result in an open three-point shot or as X1 sprints to close out an additional opportunity to penetrate the zone with a pass or dribble drive (**Diagram C**).

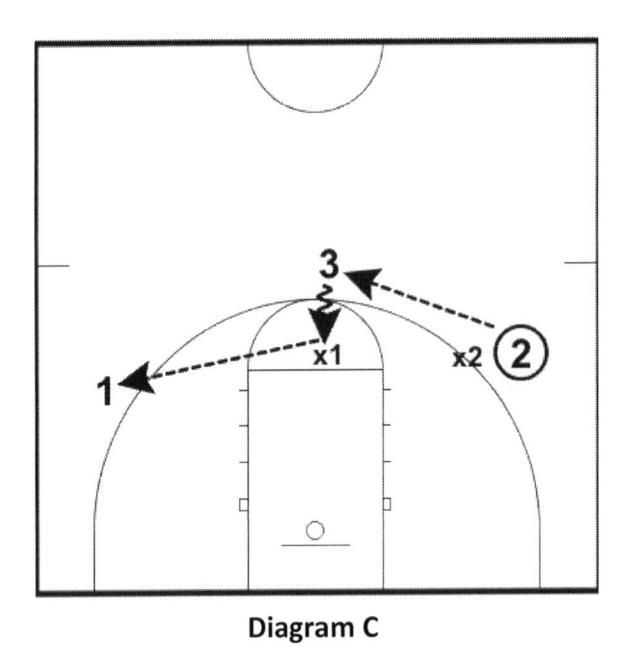

Diagram C

17

Screen the Zone

Number 31
Screen-in

Screening the zone is an effective yet seldom used tactic. The screen-in tactic is highly effective at setting up a three-point shot attempt and entering the ball into either the low post or high post. **Diagram A** depicts the initial alignment against the backline of a 2-3 zone. For clarity the top two defenders have been omitted from the diagrams.

The wing opposite the ball, #2, slides down behind the low post opposite the ball. The ball is skip passed by #3 to #2 in the corner while #5 sets a legal back screen on the last defender of the zone defense (**Diagram B**). If #2 has enough time, this will result in an excellent three-point shot opportunity.

When setting the back screen, not only does #5 have to give the defender being screened one step, the screen must be set at such an able the defender fights over the screen on the high side, or the side away from the baseline.

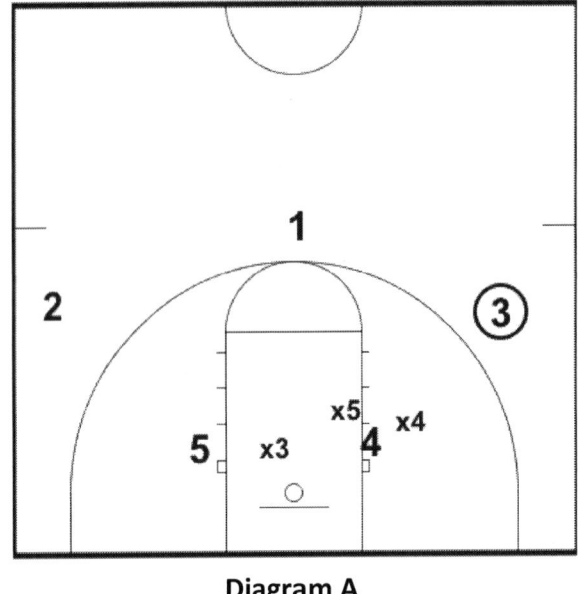

Coaching Basketball's Zone Attack Offense Using Blocker-Mover Motion Offense

Diagram A

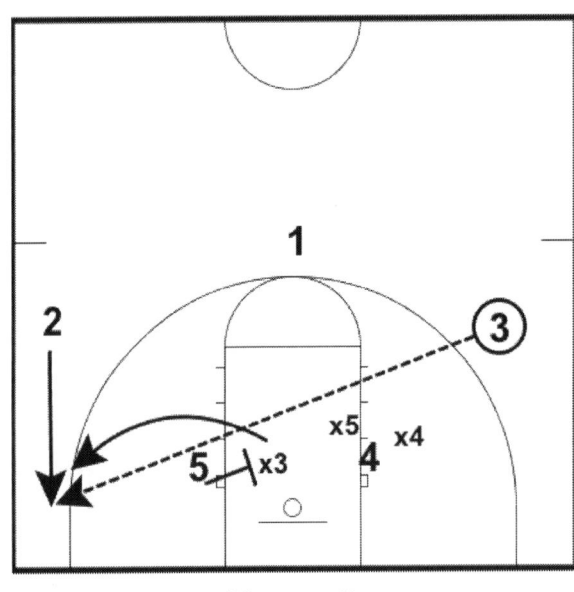

Diagram B

The reason for setting the screen at this angle is to create plenty of space for a baseline bounce pass to enter the ball into the low post.

After X3 fights over the screen from #5 and #5 goes to the next closest post defender and executes a rear turn (pivot) and seals the defender. The other offensive post player, #4, flashes into the ball side high post from behind the zone defense (**Diagram C**). If #5 is open in the low post #2 makes the entry pass for a scoring opportunity.

Screen the Zone

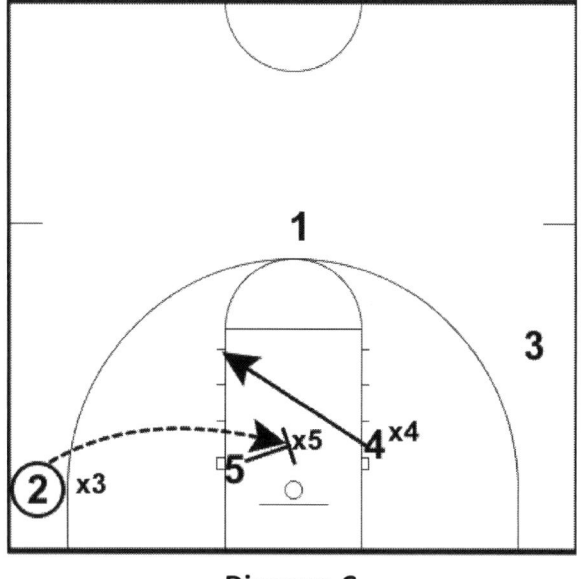

Diagram C

If the ball is entered into the high post #5 changes the angle of the post seal to set up for a high low pass. The defender still must be pinned in the middle of the lane in order to create both a passing lane and a shot after catching the ball (**Diagram D**).

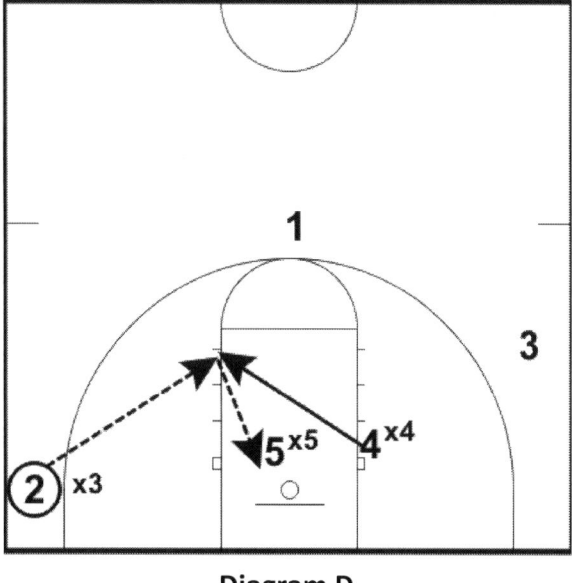

Diagram D

69

Number 32
Screen-out

The screen-out is a somewhat unorthodox tactic and must be executed carefully to avoid fouling, yet it can be highly effective. The set-up for a screen-out is shown in **Diagram A**.

The opposite post player #5 flashes into the high post and receives a pass from the wing #3. On the pass the offensive low post #4 steps out from the low post, rear turns (pivot) and seals the defender X3 who was pressuring the perimeter back to back. This "seal" creates space for a short bank shot just outside of the lane if executed properly.

Once X3 has been screened-out, #5 will be able to make a high low pass to #4 for a score (**Diagram B**).

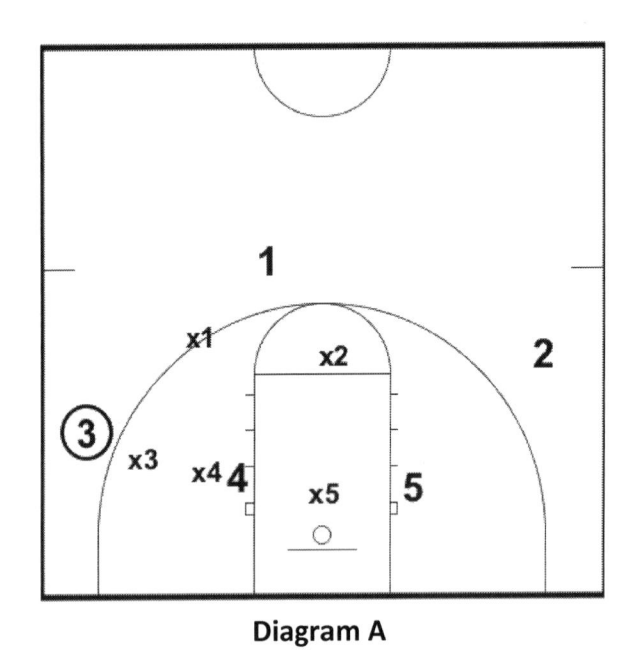

Diagram A

The low post can shoot or look to pass. In **Diagram C** #4 fans the ball out to a three-point shooter #2 with a diagonal skip pass opposite. Another possible option would be for #5 to cut from the high post to the opposite low post block for a back half of a duck cut.

Screen the Zone

Diagram B

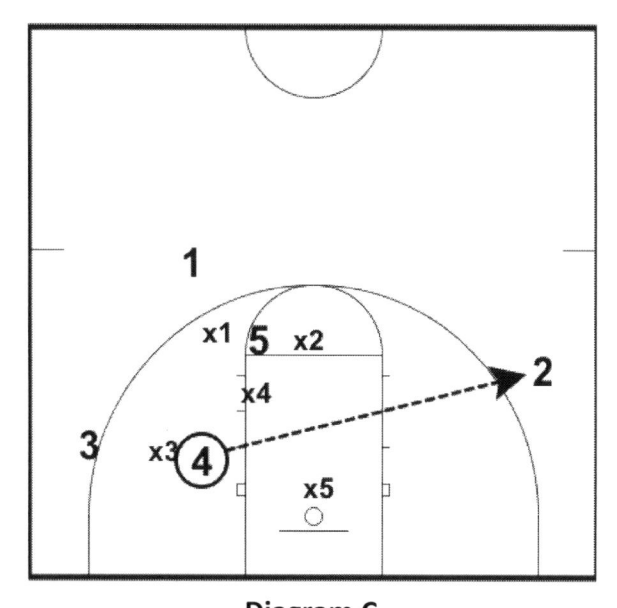

Diagram C

71

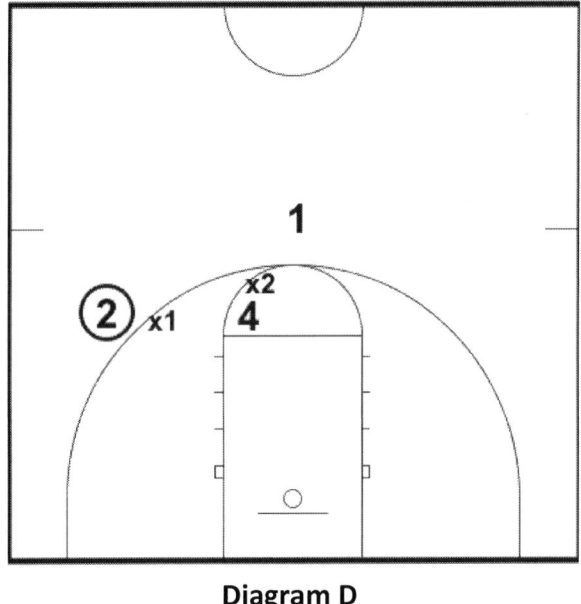

Diagram D

The screen out tactic can also be employed in the high post area (**Diagram D**). On the pass from #2 to the perimeter player on top of the three-point line #4 steps out and executes a rear turn and seals X1 back-to-back. X2 must move quickly to pressure the ball, creating a passing lane to #4 (**Diagram E**).

The post player can shoot, make a high low pass for a shot, drive or fan the ball to a perimeter player for a scoring opportunity.

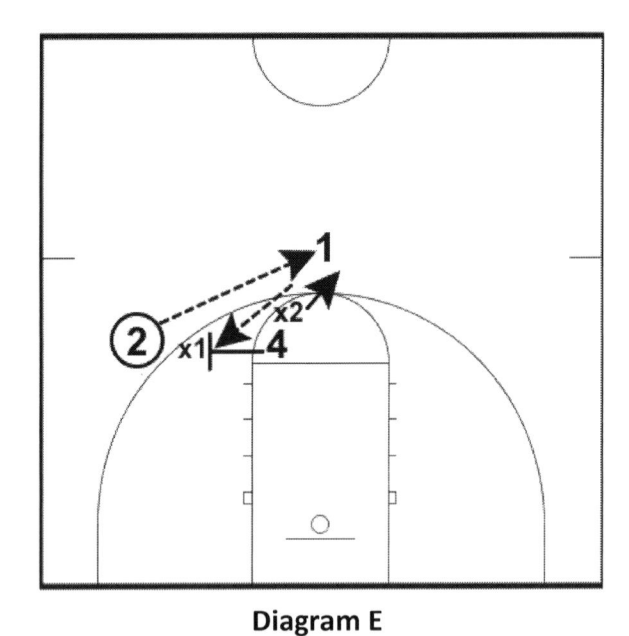

Diagram E

Screen the Zone

Number 33
Screen Down

The screen down is very similar to setting a down screen against a man-to-man defense. The perimeter player at the top of the three-point line simply sets a down screen on the zone defender closest to the perimeter player opposite the ball. The perimeter player without the ball, #2, makes a v-cut to utilize the down and screen and receives the ball. The screener, #1, should balance the floor after setting the screen by filling what was #2's space on the court (**Diagram A**).

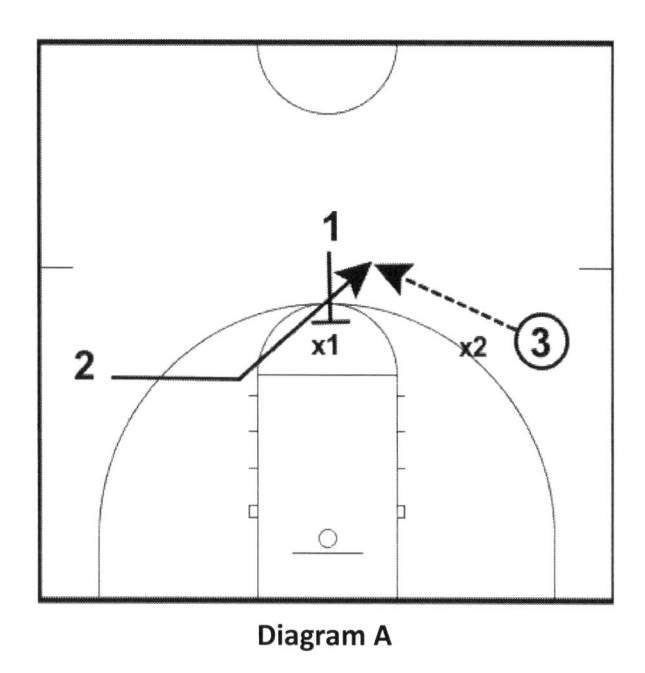

Diagram A

Number 34
Flare Screen

Like the down screen, the flare screen is very similar as a flare screen set against man-to-man defense. Perimeter player #2 sets a flare screen on the last top zone defender X1. #1 makes a v-cut to utilize the flare screen, making certain his or her chest is facing the ball handler at all times.

#3 drives the flare screen to freeze the defender being screened by taking one or two dribbles and then skip passing the ball to the cutter for a three-point shot attempt (**Diagram A**).

Coaching Basketball's Zone Attack Offense Using Blocker-Mover Motion Offense

Diagram A

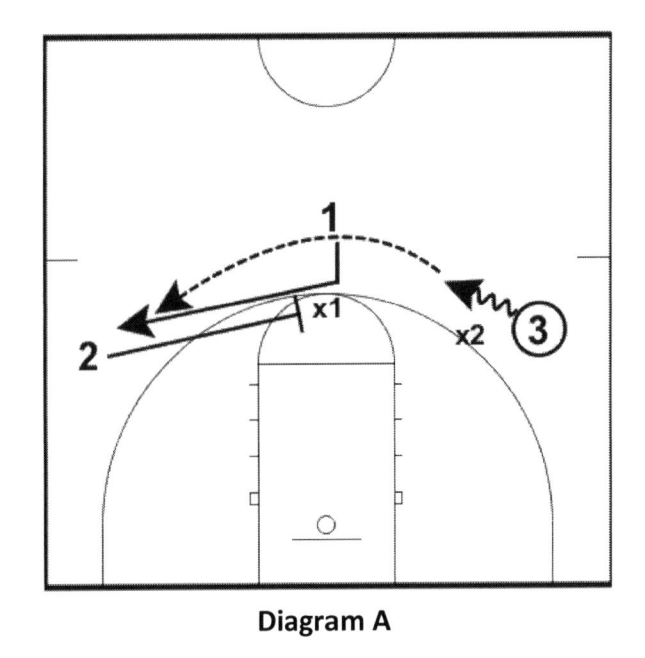

Number 35
Center Screen

The center screen tactic is designed to create an open shot in the low post area by screening the middle defender of the zone defense. **Diagrams A** and **3B** depict the center screen tactic against a 2-1-2 zone. Diagrams 35-C and 35-D depict the center screen tactic against a 2-3 zone.

For this tactic to be effective the timing of the setting of the screen, the pass to the wing and the cut of the other post player must be carefully coordinated and timed.

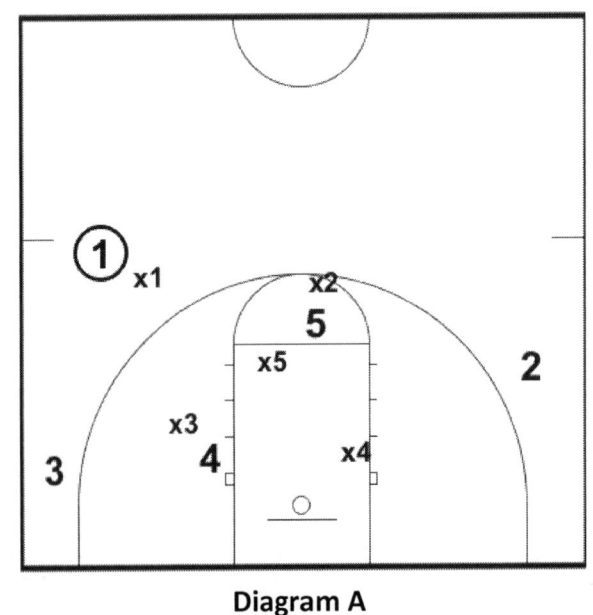

Diagram A

Screen the Zone

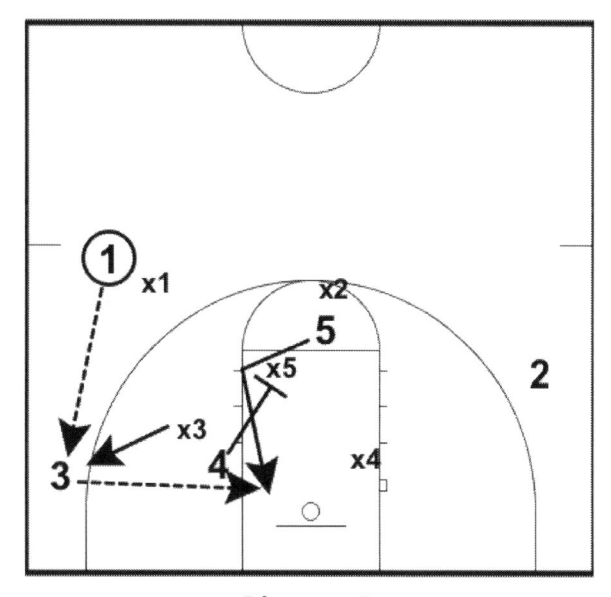

Diagram B

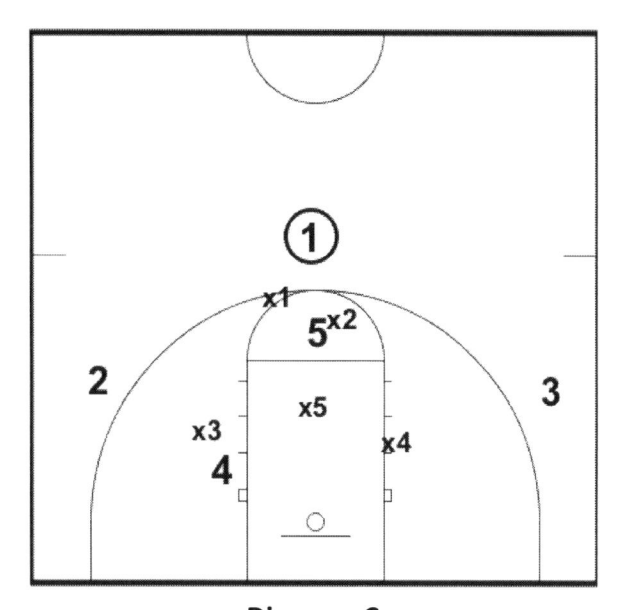

Diagram C

75

Diagram D

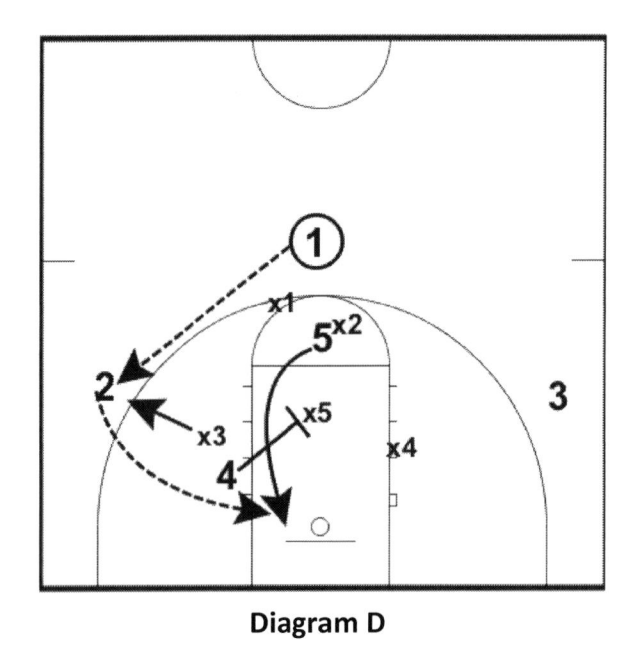

Number 36
Combine Screens

As an offensive unit becomes more comfortable with the tactic of screening a zone defense, more and more screens should be used in combination against the zone. A screen-in could be set by a post player while a wing on the same side of the court sets a flare screen for a three-point shooter on the top of the three-point line.

This double screen may create a three-point shot or a great opportunity to enter the ball into the post for a score and possible foul (**Diagram A**).

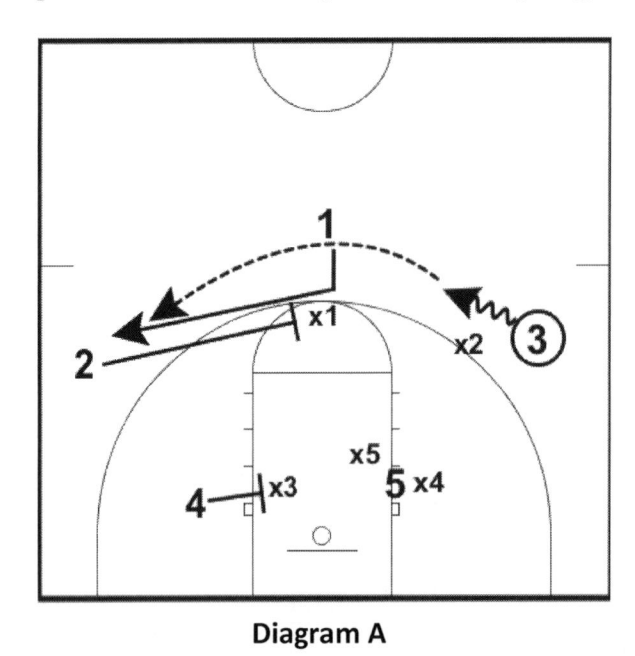

Diagram A

18

The Inside Game Against the Zone

Number 37
Go to the Defender and Seal

Post players are taught to post up at a specific location on the court. This is not always the best approach to posting up and getting open against a zone defense.

Man-to-man defenses defend individual offensive players. If a post player occupies a specific area on the court against a man-to-man defense, the defense will guard the post player wherever the post chooses to post up.

Contact is essential to hold a post seal on offense. Zone post defenders are often able to avoid being sealed because of the zone's practice of guarding areas and not necessarily individual offensive players.

This can be overcome if the post player goes to the nearest zone defender in the post area and seals the defender, regardless of where the post defender is located.

Number 38
Seal Out

Post players think of sealing post defenders into the lane. Sealing a zone defender out of the lane area can be equally effective.

Number 39
Find the Gap

As the ball is reversed and the post player is now behind the zone defense, the post player should look for gaps in the zone defense. Once a gap has been identified the post player should flash into the gap to get open and receive the ball.

Number 40
Let the Ball Come to You

Playing in the post is extremely taxing physically. Rather than expend effort battling the defensive post players, the offensive low post player should watch the movement of the ball on the perimeter. When the ball comes to the post player's side of the court the post should then step into the nearest post defender and seal.

The timing of this technique is simple. As the ball is reversed on the perimeter, when the ball is passed from the point to the wing on the same side of the court as the post, the post player steps into the nearest post defender while executing a rear turn and sealing.

Number 41
Screen to Get Open

One of the best ways to get open against any defense is to set a screen for another player. Tactics such as the screen-in, screen-out and center screen are particularly effective at getting post players open.

Number 42
Play the High Low Game

One of the hardest concepts for any zone defense to effectively and consistently defend is the high to low post-to-post pass. For this tactic to be effective the low post offensive player must seal effectively to create both space to receive the ball and to execute some type of post move after catching the ball.

The high post must face-up to the goal and pass the ball away from the defender guarding him or her and the defender guarding the low post.

Number 43
Inside Out – Fan the Ball

One of the most effective ways to set up three-point shot attempts is for the low post to fan the ball out to a perimeter shooter with a diagonal opposite pass (**Diagram A**).

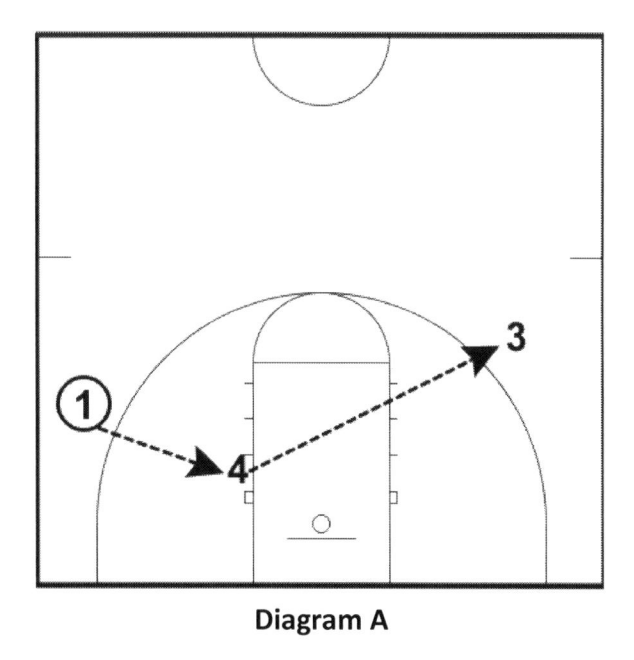

Diagram A

Upon receiving the ball the post player must chin the ball and look over the high side shoulder. This allows the post player to see the greatest portion of the court, the defense and other offensive players. If the post player is able to see an open three-point shooter and a passing lane is available, the post player should make the diagonal skip pass. The post player must square his or her shoulders up with the intended receiver when making this pass.

This tactic prevents the defense from collapsing or trapping the offensive low post out of the need to cover open three-point shooters to prevent the post from fanning the ball out to shooters. Good post players require a minimum of two defenders to neutralize the post. Eliminating the second defender by consistently pass the ball to open teammates creates more scoring chances for the post player.

19

Planning to Rebound and Floor Balance

Number 44
Form a Rebounding Triangle

Offensive rebounding is essential for success. Teams who have a haphazard approach to offensive rebounding are not very successful in consistently obtaining a high percentage of offensive rebounds.

The first goal is to form a rebounding triangle when a shot attempt is made. Unless #1 or #2 has penetrated the lane area, the three players who form the rebounding triangle are players #3, #4 and #5. If the shot attempt was taken from the middle third of the court, the triangle should be formed as shown in **Diagram A**. If the shot is taken from a wing, in the example shown the shot was taken from the left wing, the rebound triangle is formed as shown in **Diagram B.**

Diagram A

Diagram B

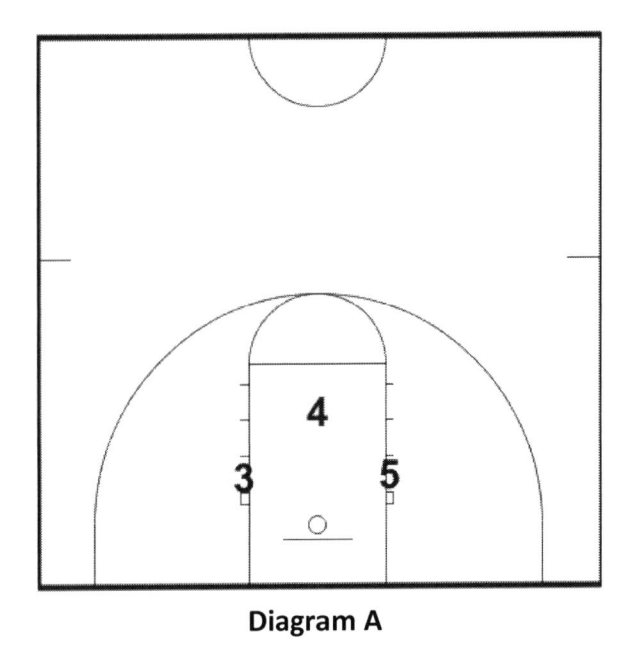

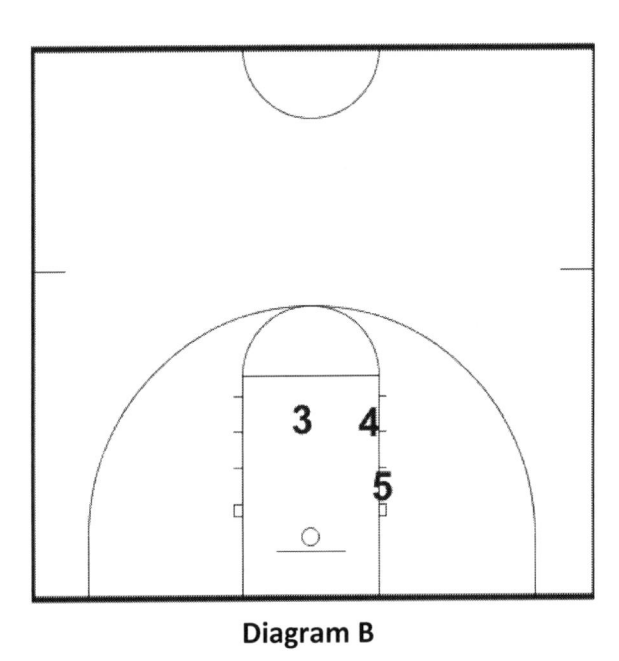

Number 45
Floor Balance for Transition

Fast break teams always want to run following a defensive rebound. Good fast break teams run off made baskets as well. It is essential when a shot attempt is made that the offense balances the floor both for offensive rebounding and to prevent the defense from obtaining a fast break scoring opportunity.

In **Diagram A** #1 has made a three-point shot attempt from the wing. #1 rotates to the top of the key for a possible return pass for another three-point attempt and to pick up the opponent's point guard on an outlet pass and #2 has

Planning to Rebound and Floor Balance

sprinted to half court to prevent a long pass for a lay-up. #3, #4 and #5 have formed a rebound triangle for a shot attempt from the wing area. **Diagram B** shows the player's final positions.

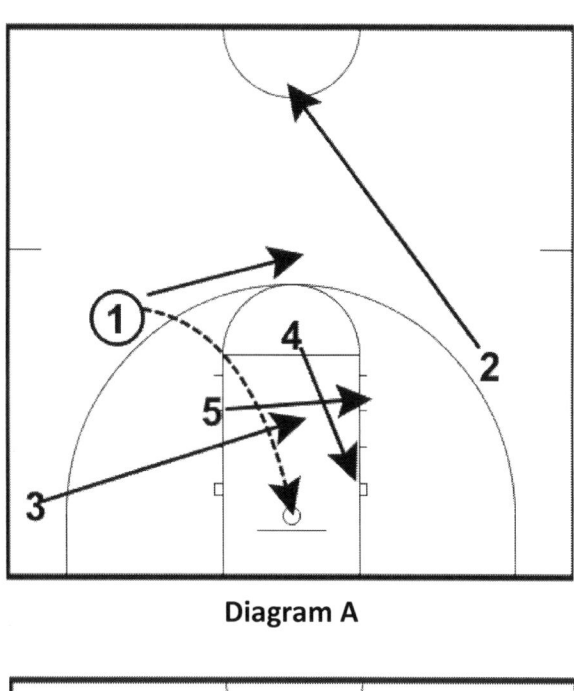

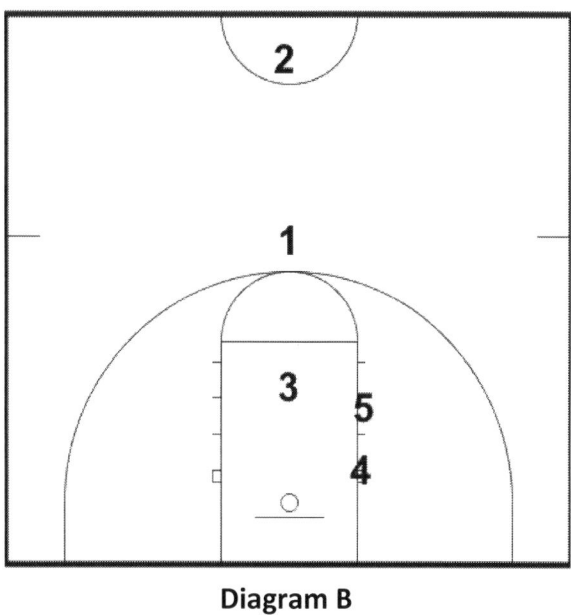

Diagram A

Diagram B

20

Principles of Attacking – Strategy and Attacking a Zone Defense

Number 46
Beat the Zone Down the Court

The easiest way to defeat a zone defense is to beat the opponent down the court and score before the opponent can establish a set defense and organize all five players into a zone.

Number 47
Establish the Inside Game as
Quickly as Possible

Emphasize avoiding perimeter lapses, the tendency for zone attack offenses to become passive and rely on the jump shot and three-point shot only.

Establishing an inside game places the zone defense on the "defensive" and forces the defense to adjust and react to the offense instead of being assertive and proactively attempting to disrupt the offensive attack.

One of the best areas to pass for a score against a zone defense is either of the post areas, the high post or the low post. Fanning the ball out to shooters or to basket cutters becomes easier when the ball is in the post due to all zones being designed to defend the ball first and an area second. The zone is forced to focus on the ball in the post area allowing three-point shooters to move to open areas in gaps and basket cutters to find seams to the goal.

Number 48
Take the Ball Away From the Scorer and Bring it Back

Defenses are taught to be aware of where the best shooters are on offense. Take the ball to the shooter then take the ball to the opposite side of the court. Zone defenses will focus on the ball. Quickly bring the ball back to the shooter with a tactic such as a dribble off up top or combine this with a flare screen or screen-in.

Taking the ball away from the shooter will often get the defense to relax in regard to the shooter or lose focus on the location of the shooter.

This is a particularly effective tactic for a low post scorer. Ass the ball is brought back to the side of the court the low post player is on, the defense will have shifted to the opposite side of the court.

This allows the low post player to go to the zone defender responsible for defending the ball side low post and seal that defender in the lane, creating not only a gap or passing lane, but excellent scoring position upon receiving the post entry pass (**Diagram A** through **Diagram C**).

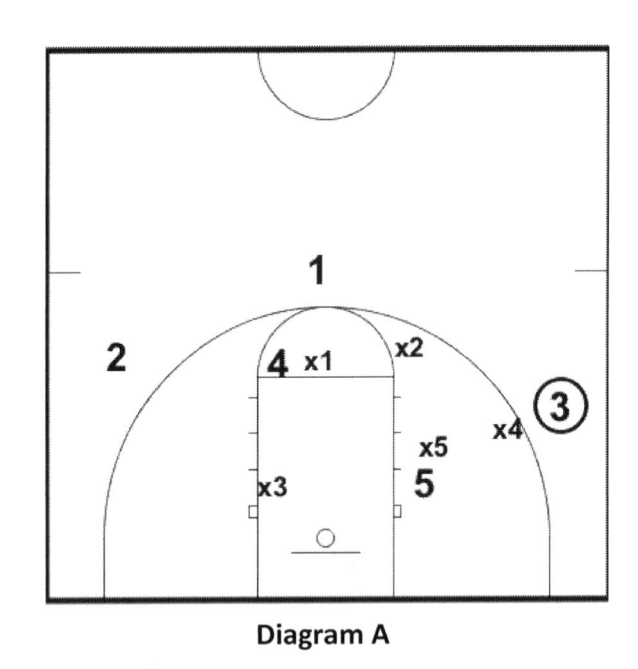

Diagram A

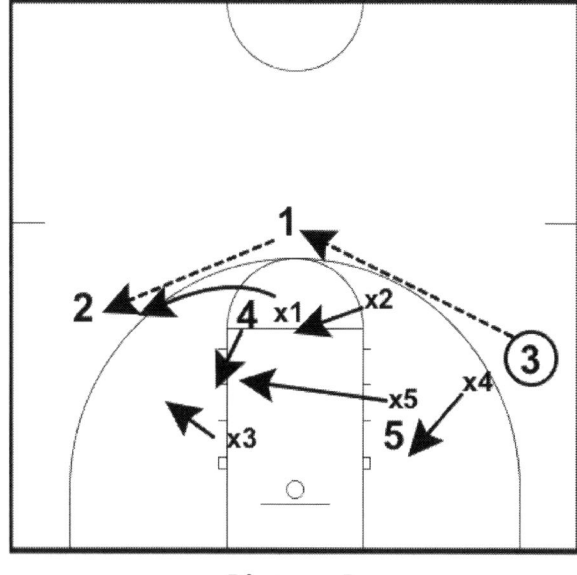

Principles of Attacking – Strategy and Attacking a Zone Defense

Diagram B

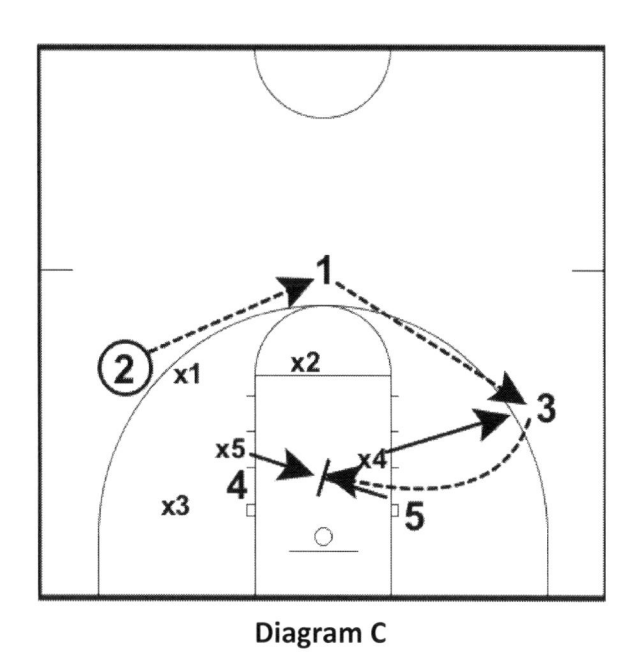

Diagram C

Number 49
Go at the Weakest Point Right Away

Never give an opponent a chance to hide a weakness or adjust to protect a weak defender. Sometimes teams can hurt themselves offensively by trying to attack a weak defender or weakness in a zone. This is due primarily to the fact the team seldom directly attacks the weak point in the zone.

Building this habit takes time but is essential. Never give the opponent a break. Always attack where the opponent is weakest. Force the opponent to always adjust and try to cover their weak point defensively.

The key to this concept working is the offense must have a thorough understanding of zone offensive concepts and how to utilize each concept or tactic to attack a specific part of a zone defense.

Number 50
Combine Concepts to Increase Effectiveness

In keeping with the tactic of never giving the defense a break, combine tactics when attacking the defense. As the game progresses and the offense is able to learn what tactics are most effective, combine effective tactics to maintain maximum pressure on the defense.

If dribble loops and screening in are effective, combine the two tactics and obtain three-point shots and pound the ball into the low post.

If dribble offs from the baseline create problems for the backline defenders, combine this with a cutter to the short post to further distort the zone defense.

Never give the defense a break. Attack and attack until the defense is demoralized and broken. Combining tactics makes the defense tentative and uncertain which will lead to a loss of confidence and cause mistakes on the part of the defense.

21

Adapting Blocker-Mover Motion for Zone Attack Offense

Zone Attack Offense Rules Using Blocker-Mover Principles

Zone attack offense, more so than man-to-man offense in the minds of many coaches, lends itself to using principles to attack. Regular motion offense adapts well with the addition of several concepts to attacking zone defenses. The same is true of Blocker-Mover motion offense.

Keeping the rules and concepts as few in number as possible is always a sound approach to teaching any system in basketball. With this in mind, here are the four principles or rules for attacking any zone defense:

- Play in the gaps of the zone defense.
- Distort the zone defense.
- Screen the zone defense.
- Use fakes to freeze and shift the zone defense.

These four concepts work for any zone attack offense and when combined with Blocker-Mover principles can create an effective attack against any zone defense. Some of the Blocker-Mover principles require slight modification, but all of the principles still apply. For example, the rule Movers hunt Blockers is modified for zone attack into Movers hunt Blockers and Gaps.

All of the examples provided to demonstrate these rules can be found in the chapters explaining zone attack concepts. The examples provided here simply **demonstrate the concepts in Chapters X-XX applied using a Blocker-Mover approach** to attacking a zone defense. It is also important to note for the examples depicted, the man-to-man Blocker-Mover motion offense rules are still being utilized.

The habits created through mastery of the man-to-man rules are important for the execution of the zone attack principles. Principles such as how many movers can occupy a perimeter zone, for example, govern the movement and spacing of the perimeter Blockers and Movers. By using this one rule, the offense is forced to move both players and the ball, a key principle of an attacking offense, against either a zone or man-to-man defense.

For coaches who have not obtained a copy of ***Coaching Basketball's Blocker-Mover Motion Offense,*** the rules for attacking against a man-to-man defense are included at the end of this chapter.

Play in the Gaps of the Zone Defense

Use Alignments to Line Up in the Gaps

One of the easiest ways to initiate the offense in the gaps of a zone defense is to use one of the Blocker-Mover alignments to set the offense up in the gaps of the zone defense.

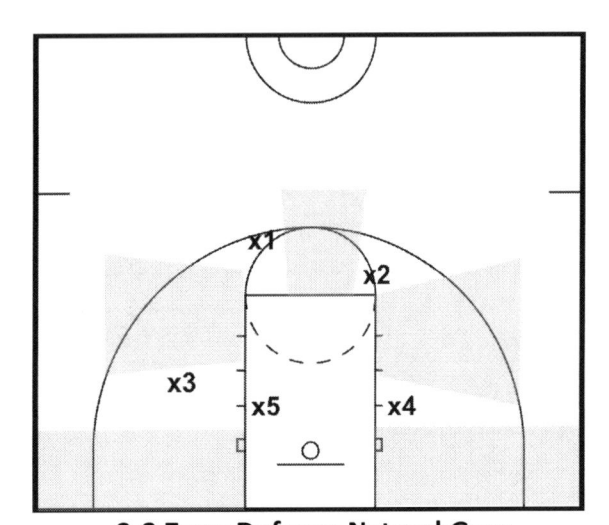

2-3 Zone Defense Natural Gaps 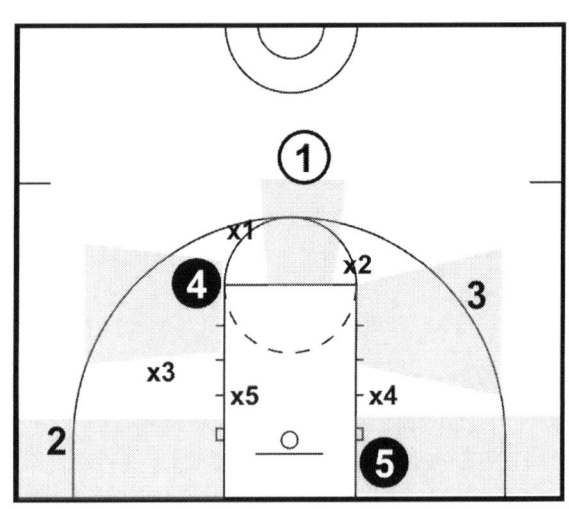   **Lane-Lane Alignment in the Gaps**

Every zone defense, except for pure match-up zones, has naturally occurring gaps. The common 2-3 zone defense is depicted with its five naturally occurring gaps. The Lane-Lane alignment depicts just one of the ways the offense can set up in the gaps using this particular alignment.

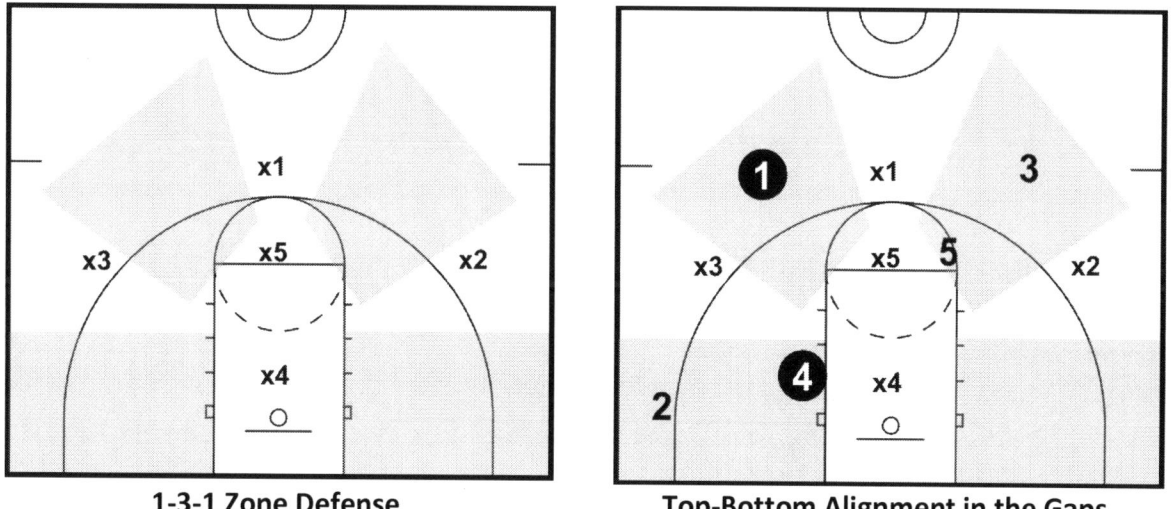

Adapting Blocker-Mover Motion for Zone Attack Offense

1-3-1 Zone Defense   **Top-Bottom Alignment in the Gaps**

Another common zone defense is the 1-3-1. The diagram above right depicts a Top-Bottom alignment against the 1-3-1.

Play the Gaps

In a perfect world for the offense, a zone defense would never adjust when offensive players set up in the natural gaps. Unfortunately, good defenses always adjust quickly. Even after adjusting, all zone defenses still have gaps in coverage. Movers must hunt out those gaps and move to fill them. Blockers, unless screening, should do the same when possible when a gap forms in their assigned area.

Diagram A   **Diagram B**

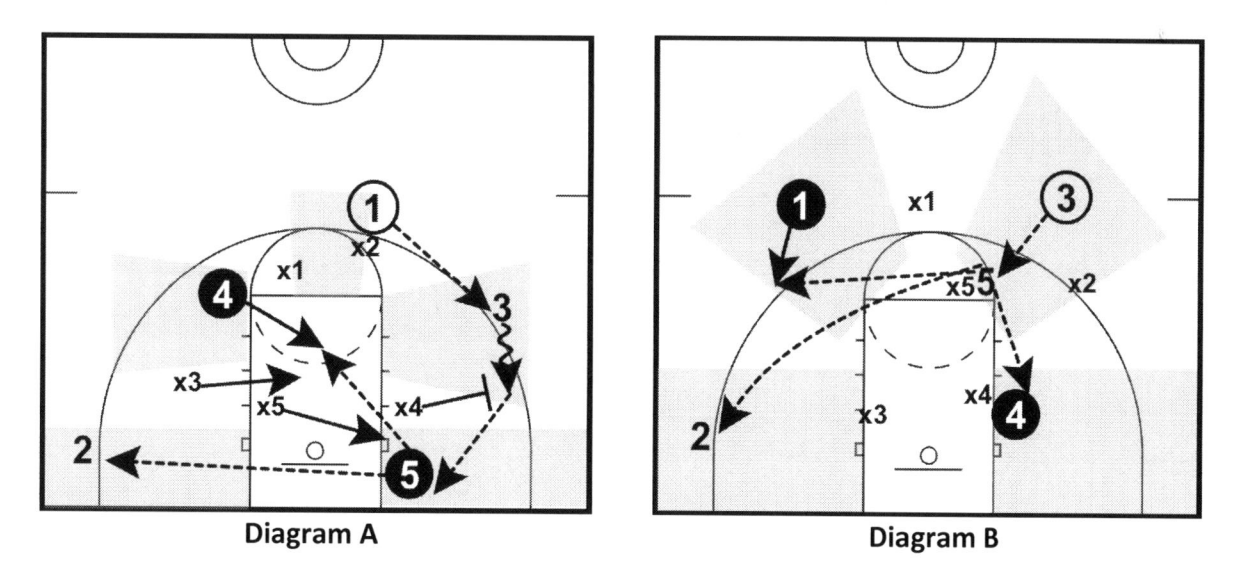

Diagram A depicts the ball being moved by a combination of pass and effective dribble use to #5 in the short post area behind the zone. The high blocker #4 steps

91

into the gap in the heart of the zone for a shot. Mover #2 is open in the opposite corner for a 3-point attempt.

Diagram B depicts an entry pass into the high post against a 1-3-1 zone defense. Blocker #4 has stepped in to seal for a high low pass. Mover #2 is open simply by virtue of the defensive wing sagging too far into the lane. Blocker #1 has moved to fill a gap while staying in the Top area of the Top-High alignment.

Movers Hunt Blockers and Gaps

Movers, by rule, must hunt Blockers. Against zone defenses this rule is modified slightly to include hunting for gaps in the zone defense.

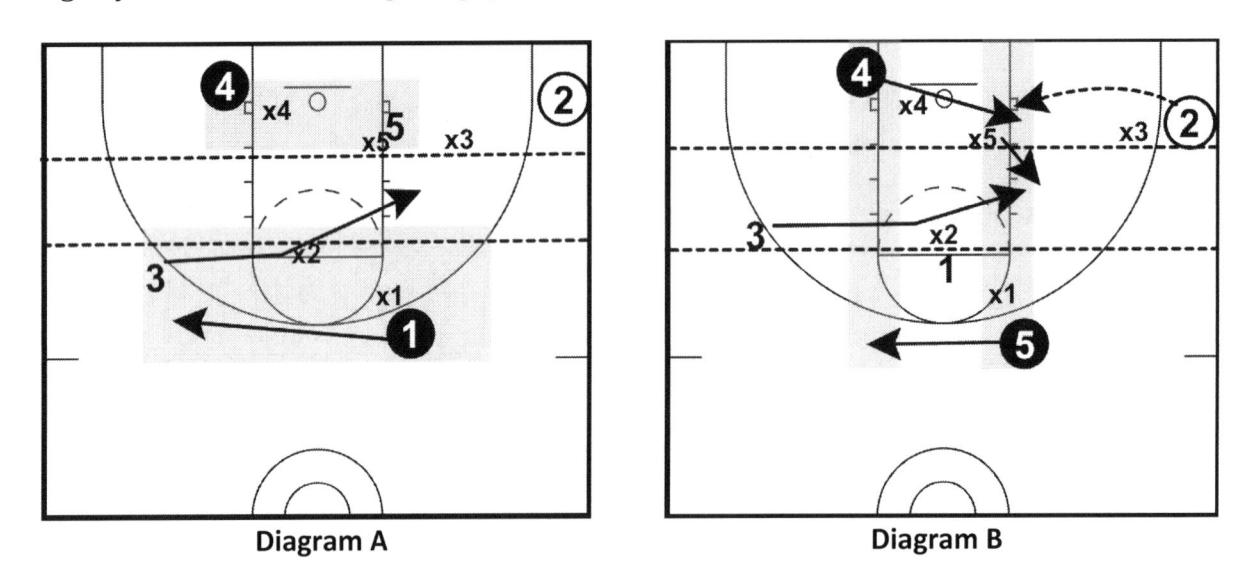

Diagram A   **Diagram B**

Mover #3 has spotted a gap (depicted by the two horizontal broken lines) and flashed across the lane to occupy the gap. Notice the use of a v-cut to freeze and cut under the defender X2. Because Mover #3 has emptied one of the three perimeter areas to move to the ball side of the court, the Top Blocker, #1 must vacate the perimeter area to fill the now vacant area to balance the floor (**Diagram A**).

Diagram B depicts a second cutter, Blocker #4 receiving the ball. Using the Lane-Lane alignment, the offense has created a middle gap. Mover #3 cuts to fill the gap and in doing so draws the ball side low post defender X5 up the lane to cover Mover #3. Note X2 and X1 are occupied by Mover #1 in the high post lane area and Blocker #5, who in this example is a stretch big who can shoot three's and must be covered.

Once Blocker #4 changes lanes, Blocker #5 must also change lanes in order for the offense to remain balanced.

Adapting Blocker-Mover Motion for Zone Attack Offense

Diagram C

Diagram D

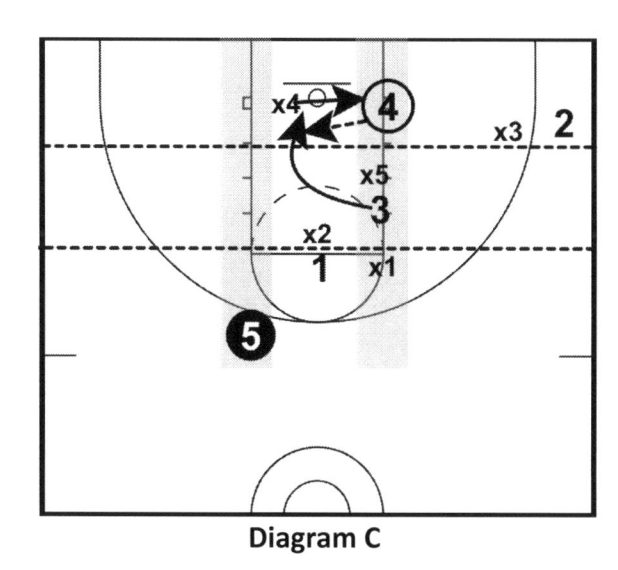

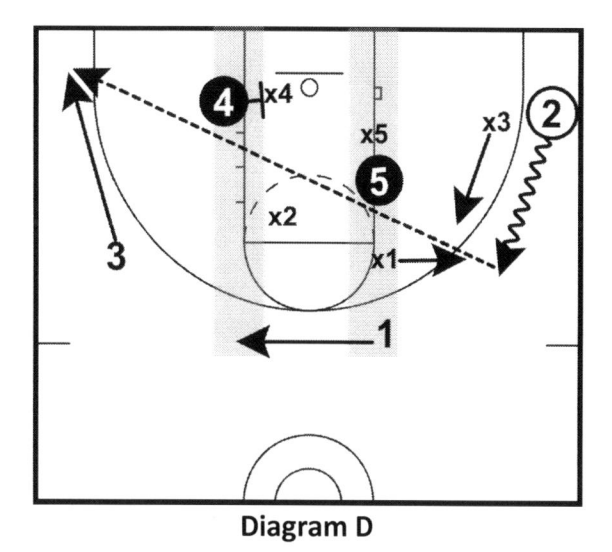

In **Diagram C** Mover #3 cuts to yet another gap created by defender X4 cutting across the lane to help on Blocker #4 who is in possession of the ball.

There is a lot going on in **Diagram B** and **Diagram C**. The defense has been forced to distort due to the alignment and Movers filling gaps. The effective movement of the ball and players has also created overloads, giving the offense a numerical advantage.

Distort the Zone Defense

One of the primary advantages of a zone defense is the defense determines the area of the court it will defend. Distorting the zone defense reduces the advantage obtained by playing zone.

Alignments

Using an initial alignment to locate players or a particular Blocker-Mover alignment can force a zone defense to shift in order to cover individual offensive players, forcing the defender out of the preferred location.

Distorting the zone defense creates gaps and openings for the offense to move players into, either for scoring opportunities or to further distort the zone defense.

Diagram A

Diagram B

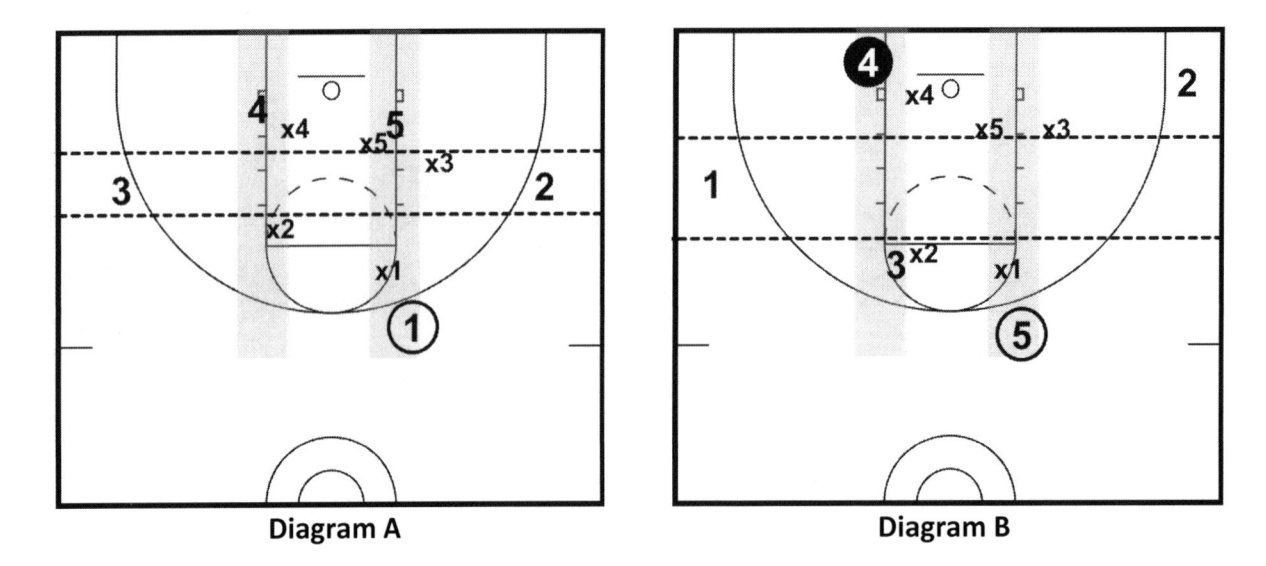

In **Diagram A** the offense has lined up in two of the natural gaps of the 2-3 but has not distorted the defense. Note the narrow gap between the front and second line zone defenders as depicted by the broken line.

In **Diagram B** the offense has stretched and distorted the zone defense using a Lane-Lane alignment and positioning players in locations forcing the defense to shift to cover the offensive player.

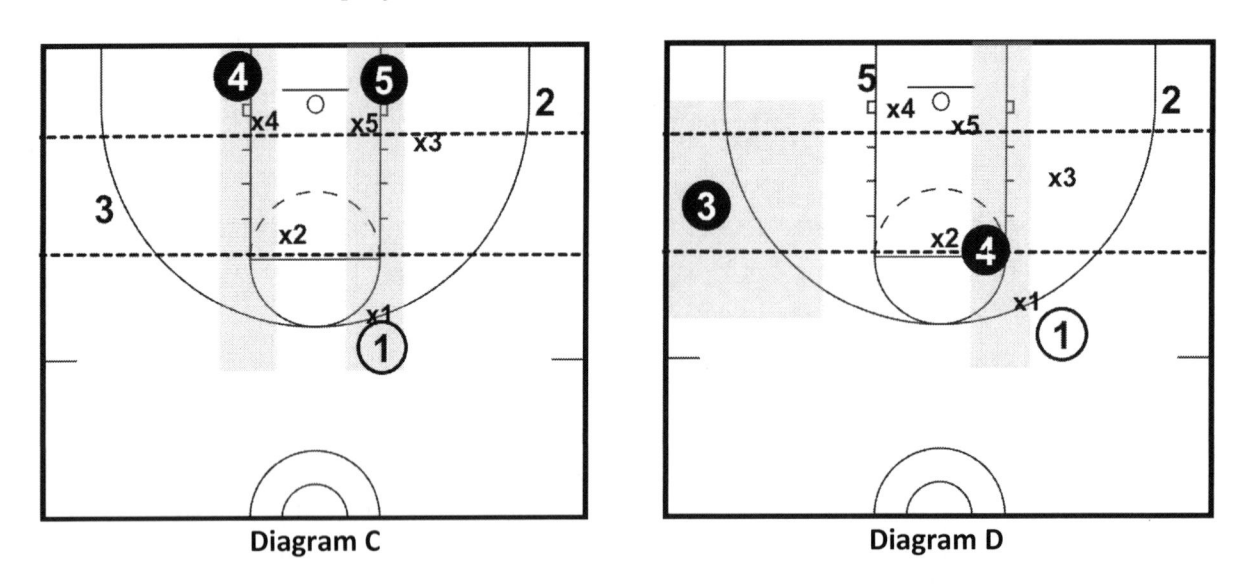

Diagram C

Diagram D

By placing the two Lane Blockers deep behind the zone defense, two of the backline defenders must defend closer to the goal, creating a wider gap on the wings. The spacing of the three perimeter Movers further distorts the zone (**Diagram C**).

The spacing depicted in Diagram D shows how the Lane-Wide alignment distorts a 2-3 zone defense, creating gaps and positioning issues the offense can exploit by applying simple offensive building block tactics to attack the defense.

Diagram E

Diagram F

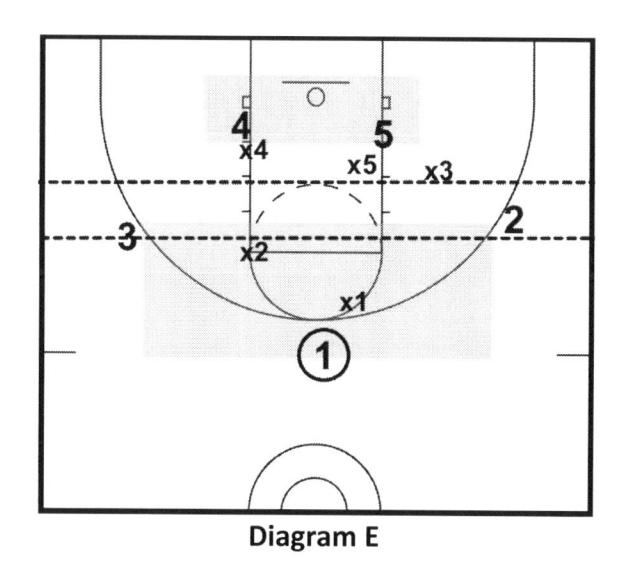

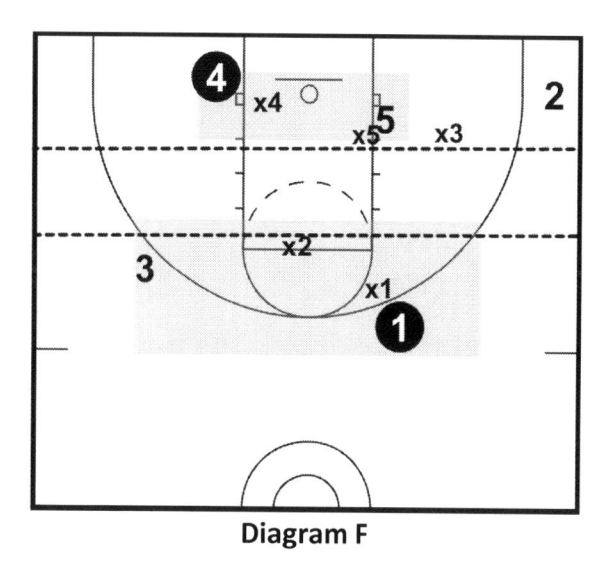

In the example depicted in **Diagram E**, the Top-High alignment has not spaced effectively to create distortion. Using the same alignment (**Diagram F**) but positioning correctly, it is obvious a larger gap in the 2-3 zone has been created and the defenders have all been forced to move out of their preferred starting locations.

Take the Defender Away (Use of the Dribble to Attack)

In addition to the desire to defend specific areas of the court, most zone defenses want specific players to defend a particular area. The desire to keep a tall defender near the goal for rebounding and low post defense is one example.

It makes sense for the defense to utilize this advantage of a zone defense, making it logical for the offense to want to eliminate this advantage by moving a particular defender out of the desired location. Using dribble rules and tactics, moving the ball with the dribble, forcing the defender to remain in on the ball defense, is an excellent tactic to take the defender out of the desired area.

Note, in all zone dribble attack tactics, all of the offensive players must be able to read and react to the actions of the ball handler, adhering to all applicable rules of zone attack and Blocker-Mover offense.

Freeze and Slide

Dribbling directly at a zone defender will force that individual defender to defend the offensive player with the ball. Once the defender is actively playing on the ball defense, the ball handler can now dribble in a direction that will pull the defender away from his/her designated area to defend.

The action of dribbling at the defender is called "freezing" the defender. The defender locks on to the ball and does not move unless the ball handler changes direction. The slide is the action of pulling the defender with the ball handler in the direction the ball handler is dribbling. The diagram below shows the "freeze and slide" action with a pass back to the shooter who has filled in the gap created by the slide action.

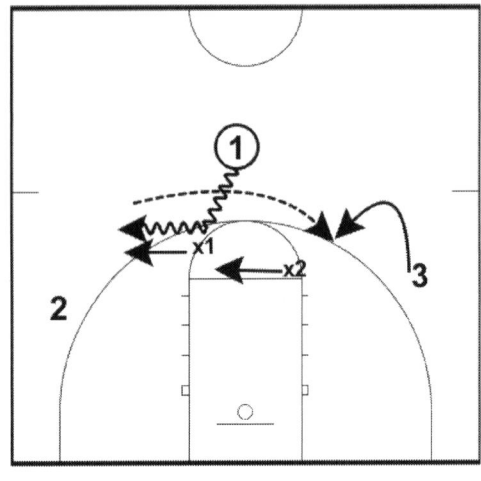

Freeze and Slide

Dribble Off

All zone defenders are prone to staying on the ball when it is dribbled. Perimeter players in the corner should "dribble off" the baseline, sliding the defender with them. This creates a space for a Mover to fill. A pass fake in the direction the ball handler is dribbling in will freeze or shift the zone in the direction of the pass. Often two consecutive dribble offs will result in an open 3-point attempt.

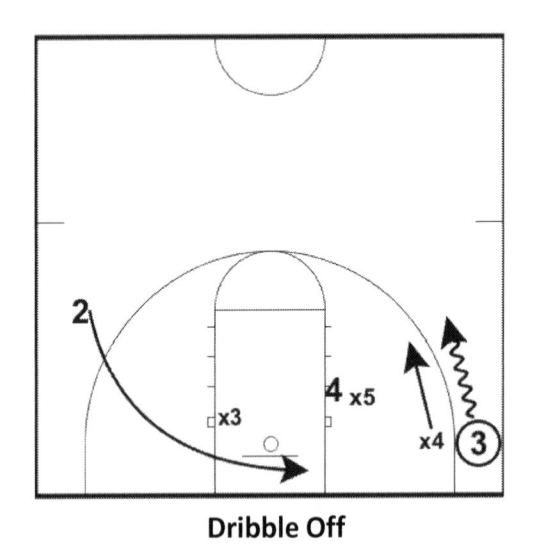

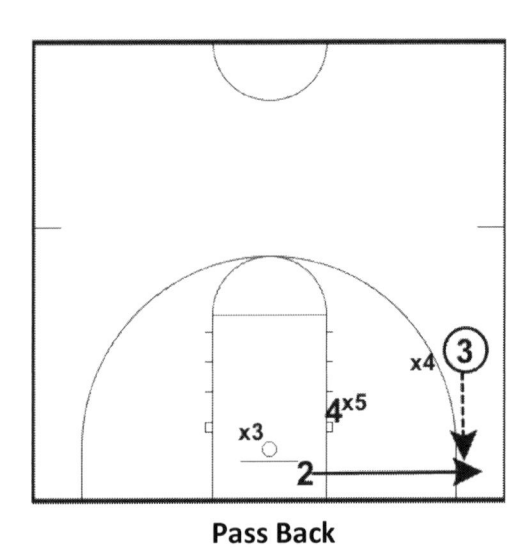

Dribble Off

Pass Back

Dribble Follow/Dribble Off the Top

Using the dribble to slide defenders away from their designated areas can be used to move the defenders on the top of a zone. **Diagram A** below depicts the dribble being used to slide the top two defenders or a 2-3 zone away from the shooter. Again, a pass fake in the direction of the dribble drive will freeze or shift the zone in the direction of the drive. By moving both defenders away, the perimeter wing may have an open shot on the pass back as a result of the space created.

Diagram A

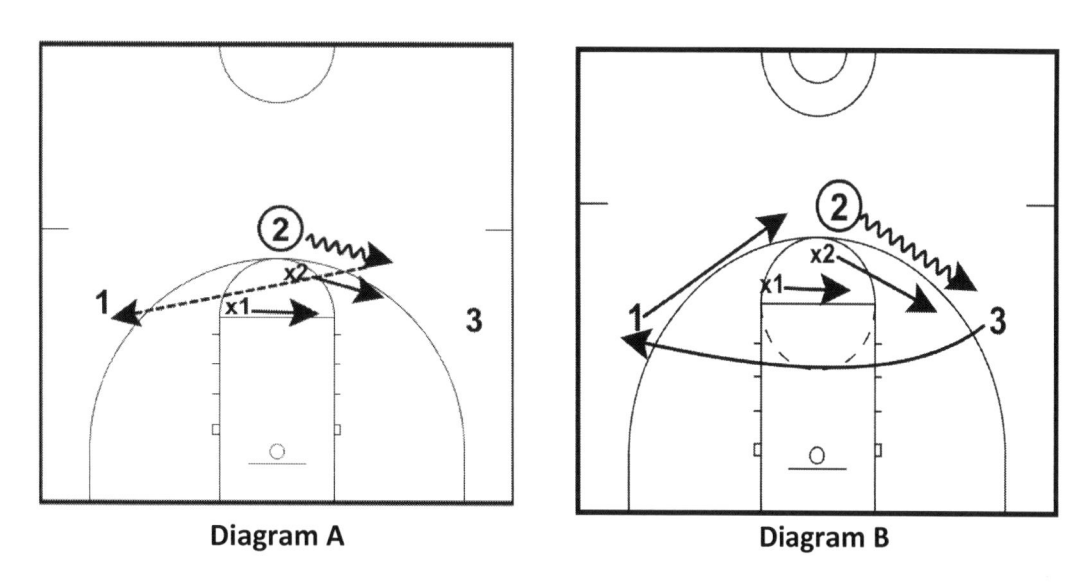

Diagram B

Diagram B depicts a combination of dribbling off the top with a dribble follow combined with the one Mover per perimeter area rule. #2 dribbles off the top, dragging #1 in a dribble follow. This results in the need for #3 to vacate the perimeter area and fill the area vacated by #1.

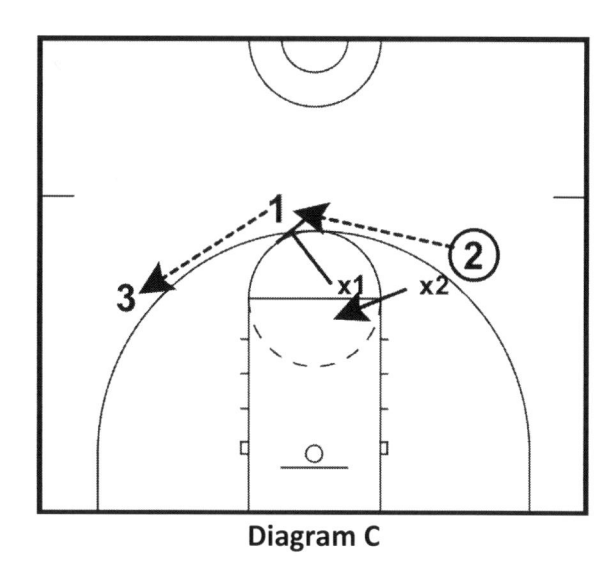

Diagram C

Quick ball reversal or a skip pass combined with the defense having been pulled out of their designated areas can create an open shot attempt or penetration opportunity.

Dribble Push

The dribble push tactic is more about pushing a teammate into an area than it is pulling the defense out of a designated area. In **Diagram A** Mover #1 "dribble pushes" Mover #3 into the corner before passing and basket cutting to fill the now empty perimeter area vacated by Mover #2 who has executed a dribble follow.

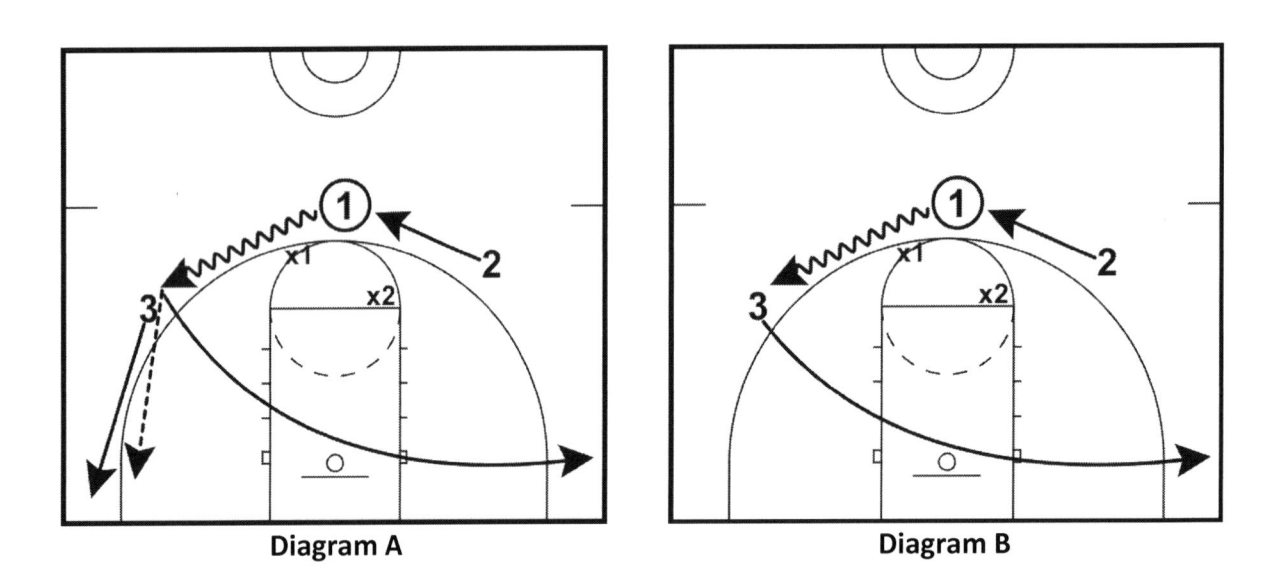

Diagram A

Diagram B

In **Diagram B** Mover #1 forces Mover #3 to vacate the left perimeter area and basket cut to fill the right perimeter area vacated by Mover #2 who executed a dribble follow.

How do players know which cut to make? If Mover #3 is a great 3-point shooter, the tactic that creates an open 3-point shot attempt is the one that should be used. If a push to the corner creates a shot (1-2-2 zones are vulnerable to this), then Mover #3 should fill the corner and let Mover #1 basket cut and fill the vacated perimeter area.

Hand signals can work well. If the ball handler makes a pushing motion with his/her protect hand, Mover #3 knows to cut to the corner. If a brushing motion is used, Mover #3 knows to basket cut, clearing out the perimeter area for the ball handler to occupy.

Overload the Zone Defense

Anytime the offense can gain a numerical advantage over the defense it must do so. Placing the defense at a disadvantage increases scoring opportunities and the likelihood the defense will commit a foul. Drawing fouls is an important strategy in attacking any defense. It is particularly true for a zone defense since many teams play zone defense to hide a weak defensive player who is gifted offensively. Isolating such a player in a disadvantage situation increases the likelihood of getting the great offensive player in foul trouble and sitting on the bench.

Make 1 Defend 2

In the example below (**Diagram A**) the offense is using a dribble off to distort the defense and set up a scenario where one defender must defend two offensive players. Mover #2 dribbles off the baseline, forcing X3 to play on the ball defense.

In Diagram B Mover #2 passes the ball back to #3 who has filled the open area on the baseline. X3 must now hustle to cover the open #3 in the corner.

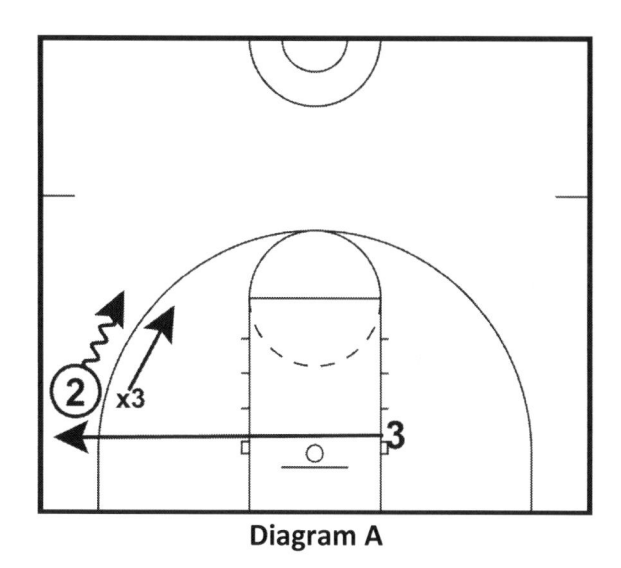

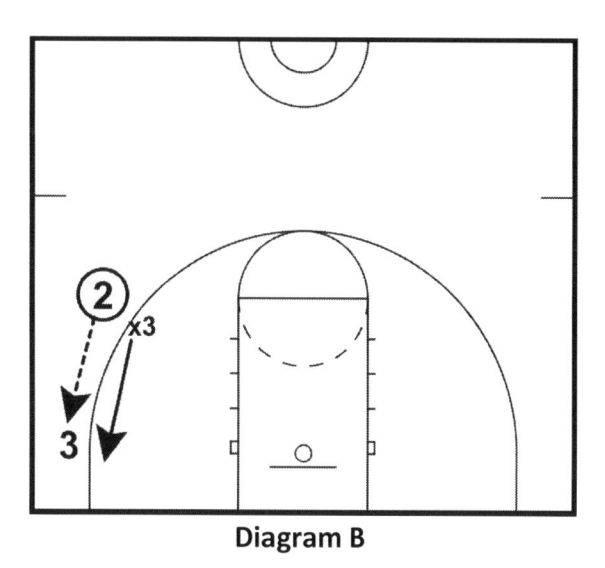

Diagram A

Diagram B

Make 2 Defend 3

Diagram C depicts another dribble off move to force two defenders to guard three offensive players. As #3 dribbles off the baseline, X3 is forced to cover the dribble off a second time in succession. The one Mover per perimeter area rule forces #2 to fill the right perimeter area that has been vacated by Mover #1 who is cutting to the ball side corner.

Diagram D depicts the "up to middle" zone slide as some coaches call it. X3, who has covered the dribble off twice sprints to cover the ball side low post as the low post defender, X5 closesout on the ball in the corner. Note Mover #3 basket cuts hard to fill the right perimeter area. If X5 does not take the new ball handler, Mover #1, in the corner, a wide-open shot is now available. This is a difficult maneuver for any defense to cover twice in succession.

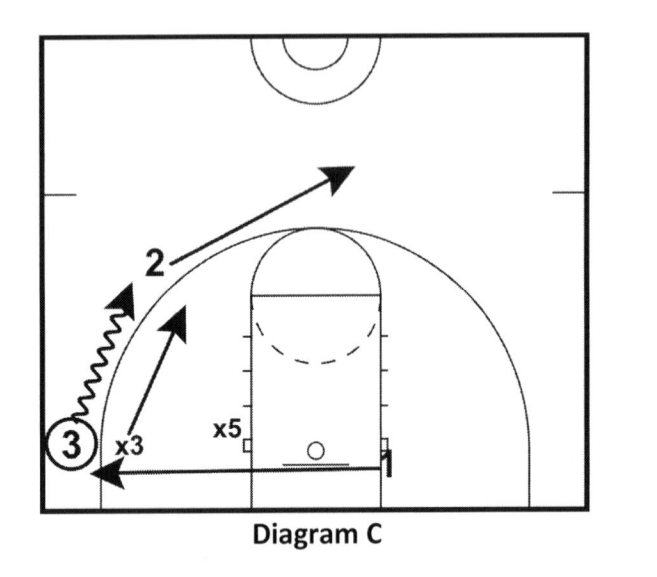

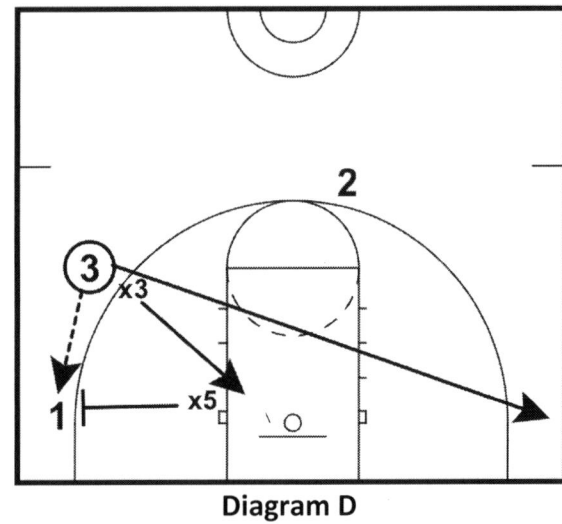

Diagram C

Diagram D

Make 3 Defend 4

In **Diagram E** the offense is forcing three defenders to guard four offensive players. Yes, there are four defenders depicted. The tactic employed removes one of the four defenders from play, making it a three defending four situation (also a one defending two and a two defending three situation).

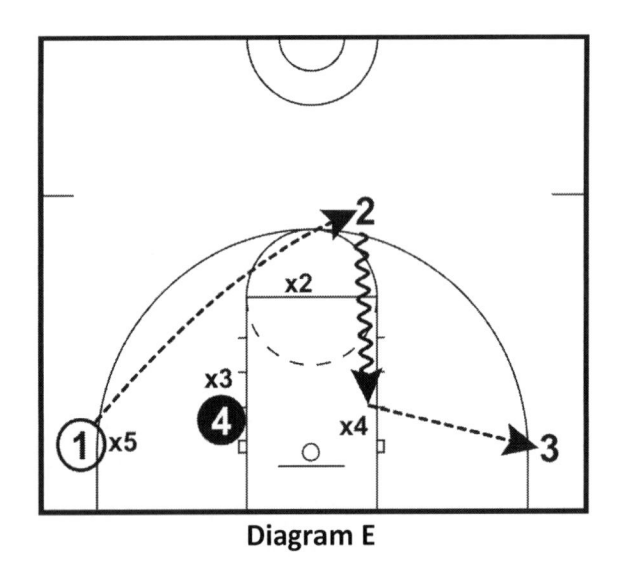

Diagram E

Every instance in which the ball is put on the baseline, all zone defenses rotate their coverage and become a 2-3 zone defense. The skip pass to Mover #2 creates a penetration opportunity that creates multiple disadvantage scenarios for the defense. The first scenario is the 2-on-1 opportunity created by driving directly at the X4 defender and passing the ball to Mover #3 for a 3-point shot attempt. If Blocker #4 is able to seal X3 out, Mover #2 now has a 3-on-2 opportunity and can pass to either Mover #3 or Blocker #4. The catch and drive takes X2 out of the play.

Screen the Zone Defense

Setting hard, legal screens against man-to-man defense is one of the most effective tactics an offense can have, particularly when combined with purposeful movement and effective spacing. The same is true for attacking a zone defense. Screens can be highly disruptive and force the zone to distort and shift into awkward formations that are not only difficult to defend, but difficult to recover from.

Screen-in

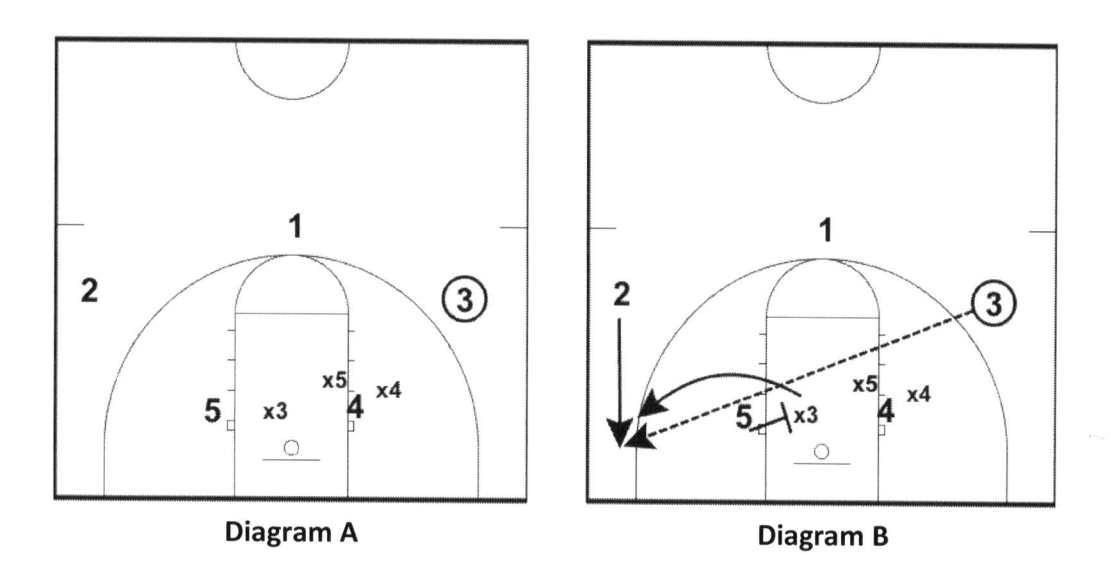

Diagram A

Diagram B

Of all the possible screening tactics that can be used against a zone defense, the screen-in is my all time favorite. **Diagram A** shows one example of how to set up a screen-in. **Diagram B** shows the skip pass and the screen in set by #5. Note the screen is an angle that will encourage the defender to take a path away from the baseline, creating space for a baseline side bounce pass to feed the ball into the low post.

Coaching Basketball's Zone Attack Offense Using Blocker-Mover Motion Offense

Diagram C

Diagram D

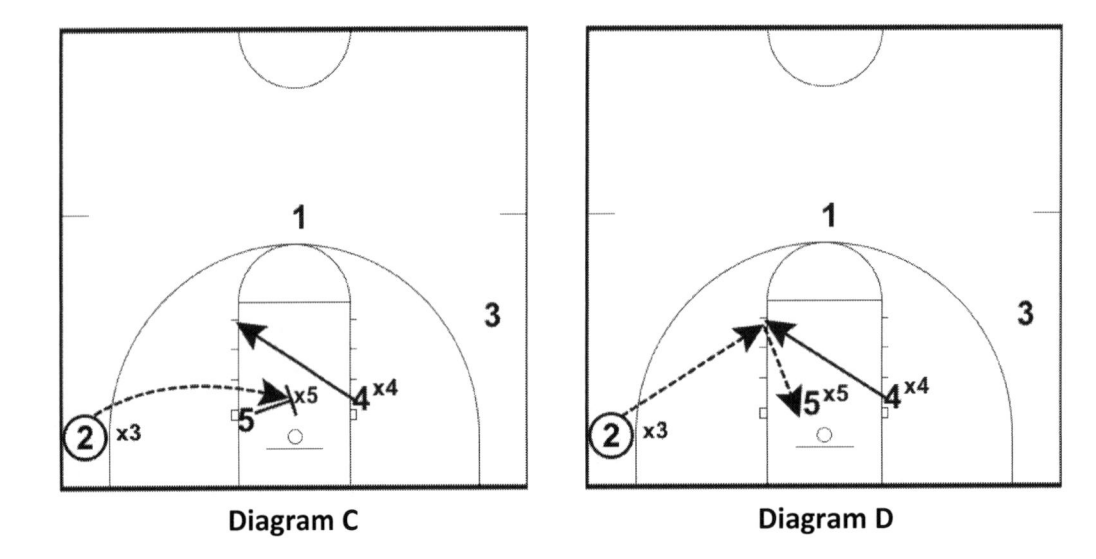

After screening the back defender (X3), the post screener goes to the next defender (X5) and seals for a post-up. The opposite offensive post player, #4, flashes into the gap on the ball side (**Diagram C**). Often the defense fronts the low post offensive player and takes away the post feed, the ball can be entered into the high post to #4 who can then make a high low pass to #5 (**Diagram D**).

Center Screen

Diagram A

Diagram B

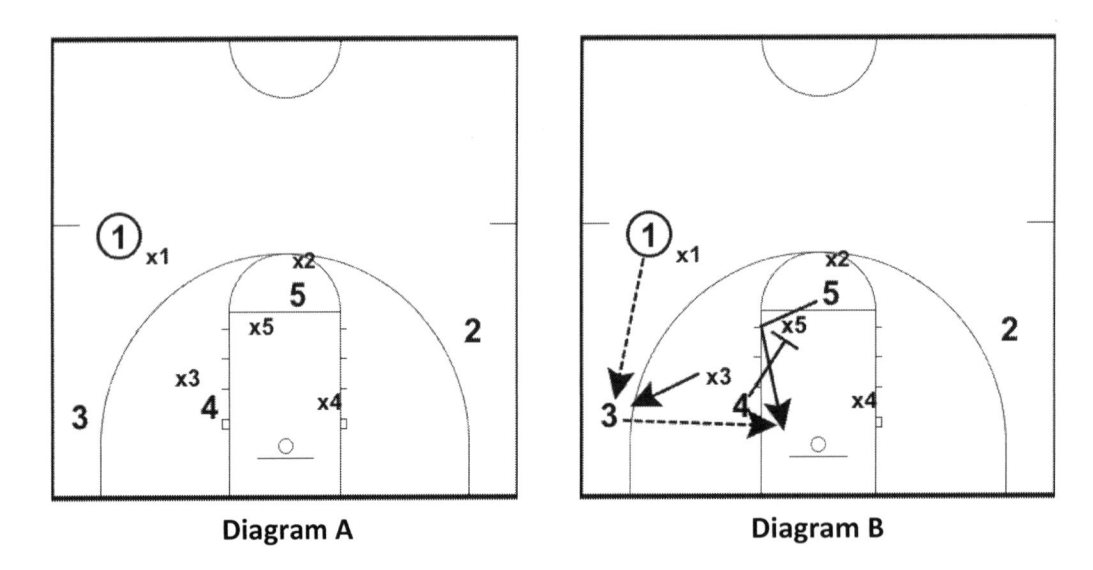

The Center Screen is effective against nearly every type of 2 front zone. The pass to the corner requires the closest defender to pressure the ball. The ball side offensive low post turns and screens the defender most likely to defend the low post, allowing the other post player to cut into the gap or area created by the screen (**Diagrams A and B**).

Screen Out

Most screens set against zone defenders are meant to pin a defender in, to keep the defender as close to the goal as possible, creating space for the offensive player behind the screen. In the case of the screen out, the intent is to keep the zone defender away from the goal, creating space for the Blocker who set the screen out.

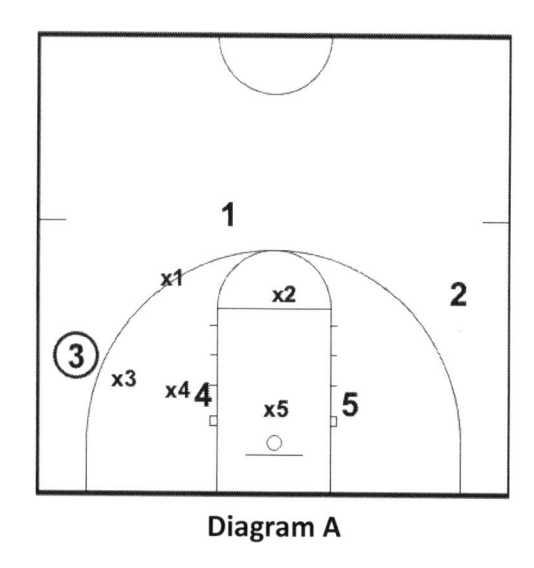

Diagram A

Diagram A depicts a screen out being set up for the offensive low post #4. A screen out is set with the screener using his/her back to set the screen. It is much like sealing a post defender except the zone defender being screened is almost always on the perimeter (at least outside the lane) and the screener is showing his/her numbers to the ball.

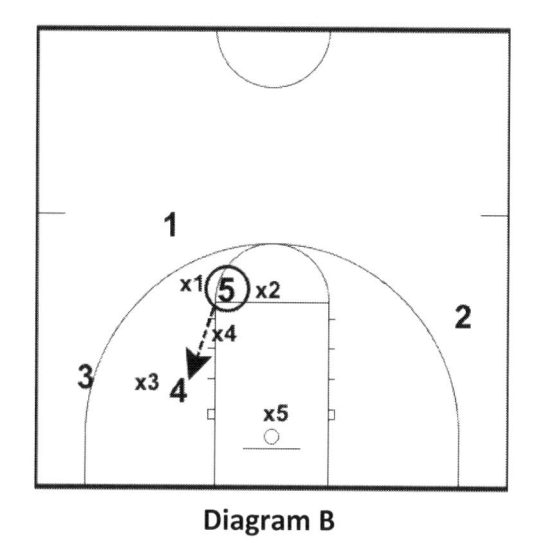

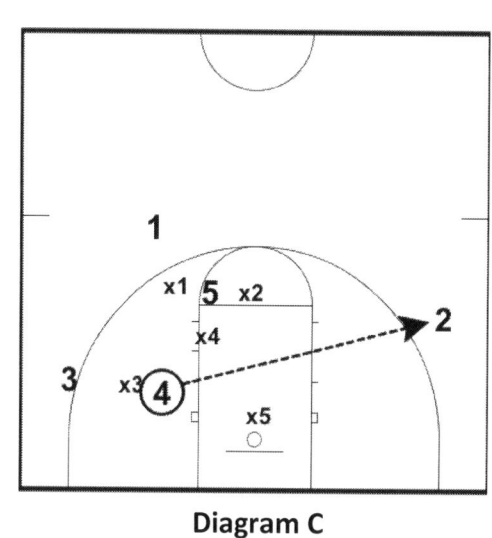

Diagram B

Diagram C

In the example shown in **Diagram B**, #5 has flashed into the gap in the ball side high post and received the ball. #4 has screened the defender X3 out, creating space between him/herself and the next zone defender X5. The high low pass is made for an easy shot opportunity or, if X5 is able to defend #4, an easy fan pass to Mover #2 for a 3-point shot attempt on the help side of the court (**Diagram C**).

Use Fakes to Freeze and Shift the Zone Defense

Of all the offensive tactics available to defeat zone defenses, the use of the fake is the most underutilized tactic in the game. Shot fakes freeze the zone defenders in place, often getting the defenders to stand up or even turn to block out.

Pass fakes are particularly effective against aggressive zone defenses that take great pride in actively relocating while the ball is in the air, arriving at the next correct defensive position the same time the ball does. An effective pass fake will shift the aggressive, hard working zone defenders in the direction of the pass fake.

Passing in the opposite direction of the pass fake forces the defenders to stop and change direction. Often this brief loss of time is enough to create a shot attempt or a mistake on the part of the defense, creating an opportunity the offense can exploit.

General Rules for Blocker-Mover Motion Offense

The general principle of "less is more" certainly applies to the game of basketball in general and certainly motion offense to be specific. Having stated less is more, you will notice the following list of rules is rather long. Please keep in mind, most of these rules are sound principles of basketball and must be taught regardless of the offensive system taught.

The actual rules for the Blocker-Mover Motion Offense are fairly few in number. The Blockers have five rules and the Movers have six. As always, do not feel tied to any rules I have set forth in this book. You may add rules (if you do, I strong suggest that for every rule you add, you subtract a rule if possible) or subtract rules. Certainly, you may reword rules to fit your terminology or to make the rules more understandable to you or your players.

Keep in mind there will always be some strange or unique situation serving to create an exception to the rules. Motion offense by its very nature will create unique situations and opportunities so it the unexpected exceptions should be expected. Simply teach your players to play through these situations and return to normal play.

Finally, when teaching and running a free lance, rule based offense, you as a coach must be committed to teaching your players how to play the game of basketball instead of how to run basketball plays.

General Rules for All Players:

- Maintain 15-18 ft. spacing.
- Move with a purpose.
- Go somewhere when you move.
- Pass away from the defense.
- Dribble with a purpose or not at all (Dribble use rules).
- Face-up for a 2-count on receiving the ball and look under the net.
- Relieve pressure to the high post/top area.
- Obey the principles of cutting and screening.
- Reverse the ball from side-top-side when possible.
- Solve problems using offensive building blocks.
- Floor balance on the shot!

Rules for Blockers:

- Blockers hunt Movers!
- Blockers play within their assigned area in the designated alignment.
- Blockers are second cutters after screening.
- Blockers in the Lane areas may post up when the opportunity presents.
- In specific situations Blockers may exchange areas.

Rules for Movers:

- Movers hunt Blockers.
- After passing a Mover must be a Blocker for one screen or basket-cut
- Only one Mover may occupy a Mover area.
- When a Mover enters an occupied Mover area, the Mover occupying the area must vacate the area.
- Movers may screen for other Movers, particularly when entering an occupied Mover area in order to help the other Mover vacate the area.
- Look to score!

Post Play Rules:

- Create contact first
- Establish arm and leg dominance
- Show your numbers to the ball, creating a line of deployment.
- Direct traffic.
- Post up for a two-second count.
- Upon receiving the ball, chin it and check over the high shoulder.
- When the ball is entered in the low post the high post must be a second cutter.

Dribble Use Rules:

- Limit of two dribbles.
- Go somewhere with your dribble.
- Dribble with purpose or not at all.
- Limit of One Dribble from the 3-point Line to the Rim

General Rules for All Players

Maintain 15-18 ft. Spacing

Coach Chuck Daly, winner of Olympic Gold as the head coach of the U.S. Men's Basketball Olympic Team and winner of NBA Championships as the coach of the infamous Detroit Pistons "Bad Boy" teams states this rule simply: offense is spacing and spacing is offense. This most basic of all offensive principles applies to all forms of offense in the game of basketball.

When the offense is not spaced properly, players 15-18 feet apart, the defense has the advantage. The lack of proper spacing, either too close or too far, means the defense can play in gaps to prevent penetration, use one defender to cover two offensive players or easily anticipate and intercept a pass that is too long.

When the offense is correctly spaced, the defense is placed at maximum disadvantage. Passes are more difficult to anticipate and intercept, defenders cannot play in gaps with as much ease and each defender must defend one offensive player.

Move With a Purpose

Movement without a purpose is not only of no use, it is often counterproductive. Players who have no clear and correct reason to move often disrupt the purposeful and useful of other teammates. A player cutting to an open area near the goal for a pass and a lay-up could have the opportunity eliminated by a player cutting with no clear and positive purpose. The player with no purpose could bring a defensive player into the passing lane or simply clog up the lane area, closing the opening for a potential pass for a score.

Purposeful movement includes cutting to an open area to receive a pass for a shot, to continue moving the ball for a shot, to set a screen for a teammate, to create space for a pass or dribble penetration or to move the ball up the court. Not only should movement be purposeful in terms of location but also in how the cutting movement is made.

Go Somewhere When You Move

This concept is different from the idea of moving with a purpose. Players can desire to get open, a good purpose, enter the v-cut slow, exit the v-cut quickly, use a ninety degree angle and still not be able to get open. In order for a change of direction move to be successful, the player must cover a distance of at least fifteen feet in both legs of the cut.

In other words, the player must go somewhere. By moving the defender fifteen feet in one direction and then a change of pace with a angle cut and change of direction with sprinting fifteen feet in the new direction, the cutter will make the task of defending him as difficult as possible.

Pass Away From the Defense

Turnovers due to intercepted passes are usually a result of passing the ball to a teammate. Sounds silly, but it is true. Unless the teammate is wide open for a shot, the ball should never be passed directly to the teammate. Instead, the ball must be passed away from the defense. This includes both the defender guarding the passer (**Photograph A**) and the cutter (**Photograph B**).

Photograph A

Photographs A and B by Maddy Copollo

Dribble with a purpose or not at all (Dribble use rules)

Obey the four rules of dribble use.

Face-up for a 2-count on receiving the ball and look under the net

All forms of Motion Offense require that the players "see" what is happening both on offense and defense. In order for players to see, they must "look!" All too often players are looking some place other than where they need to.

The best place to look when in possession of the ball is under the net of the offensive goal after facing up to the basket. This allows the player to see all of the other nine players on the court, five defensive players and four offensive teammates.

By looking under the net, movement of offensive players becomes more evident and opportunities to pass for a score become visible because the ball handler can see the location of the defensive players.

Facing the net and holding the ball for a 2-count, unless an immediate pass results in a score, allows enough time for scoring opportunities to develop, or not, requiring the ball to be passed to another location.

Relieve Pressure to the High Post/On Top Area

Defenses are adept at applying pressure and denying the ball when it is located on the wing or corner areas. Defenses are less adept at pressuring the ball when it is located in the middle of the court.

Off all defenders, the post defender is the least comfortable playing defense away from the basket. The further from the basket, the less comfortable the post defender is, reducing that player's confidence level. Typically, post defenders respond to being placed in this situation by being tentative in pressuring the ball and will allow the offensive high post to step away into the on top area to receive the ball.

Thus, whenever the ball is under pressure or in trouble, the high post player, or a perimeter player, should cut into the high post extended area on top to receive a pass to alleviate pressure.

Obey the Principles of Cutting and Screening

The most difficult offensive tactic to defend is a cut combined with a screen. This is true only when a screen is set correctly and the cut is also executed correctly.

Reverse the Ball From Side-Top-Side When Possible

Keeping the ball on one side of the court when in half court offense allows the defense to establish ball side and help side, giving the defense an advantage. The defense is essentially playing 5-on-3 or 5-on-4.

One of the toughest things for any defense to cover is moving the ball on offense from one side to the top and then the other side, reversing the ball side-top-side.

This forces the defense to quickly and successfully transition from ball side with help side established to defending the ball in the middle of the court, something no defense likes to do, and then establishing ball side and help side position yet again on the side opposite where the ball was originally located. Reversing the ball a second time side-top-side makes this entire process even more difficult for a defense.

Solve Problems Using Offensive Building Blocks

Offensive building blockers are the foundation of all forms of offense in basketball, regardless of the offense or type of offensive system used. Just a few examples include:

- pass and screen away.
- give and go.
- flare screen and skip pass (drive the flare).

When problems arise, the solution to attacking the defense is always to apply the correct offensive building block. Players have to be taught not only to recognize the problem the defense has created (another way of thinking is the opportunity the defense has created) and apply the correct offensive building block to the situation. Motion Offense is perfect for this approach. Set plays or continuity offenses have a hard time taking advantage of opportunities the defense may create because of the set nature of these systems. **See the chapter on Offensive Building Blocks for more details.**

Floor Balance on the Shot!

One of the inherent weaknesses of any type of Motion Offense is the increased odds of poor offensive rebounding position. Continuity offenses and set plays, because of their preset and controlled nature, can generally place players in advantageous offensive rebounding position at any stage of the play.

Motion Offenses, because of their rules based approach and freelance nature cannot predict, let alone position, players at any given time during an offensive possession. To some degree, because of the use of alignments, Blocker-Mover does help with this problem. The Blockers may be in a relatively good position for offensive rebounding.

Floor balancing is the practice of assigning players offensive rebounding positions to attack when the offense takes a shot. It also establishes the first stages of transition defense by assigning, depending on the defensive philosophy, one or two players to "get back" to stop the opponent from establishing a successful fast break attempt.

Like Motion Offense, floor balancing is rules based. These rules take effect when the offense takes a shot and include:

- Players #3, #4 and #5 attack the basket and establish a rebounding triangle as depicted in **Diagram A** and **Diagram B.**
- Player #2, usually the shooting guard and best 3-point shooter, rotates the top of the key area and spots up.
- Player #1, the point guard sprints back towards half court in the center of the court to establish a defensive presence to stop a quick fast break and to help teammates in the process of defensive transition.

Diagram A   **Diagram B**

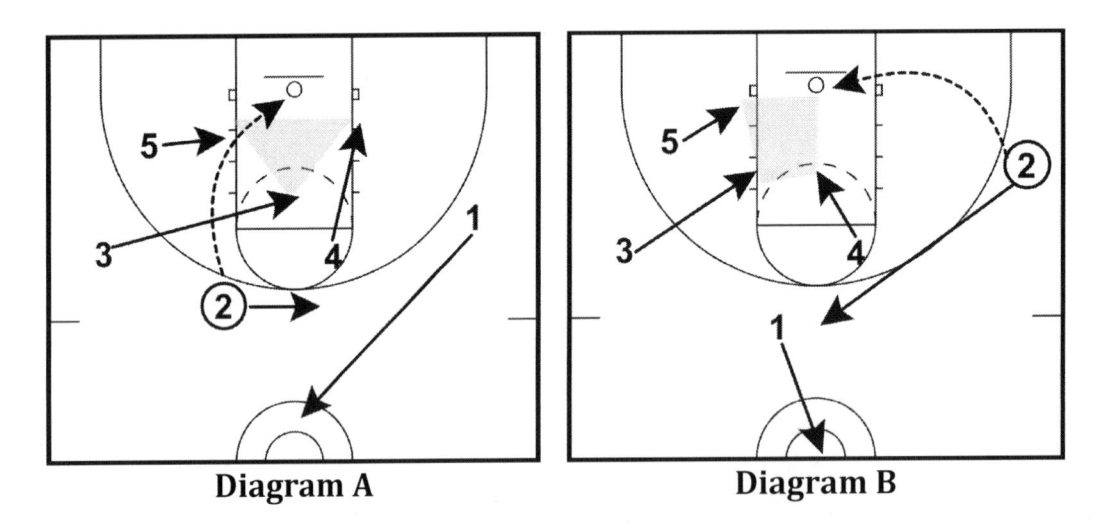

Diagram A depicts a shot taken from the center area of the court. **Diagram B** depicts a shot taken from one side of the court. Note the primary rebounders are attempting to establish a triangle. By rotating the shooting guard on top a second shot from an inside out pass may be obtained, increasing the field goal percentage in the process.

If #1 or #2 has attacked the rim, then player #3 takes fills the role of that player. For this approach to be successful, a heavy emphasis must be placed on floor balancing. ***Regardless of the drill or what is being worked on in any form of offense, when a shot is taken players must floor balance or suffer a consequence.***

Rules for Blockers:

Blockers Hunt Movers!

The primary objective of a Blocker is to get Movers open! This means the Blocker's first task is to hunt for and find a Mover! This involves not only locating Movers, but knowing where the ball is located, or about to be located. Once a Mover has been found and the ball located, the Blocker selects the most advantageous type of screen to set for the Mover and communicates both verbally, with hand signals and eye contact with the targeted Mover and sets the screen. See **Diagram A**.

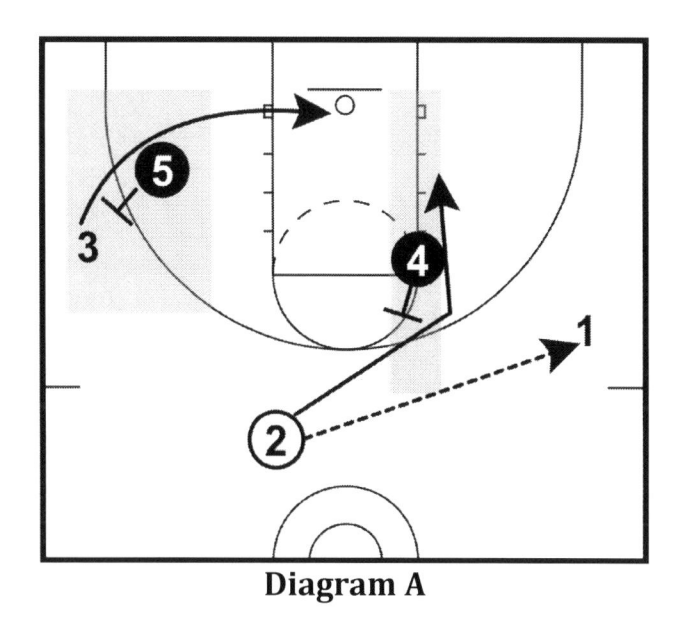

Diagram A

Blockers Play Within Their Assigned Area in the Designated Alignment

The Lane-Wide alignment is depicted in **Diagram A**. Note the two Blockers, Blocker #4 and Blocker #5, are physically located within their designated areas. Unless a unique or specific situation arises, these two Blockers must not leave their assigned areas until a shot is taken and they must floor balance.

This rule is necessary to help Movers find Blockers and for both Movers and Blockers to best determine what the best screen and cut will be based on the area the Blocker is located and where the ball is, or will be, located when the screen is set.

Blockers Are Second Cutters After Screening

Regardless of the type of offense, one of the best ways to get open it to screen for someone else, forcing the screener's defender to help on the cutter to prevent an easy score. Blockers, particularly those with high basketball IQ, can be effective scorers in the Blocker-Mover offense! ***Coaches MUST teach and sell this point to Blockers in order to prevent low morale or selfish behavior among Blockers!***

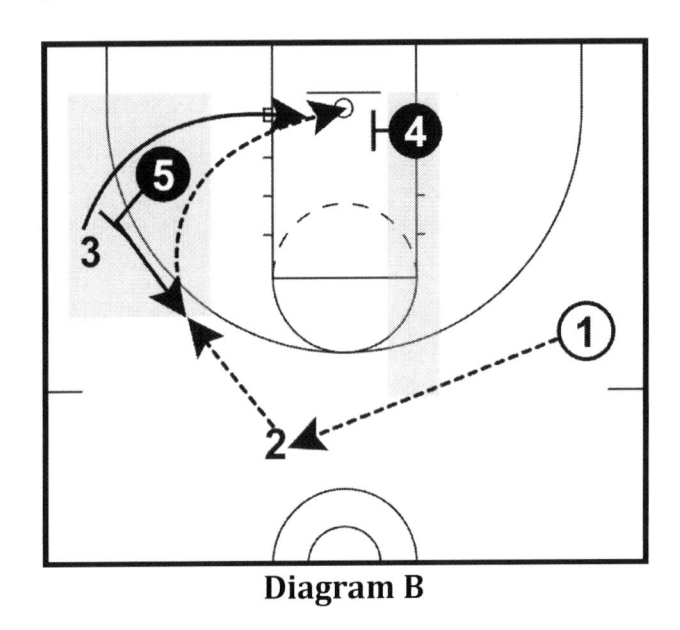

Diagram B

In the example depicted in Diagram B above, Blocker #5 is not a particularly mobile player but has excellent 3-point shooting ability. By setting a back screen for Mover #3 when the ball is passed to the on top area, Blocker #5 has created a possible back door lay-up opportunity for Mover #3, forcing Blocker #5's defender to momentarily open up in the lane to prevent the back door pass.

This allows Blocker #5 to step to the ball as second cutter, while remaining in the Wide Lane area to receive a pass. Because Blocker #5 is a good 3-point shooter, by setting a good back screen for Mover #3, Blocker #5 has created a shot for him/herself by being a second cutter.

Blockers in the Lane Area May Post Up When the Opportunity Presents

The Lane-Wide, Lane-Lane and Top-Bottom alignments all take advantage of positioning Blockers in areas that place the Blocker in proximity to the low post area. This allows the Blocker who is a skilled offensive low post player to take advantage of his/her post skills and the fact one of the best ways to get open is to screen for another player. When the opportunity presents itself, Blockers assigned to the Lane or Bottom areas should always post up for a 2-second count. **Diagram C** depicts an example of where Blocker #4 was able to take advantage of setting a pin screen for Mover #3 and receive the ball in the low post area for a possible score.

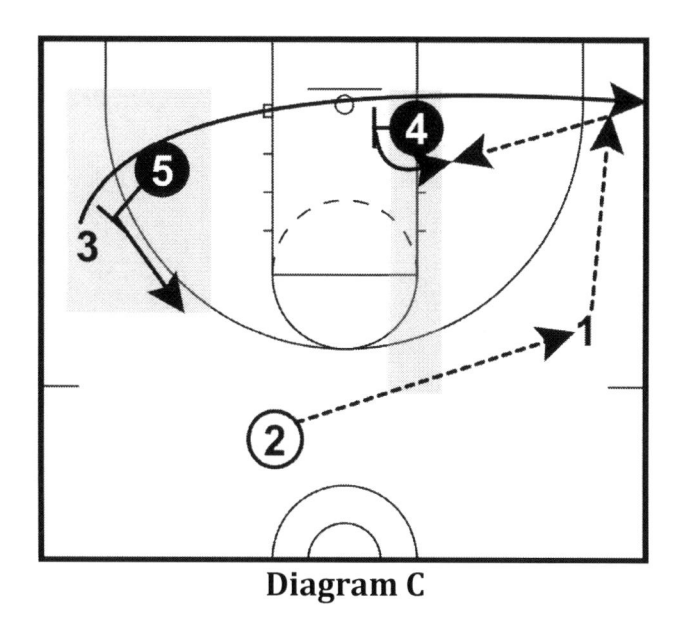

Diagram C

In Specific Situations Blockers May Exchange Areas

As a general rule Blockers must stay in their designated Blocker Areas. There are times when it is advantageous for the offense for Blockers to exchange areas, particularly when one Blocker screens for the other to establish the exchange of Blocker areas. See **Diagram D** and **Diagram E** for an example. It is important for the head coach to establish when these types of exchanges can occur to instill in the Blockers when this is acceptable.

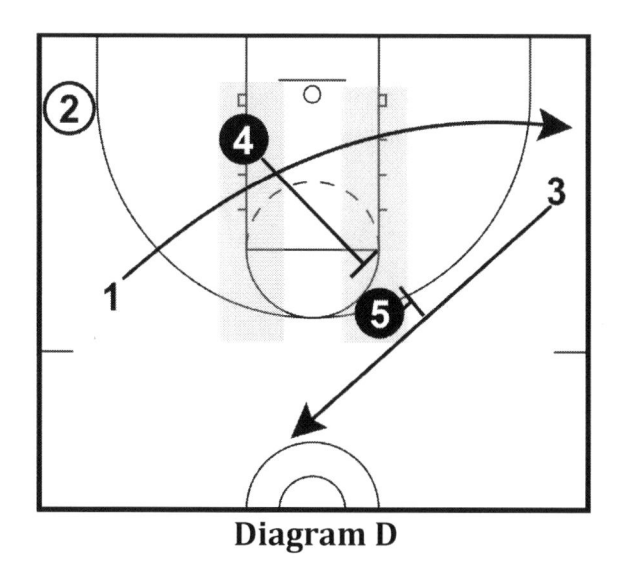

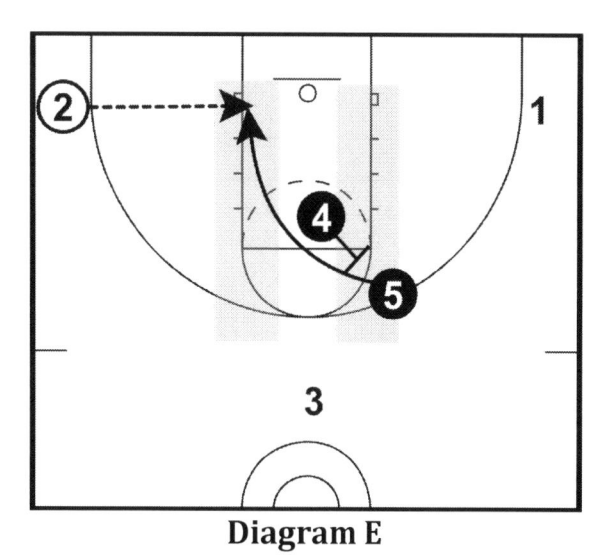

Diagram D

Diagram E

Rules for Movers:

Movers Hunt Blockers

The primary objective of Movers is to score! In order to do achieve this objective Movers need to not only obtain the ball but to do so in a location where they can score and the defense is at an appropriate disadvantage for the Mover to take a shot.

This means Movers need to have Blockers set screens for them. Since the Mover not only wants to get open but to obtain the ball in a good scoring location, the Mover needs to locate a Blocker and establish a position so the Blocker can set a screen that will lead to the Mover getting open to receive the ball and possibly score.

Once a Mover has located a Blocker who can set a screen, the Mover must communicate with the Blocker both verbally and with signals to indicate a screen is desired and if possible where and what kind of screen should be set.

After Passing a Mover Must be a Blocker for One Screen or Basket-cut

Regardless of the incarnation of Motion Offense, standing, or standing with no purpose, is one of the worst things an offensive player can do. Once a Mover passes the ball, the Mover must move and move with purpose.

In order for that movement to have purpose the Mover should either basket cut, which creates a possible scoring opportunity, sets the Mover up to be screened for by a hunting Blocker and forces the defense to readjust and reposition, or the Mover should become a roving Blocker for the length of time required to find one Mover and set one screen.

Only One Mover May Occupy a Mover Area

Spacing is offense and offense is spacing. Two Movers occupying a single Mover area eliminates proper spacing. One of the Movers must vacate the area when another Mover enters.

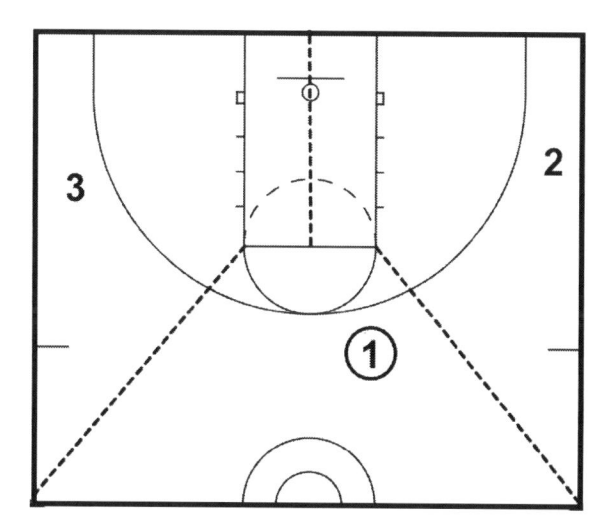

Adapting Blocker-Mover Motion for Zone Attack Offense

When a Mover Enters an Occupied Mover Area, the Mover Occupying the Area Must Vacate the Area

Since only one Mover can occupy a Mover area at a time and standing without purpose is a negative, it is logical for the Mover who is occupying the Mover area to be the Mover who must vacate the area.

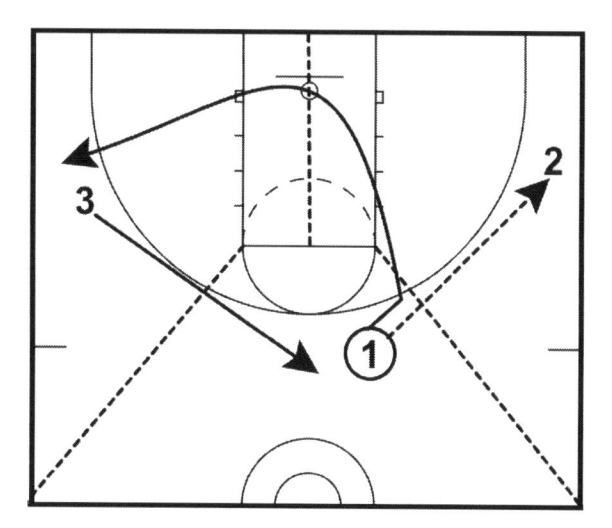

Movers May Screen for Other Movers, Particularly When Entering an Occupied Mover Area in Order to Help the Other Mover Vacate the Area

Movers may act as Blockers and screen for other Movers in specific situations. Serving as a Blocker for one screen after passing has been mentioned. Another specific situation is when a Mover is entering an occupied Mover area. By screening for the Mover who must vacate the area, the Mover entering the area indicates which Mover must leave the area, and by setting a screen for a teammate, creates the possibility of getting open by setting a screen and becoming a second cutter following the screen.

Look to Score!

Cutting and getting open is great and so is catching the ball. The objective of offense is not to simply pass the ball to open players, it is to score! Movers must be hungry to score and constantly looking for ways to get open and receive the ball that lead to scoring!

Post Play Rules*

Create Contact First

When it comes to post play, the player who makes contact first almost always will obtain and maintain the advantage. For this reason the offensive post player always wants to create contact first.

This allows the post to establish where he or she will post up and possibly how the post defender will play defense. Establishing contact first also allows the post player to establish arm and leg dominance.

Establish Arm and Leg Dominance

In order to be effective posting up or sealing, the offensive post player must establish both arm and leg dominance. This requires that the offensive post player's leg physically be over and on top of the leg of the post defender.

If the post defender is attempting to defend on the high side of the offensive post player, the post defender's leg will be over the high side leg of the offensive post player.

The offensive post player must move his high side leg over the post defender's leg, establishing leg dominance. This will allow the offensive post player to control the post defender's leg thereby gaining a significant advantage in holding the desired post-position.

Just as the post defender cannot be allowed to have leg dominance, the offensive post player cannot allow the post defender to have arm dominance. The offensive post player achieves arm dominance by obtaining the high position in the battle for arm dominance, meaning the offensive post player's arm is physically over that of the post defender's arm. The post defender must attempt to establish arm dominance in order to deflect any pass to the offensive post player.

To prevent the post defender from gaining or regaining arm dominance, the offensive post player des hold the post defender's arm but rather maintains a rigid position, not allowing the post defender to push, pull or otherwise move the offensive post player's arm. This requires considerable strength in the upper back, shoulders and arms on the part of the offensive post player.

Photograph C

Photograph D

In **Photograph C** the post defender has the advantage with both arm and leg dominance over the offensive post player. In **Photograph D** the offensive post player has gained control of the post defender's leg and arm by establishing arm and leg dominance. The offensive post player is also sitting on the defender's leg, locking the defender into place.

Show your numbers to the ball, creating a line of deployment.

Show Your Numbers to the Ball

Post players must not only be on the line of deployment and generally in the post box or posting area, but must also "show their numbers" to the ball. Regardless of where the ball is on offense, the offensive post player on the ball side of the court must show his numbers to the ball. This allows the offensive player with the ball, usually on the perimeter, to be able to best judge if the offensive post is open. If the numbers on the chest of the offensive post are clearly visible, the offensive player with the ball must pass the ball into the post player.

In **Photographs A** and **B** the post player is clearly showing her numbers to the perimeter player in possession of the ball. For example, in **Photograph B** if the post player was facing the sideline instead of the ball, she would NOT be showing her numbers to the ball.

Photograph A    **Photograph B**

Line of Deployment

Tex Winter, the master teacher of the Triangle Offense, teaches a concept called the line of deployment. An offensive post player must post up on the line of deployment in order to be both effective and open in an area where the post player can score. This imaginary line is between the rim and the ball with the post player straddling this line, bisecting it at a ninety-degree angle (**Diagrams A** and **B** and **Photographs A** and **B**).

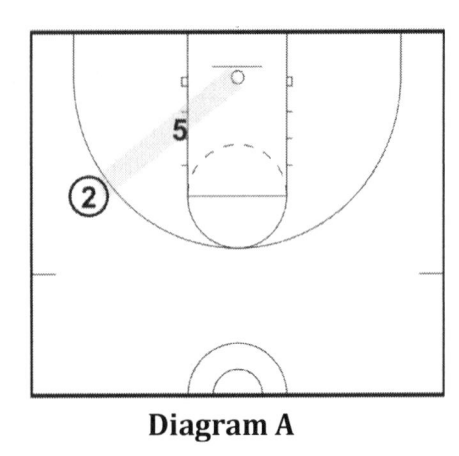

Diagram A    **Diagram B**

Direct Traffic

Post players have to struggle to obtain the position they want and to maintain their seal on the post defender. Great post players want the ball and they want to receive the ball in a specific spot, both on the court and in terms of pass location. In order to receive the ball in the exact desired location, post players must develop the habit and ability of communicating to perimeter players where the ball needs to be passed to so the most advantageous post entry pass can be made.

This practice is referred to as directing traffic. Post players who direct traffic can do so by pointing to their desired location for the ball and verbally insisting the ball be passed to the desired location.

In the photograph below the post player is directing traffic by point to the desired pass location. The post defender has moved to defend from the baseline side, making a post entry pass from on top desirable.

The ball is located at the top of the key area and the defender is in good position to deny a direct pass to the offensive post player.

The offensive post player reads the situation and directs traffic for the perimeter players. The post player has indicated she wants the ball passed to the wing.

The wing is making a baseline bounce pass to enter the ball into the offensive low post.

Upon receiving the ball, "chin it and check" over the high shoulder.

Upon receiving the ball with both hands, the offensive post player chins the ball with both elbows pointing straight out as extensions of the shoulders, giving the offensive post player strength in maintaining possession of the ball and preventing the costly mistake of lowering the ball to waist height where it can be stripped.

After chinning the ball, the offensive post player is to quickly look over his high side shoulder. This allows the offensive post player to quickly scan for all four offensive teammates and the five defenders. If the offensive post player quickly looks over the baseline shoulder, all the offensive post player can see at best is the post defender, the baseline and any player standing directly under the goal.

A quick scan over the high shoulder not only provides the opportunity to see the greatest possible number of players and court area, if the offensive post player does not see the post defender the offensive post player can immediately make an offensive move to the middle of the lane.

When the ball is entered in the low post the high post must be a second cutter.

Diagram C depicts this post play rule. The ball has been entered into the ball side low post, creating a great scoring opportunity in any offensive situation. The low post chins the ball and checks over the high shoulder.

As soon as the ball is being delivered to the low post, the high post player, if there is one, must execute a "back half cut" and cut hard to the low post opposite the ball side low post.

This accomplishes to important objectives. First, it establishes the best possible offensive rebound position should the offensive low post shoot the ball (it is believed 80% of all missed shots rebound on the side opposite from where the shot was taken).

The second objective is the back half cut often creates an open lay-up opportunity which is even better than a low post post move for a shot. This is often due to the opponent's defense doubling on the offensive low post with the high post defender or the high post defender simply relaxing for a moment when the ball entered the low post.

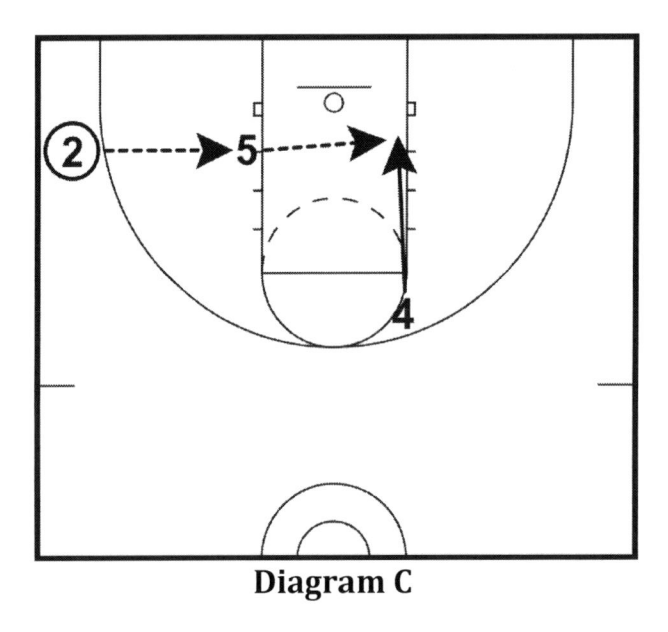

Diagram C

*Most of the material in the section on post play rules was excerpted from **Fine Tuning Your Team's Position Play**. Considerably more information about offensive post play and how to develop post play is provided in this book as well as information concerning developing point guards and perimeter players.*

Dribble Use Rules

Limit of Two Dribbles

Players love to dribble. They love to dribble too much. Other than advancing the ball up the court, a player can go nearly anywhere necessary in half court offense with no more than two dribbles. The two-dribble limit teaches players to attack when they move using the dribble. It also forces players to follow the rule of going somewhere with purpose and going somewhere when you move. By limiting players to only two dribbles, the likelihood of turnovers is decreased while forcing players to become purposeful in both their use of the dribble and movement.

Go Somewhere with Your Dribble

When a player puts the ball on the floor to dribble, the player should have a specific location on the court the player intends to move to by dribbling the ball. Too many players dribble for the sake of dribbling.

By putting the ball on the floor just to dribble, the player loses the element of surprise in attacking the defense. Before the offensive player can pass or shoot he must pick up his dribble giving the defense a split second to adjust and defend accordingly.

Dribble with purpose or not at all.

There are only a limited number of valid reasons to dribble the ball. These reasons are:

- attacking the rim.
- improving passing angle.
- shorten a pass.
- to escape trouble.
- advancing the ball up the court.

Limit of One Dribble from the 3-point Line to the Rim

Great penetrating attackers only need one dribble to make it from the 3-point line to the rim to shoot a lay-up. This offensive skill greatly enhances the ability of an offensive attacker to score, create opportunities for teammates, draw fouls and in general create problems for the defense. It will also cause many defensive players to give the offensive player considerable space to eliminate the attacking drive, creating opportunities for 3-point shots.

22

Alignments Versus Zone Defense

Blocker/Mover differs from other variations of motion offense by virtue of the alignments the offense uses. In order to fully understand Blocker/Mover, it is necessary to first have a basic understanding of the purpose of alignments, the various alignments and the advantages and disadvantages of each alignment.

Alignments and Traditional Motion Offense

Most variations of motion offense allow for complete random movement with the possible exception of dividing players into perimeter or post players. Common motion offense alignments might be 3-out-2-in (3 perimeter players and 2 post players – **See Diagram A**) or 4-out-1-in (4 perimeter players and 1 post player- **See Diagram B**). For teams with no true post player, a common form of motion offense is 5-out-0-in (all players can fill any position, perimeter or post – **See Diagram C**). While not very common, some teams use a 2-out-3-in version of motion offense (2-out-3-in- **See Diagram D**).

Diagram A

Diagram B

Diagram C

Diagram D

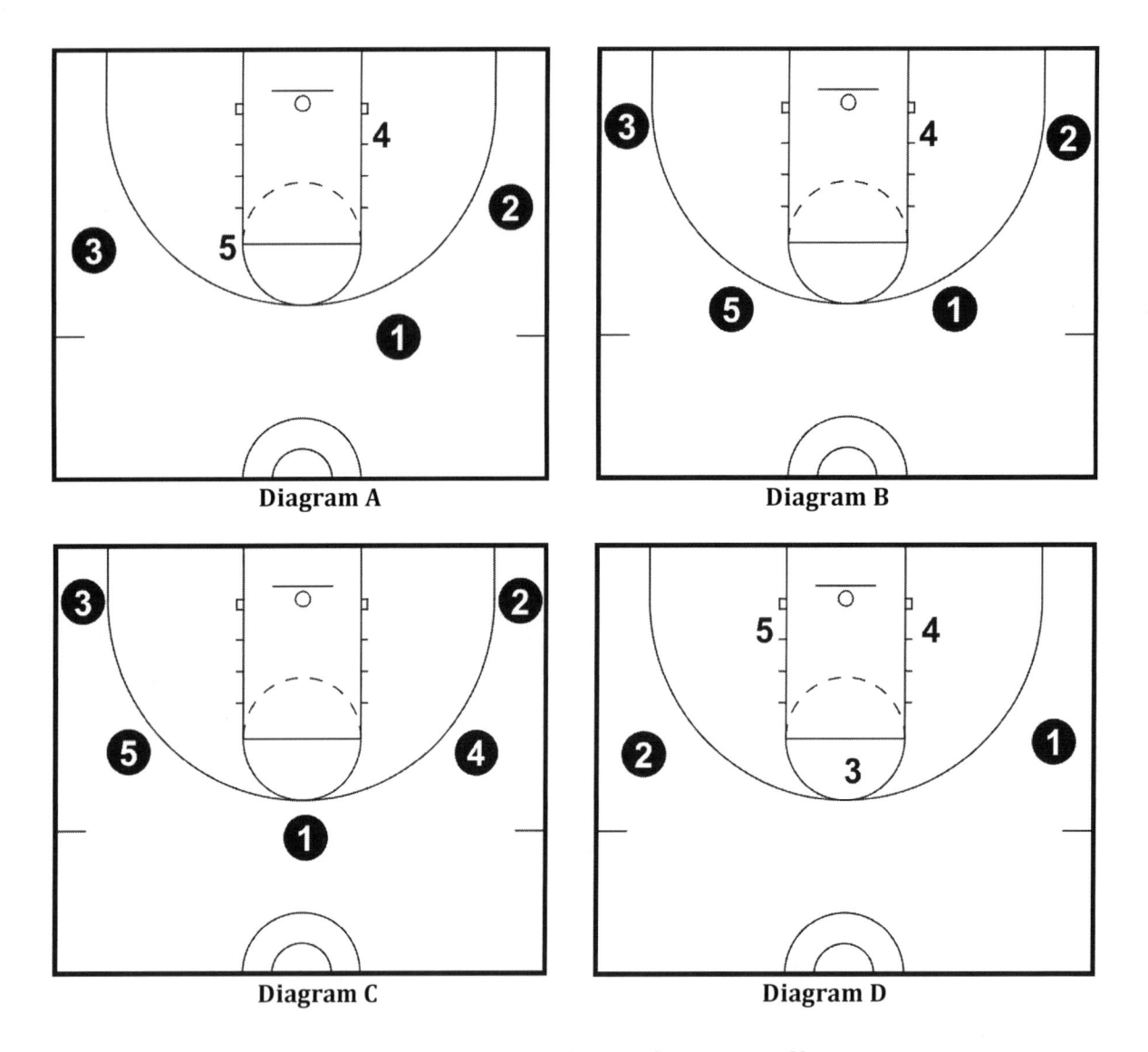

The primary purpose of alignments in traditional motion offense is to ensure proper spacing, an essential component to any offense, motion or not. A quick examination of the four examples shown depicts four alignments with players spaced roughly 15-18 feet apart.

Alignments also serve to designate roles in conventional motion offense. Players who play "out" are considered perimeter players and adhere to motion offense rules for perimeter players. Players who play "in" are considered post players and adhere to motion rules for post players.

Alignments and Blocker/Mover

Blocker/Mover uses alignments differently. While players may very well be perimeter or post players and spacing is just as essential in Blocker/Mover as it is in any other offense, **the alignments in Blocker/Mover dictate where and how action will take place in the offense!**

Blockers are assigned to specific areas of the court. Movers may move wherever necessary in order to "find" a Blocker to screen for them. Blockers may move anywhere inside their assigned area to find a Mover to screen for but, within reason, are not allowed to venture out of their designated area.

Why adopt such an approach when the primary reason for using a motion type offense is the freedom and lack of predictability such an offense allows? The use of alignments provides structure players need while still allowing the freedom of movement traditional motion offense permits.

In traditional motion offense, one of the most common drawbacks is players will simply stand still and no movement of any kind takes place. Too much freedom in this instance results in confusion on the part of players concerning who should be doing the screening, who should be cutting and where should the screens be set.

Determining in advance who the Movers (players who cut) and Blockers (players who screen) are and selecting an alignment, these issues are eliminated. The players know who is supposed to be a cutter, who is supposed to set screens and a good idea of where the screens will be set.

Alignments are chosen based on the personnel available to the team or the group of players who are in the game. Some alignments are better suited for an interior game, such as the Lane-Lane alignment. Strategic or tactical reasons, such as a desire to keep the ball in the hands of a great point guard as much as possible may see a team use the Top-Bottom alignment.

Alignments and Zone Attack

Zone defenses tend to guard areas of the court and not specific offensive players requiring a different approach of attack when utilizing a motion type offense. Alignments are useful to maintain good offensive spacing while clarifying offensive roles, similar to attacking a man-to-man defense.

Alignments are also useful in attacking zone defenses by immediately distorting the basic alignment of the zone defense, forcing the defenders to guard areas the zone is not intended to defend. Distorting the zone creates gaps for Movers to flash into, spaces for Movers to move to when a dribble move is executed as well as creating situations where defenders are vulnerable to screens set by Blockers.

Common Basic Alignments Against Zone Defenses

Lane-Lane

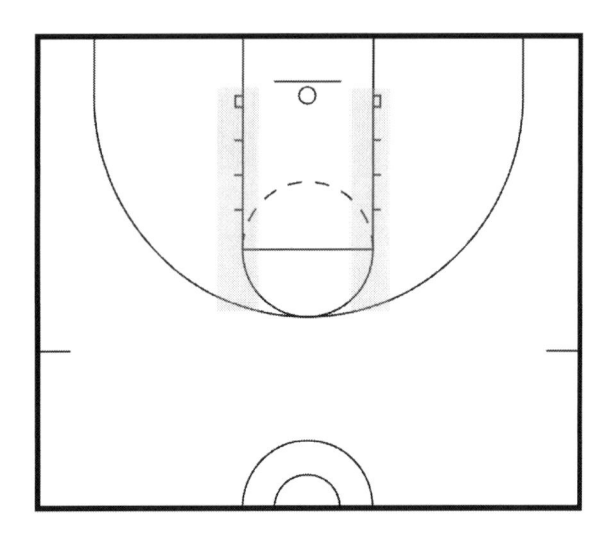

The Lane-Lane Alignment is good for:

- teams who have strong post play, both in the high and low post.
- teams who have two strong post players who can play together.
- using the high post to pass the ball, creating lots of scoring options.
- setting high ball screens.
- setting pin screens for cutters.
- creating double and triple screen opportunities for Movers.
- providing good, consistent offensive rebounding position.
- creating screen in action for 3 pt. shooters.
- creating back screen/pin screen opportunities.

The Lane-Lane Alignment is not good for:

- teams who lack good post play.
- teams who lack at least one mobile post player who can step out and face the basket.
- teams who lack at least one mobile post player who can step out to create space for cutters against the zone.

Top-Bottom

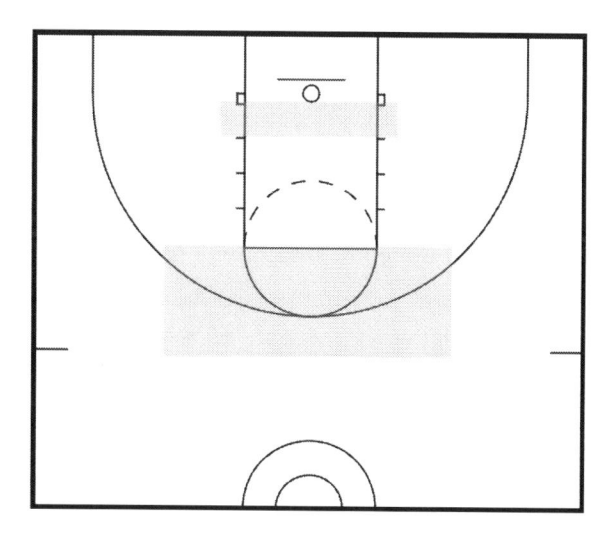

The Top-Bottom Alignment is good for:

- teams with one very effective low post player.
- the high low game utilizing an effective low post player.
- teams with an intelligent role player who is both an excellent screener and pass from the Top area of the alignment, often this player can be a permanent post player.
- teams with Movers who are excellent at flashing into gaps in a zone defense.
- creating back door cutting opportunities.
- providing consistently good offensive rebounding position.
- teams with only one good ball handler who may, or may not, be able to score. By having this ball handler play the Top Blocker position, the ball handler is never more than one pass away from the ball (If the ball handler is not a scorer, this is an excellent option).

The Top-Bottom Alignment is not good for:

- teams who lack an effective low post scorer.
- teams who lack an effective passer from the high post/Top area.
- whose Mover's require flare screens or wide down screens to be effective.
- teams who need ball screens to be effective, particularly wide ball screens on the wing area.
- teams who need or want to place a heavy emphasis on middle penetration UNLESS the Top Blocker is a penetrating point guard.

Wide-Wide

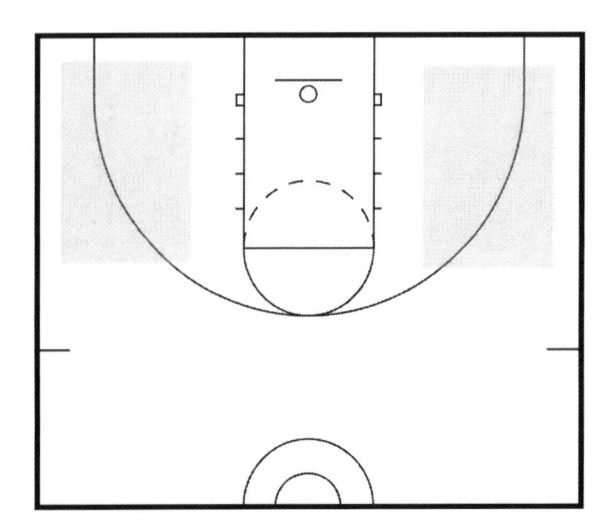

The Wide-Wide Alignment is good for:

- teams with three good perimeter players.
- teams with at least two excellent 3 pt. shooters and a tough perimeter player.
- teams with small but mobile post players.
- teams with thee good perimeters and two tough, physical, smart role players.
- creating plenty of space for middle penetration.
- setting up penetrate and pitch opportunities.
- using the Euro tactic to generate 3-point shot opportunities.
- ball screens on the wing area.
- setting back screens for backdoor cuts for lay-ups.
- setting double and triple screens as a Mover changes sides of the court.

The Wide-Wide Alignment is not good for:

- traditional low post offense.
- may result in frequent poor offensive rebounding position.
- teams who only have one good ball handler or passer.

Lane-Wide

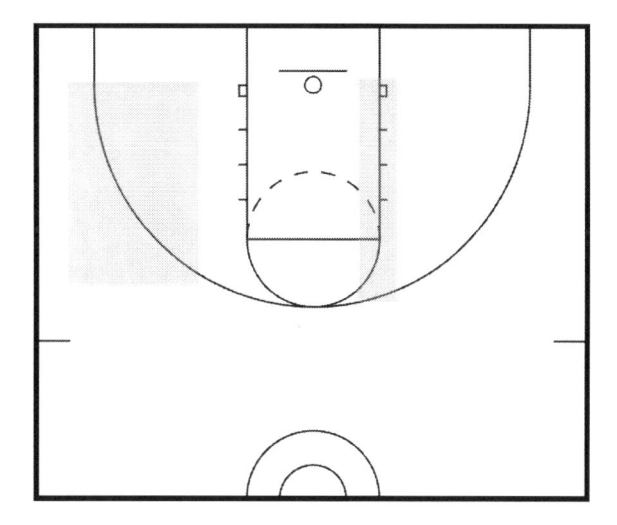

The Lane-Wide Alignment is good for:

- teams who have a good post player, three good perimeter players who can penetrate and a tough, physical and intelligent role player.
- striking a balance between low post offense and creating penetration opportunities.
- ball screens on the Wide side of the alignment.
- high ball screens on the Lane side of the alignment.
- creating back door opportunities when the Lane Blocker is used as a high post passer.
- providing more consistent offensive rebounding.

The Lane-Wide Alignment is not good for:

- teams who do not have intelligent players. The compromise between the strong post play options of the Lane-Lane alignment and the Wide-Wide alignment can create confusion for players who are not good at reading defenses and making decisions.
- teams who do not have three good perimeter players who can penetrate, cut and pass off penetration.
- teams who lack a role player with the needed character qualities of intelligence, toughness and physical play to fill the role of the Wide Blocker.

23

Attacking the Gaps of Zone Defense With Blocker-Mover

Use Alignments to Line up in the gaps

There is no need to make offense more complicated. The easiest way to attack gaps in a zone defense is to have the offense line up in the gaps to initiate its zone attack.

Lane-Lane versus 2-3

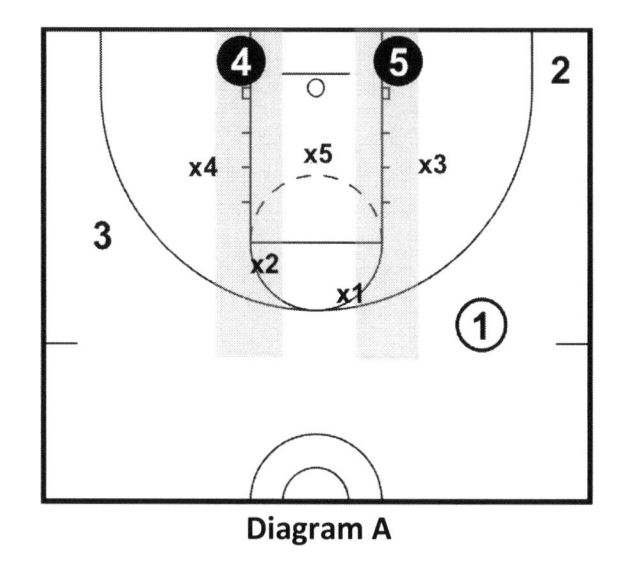

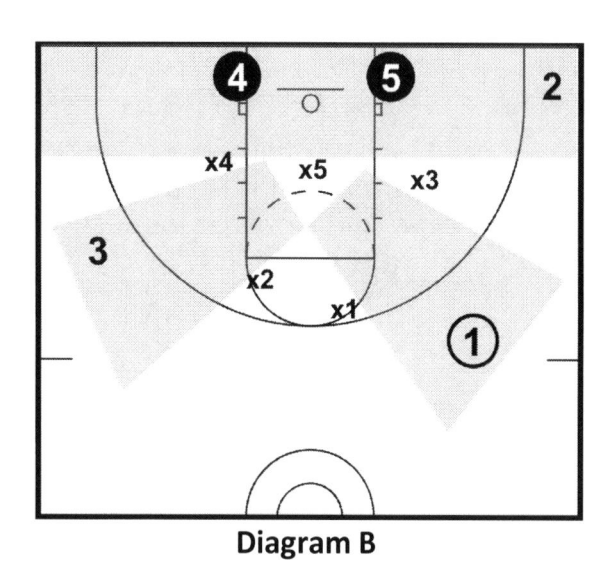

Diagram A   Diagram B

Not only does the offense line up in the gaps of the zone in **Diagram A**, it stretches the zone by lining up the two Blockers in this Lane-Lane alignment deep behind the zone defense. **Diagram B** depicts the gaps in the 2-3 zone the offense has lined up in.

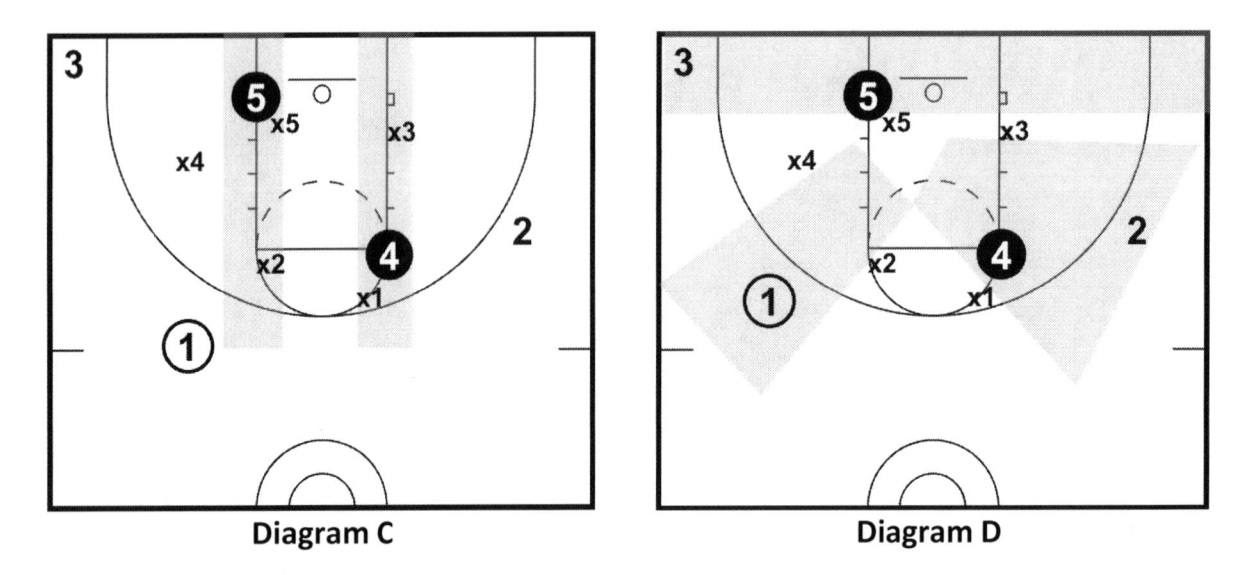

Diagram C   **Diagram D**

Diagram C shows a different initial alignment in the Lane-Lane alignment. In this example the alignment utilizes other zone attack principles such as overloading the zone (Players 1, 3 and 5). **Diagram D** shows the gaps in the zone.

Lane-Lane versus 1-2-2

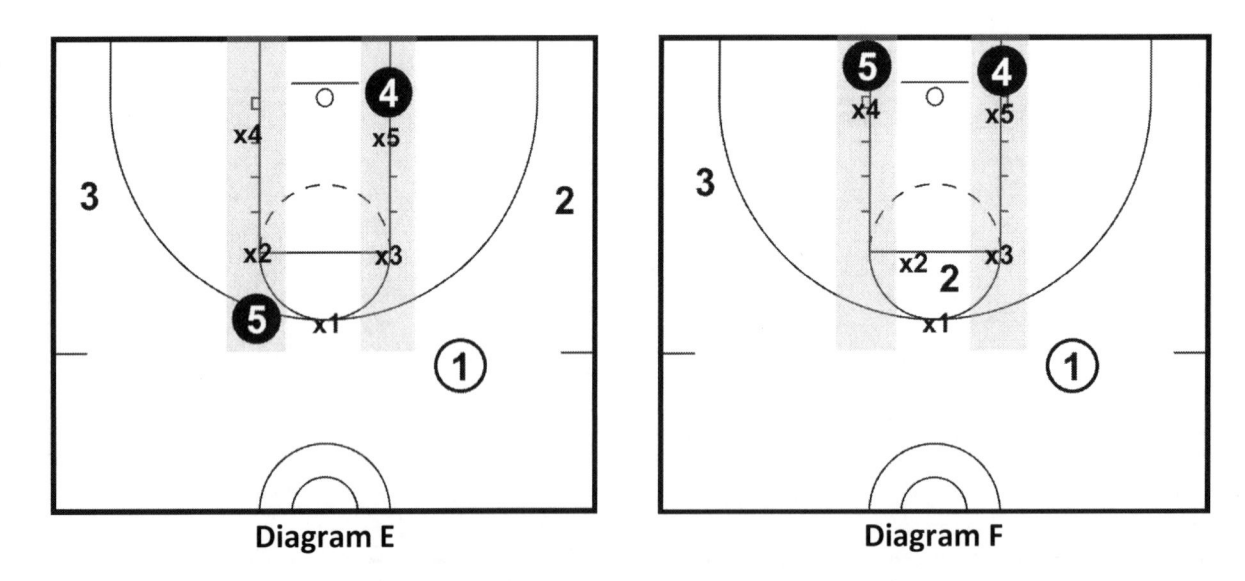

Diagram E   **Diagram F**

The next two diagrams, **Diagrams E** and **F**, show different initial alignments in the gaps of a 1-2-2. Note in **Diagram F** the Blockers are stretching the zone and distorting it by playing deep behind.

Lane-Lane versus 1-3-1

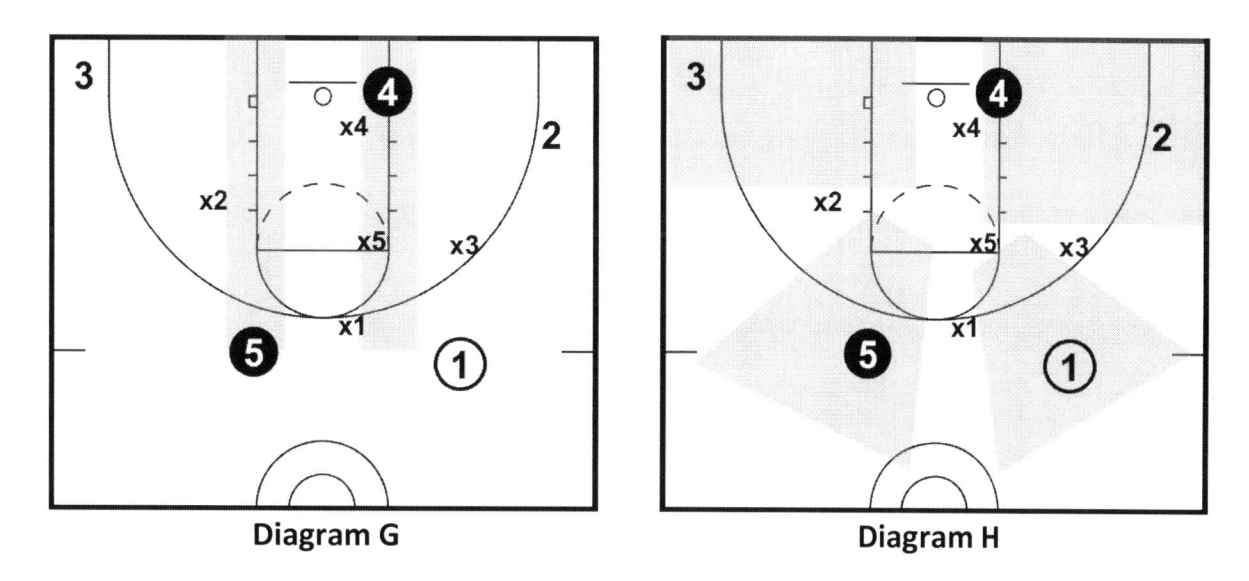

Diagram G

Diagram H

The two diagrams above depict the Lane-Lane alignment against a 1-3-1 zone. **Diagram H** shows the gaps the players are lined up in.

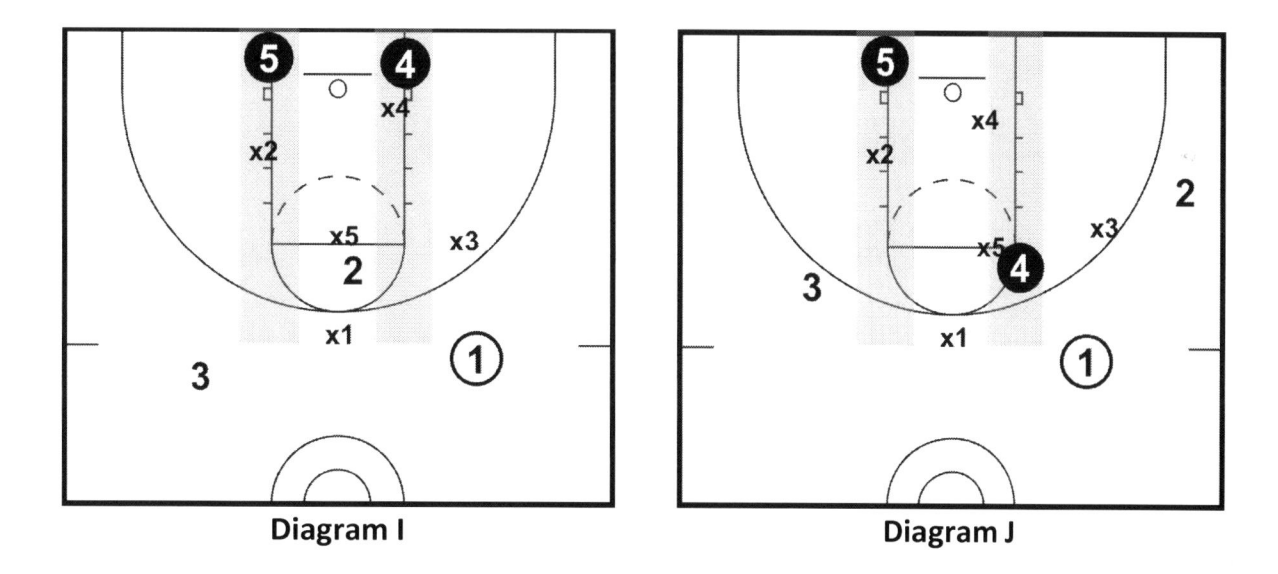

Diagram I

Diagram J

Diagram I and **Diagram J** show two additional starting alignments using the Lane-Lane alignment lining up in the natural gaps of a 1-3-1 zone defense.

Lane-Wide versus 2-3

Diagram K

Diagram L

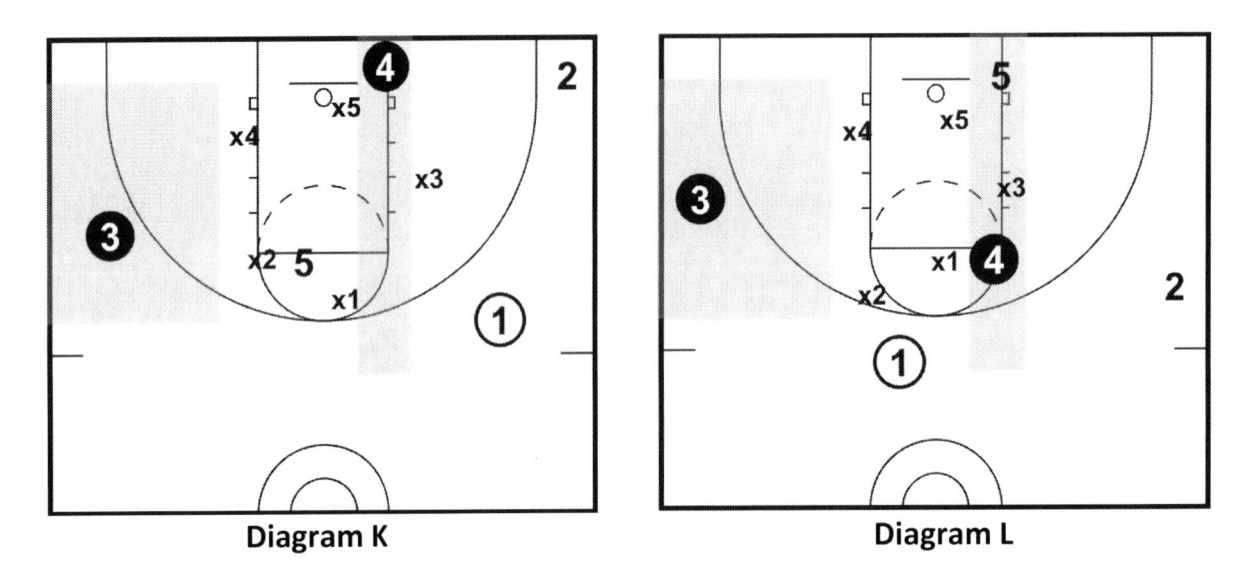

Diagram K and **Diagram L** depict two different starting alignments using the Lane-Wide alignment. In **Diagram K**, the post Blocker starts out behind the zone to stretch it. In **Diagram L**, the post Mover lines up behind the zone while the post Blocker occupies the high post.

Lane-Wide versus 1-2-2

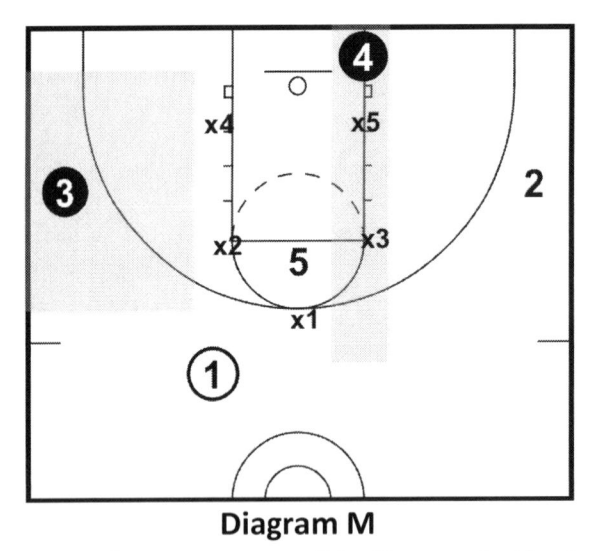

Diagram M

In **Diagram M** the two post players are used to line up in the interior gaps of a 1-2-2. The post Blocker is in the gap behind the zone and the post Mover has lined up in the gap at the foul line area.

Lane-Wide versus 1-3-1

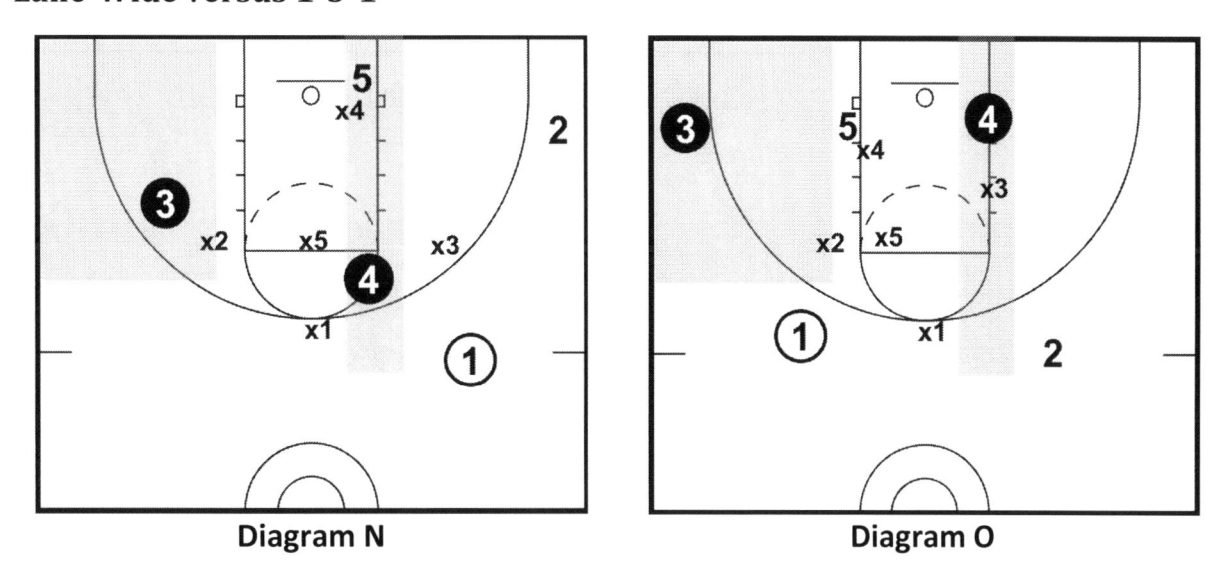

Diagram N

Diagram O

Two different starting alignments are show in **Diagram N** and **Diagram O**. The positioning in **Diagram N** does little to alter the 1-3-1 zone but does take advantage of the natural gaps in the zone. In **Diagram O** the positioning of the post Blocker forces the help side wing to drop down into the lane area, creating space for Mover #2.

Top-Bottom versus 2-3

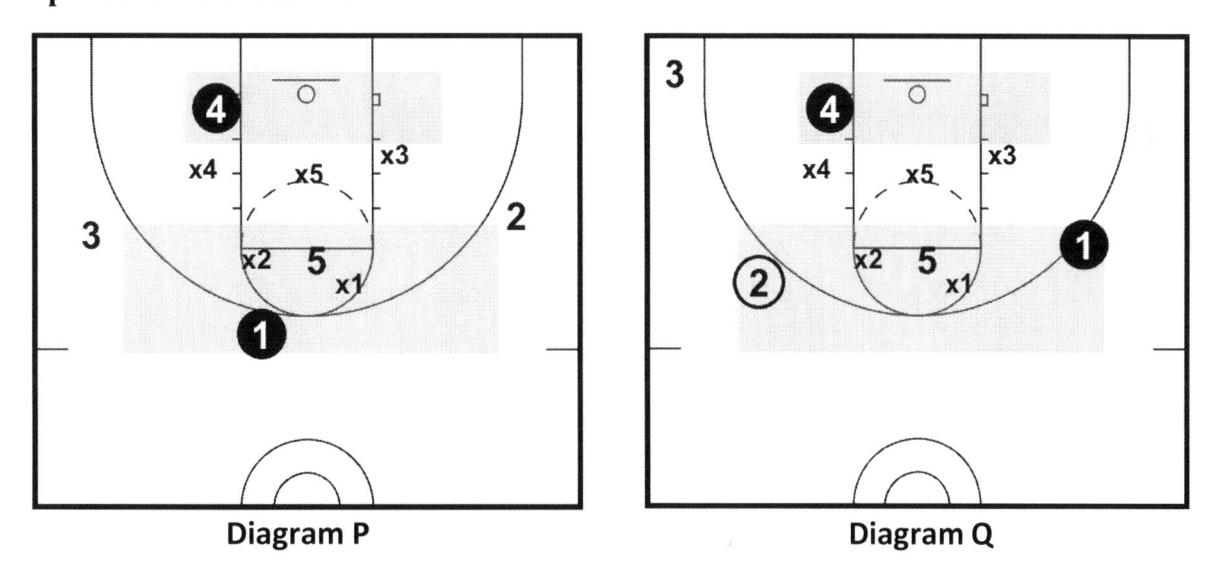

Diagram P

Diagram Q

Two simple alignments in the gaps are shown in **Diagram P** and **Diagram Q**. Both of the alignments shown are excellent starting alignments for a Top-Bottom team who has great 3-point shooters. The top Blocker is in a good position to start screening for the perimeter shooters.

Top-Bottom versus 1-2-2

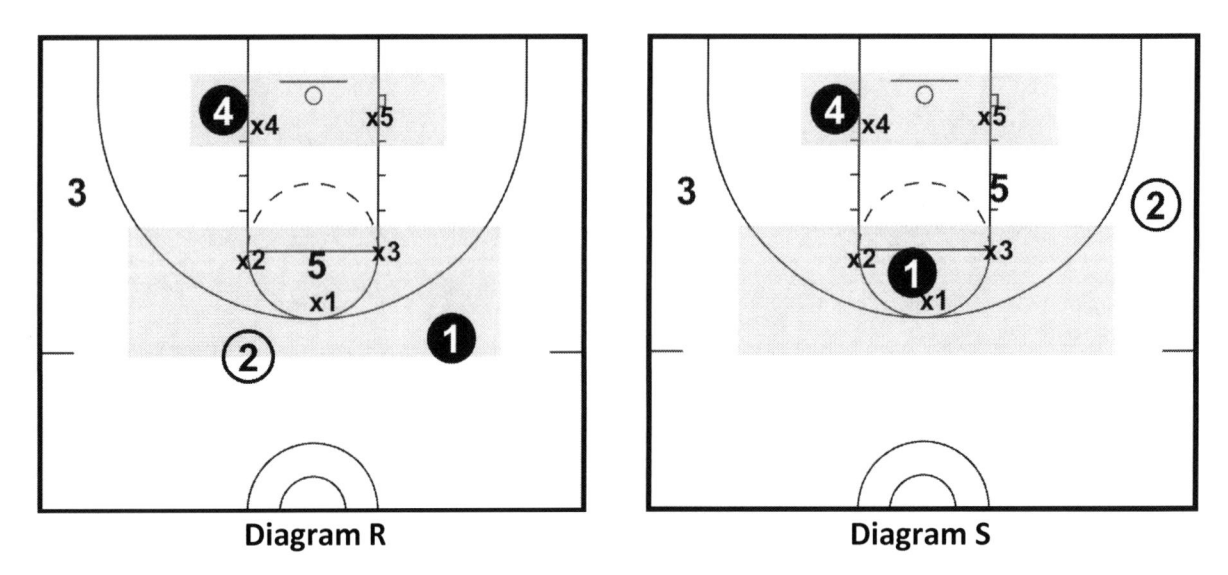

Diagram R

Diagram S

The two starting alignments above show the post Blocker in a great position to set screen-in screens for the #3 Mover. The perimeter Blocker is in good position to set a flare screen in Diagram R and in Diagram S an entry pass to #1 is essentially the creation of a 3-2 break situation, forcing the zone to defend 3 offensive players with 2 defenders.

Top-Bottom versus 1-3-1

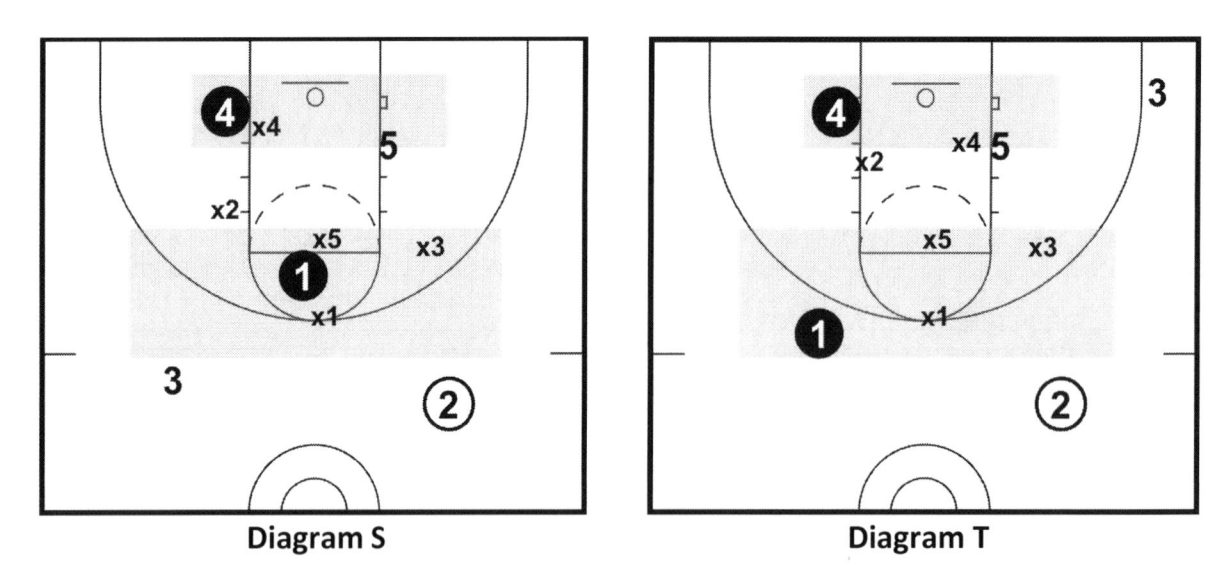

Diagram S

Diagram T

The Top-Bottom alignment is depicted versus a 1-3-1 in the two examples shown in **Diagram S** and **Diagram T**.

Attacking the Gaps of Zone Defense With Blocker-Mover

Play the Gaps

Starting in the gaps is just one step in using gaps to attack a zone defense. Once the offense has been initiated, the offensive players, both Blockers and Movers must play the gaps, taking advantage of the natural openings a zone defense offers.

Movers Hunt Blockers and Gaps

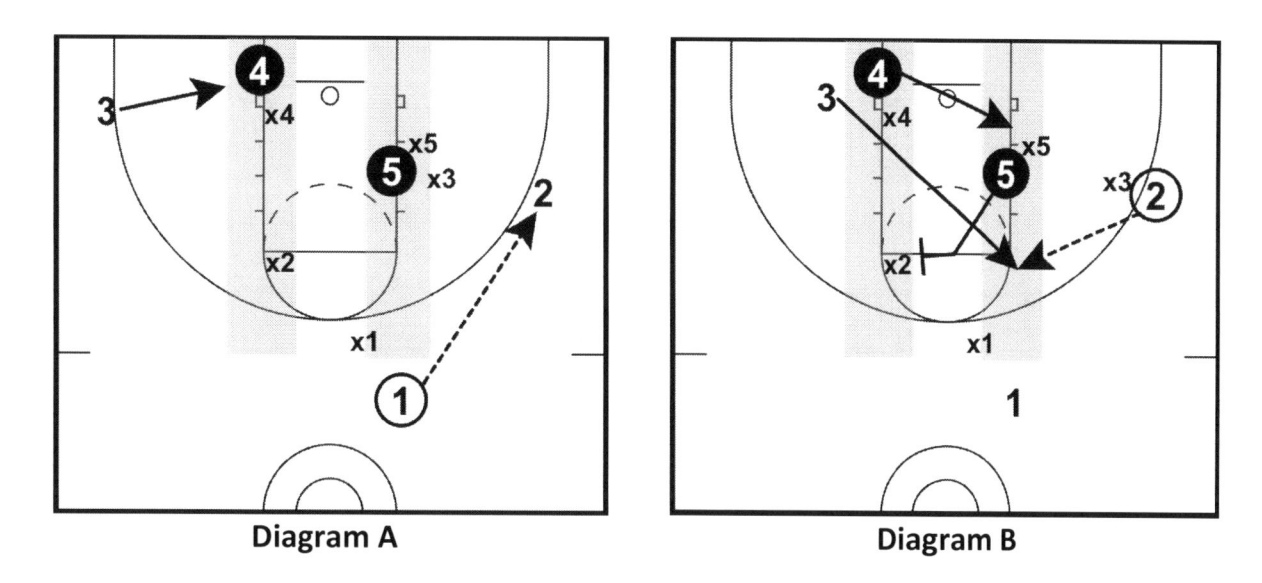

Diagram A   **Diagram B**

Movers must hunt gaps in Blocker-Mover zone attack motion just as they would hunt for a Blocker against man-to-man defense. When attacking a zone, a Mover must hunt BOTH. Movers must seek and flash cut into gaps in a zone defense. They must also hunt for Blockers who are screening the zone to either create a gap in the zone defense or to create an open space behind the zone such as what happens when setting a screen-in screen.

In **Diagram A** the movement of the ball on the perimeter sets up two opportunities to flash into gaps, one of which is aided by a screen. In Diagram B the screen set on X2 by the post Blocker creates a gap in the middle of the 2-3 zone. An opening in the ball side low post is created when the middle zone defender X5 either follows the post Blocker up the lane for a short distance or is forced to cover the Mover filling the high post on the ball side mid-post. This leaves the post Blocker #4 open when flash cutting into the newly created ball side low post gap in the zone. If the ball is not entered into the low post to Blocker #4, the two post Blockers exchange Blocker lanes in the Lane-Lane alignment, balancing the floor.

Coaching Basketball's Zone Attack Offense Using Blocker-Mover Motion Offense

Diagram C

Diagram D

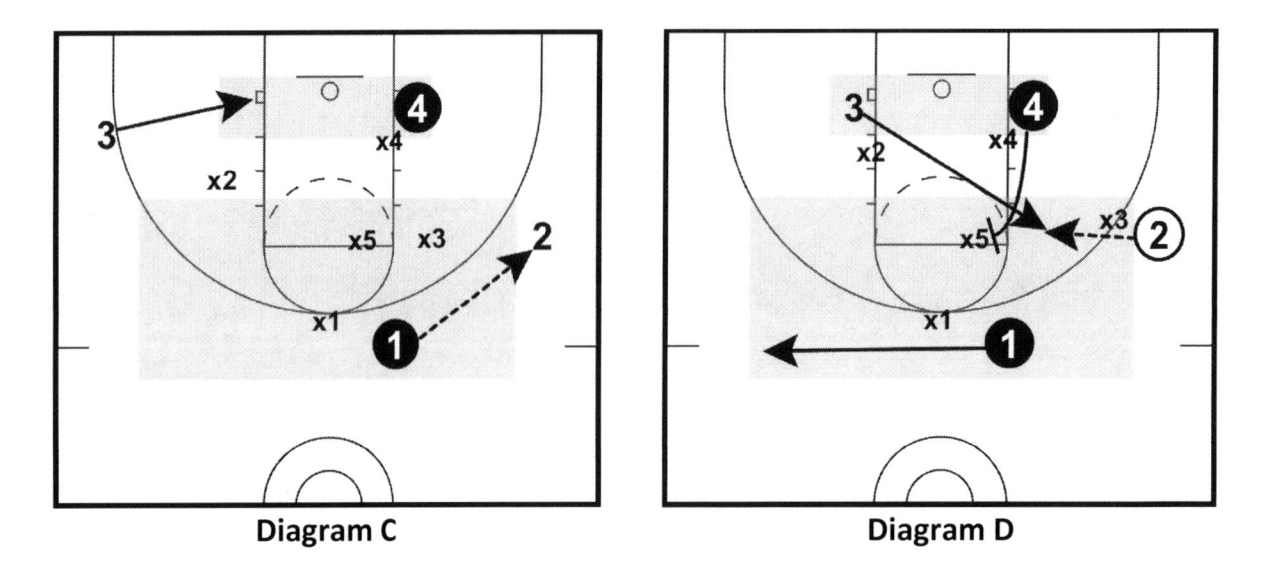

A similar outcome is depicted in **Diagram C** and **Diagram D**, using ball movement combined with a screen to create a gap for a Mover to flash into. Note the Top Blocker moves to the opposite side of the court, filling a gap. This particular area is tough for all zone defenses to cover when a quick reversal pass or skip pass is made to this area after the ball has been moved below the free throw line extended. It is also wise in this example to create the spacing for the #3 Mover so the one Mover per perimeter area rule can be adhered to when the #3 Mover exits the high post area.

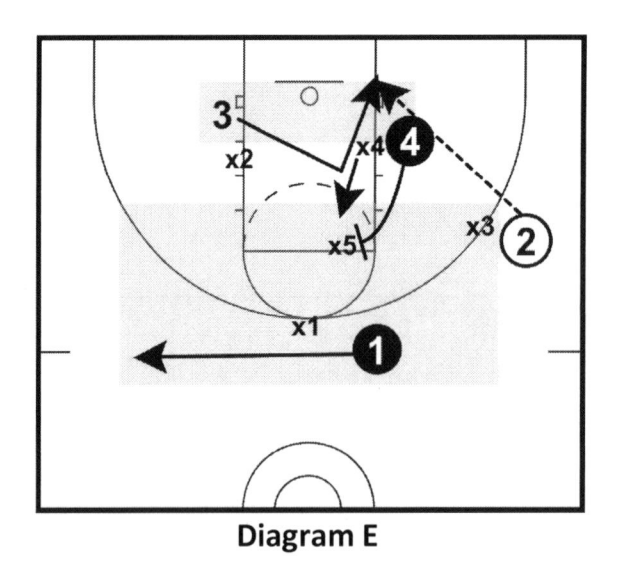

Diagram E

An alternate version of this same attack shows the X4 defender moving up the lane to help cover the post Blocker, creating a gap for the Mover to cut under to fill in the ball side low post (**Diagram E**).

24

Distort The Zone Defense

Teams who play zone defense often do so for the strategic advantage of deciding what parts of the court will be defended. Distorting the zone defense takes this advantage away, creates gaps and forces the zone to make rotations in a less than desirable fashion.

Alignments

Alignments can be used to distort the zone defense before the offense even begins to attack the zone defense. The following examples show how different Blocker-Mover alignments can be used to force a zone out of its initial preferred alignment.

Lane-Lane versus 2-3

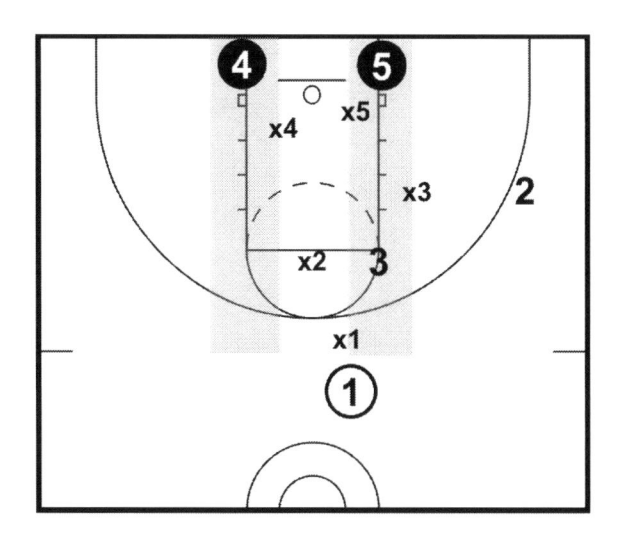

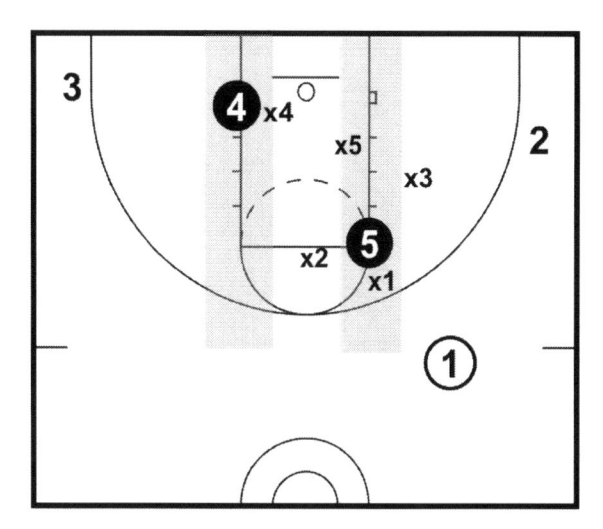

Lane-Lane versus 1-2-2

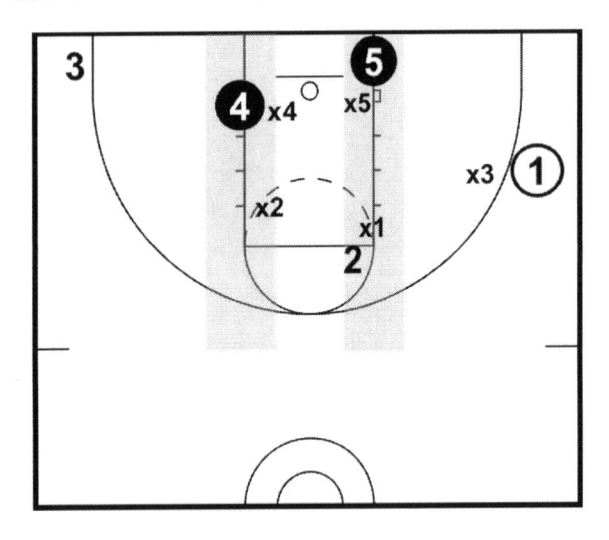

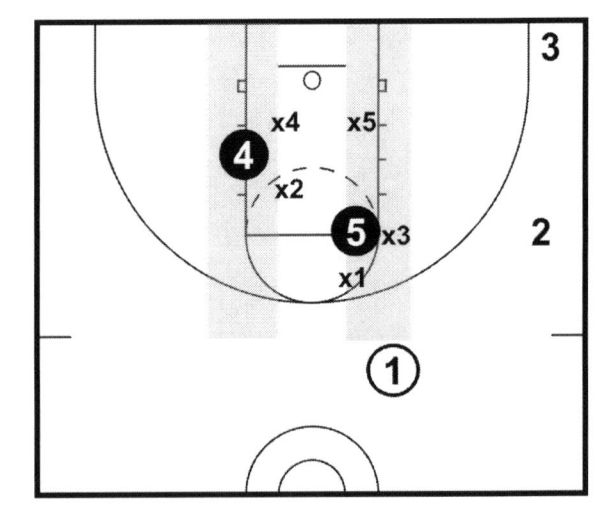

Lane-Lane versus 1-3-1

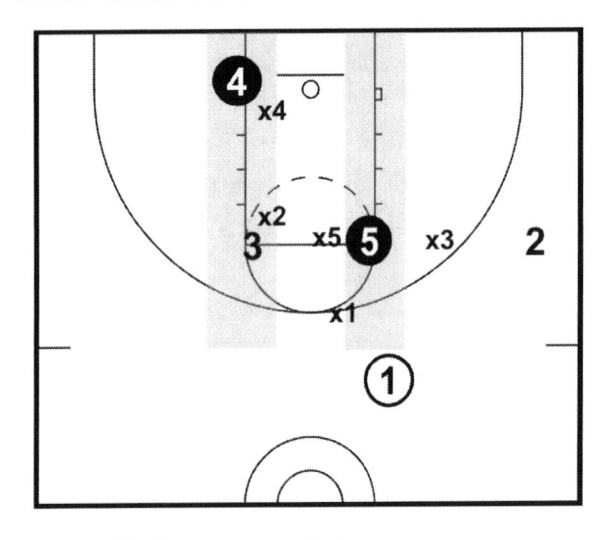

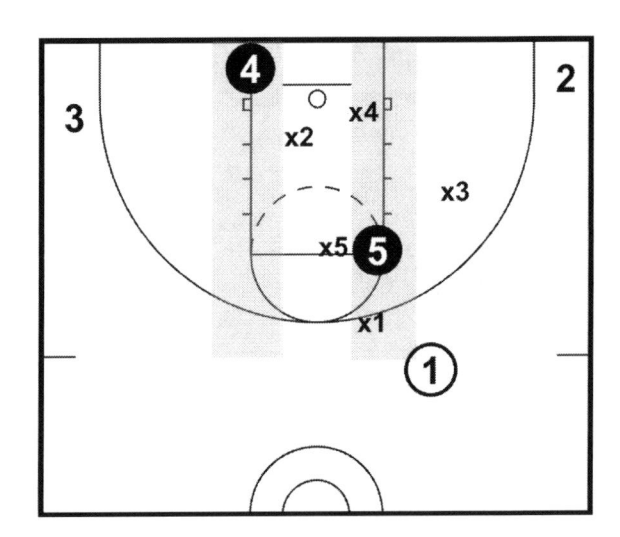

Lane-Wide versus 2-3

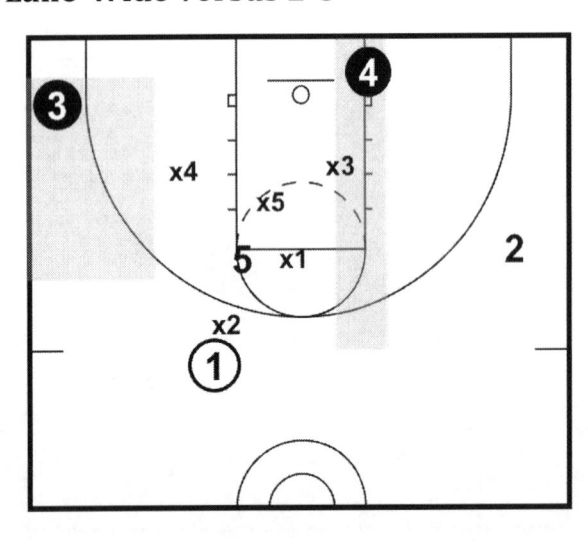

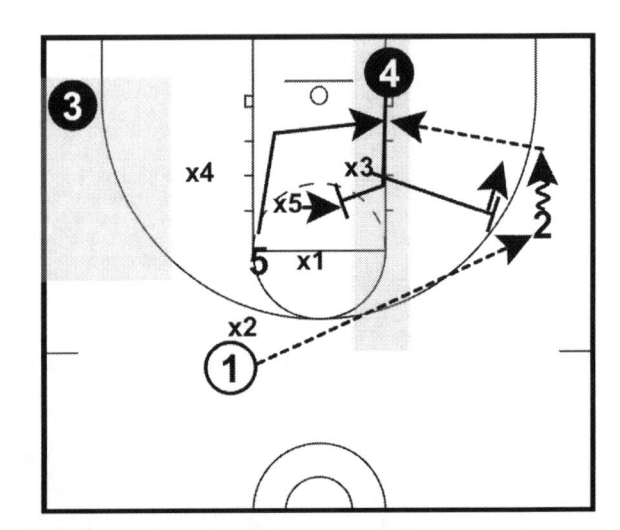

Lane-Wide versus 1-2-2

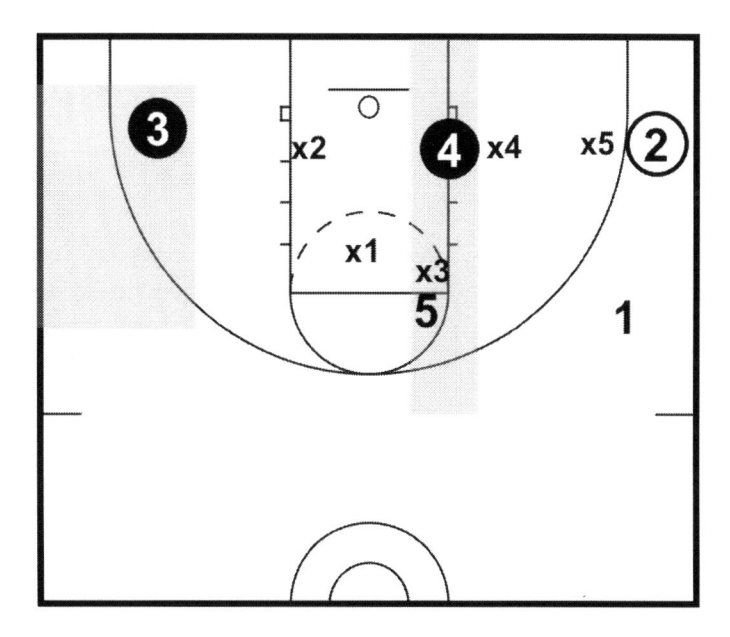

Lane-Wide versus 1-3-1

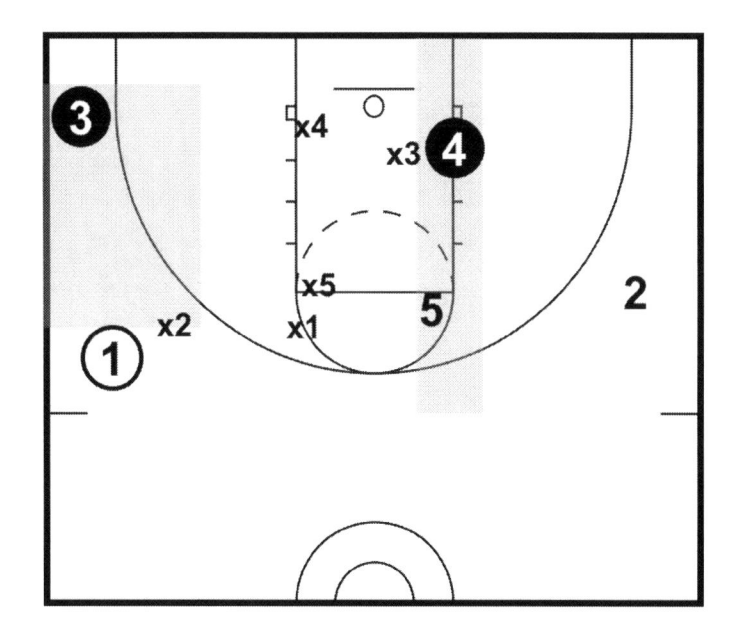

Top-Bottom versus 2-3

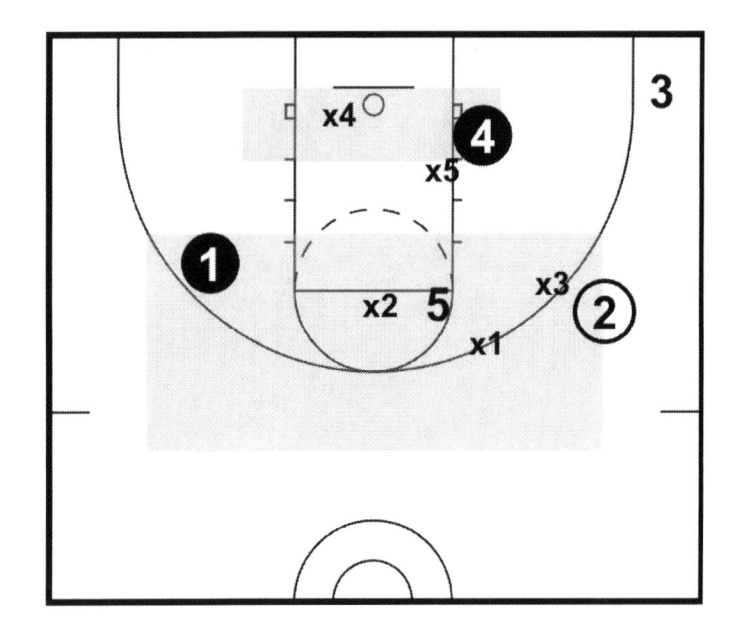

Top-Bottom versus 1-2-2

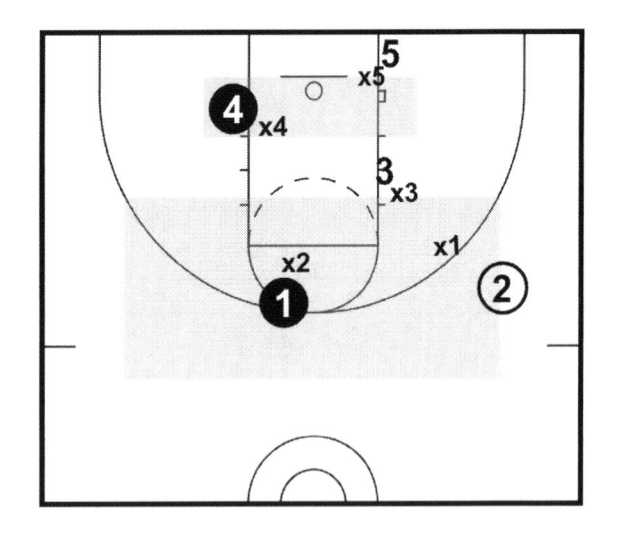

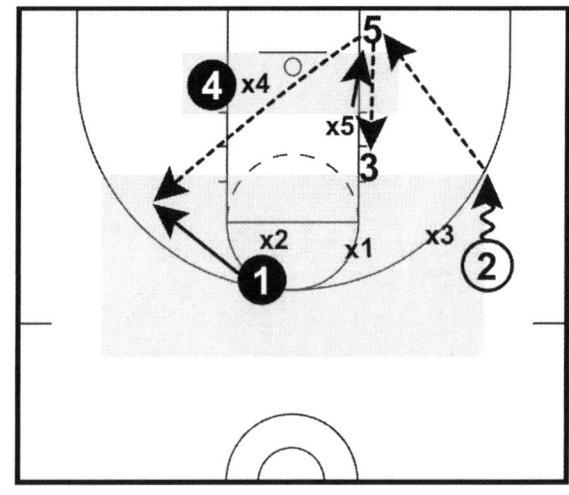

144

Distort the Zone Defense

Top-Bottom versus 1-3-1

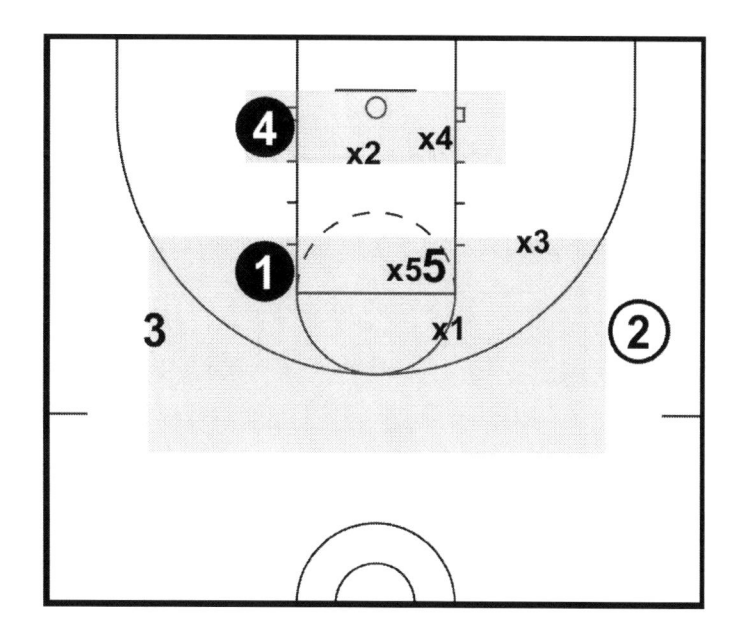

25

Take the Defender Away (Use of the Dribble to Attack)

Today's players use the dribble far too much. Not only do players dribble too much, they do not dribble with purpose. Having made this point, the dribble can be an excellent weapon against a zone defense, so long as players dribble with purpose, go somewhere specific with their dribble and use as few dribbles as possible.

Freeze and Slide

Diagram A   Diagram B

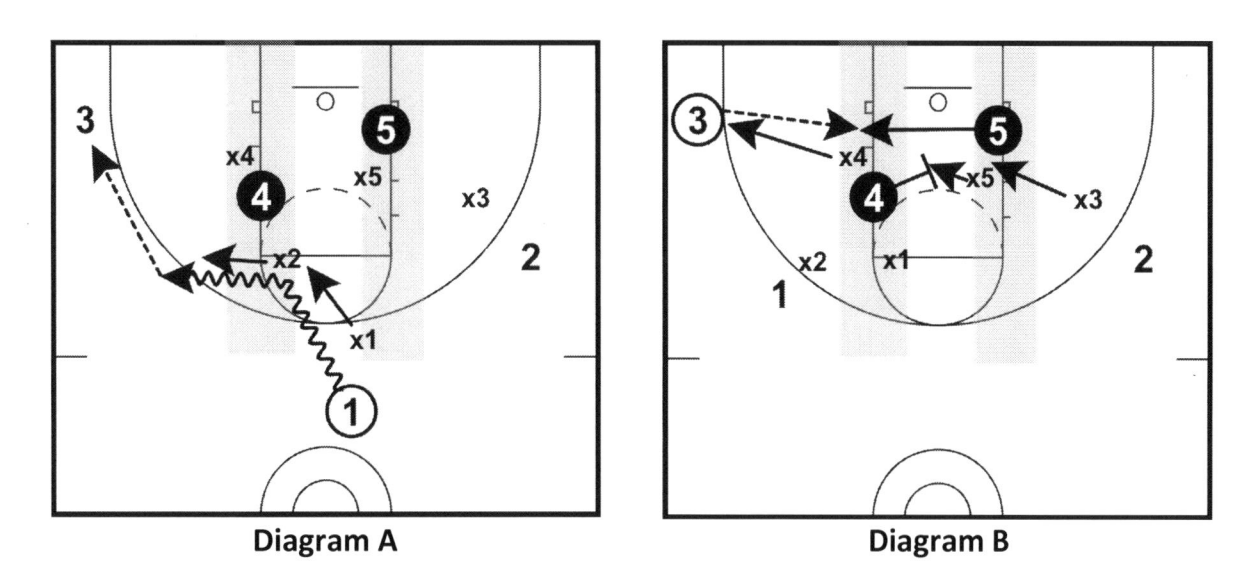

In **Diagram A** and **Diagram B** the "freeze and slide" zone attack tactic is used in combination with a dribble push and a Center Screen to create a low post shot for post Blocker #5. (See Zone Attack Tactic Number 26).

Dribble Off

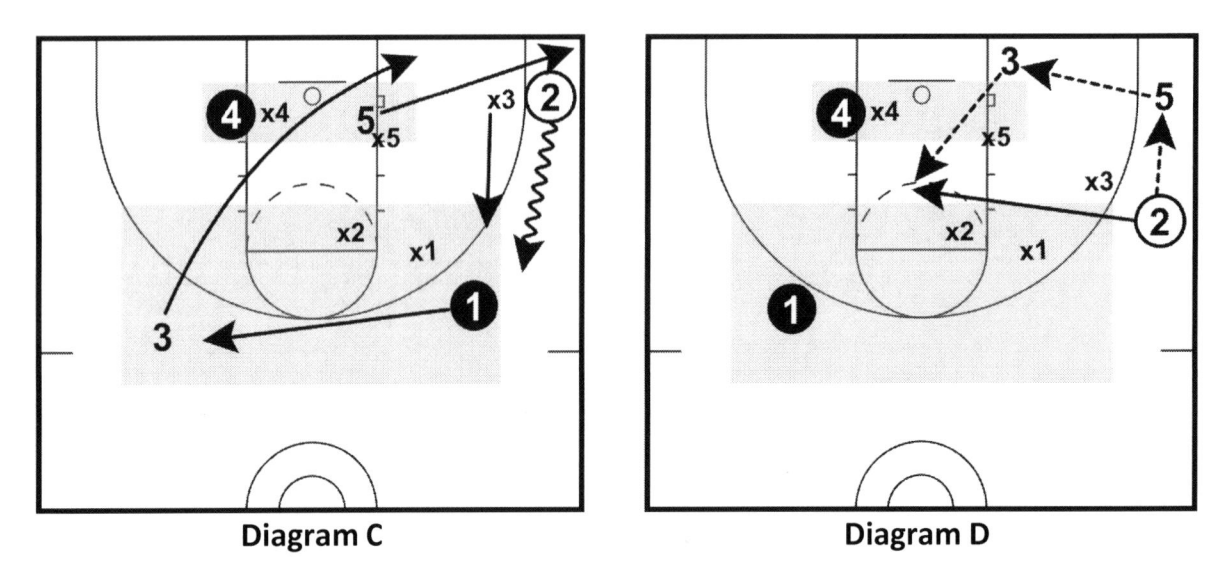

Diagram C

Diagram D

Zone Attack Tactic Number 27 is depicted in **Diagram C** and **Diagram D**. Dribbling off the baseline draws a zone defender away from the baseline and the zone defender's assigned area, creating an opening (or gap) for a Mover to fill. Note the combination of distorting the zone, filling the gaps and the Mover hunting and filling the gap in Diagram D. A good pass fake to freeze the zone before passing to the post Mover in the corner will set the zone, allowing the ball to be moved quickly and for Mover #2 to take advantage of the gap created in the middle of the zone.

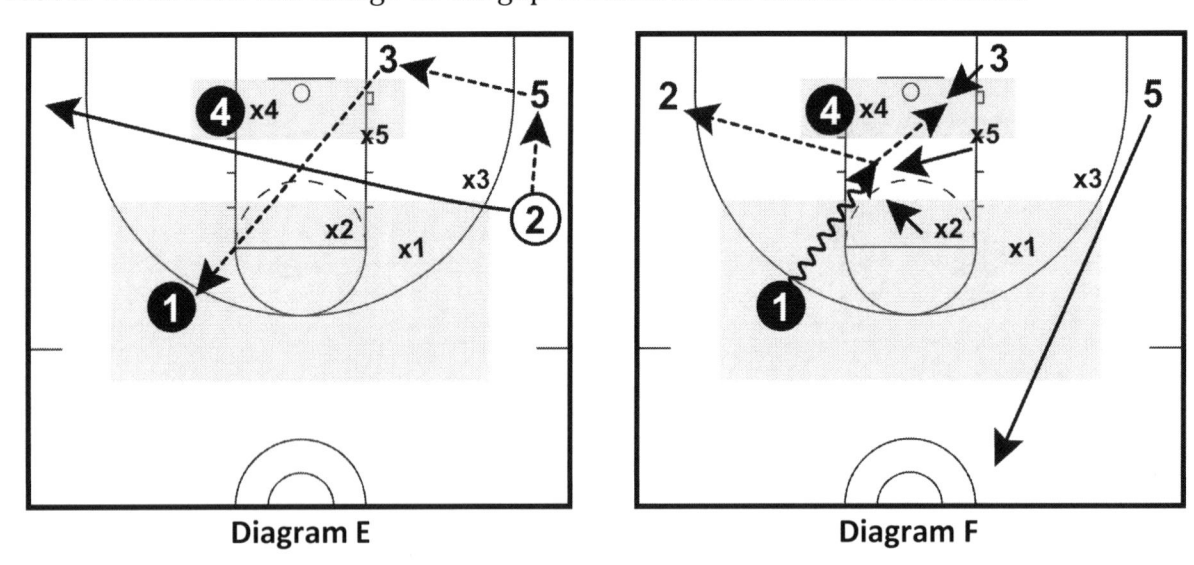

Diagram E

Diagram F

The same initial movements and tactics are used to set up the diagonal skip pass depicted in Diagram E. This creates the dribble penetration opportunity that forces two defenders to guard three offensive players. Note Mover #3 sneaking in from behind the zone defense. Also, post Mover #5 must balance the floor to defend against a possible fast break by the opponent.

Take the Defender Away (Use of Dribble to Attack)

Dribble Follow/Dribble Off the Top

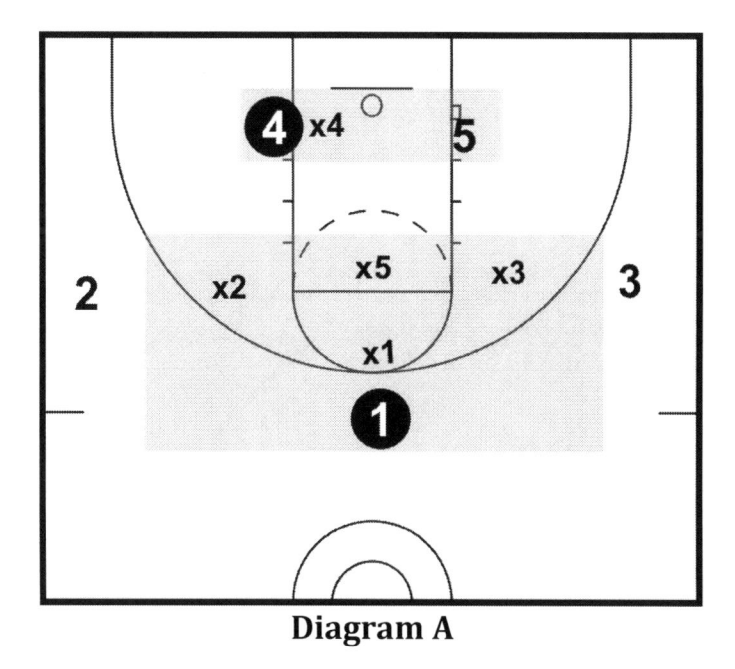

Diagram A

Diagram A depicts a Top-Bottom alignment set up against a 1-3-1 zone. Note the offense has not aligned in the gaps. The dribble will be used to move the ball and create opportunities for the offense.

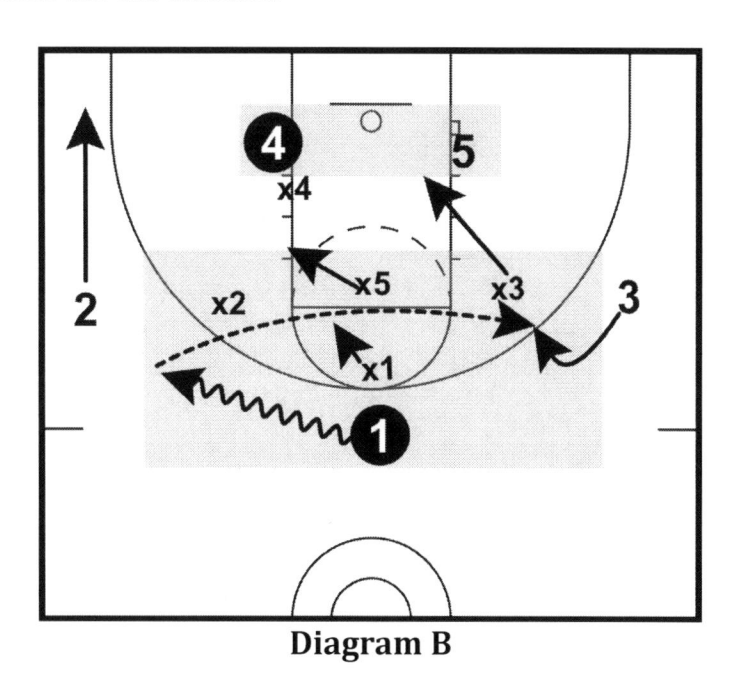

Diagram B

The dribble off the top, also known as a dribble follow (Zone Attack Tactic Number 28) is depicted in Diagram B. Note all the shifts by the offense and defense. Mover #3 makes a circle, or "J" cut to position his/her feet for a shot. Mover #2 has been "pushed" into the ball side corner. A pass fake to Mover #2 will set the defense,

149

allowing a skip pass back to Mover #3 for a 3-point shot attempt. Note the dribble off forced X3 to drop down into the lane to cover post Mover #5, creating space for Mover #3 to fill.

Dribble Push

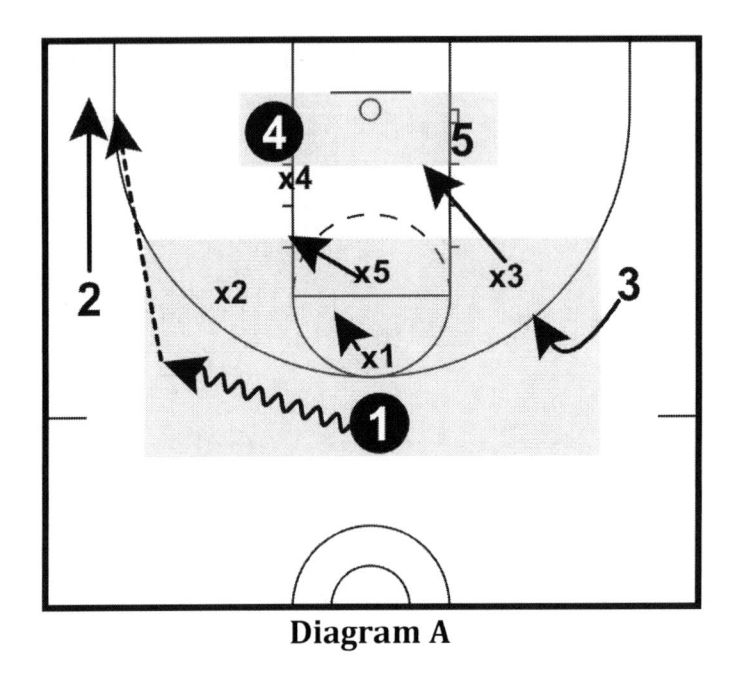

Diagram A

Using the same starting alignment and use of dribble, Mover #2 has been "dribble pushed" into the ball side corner. When the ball handler wants to "push" a teammate a hand signal should be used to indicate the desire for a push. Simply making a pushing movement with the arm bar hand will suffice.

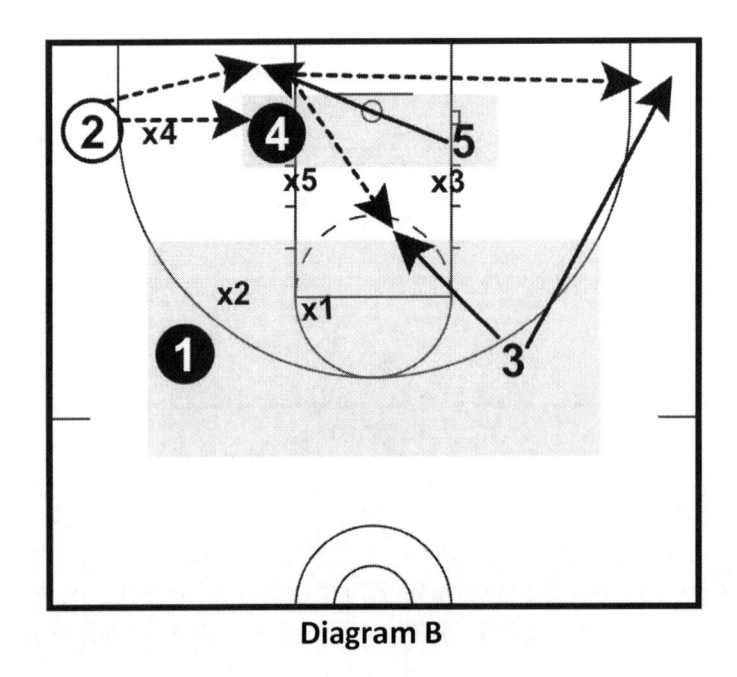

Diagram B

Take the Defender Away (Use of Dribble to Attack)

Diagram B depicts all the possible cuts and passes from this example. Some of the tactics used are distorting the zone, Mover hunting a gap, and stretching the zone from behind.

26

Overload the Zone Defense

One of the reasons teams play zone defense is to gain an advantage against the offense by deciding what areas of the court will be defended. The offense must work to negate this advantage by forcing the zone defense into a position of disadvantage due to numerical superiority by the offense. In other words, the offense wants to outnumber the defense.

Make 1 Defend 2

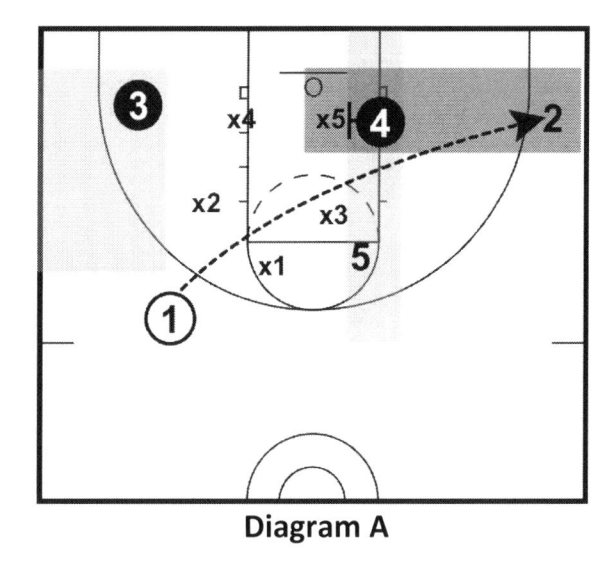

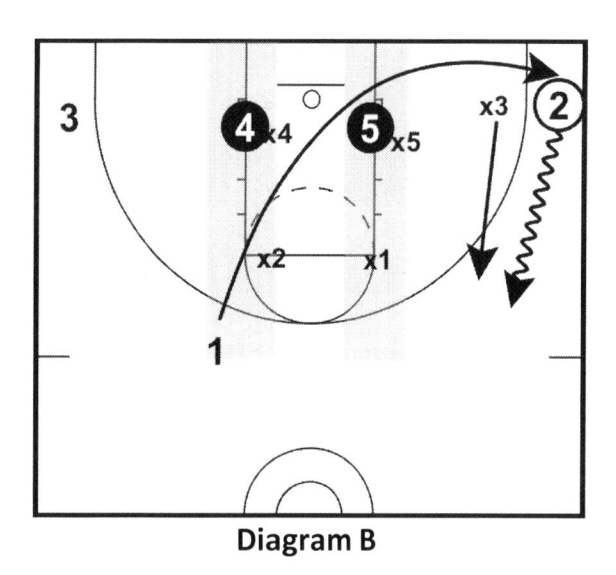

Diagram A

Diagram B

153

Diagram C

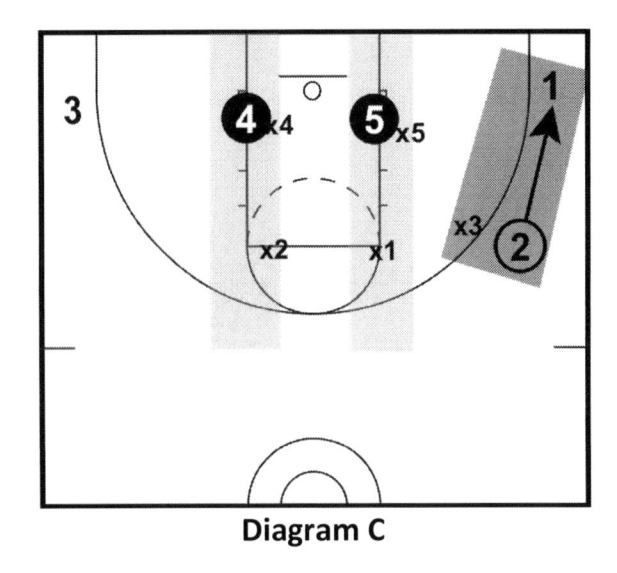

The sequence depicted in **Diagram A** through **Diagram C** create two different situations in which the defense is forced to use one defender to cover two offensive players. In **Diagram A** the skip pass utilizes a screen-in set by the post Blocker. Defender X5 must defend both the post Blocker and Mover #2. The dribble off pulls Mover #1 in **Diagram B** to the corner. A pass fake and pass back forces the defender X3 to cover two offensive players, Mover #2 and Mover #1 (**Diagram C**).

Make 2 Defend 3

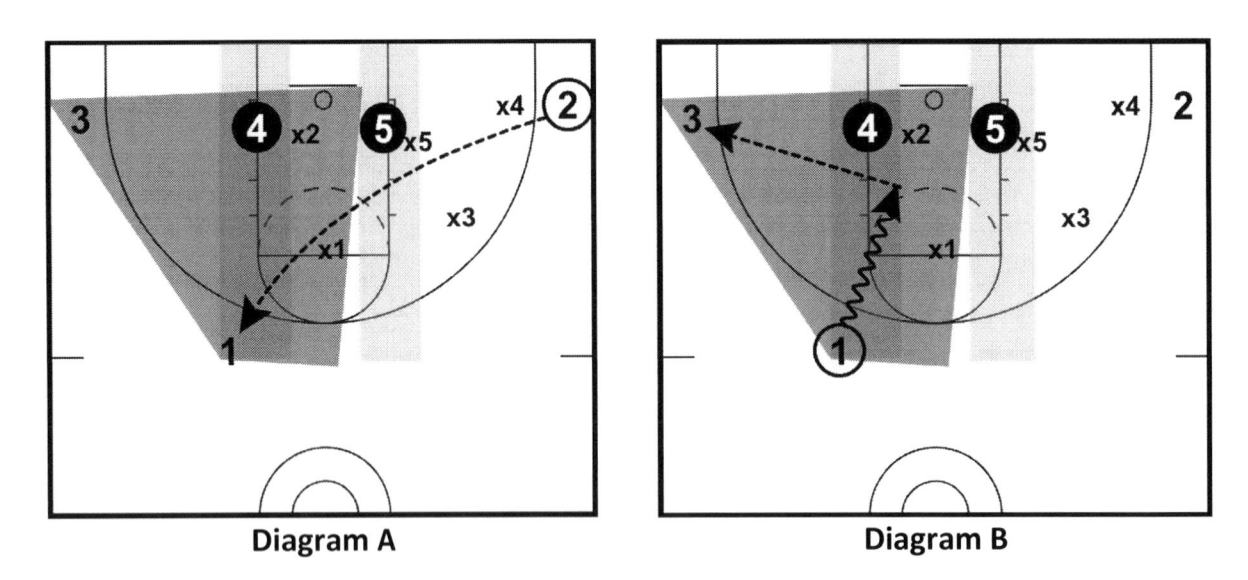

Diagram A **Diagram B**

All zones become a 2-3 when the ball is put in the corner. This leaves many zones, particularly aggressive ones, vulnerable to the diagonal skip pass. This creates a 3-on-2 offensive situation as depicted in **Diagram A** and **Diagram B**.

Overload the Zone Defense

Diagram C

Diagram D

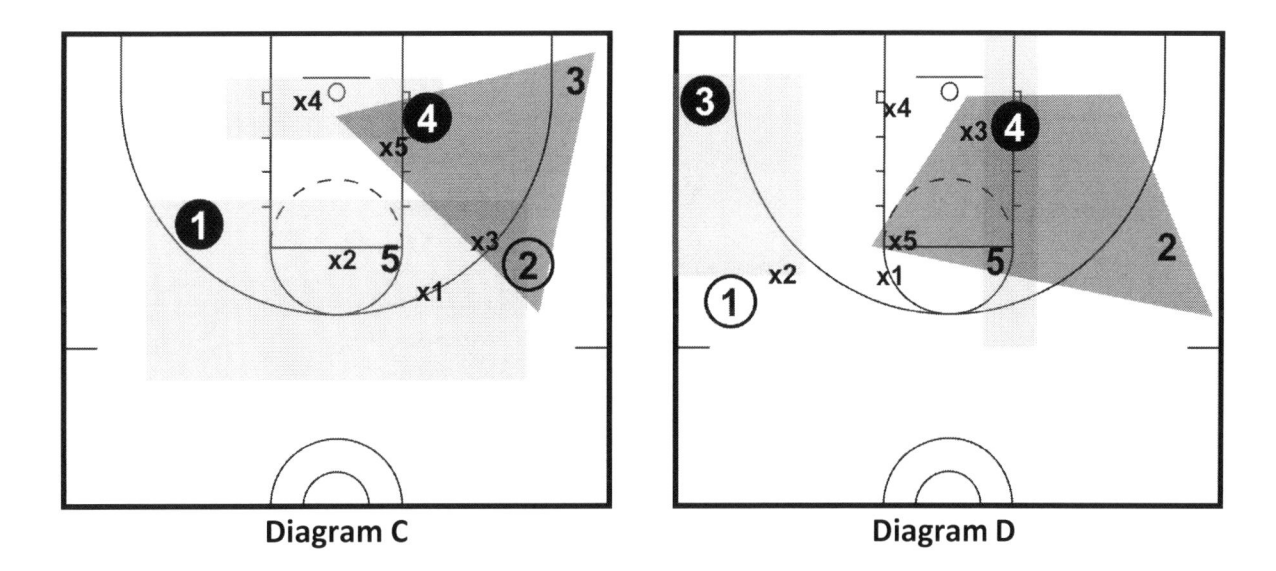

The simple use of alignments as shown in Diagram C and Diagram D has created opportunities for the offense to outnumber the defense with a 3-on-2 advantage.

Make 3 Defend 4

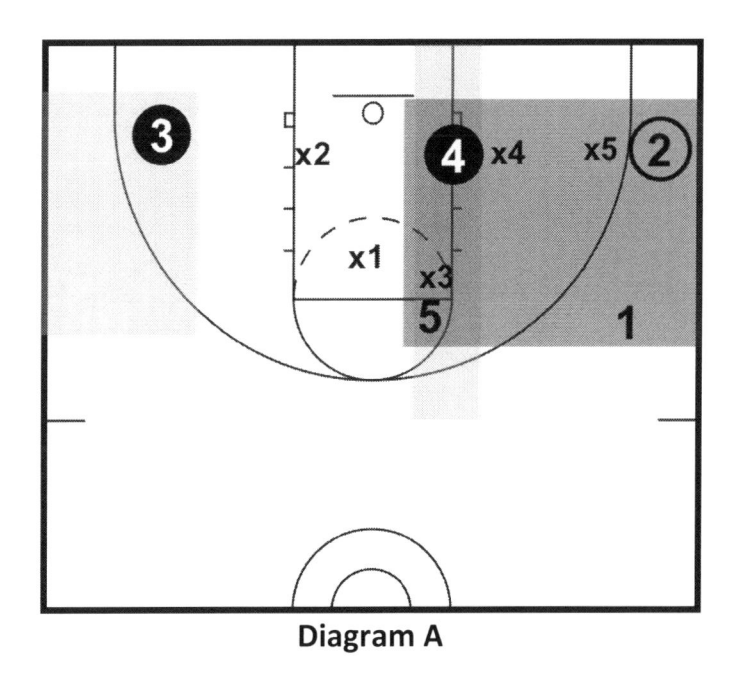

Diagram A

In this example, the overload depicted has created a situation where the defense is caught in a situation where three defenders must defend four offensive players (**Diagram A**).

Coaching Basketball's Zone Attack Offense Using Blocker-Mover Motion Offense

Diagram B

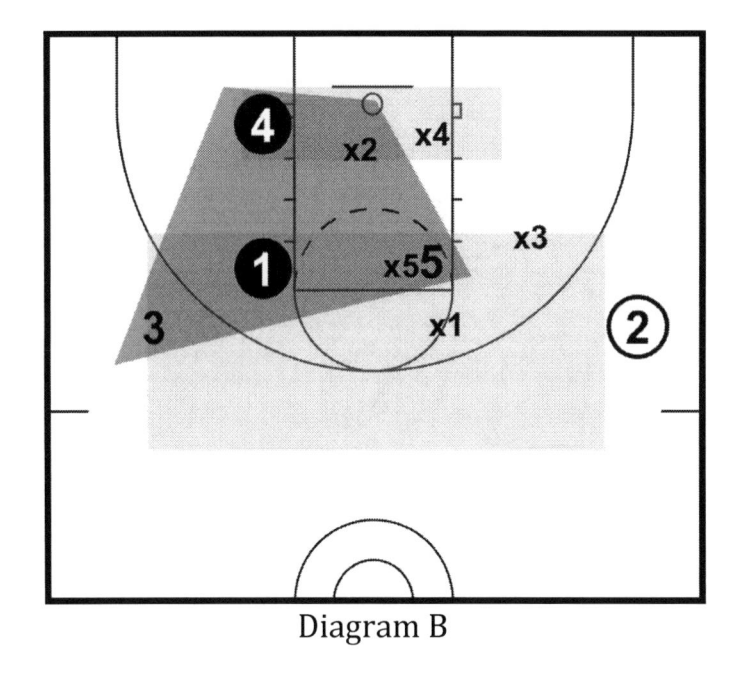

A skip pass from Mover #2 to Mover #3 will create a 4-on-3 advantage for the offense (**Diagram B**).

27

Blocker-Mover Zone Attack Motion Using Screening Concepts

Lane-Lane Screen-in Attack

The screen-in attack takes advantage of three principles of attacking any zone:

a) all zones become a 2-3 zone when the ball is on the baseline.
b) screening the middle of the zone will create opportunities to enter the ball into the post areas.
b) two consecutive diagonal skip passes will create penetration opportunities.

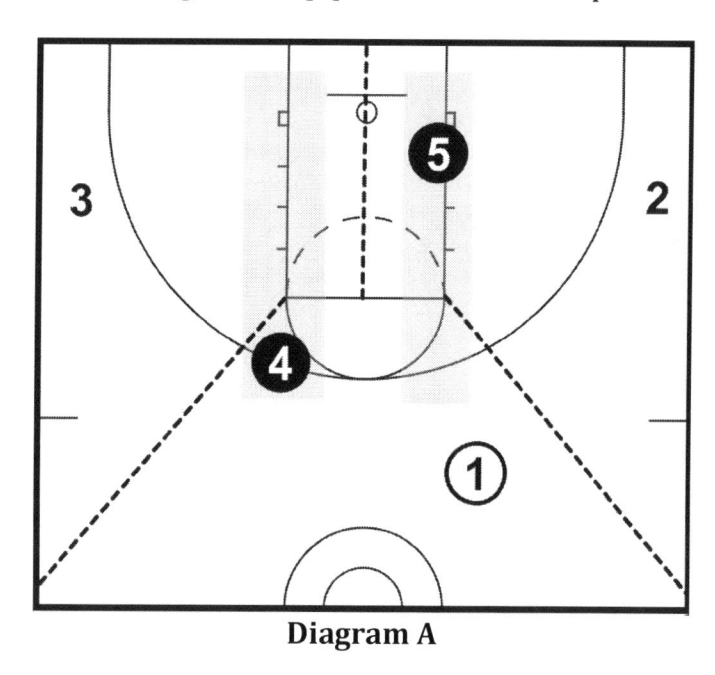

Diagram A

Coaching Basketball's Zone Attack Offense Using Blocker-Mover Motion Offense

Diagram A depicts a typical Lane-Lane alignment against any zone defense. Solid zone offense principles have been applied in terms of spacing. Both Blockers and Movers should line up in gaps in the zone in an effort to distort the initial zone alignment.

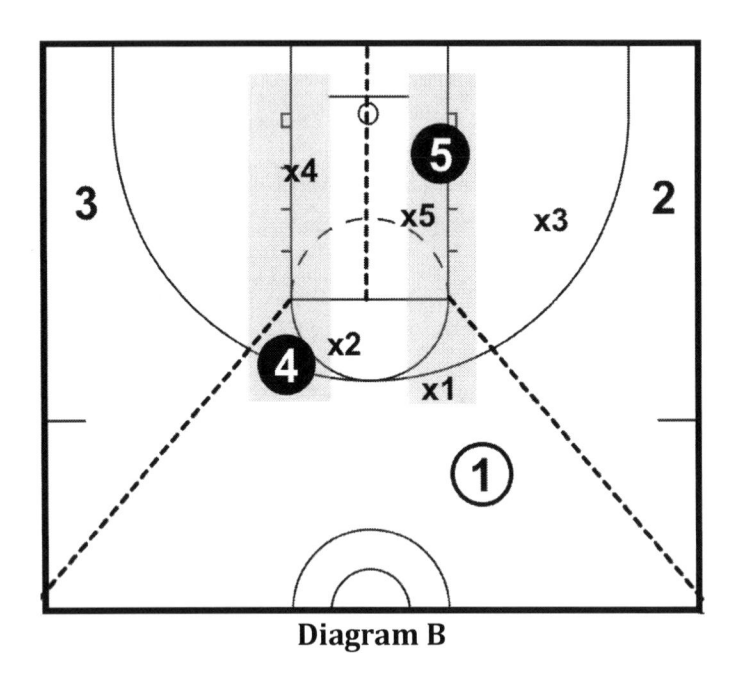

Diagram B

Diagram B depicts a typical match-up of the 2-3 zone against the Lane-Lane alignment.

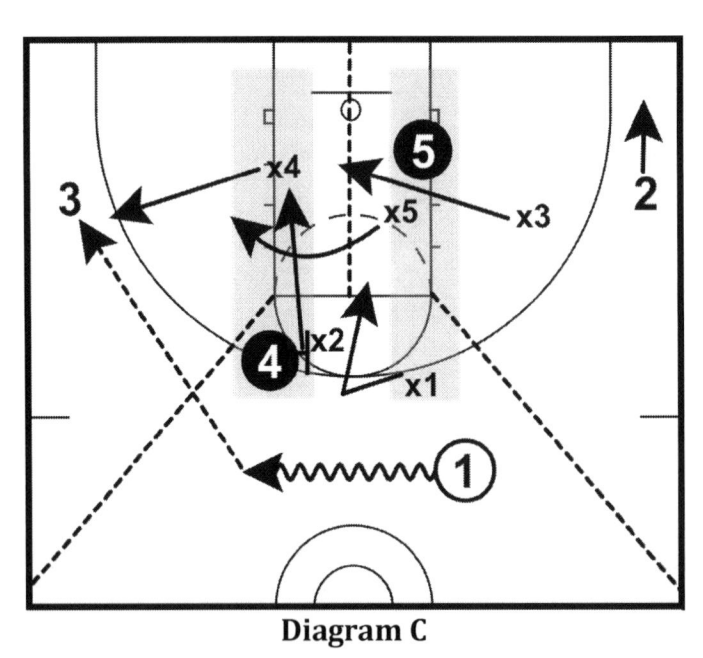

Diagram C

The ball is reversed with the dribble. Blocker #4 sets a screen on the top guard X2 and rolls down the lane to post up in the low post area as the ball is reversed to

Blocker-Mover Zone Attack Motion Using Screening Concepts

Move #3 on the wing. Mover #2 drifts to the corner and spots up for a possible 3 pt. shot attempt. Note the aggressive slides of the 2-3 zone defense.

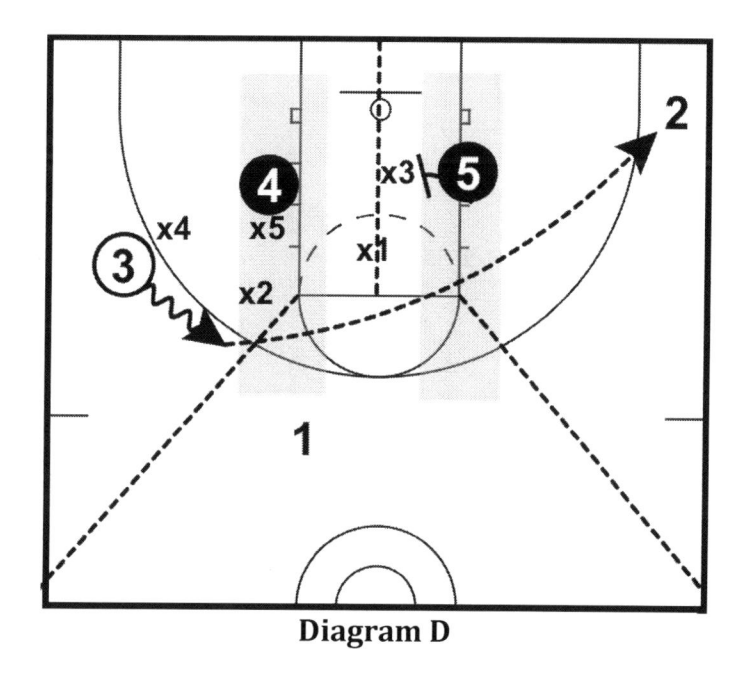

Diagram D

Mover #3 freezes the zone defenders with a short dribble off from the wing and makes a diagonal skip pass to Mover #2. Blocker #5 sets a screen-in at a slight angle designed to encourage the hoop defender, X3, to take an attack approach away from the baseline when closing out on Mover #2. (See **Diagram D**)

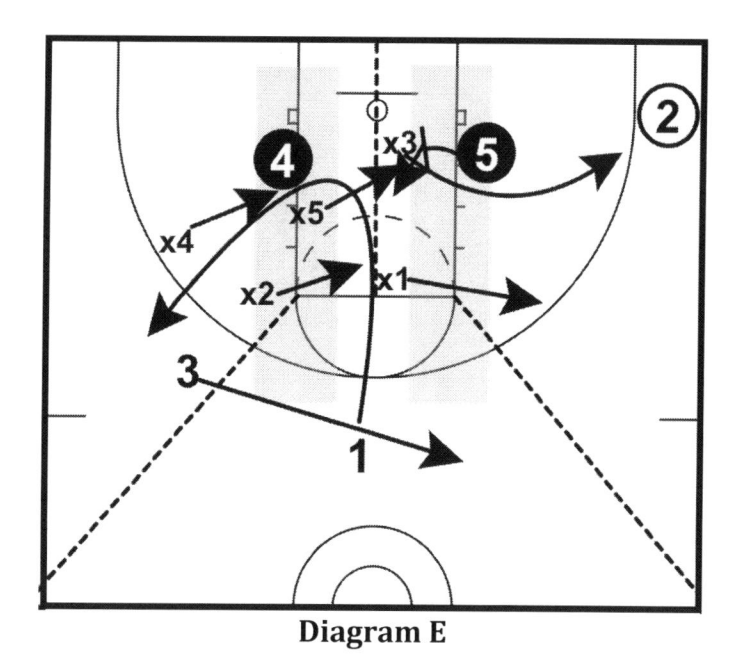

Diagram E

The reaction of the defenders is depicted in **Diagram E**. Note, X3 was forced to take the high route due to the angle of Blocker #5 screen. This creates a baseline passing angle for the low post entry pass from Mover #2. Blocker #5 goes to defender X5 and posts up at the point of contact. Defenders X4, X2 and X1 all slide as depicted. Mover #3 and Mover #1 exchange places by flashing cutting and basket cutting.

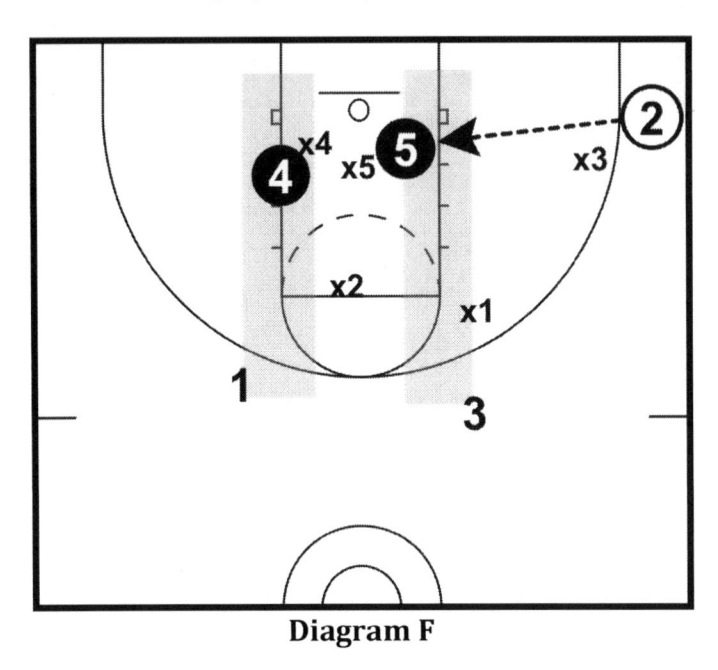

Diagram F

Diagram F depicts the low post entry pass to Blocker #5 if a three point shot attempt is not available for Mover #2. While not depicted, a pass to Mover #3 on top could possibly result in a high-low pass to #5.

Screen-in/Flare Screen

The flare screen is a commonly used screen to create open looks for 3-point shooters or players who are able to shoot and penetrate. With slight modifications the flare screen can be used with great effectiveness as a variation of the screen-in tactic. **Diagram G** depicts an initial alignment against a 2-3 zone defense. The help side Blocker #5 has set a flare screen for Mover #2.

Blocker-Mover Zone Attack Motion Using Screening Concepts

Diagram G

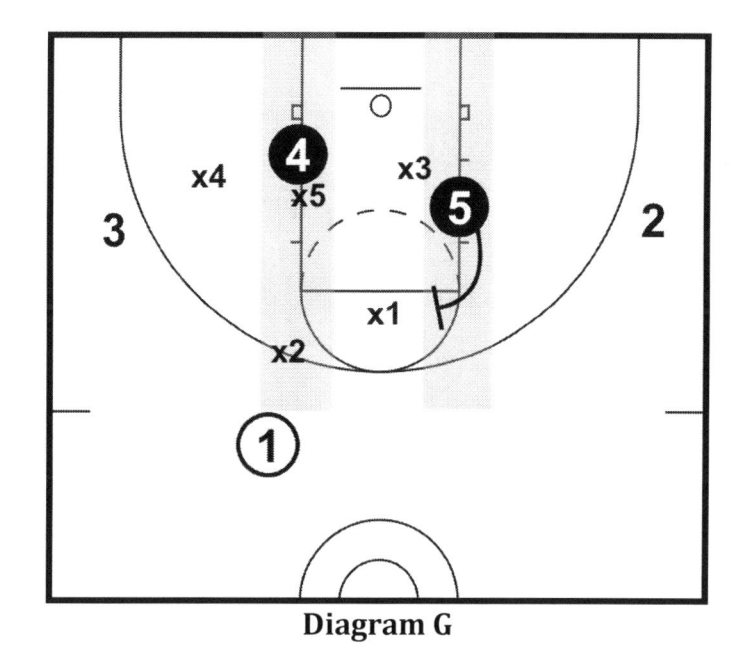

In the example above, the screen-in, or flare screen, is set against a defender who is not assigned to defend an area close to the goal. This is much like setting a flare screen against a man-to-man defense (**Diagram G**).

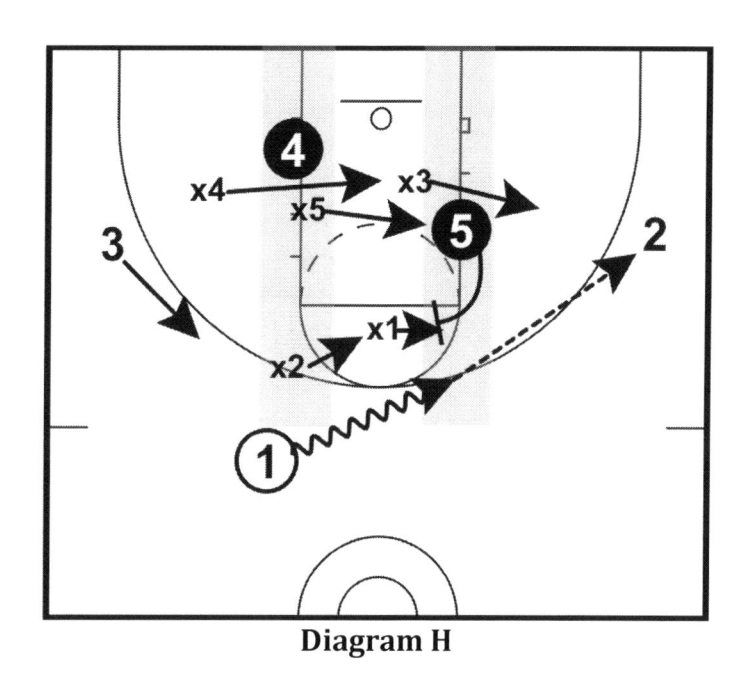

Diagram H

The ball handler "drives the screen" to set the defender into the screen by driving at the defender just like the ball handler would in a freeze and slide tactic (**Diagram H**).

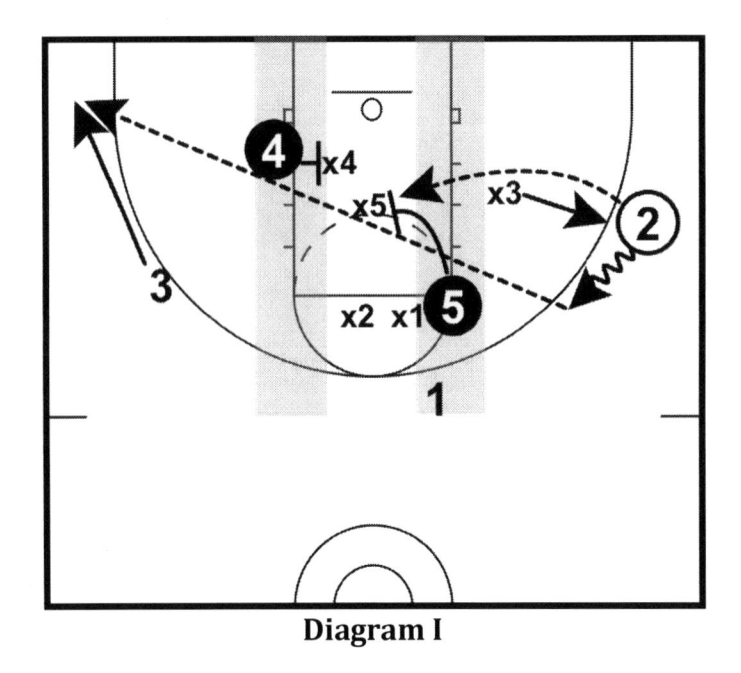

Coaching Basketball's Zone Attack Offense Using Blocker-Mover Motion Offense

Diagram I

Diagram I depicts two screens of a different variety being set, creating different options for Mover #3 to "hunt" for. Post Blocker #4 sets a screen in for the traditional skip pass attack with Mover #2 driving the screen to make the pass. Post Blocker #5 sets a screen on defender X5 by going to the next defender and sealing. This post up may result in an open post and can receive an entry pass for a post shot. It also serves as an effective screen, creating a gap in the zone defense.

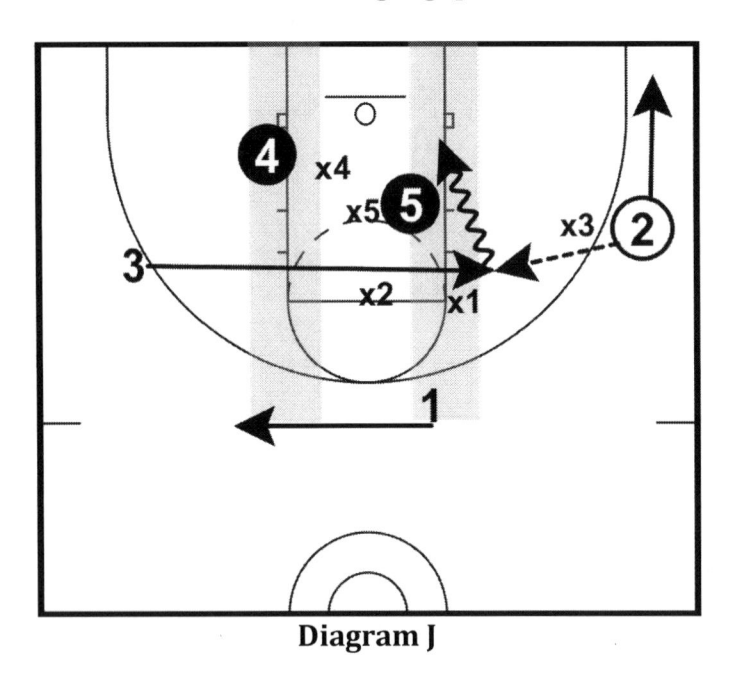

Diagram J

In this example, Mover #3 has hunted the gap created by post Blocker #5's seal/screen of the middle zone defender X5 and flashed into the gap created. Note Movers #2 and #1 both move to create space and open 3 pt. shot attempts (**Diagram J**).

Blocker-Mover Zone Attack Motion Using Screening Concepts

Diagram K

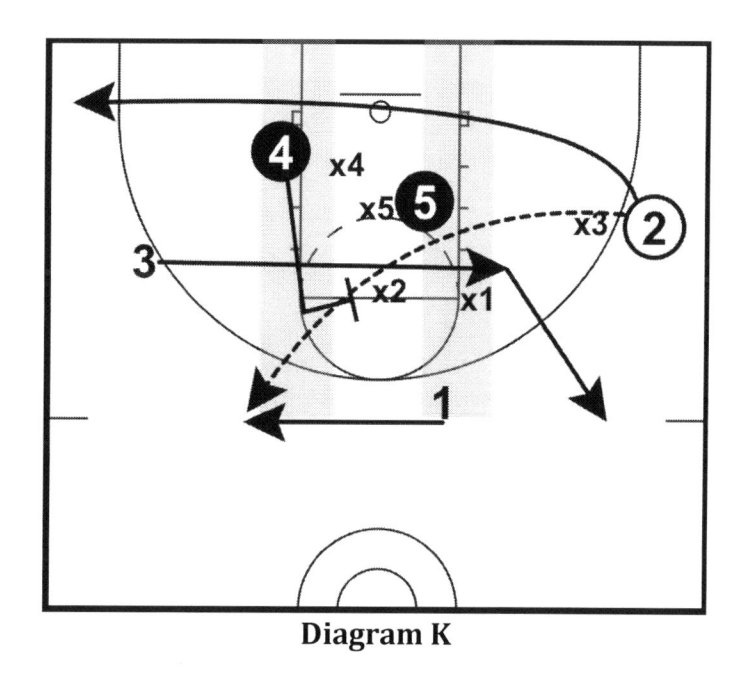

There is a lot going on in this example of using a screen in the Lane-Lane alignment. Post Blocker #4 sets a flare/screen-in screen on X2. At the same time post Blocker #5 is sealing/screening the middle defender X5, creating a gap for Mover #3 to hunt. The skip pass creates an overload situation for the defense where one defender must defend two offensive players. Mover #2 cuts hard to fill the new ball side corner to create space for Mover #3 (one Mover per perimeter area rule) (**Diagram K**). Mover #1 may shoot a 3 pt. shot, drive for a shot or drive and pitch to Mover #2. Mover #3 is responsible for defensive floor balance (**Diagram L**).

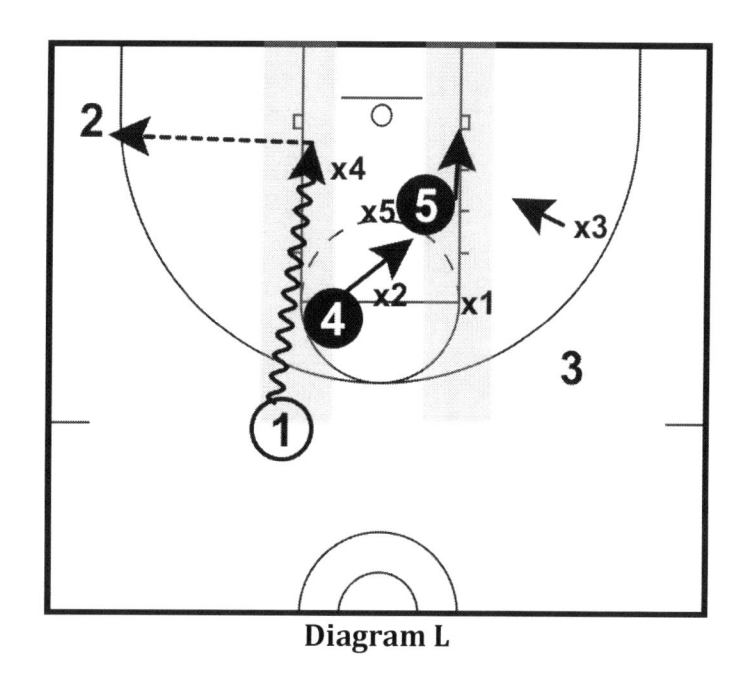

Diagram L

Top-Bottom Screen-in Attack

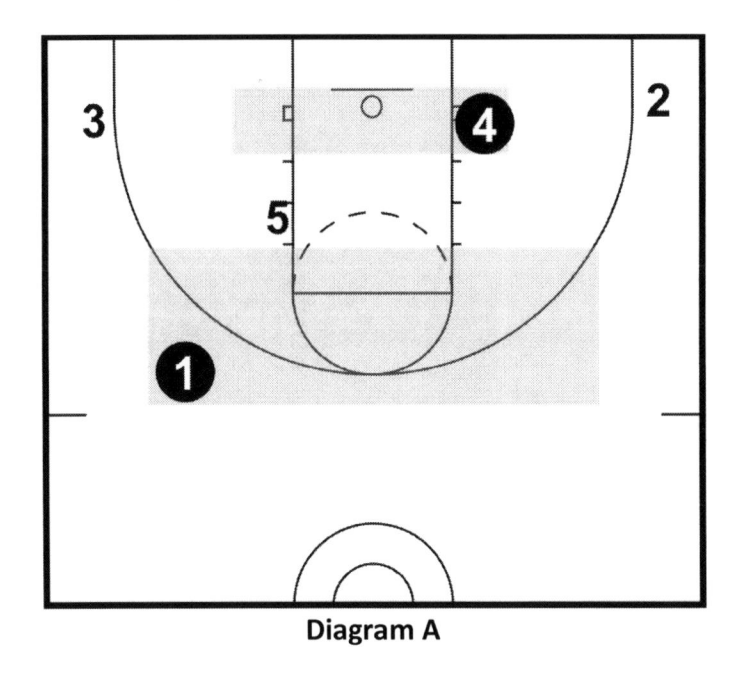

Diagram A

The first example of using a screen in Top-Bottom is depicted without defenders for clarity (**Diagram A** through **Diagram D**).

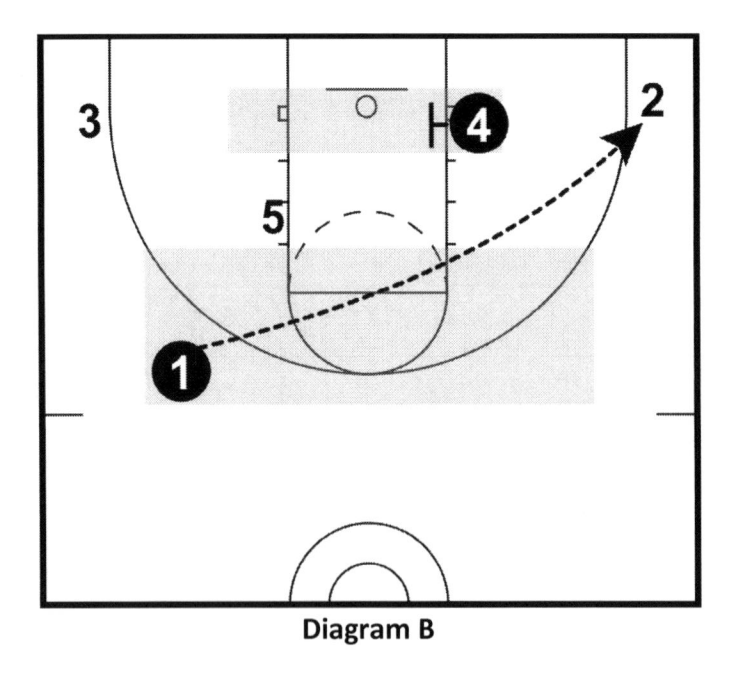

Diagram B

In **Diagram B** the screen-in and skip pass are depicted.

Blocker-Mover Zone Attack Motion Using Screening Concepts

Diagram C

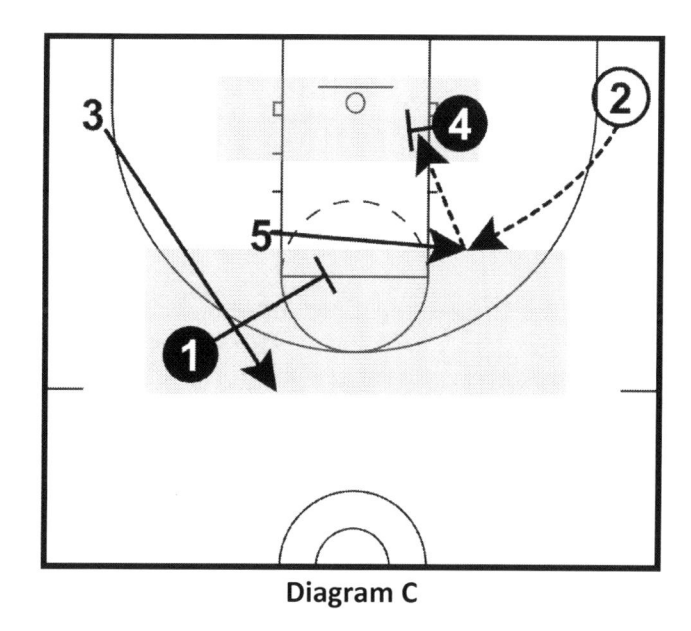

After screening the back defender of the zone, post Blocker #4 goes to the next defender and seals to post up, showing numbers to the ball. Mover #5 hunts for the gap and flashes into the high post area. In this example, the entry pass is made into the high post and a high to low pass is made. Also, the Top Blocker has set a pin screen/down screen to set up the diagonal skip pass to create an overload opportunity for Mover #3 who has hunted for a screen (**Diagram C**).

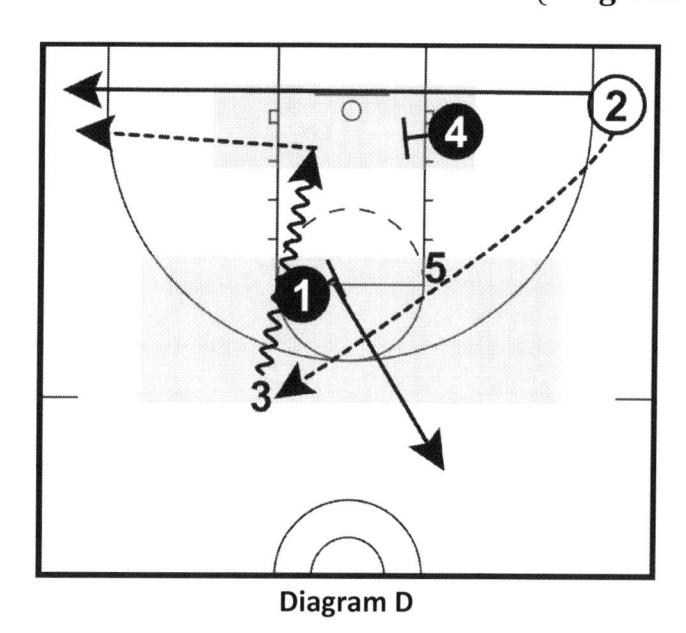

Diagram D

To finish the sequence, Mover #2 hunts for the open gap by flashing to the opposite corner after the diagonal skip pass, creating a passing opportunity for Mover #3. Top Blocker #1 balances the floor for defensive floor balance. Mover #3 can shoot the 3-pt. shot or drive the overload for a short jump shot or pass to Mover #2 for a 3 pt. shot attempt of post Blocker #4 for a power shot.

Lane-Wide Screen-in Attack

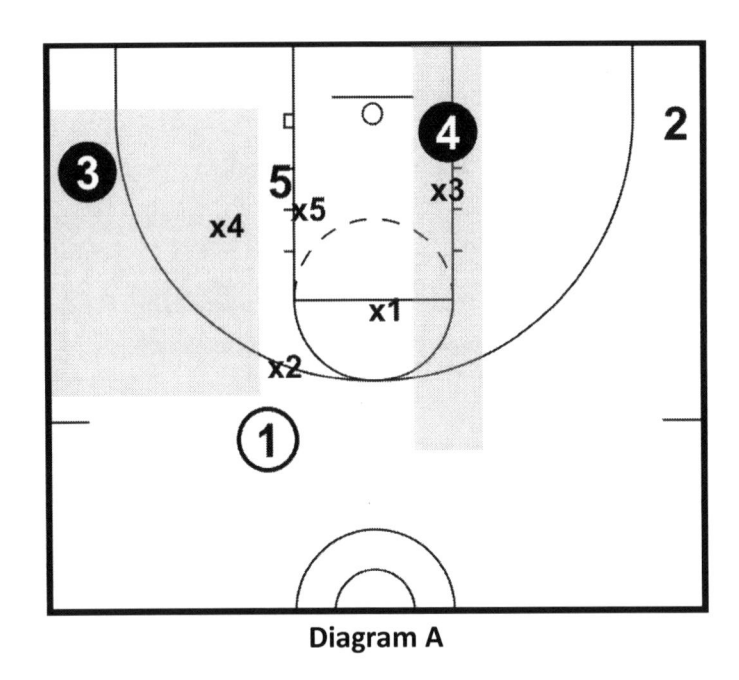

Diagram A

Diagram A through **Diagram D** depict a sequence of events showing one way a screen-in can be used in the Lane-Wide alignment.

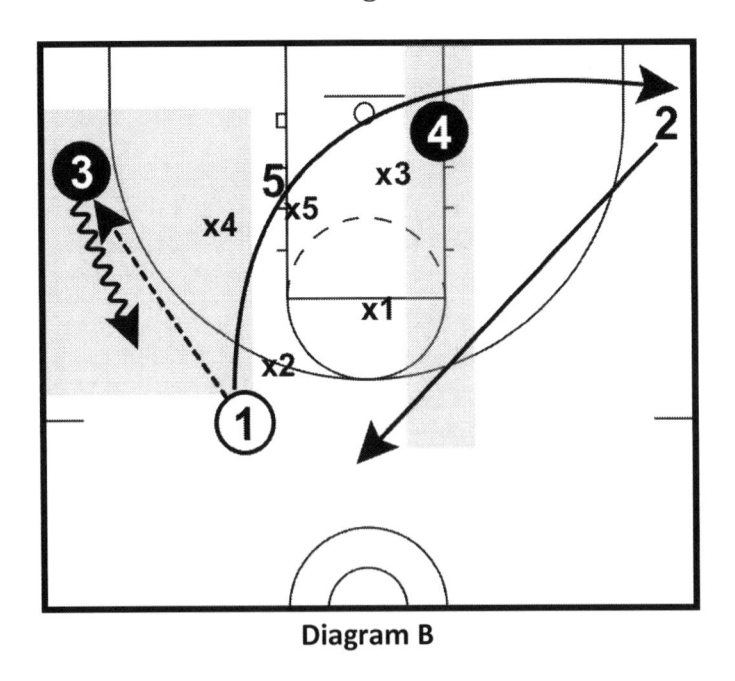

Diagram B

The sequence starts with Mover #1 passing to the Wide Blocker and hunting for a gap and a screen. Post Blocker #4 is in excellent position to set a screen-in so Mover #1 cuts to the corner opposite the ball. Mover #2 must fill the top to obey the one Mover per perimeter area rule. Blocker #3 dribbles off the baseline to create an angle for the skip pass or to shorten the pass to Mover #2 (**Diagram B**).

Blocker-Mover Zone Attack Motion Using Screening Concepts

Diagram C

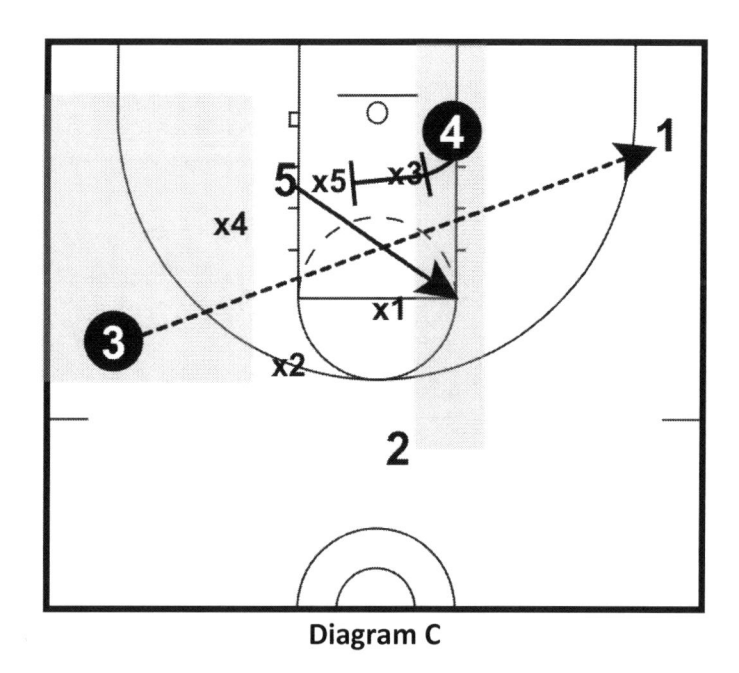

The skip pass is made and post Blocker #4 goes to the next closest defender and seals while Mover #5 hunts for a gap and flashes into the high post area (**Diagram C**).

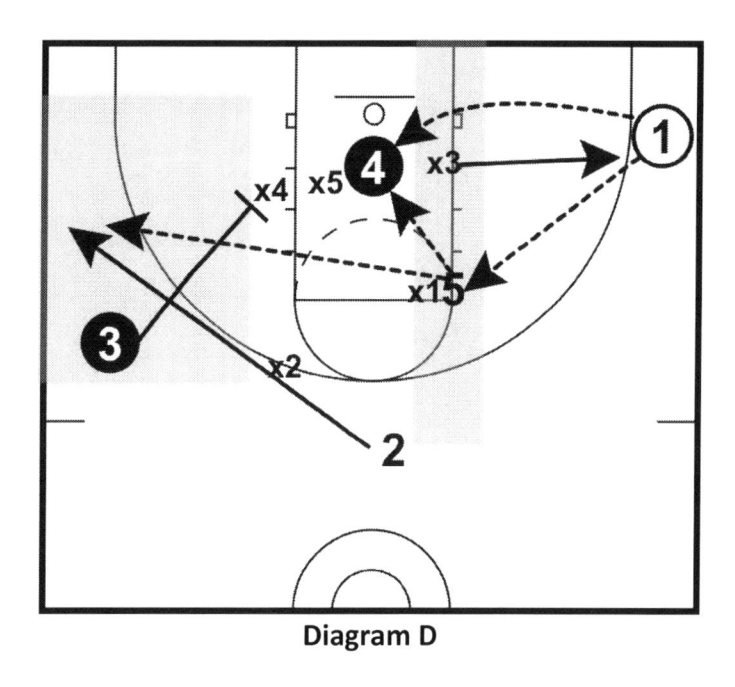

Diagram D

The sequence ends with several possibilities. The ball can be entered into the low post either by a direct pass or a high low pass. In the mean time, the wide Blocker #3 has set a down screen for Mover #2 who hunts the Blocker for a screen. This creates a 3 pt. shot opportunity on the look inside/look weak side fan pass from Mover #5 (**Diagram D**).

Lane-Lane Center Screen Attack

Diagram A

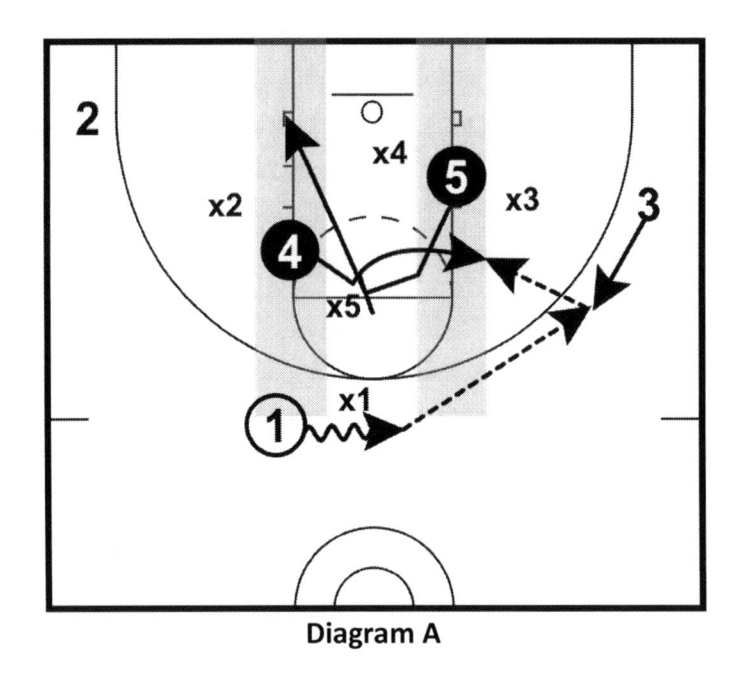

Diagram A through **Diagram E** depict an example of using the Center Screen tactic in the Lane-Lane alignment. Post Blocker #5 sets a screen against the middle defender in a 1-3-1 zone. Post Blocker #4 cuts under the screen (Lane Blockers may exchange lanes if the situation warrants it). The ball has been moved to the win in order to enter it into the mid-post area.

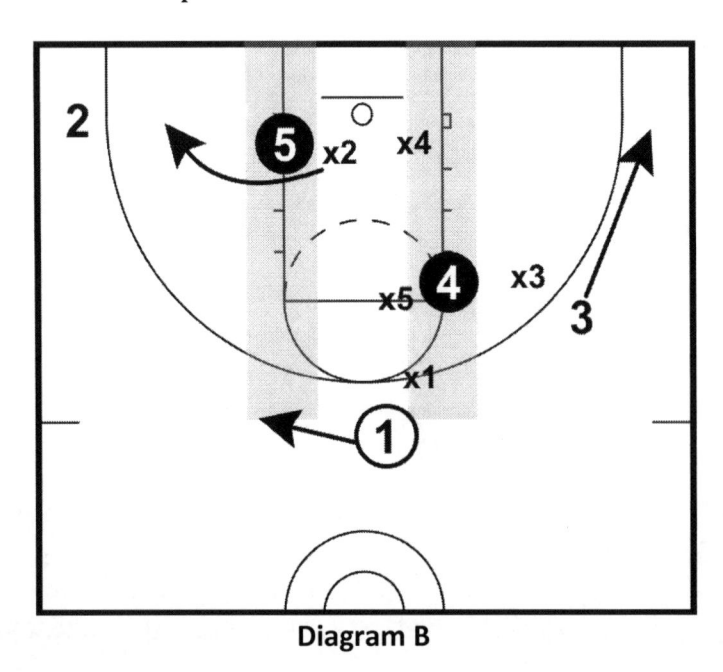

Diagram B

Blocker-Mover Zone Attack Motion Using Screening Concepts

Movers hunt gaps for a possible pass from Blocker #4 (**Diagram B**).

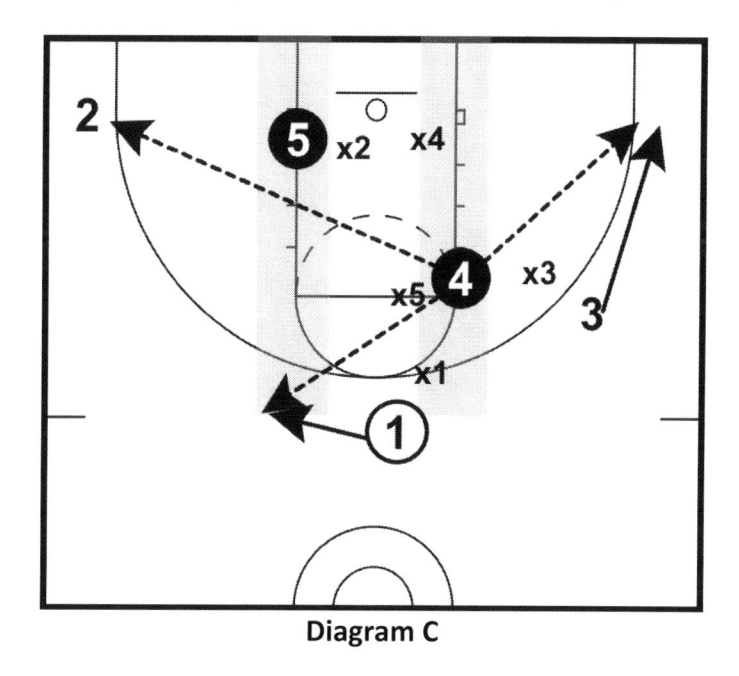

Diagram C

Diagram C depicts fan passes being made out of the high post/mid-post area by Blocker #4.

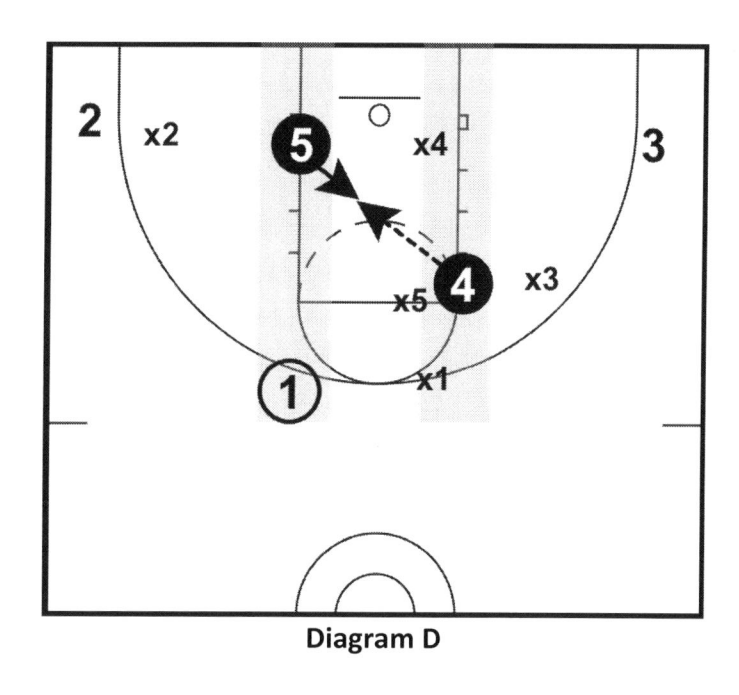

Diagram D

In **Diagram D** the wing defender X2 has cheated outside to cover Mover #2 or slipped a screen set by Blocker #5, allowing #5 to step to the ball in the gap created for a pass for a low post power shot.

Diagram E

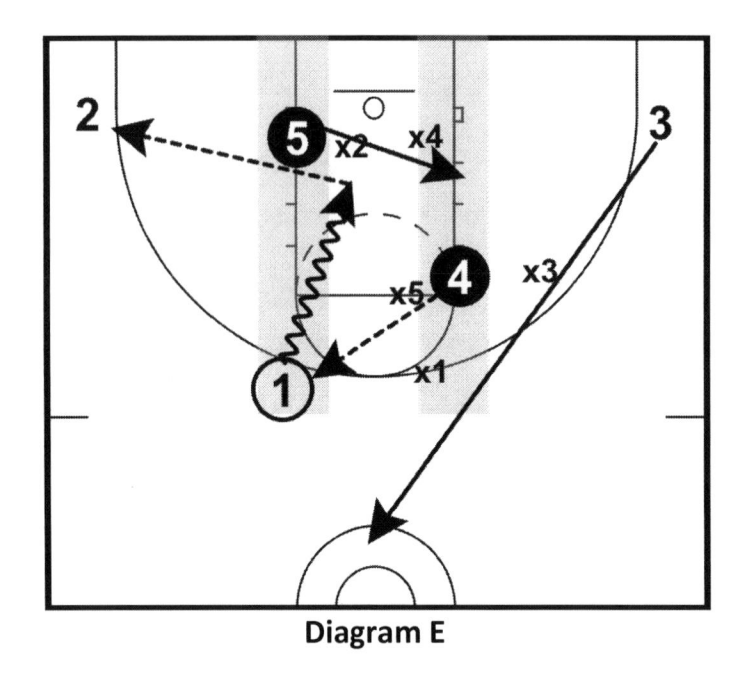

The pass to Mover #1 in **Diagram E** has set up an overload for #1 to drive. Note the various cuts by other players to create space and to balance the floor.

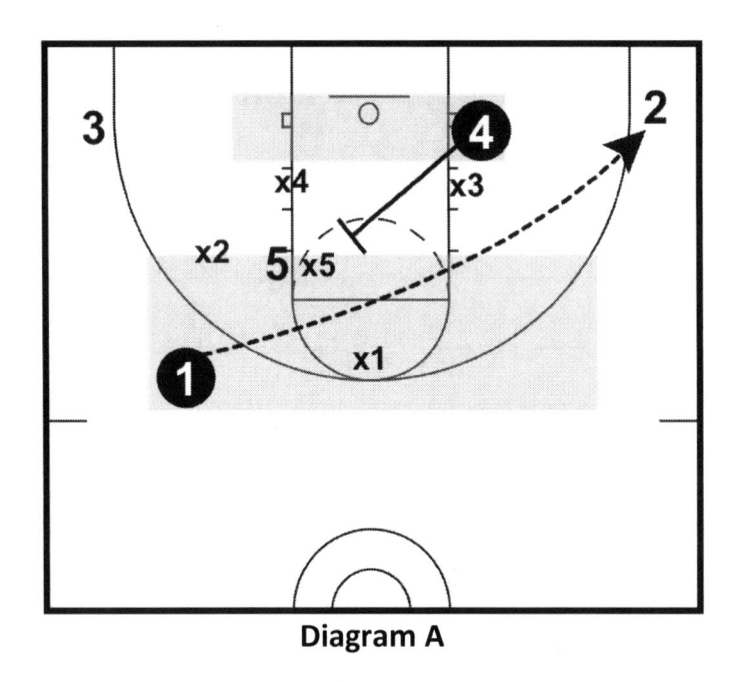

Top-Bottom Center Screen Attack

Diagram A

The Top-Bottom attack is depicted against a 1-3-1 zone using the screen-in tactic in **Diagram A** through **Diagram C**. The initial screen and skip pass are depicted in **Diagram A**.

Blocker-Mover Zone Attack Motion Using Screening Concepts

Diagram B

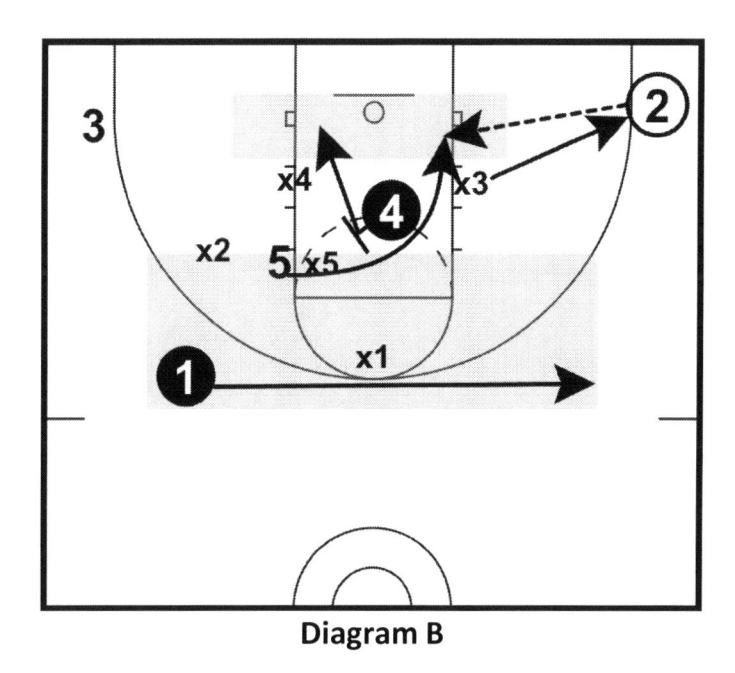

Mover #5 hunts the screen by the post Blocker #4. Top Blocker #1 cuts to move the top zone defender to create space for Mover #5 (**Diagram B**).

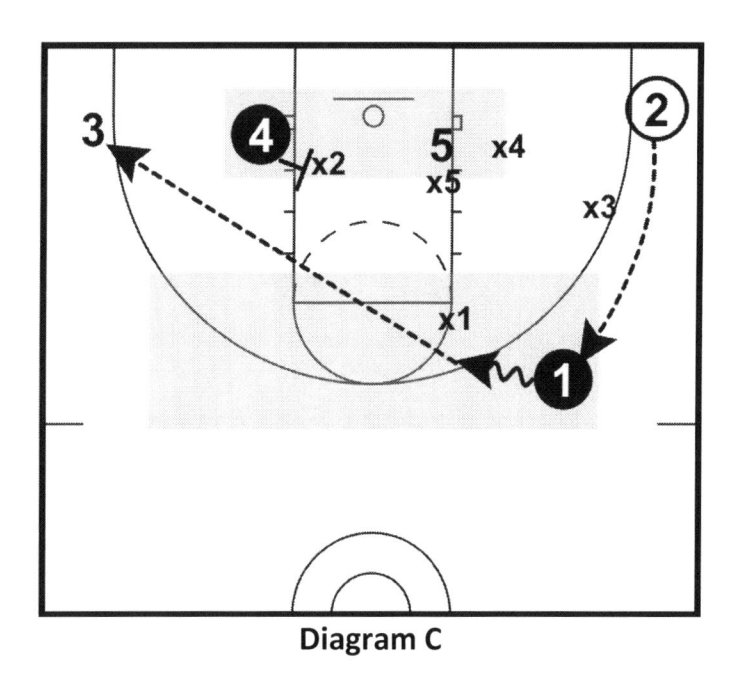

Diagram C

Diagram C demonstrates a possible continuation of the sequence if Mover #5 was not open on the center screen. Mover #2 pass the ball to the top Blocker #1 who makes a skip pass to Mover #3 who has hunted for the screen set by the post

Blocker #4 who rolled back to the Bottom after setting the center screen. Top Blocker #1 drives the screen to make the skip pass.

Lane-Wide Center Screen Attack

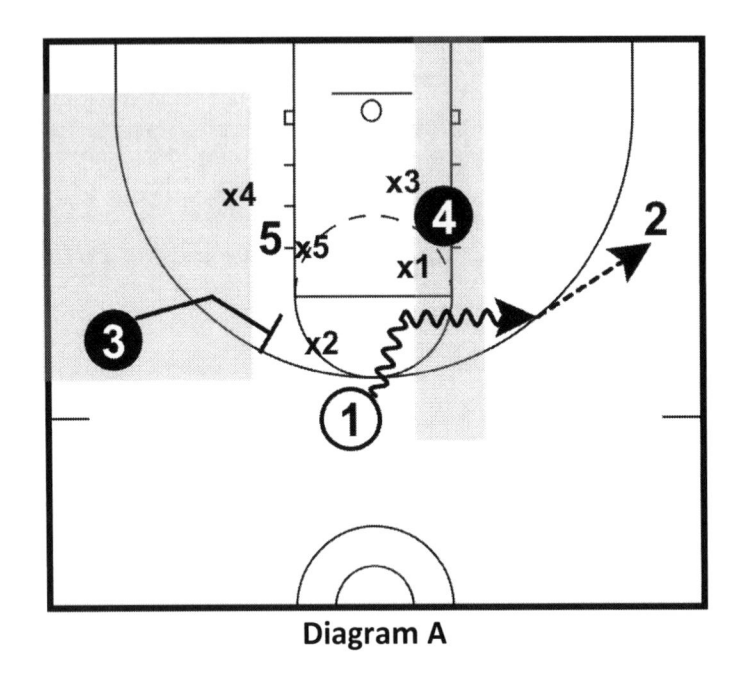

Diagram A

This sequence starts with a freeze and slide combined with a flare screen set by the wide Blocker against the X2 defender in a 2-3 zone (**Diagram A**).

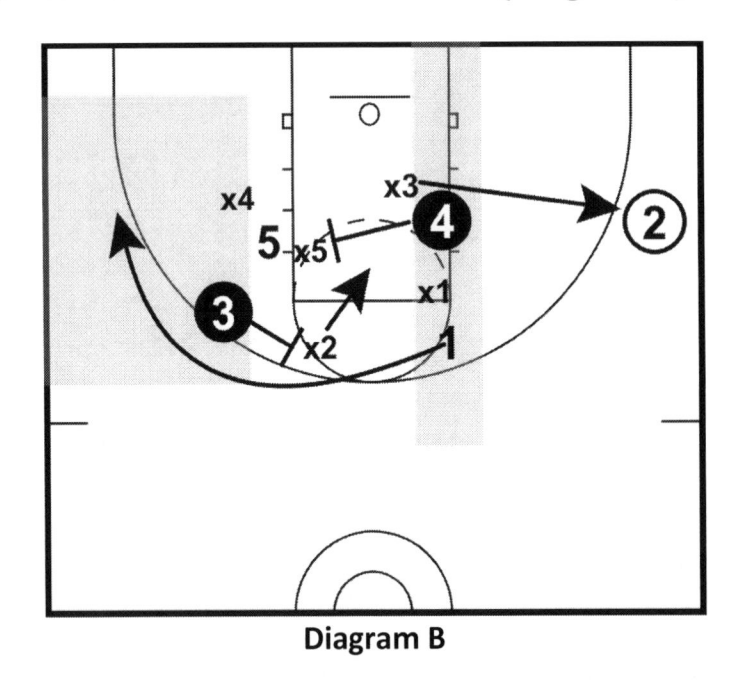

Diagram B

Here the lane Blocker sets the center screen as the defense shifts to the new ball location on the wing (**Diagram B**).

Diagram C

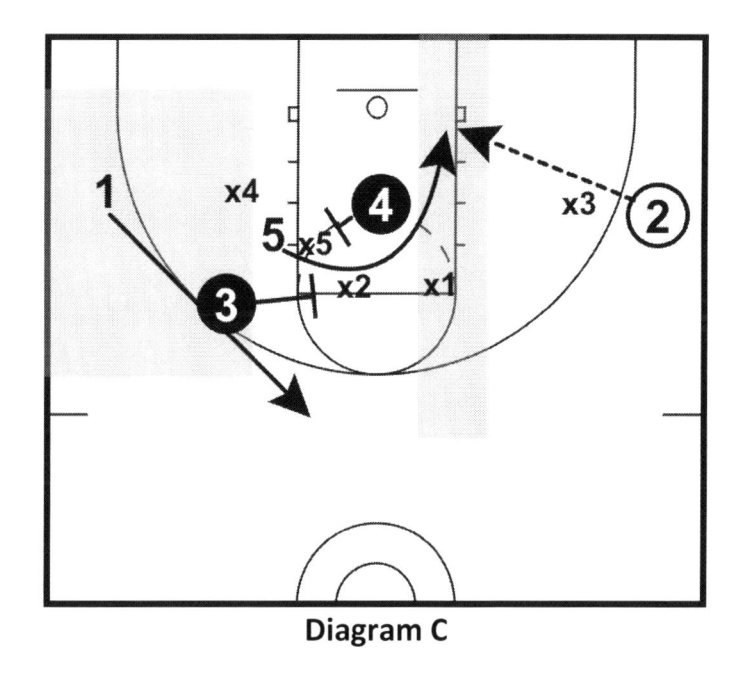

Mover #5 cuts off the center screen while the wide Blocker #3 sets a screen again on the X2 defender so Mover #1, who is hunting a gap or a blocker, cuts back on top for defensive floor balance (**Diagram C**).

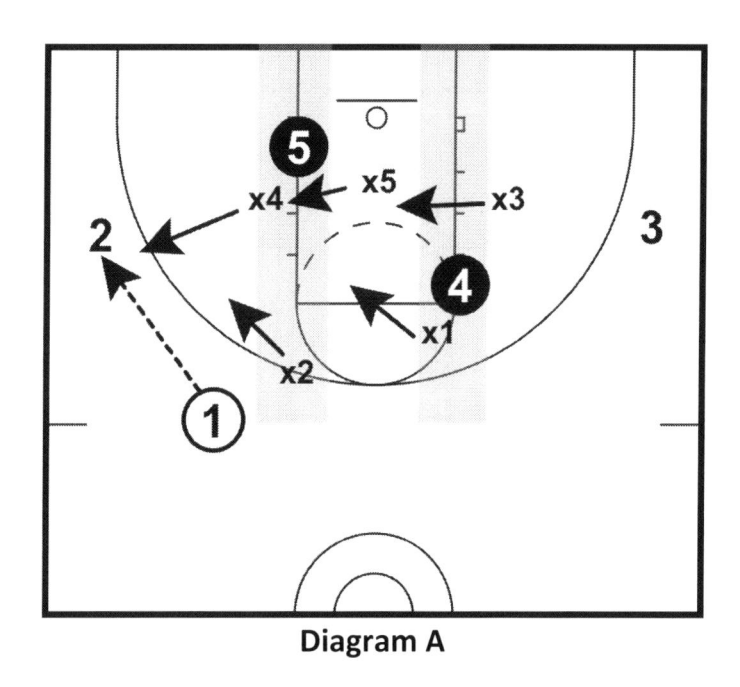

Lane-Lane Screen Out Attack

Diagram A

Screen outs are screens designed to create space inside a zone, often for the player setting the screen. **Diagram A** shows the set up for a screen out against a 2-3 zone using the Lane-Lane alignment.

Diagram B

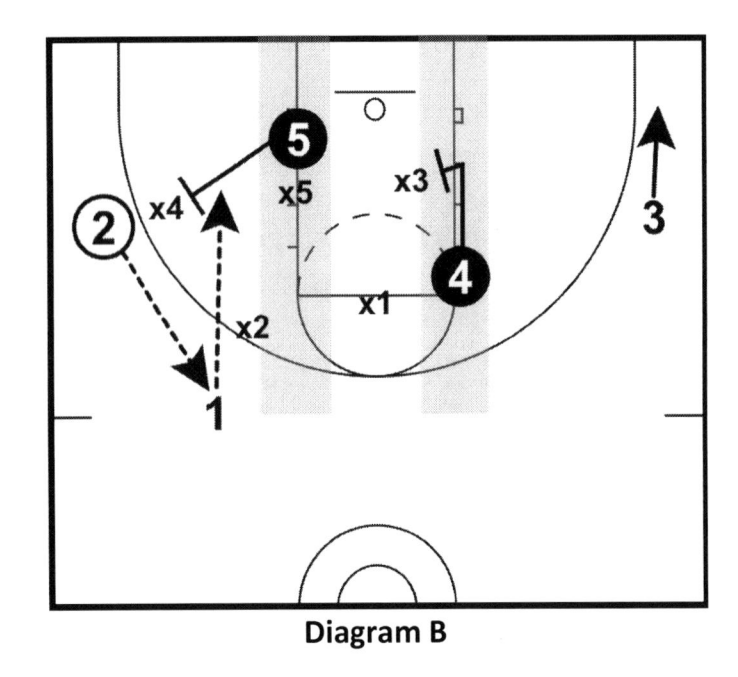

Post Blocker #5 steps out and "posts up/seals" the on the ball defender X4. This creates space between the Blocker #5 and the middle defender X5 while screening X4 out of the play. A high to low pass is depicted in **Diagram B** showing the finish of the play.

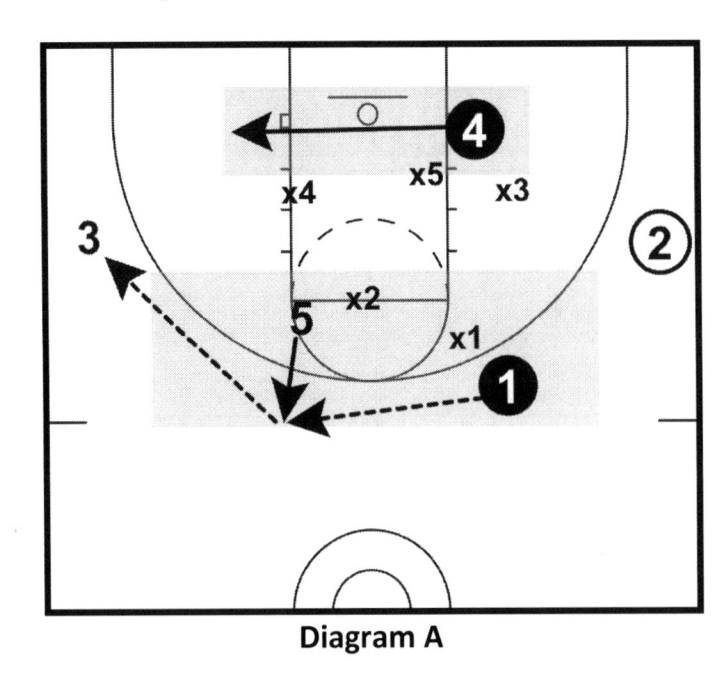

Top-Bottom Screen Out Attack

Diagram A

Two screen outs are depicted in this example (**Diagram A through Diagram D**). **Diagram A** depicts the set up in the Top-Bottom alignment.

Blocker-Mover Zone Attack Motion Using Screening Concepts

Diagram B

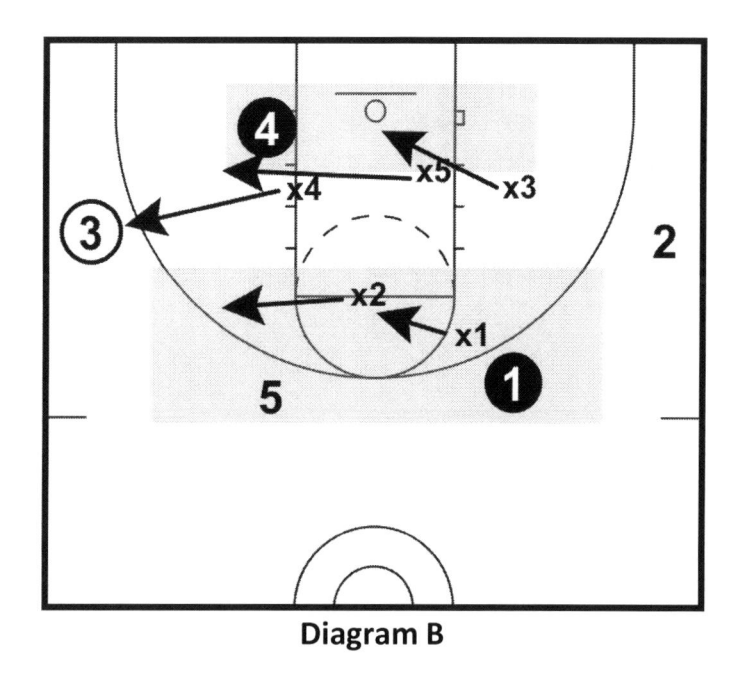

Diagram B shows how the defense reacts to the initial movements of the offense.

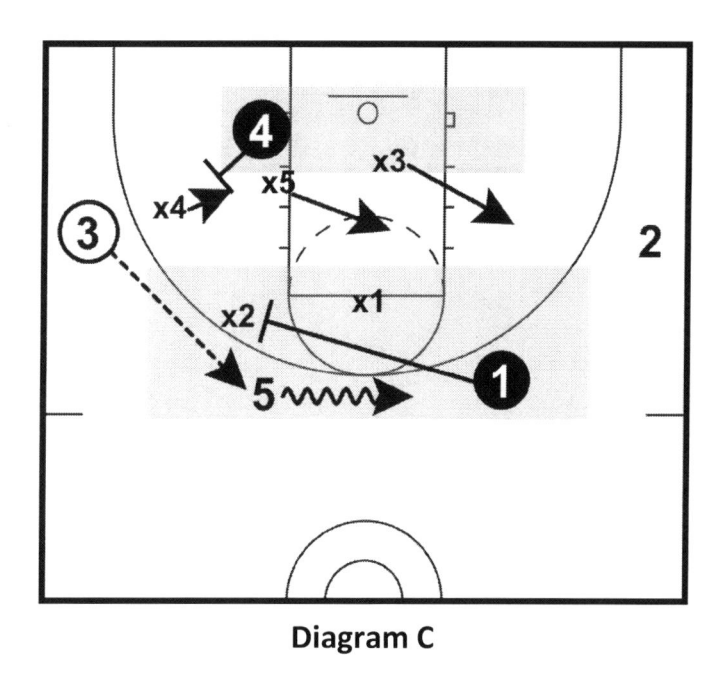

Diagram C

In **Diagram C** the two screen out screens are set. The Bottom Blocker has screened out X3, the on the ball defender. The Top Blocker screens out the X2 defender. By dribbling off the top, Mover #5 sets the zone defenders into the screen outs as all zone defenders follow the ball.

Diagram D

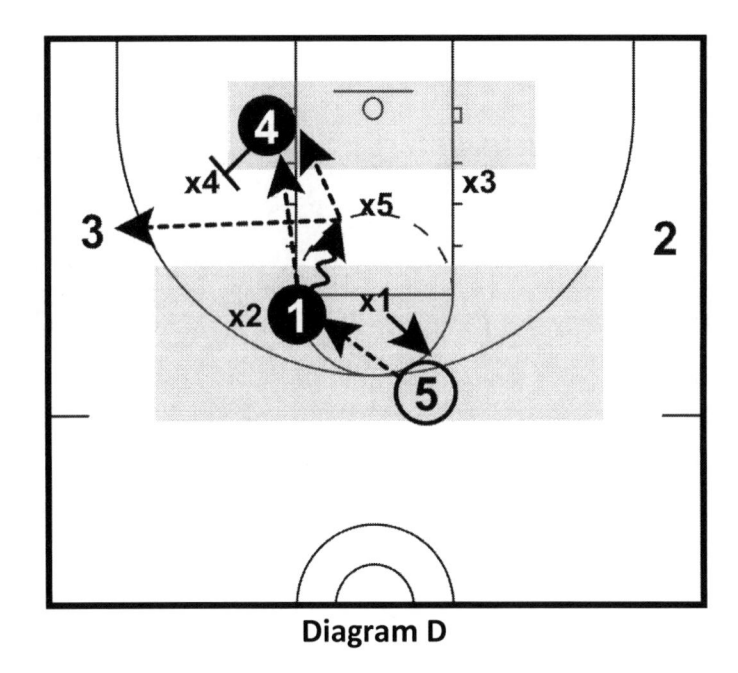

Diagram D shows the ball being "passed back" (a pass fake to Mover #2 would also cause the zone to continue to shift in that direction) to the Top Blocker who can then make a high to low pass or drive the lane.

Lane-Wide Screen Out Attack

Diagram A

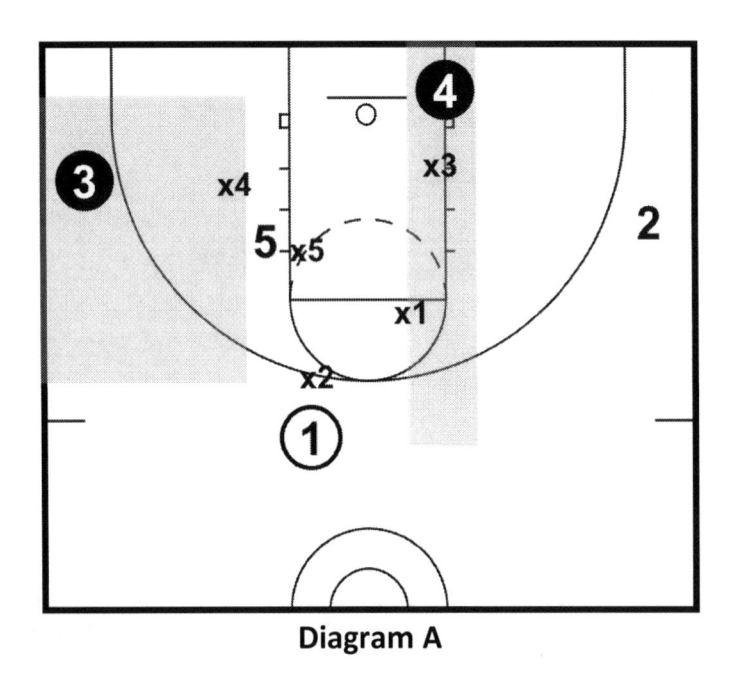

Diagram A through Diagram G depict a sequence of tactics strung together to attack a zone defense. There are multiple screen outs depicted as the sequences flow from one scenario to another as an example of how the principles of Blocker-Mover zone attack flow once players have learned the offense and its principles.

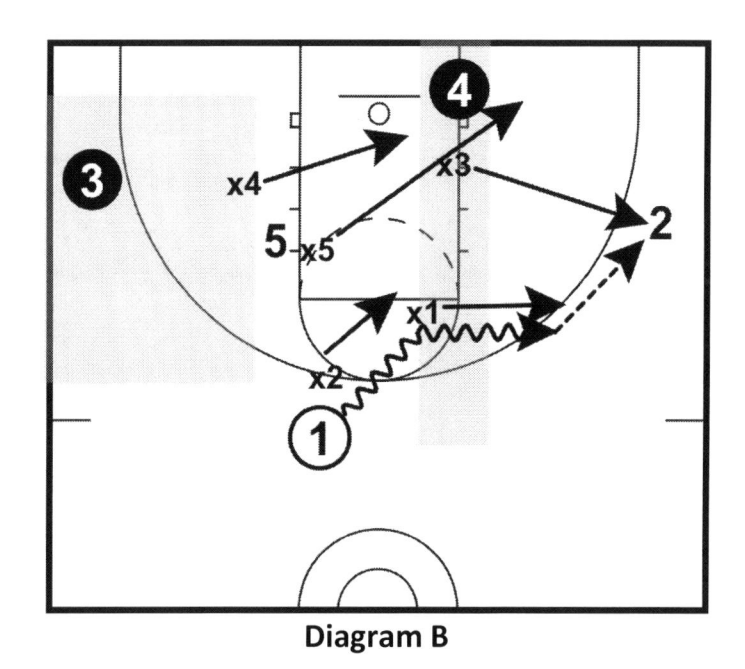

Blocker-Mover Zone Attack Motion Using Screening Concepts

Diagram B

Diagram C

177

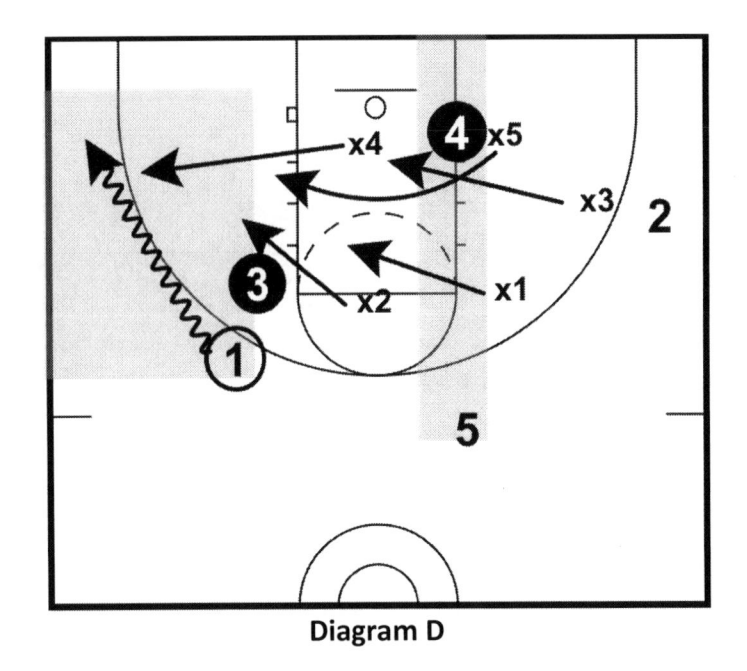

Coaching Basketball's Zone Attack Offense Using Blocker-Mover Motion Offense

Diagram D

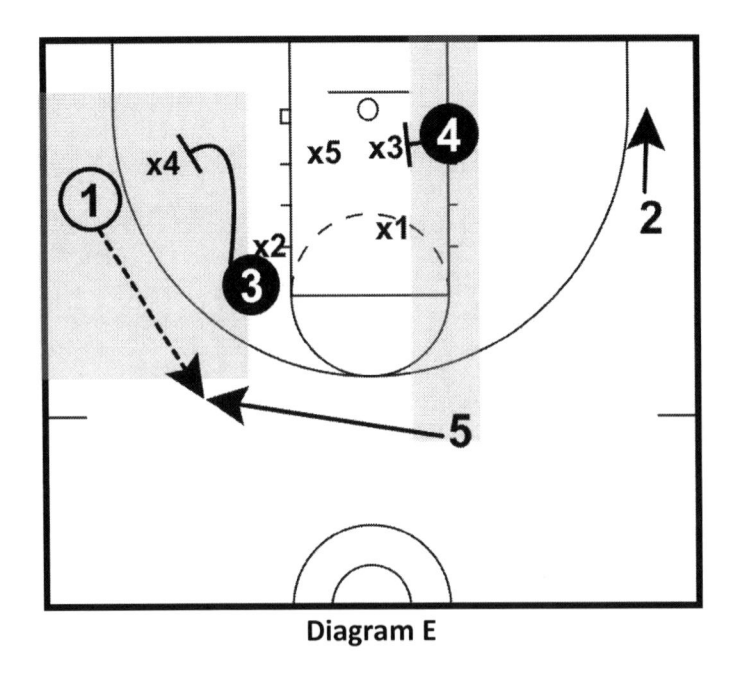

Diagram E

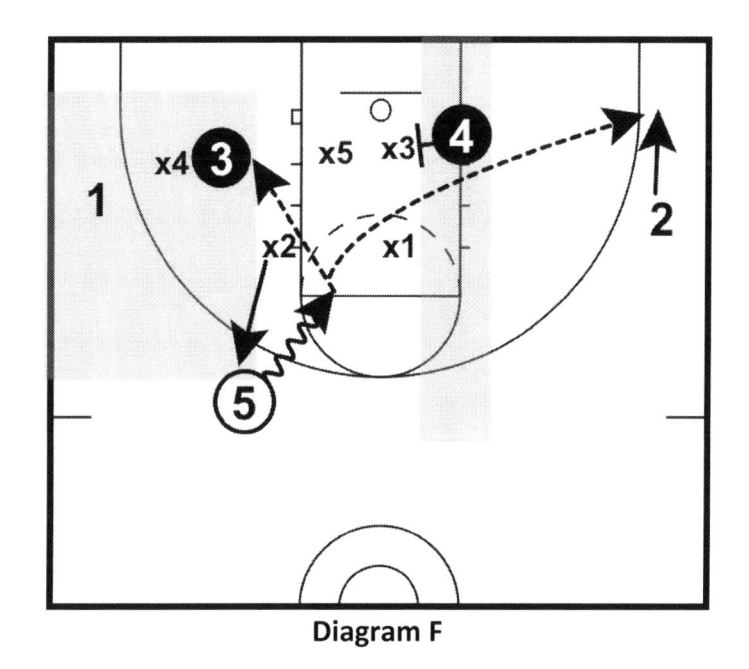

Blocker-Mover Zone Attack Motion Using Screening Concepts

Diagram F

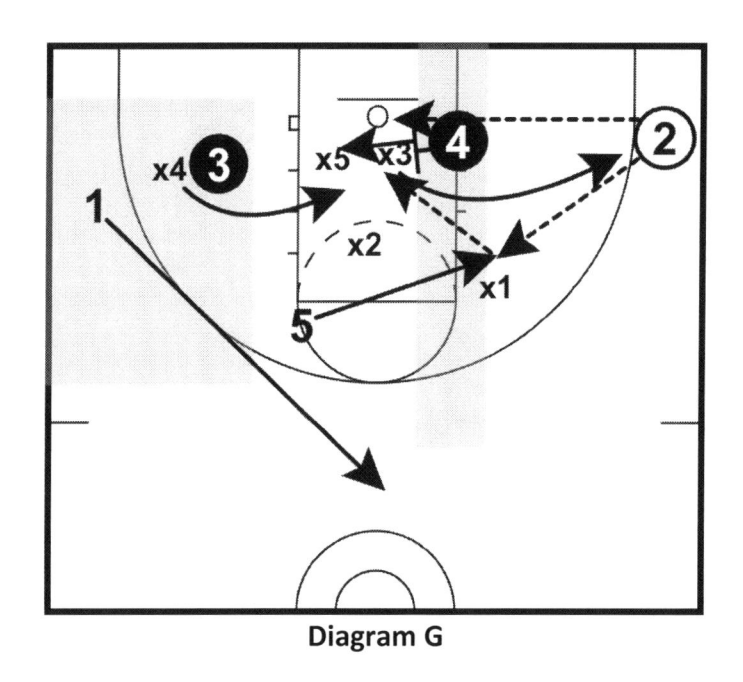

Diagram G

179

28

Use Fakes to Freeze and Shift the Zone Defense

Coaching legend Bob Knight has been often quoted as saying the use of fakes against zone defense is one of the most under utilized tactics in the game of basketball. The very nature of an aggressive zone defense makes it susceptible to fakes. Defenders in a disciplined, well coached, aggressive zone defense are taught to arrive in position at the same time the ball does.

This trait or habit is what makes fakes effective against a zone defense. Pass fakes will freeze a zone defense in place. Really well trained defenses may even have one or two defenders move to start blocking out for a defensive rebound. Pass fakes can freeze a zone defense in place or cause the defenders to move several steps in the direction of the fake.

Shot Fakes

Players make several common mistakes in executing a shot fake. The two most common are moving the ball too far up in the execution of the shot fake and fake so hard the player "takes the bend out of the knees."

The key to a successful shot fake is to use a two-inch fake. The player must be in a good triple threat stance and "fake" the shot by moving the ball upwards no more and no less than two inches. The key to selling the shot fake is the eyes and the quickness of the fake. If necessary, fake twice.

If the ball travels more than two inches the offensive player will have a strong tendency to "take the bend out of the knees" meaning the player will stand up. This reduces the ability of the player to attack from the triple threat position and serves as a "tell" to savvy defenders that the fake is just that, a fake.

Since zone defenses are trained to follow the ball, a perfectly executed shot fake will freeze a zone in place out of necessity to determine of a shot has actually been taken and the defenders need to box out for a defensive rebound.

Once the defense has been frozen in place, the offense can make a pass, usually in the direction opposite the flow of movement the defense had been moving in. The loss of momentum combined with a change of direction can force a zone defense into undesired recovery situations that create gaps, distort the zone or even create open shot opportunities.

Pass Fakes

Pass fakes can be used to freeze a zone or shift in a desired direction. Like a shot fake, a good pass fake is not overextended, causing the offensive player to over extend the arms, change center of gravity (stand up or lose balance).

If the desire is to freeze the zone, a pass fake back in the direction the ball was just passed from. This will cause the zone to stop in preparation to reverse direction. The loss of momentum costs the disciplined, aggressive zone defense in terms of reaction time, giving the offense the advantage.

If the desire is to reverse the ball in the direction it came from, a pass fake in the continued direction of movement the ball was moving in will cause the defense to continue shifting in that direction. In order to recover and attack the ball, the zone must stop after moving another one or two steps in the direction the ball was moving in and then accelerate in the opposite direction to again pursue the ball. Again, the offense gains an advantage as a result of the fake.

Teaching Point

Regardless of what form of zone attack is used, Blocker-Mover or another offense, it is a wise teaching tactic to require a pass fake or shot fake after every three or four passes in any zone offense work during practice in order to teach correct technique and build the habit of faking against a zone defense.

29

Putting It All Together

This chapter will provide examples of just a few of the thousands of possible combinations of zone attack offensive building blocks utilized in a variety of scenarios of zone defenses being attacked by Blocker-Mover Motion Offense. A great way to see the opportunities Blocker-Mover provides, particularly screening a zone defense, is to simply sit down and draw up sample scenarios like the examples provided in this chapter.

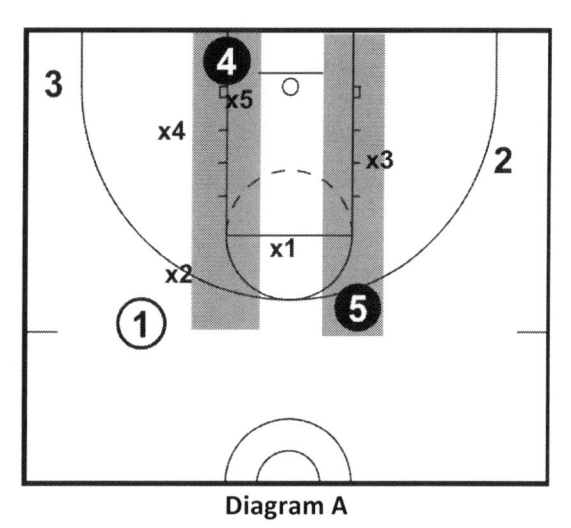

Diagram A

In this first example, the offense is using a Lane-Lane alignment to attack a 2-3 zone and has chosen not to line up in the gaps of the zone defense all though post Blocker #4 has lined up deep behind the zone, pulling defender X5 out of position and creating both a gap in the middle of the zone and distorting the backline (**Diagram A**).

Coaching Basketball's Zone Attack Offense Using Blocker-Mover Motion Offense

Diagram B

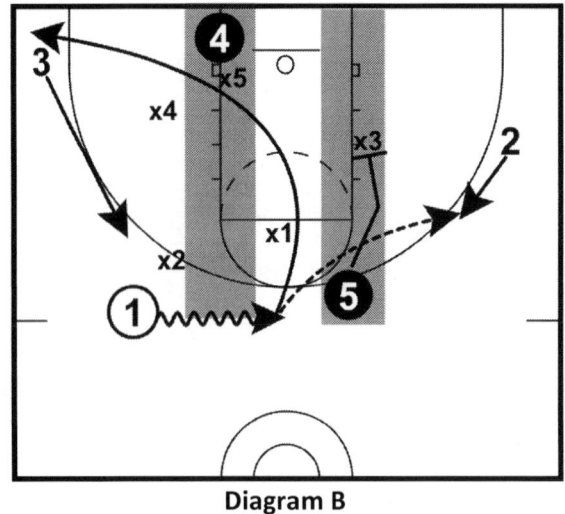

Principles applied in Diagram B:

- Dribble use
- Blocker hunts Mover – sets screen
- Mover hunts Blocker and Gap
- One mover per perimeter area
- Screen the zone

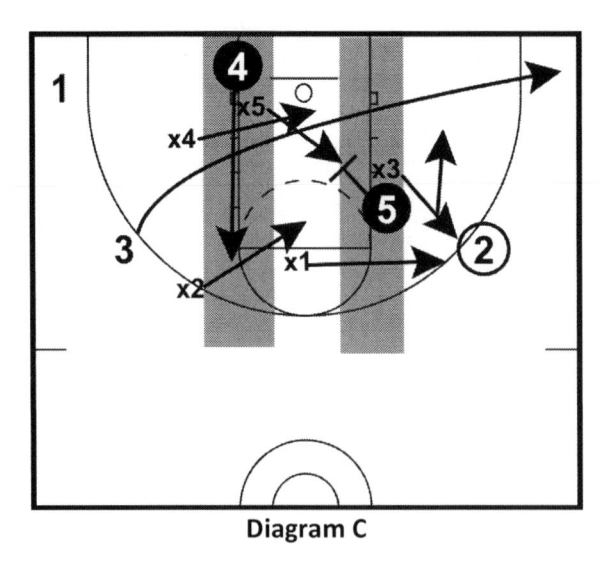

Diagram C

Principles applied in Diagram C:

- One Mover per perimeter area
- Blocker hunts Mover (screening opportunity)
- Blocker acts as a second cutter after screening (post Blocker #5 seals next defender).

Putting It All Together

Diagram D

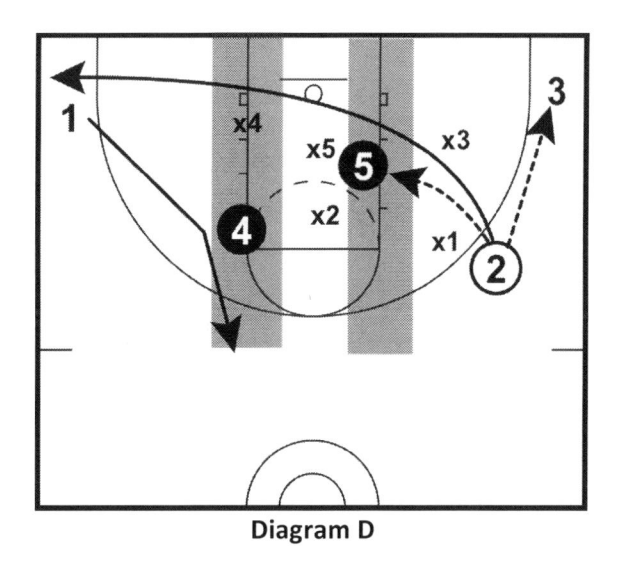

Principles applied in Diagram D:

- Distort the zone
- One Mover per perimeter area
- Blockers hunt Movers (screening opportunities)
- Movers hunt gaps and Blockers

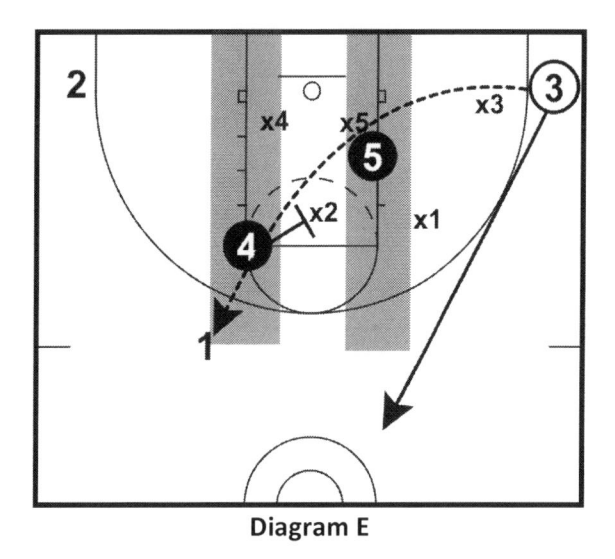

Diagram E

Principles applied in Diagram E:

- Screen the zone
- Blockers hunt Movers (look for screening opportunities)
- Balance the floor defensively
- Move the ball from side to side (diagonal skip pass)
- Create overloads (one defender guards two offensive players)

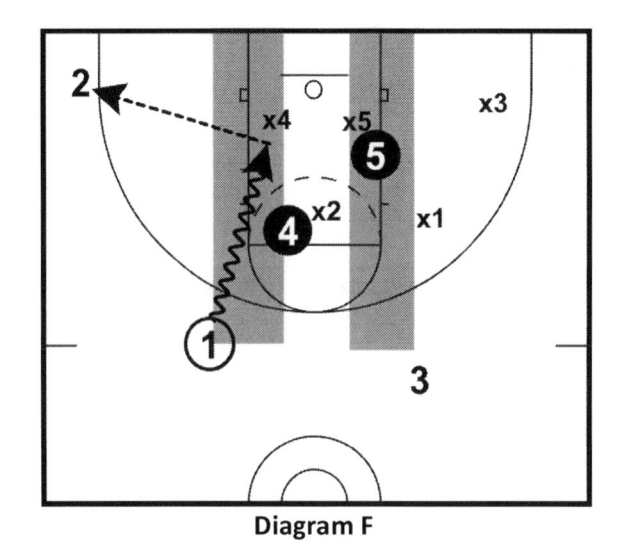

Coaching Basketball's Zone Attack Offense Using Blocker-Mover Motion Offense

Diagram F

Principles applied in Diagram F:

- Use of dribble – freeze – penetrate and pitch
- Create an overload (one defender guards two offensive players)

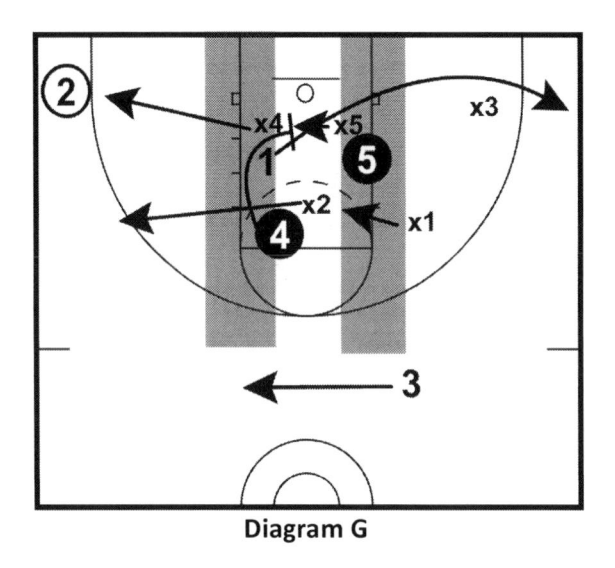

Diagram G

Principles applied in Diagram G:

- One Mover per perimeter area
- Spacing on the perimeter
- Lane Blockers are second cutters (#4 goes to the next post defender and seals)

186

Putting It All Together

Diagram H

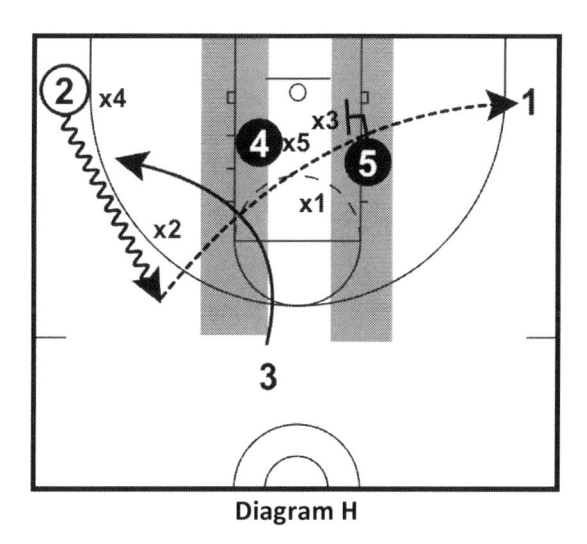

Principles applied in Diagram H:

- Screen the zone – (Lane Blocker #5 sets a screen-in)
- Dribble off combined with dribble loop
- One Mover per perimeter area – dribble push to loop
- Move the ball from side-to-side – diagonal skip pass

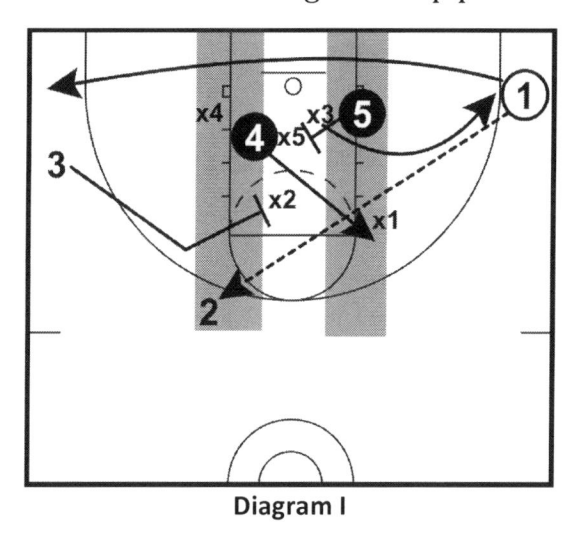

Diagram I

Principles applied in Diagram I:

- Screen the zone (Mover #3 sets a screen for Mover #2)
- Move the ball from side-to-side – diagonal skip pass
- One Mover per perimeter area
- Screen the zone – screen-in (Lane Blocker #5 goes to the next defender and seals)
- Screen the zone – screen –in (Lane Blocker #4 flashes into the ball side high post)
- Lane Blockers may exchange lanes when the situation requires.

187

Diagram J

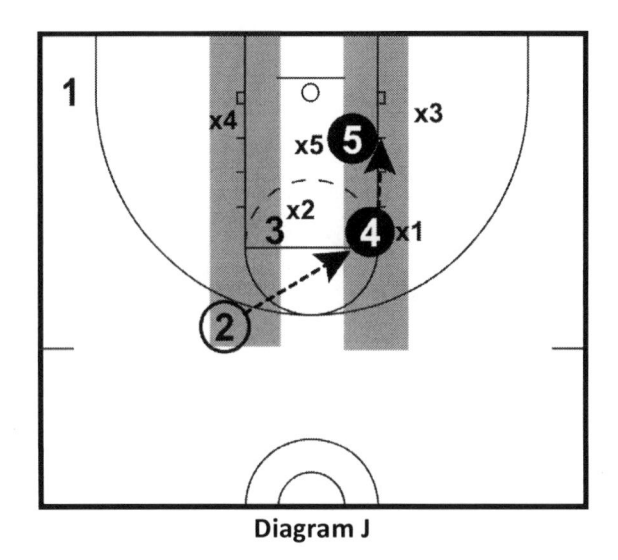

Principles applied in Diagram J:

- Screen out the zone – Lane Blocker #4 has screened out X1
- Screen the zone – Lane Blocker #5 has sealed the middle defender for a high low pass
- Move the ball – high to low pass from Mover #2 to Lane Blocker #4 to Lane Blocker #5

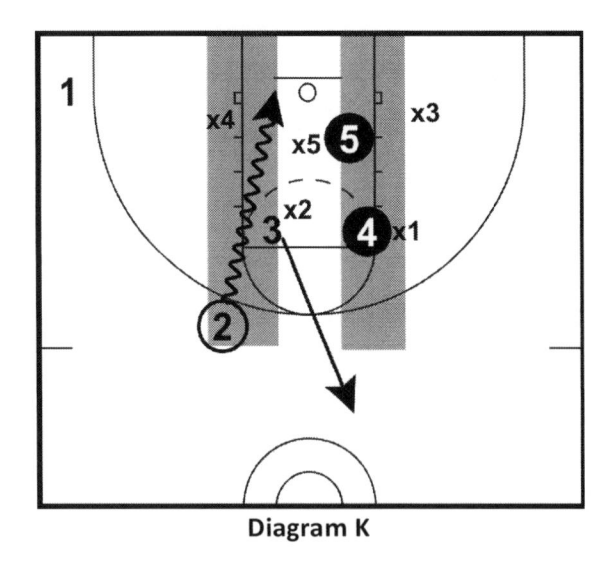

Diagram K

Principles applied in Diagram K:

- Balance the floor for defensive floor balance
- Create an overload – one defender guards two offensive players
- Dribble penetration – dribble use rules

Putting It All Together

Lane-Lane versus 1-3-1 Zone Defense

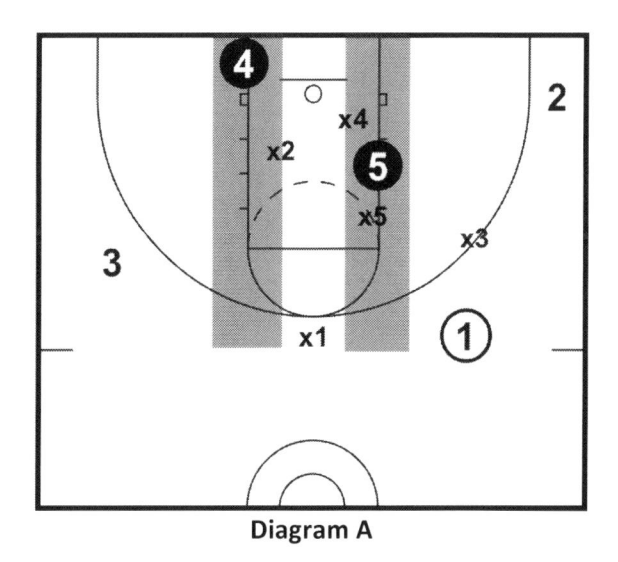

Diagram A

Principles applied in Diagram A:

- Line up in the gaps of the zone
- Distort the zone – the players aligned to distort the zone

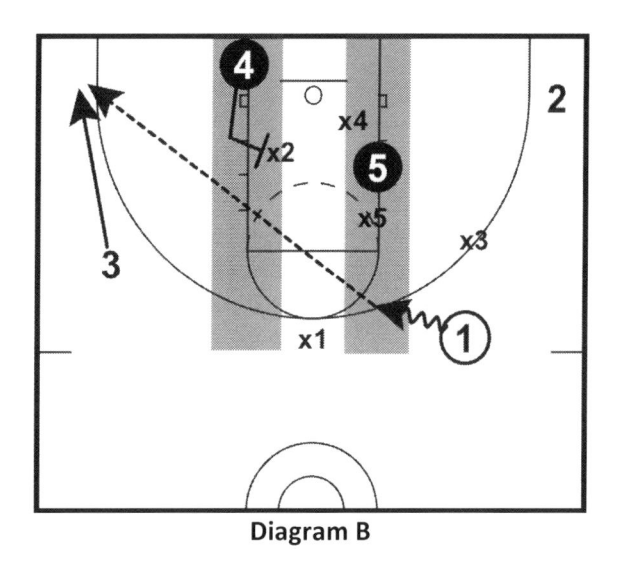

Diagram B

Principles applied in Diagram B:

- Dribble use – penetrate the gap
- Screen the zone – screen-in
- Blockers hunt Movers – look for opportunities to screen
- Movers hunt gaps and Blockers – look for opportunities to cut

Diagram C

Diagram D

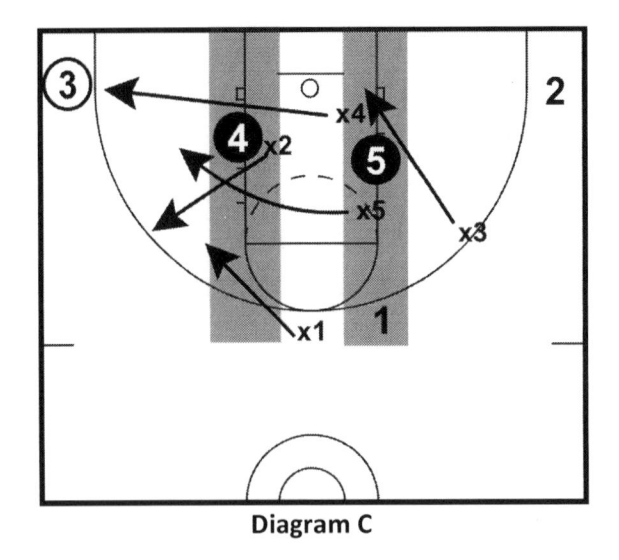

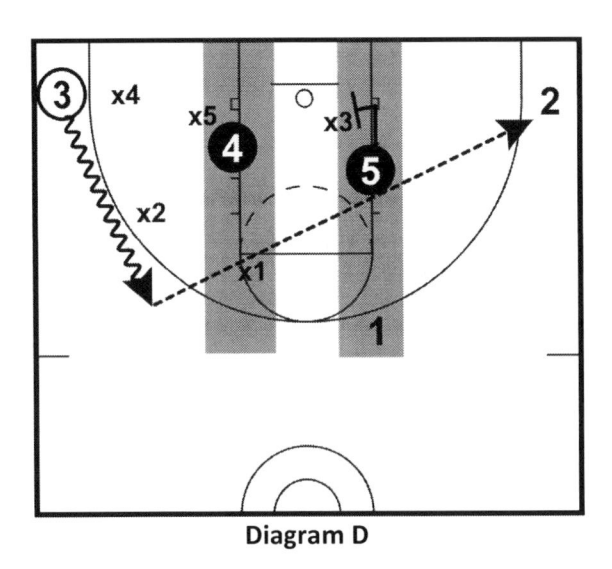

Principles applied in Diagram D:

- Screen the zone – screen-in
- Dribble off
- Move the ball side-to-side – diagonal skip pass

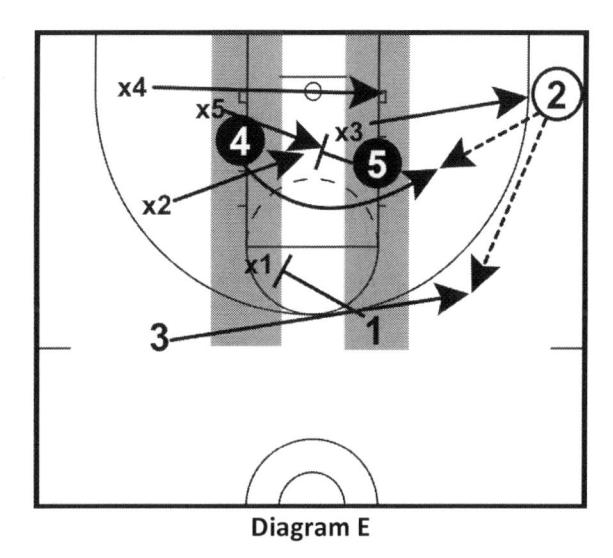

Putting It All Together

Diagram E

- Screen the zone – center screen (Lane Blocker #5 screens for Blocker #4)
- Screen the zone – look for opportunities to screen (mover #1 screens X1)
- Lane Blockers can exchange lanes if necessary

Lane-Lane versus 1-2-2 Zone Defense

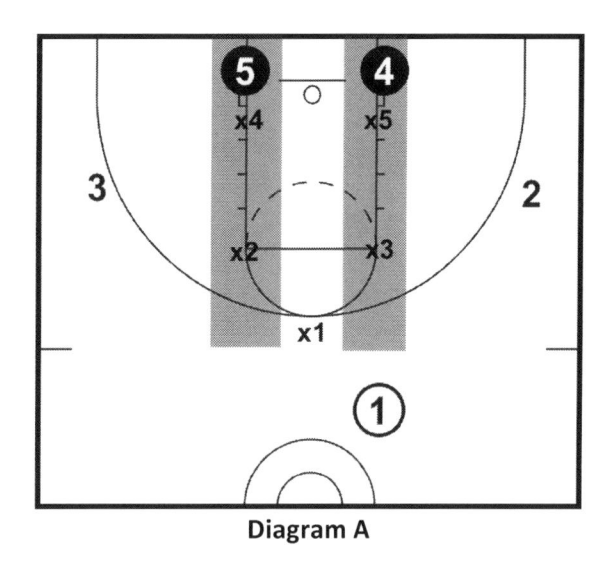

Diagram A

Principles applied in Diagram A:

- Line up in the gaps of the zone defense
- Distort the zone defense – the Lane Blockers have lined up deep behind the zone

Coaching Basketball's Zone Attack Offense Using Blocker-Mover Motion Offense

Diagram B

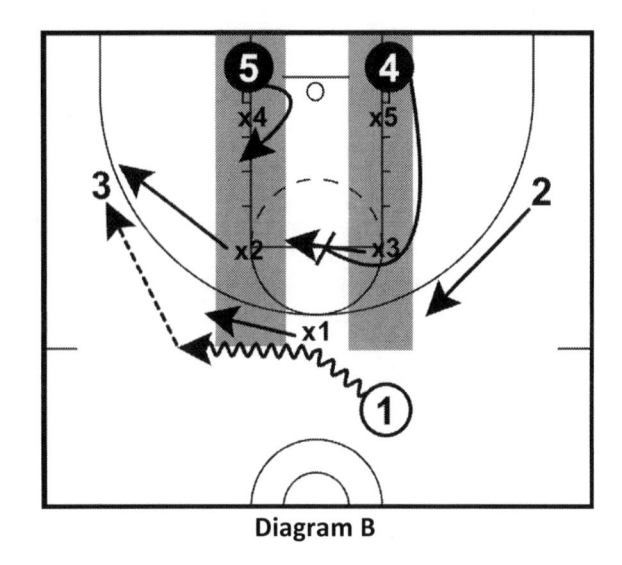

Principles applied in Diagram B:

- Use of dribble – freeze and slide
- Move the ball from side-to-side
- Screen the zone
- Blockers hunt Movers – look for opportunities to screen
- Movers hunt gaps and Blockers – Mover #2 cuts behind the screen

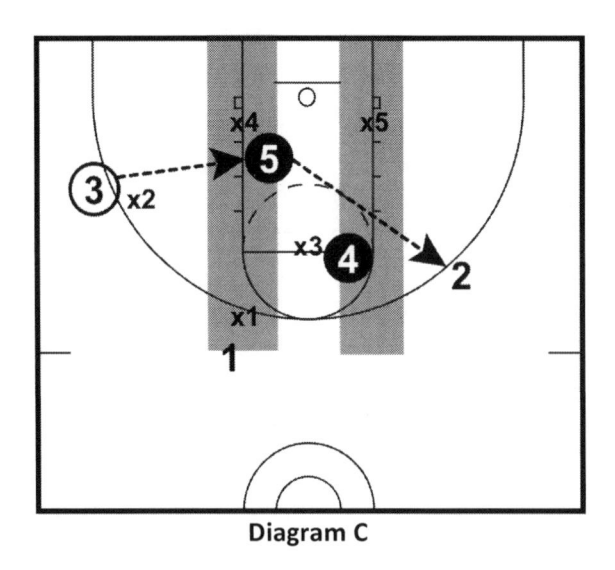

Diagram C

Principles applied in Diagram C:

- Move the ball from side to side
- Fan the ball

192

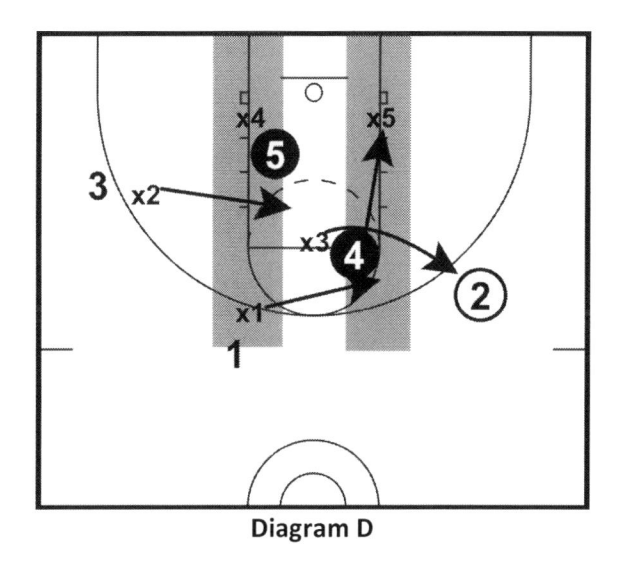

Putting It All Together

Diagram D

Principles applied in Diagram D:

- Blockers are second cutters – Lane Blocker #4 posts up after screening

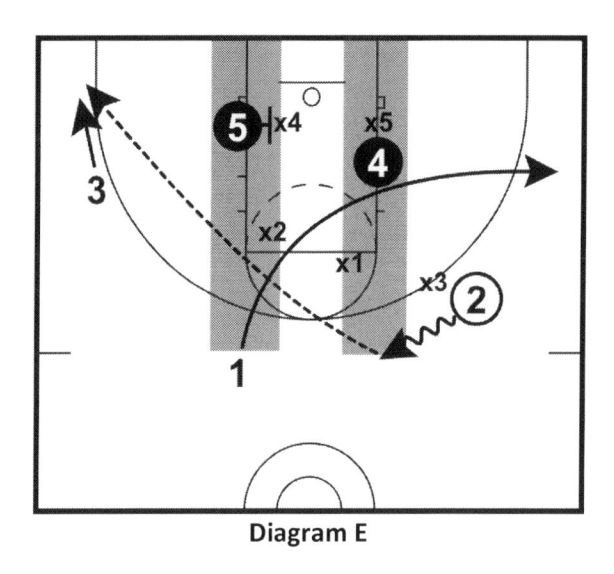

Diagram E

Principles applied in Diagram E:

- One Mover per perimeter area – balance the floor
- Dribble use – drive the skip pass
- Look to screen – screen-in – Lane Blocker #5 screens in
- Blockers hunt Movers – look for opportunities to screen
- Movers hunt gaps and Blockers
- Move the ball from side-to-side – diagonal skip pass

Coaching Basketball's Zone Attack Offense Using Blocker-Mover Motion Offense

Diagram F

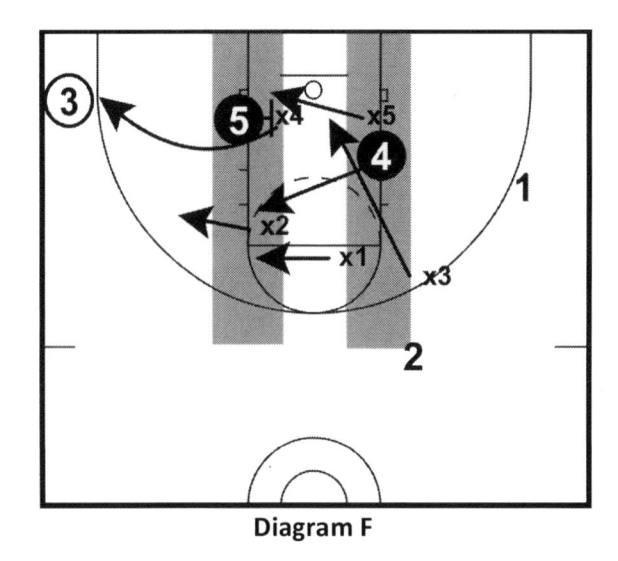

Principles applied in Diagram F:

- Flash into the gaps in the zone defense
- Lane Blockers may change areas when necessary

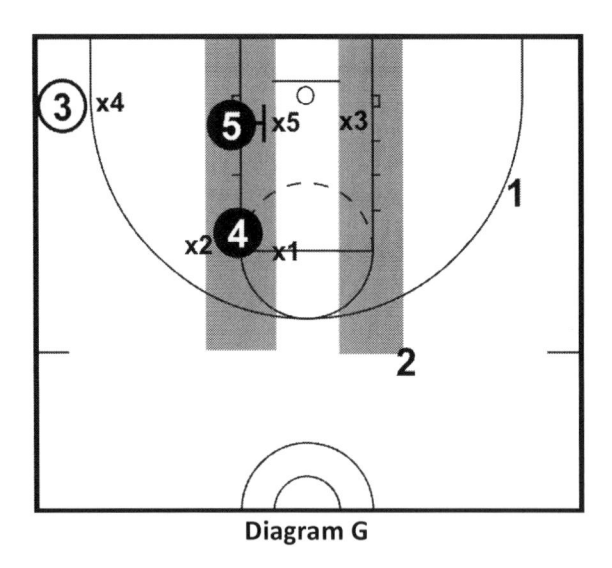

Diagram G

Principles applied in Diagram G:

- Screen the zone – Lane Blocker #5 goes to the next defender and seals, effectively setting a screen by posting up.

Putting It All Together

Diagram H

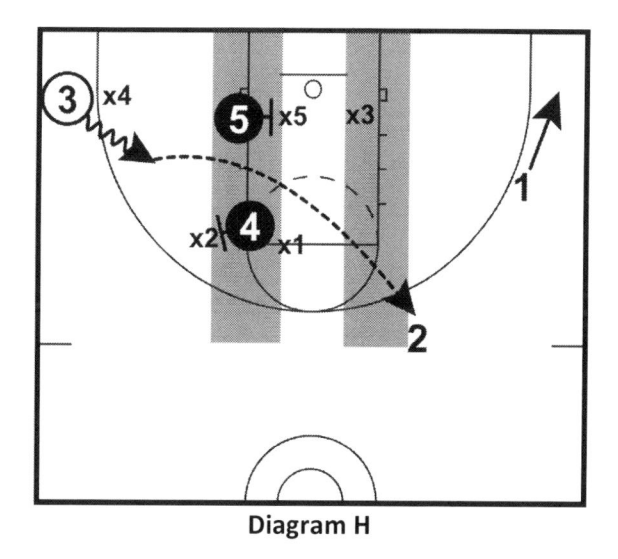

Principles applied in Diagram H:

- Dribble use – drive the skip pass
- Screen out – Lane Blocker #4 screens out X2
- Move the ball from side-to-side – diagonal skip pass

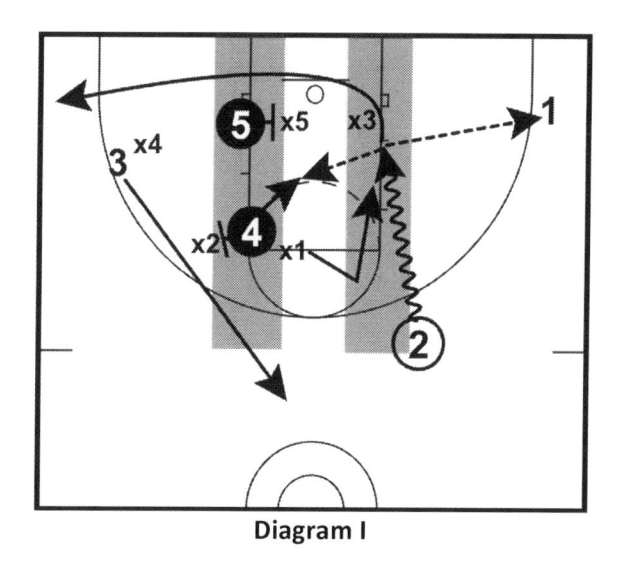

Diagram I

Principles applied in Diagram I:

- Overload the zone defense
- Make one defender guard to offensive players
- Dribble use –dribble penetrate
- One Mover per perimeter area
- Balance the floor for defensive purposes

195

Top-Bottom versus 2-3 Zone Defense

Diagram A

Principles applied in Diagram A:

- Distort the zone – use alignments to distort the zone
- Line up in the gaps – use alignments to line up in the gaps of the zone

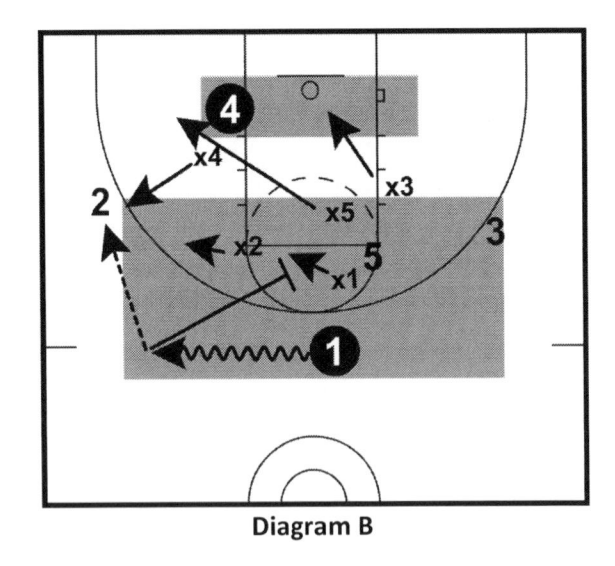

Diagram B

Principles applied in Diagram B:

- Dribble use – dribble off the top
- Screen the zone – Top Blocker #1 set a down screen on X1

Putting It All Together

Diagram C

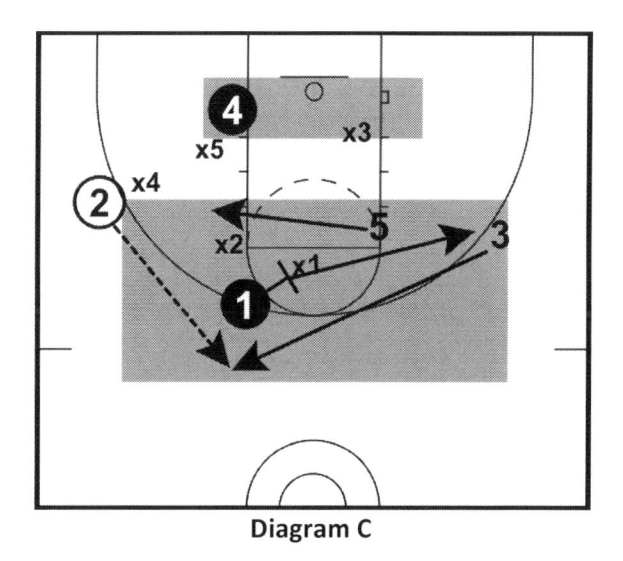

Principles applied in Diagram C:

- Blockers hunt Movers – look for opportunities to screen
- Movers hunt gaps and Blockers – Mover #3 used the Top Blocker's screen
- Flash into gaps – Mover #5 flashed into the ball side high post

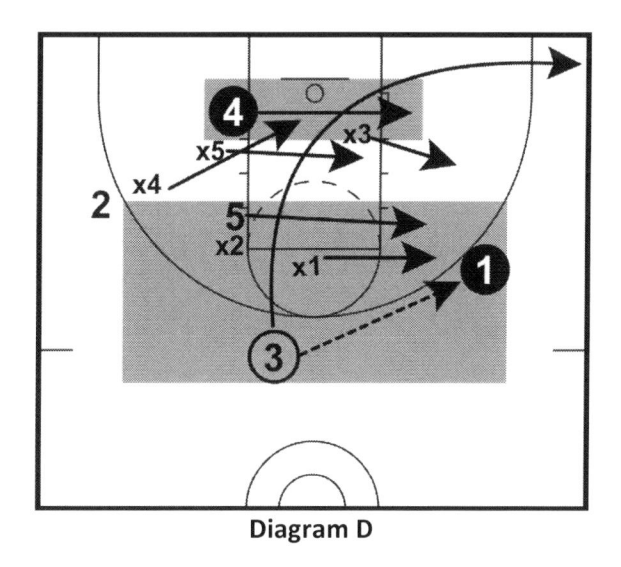

Diagram D

Principles applied in Diagram D:

- One Mover per perimeter area
- Move the ball from side-to-side

Diagram E

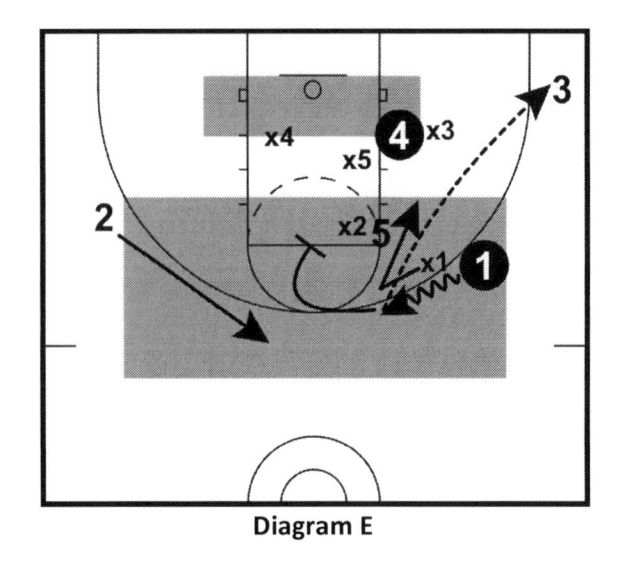

Principles applied in Diagram E:

- Dribble use freeze and slide X1– sets up a pass fake to freeze the defense
- Blockers hunt Movers – Top Blocker #1 sets a flare screen for Mover #2
- Movers hunt gaps and Blockers – Mover #2 moves behind Top Blocker #1's screen

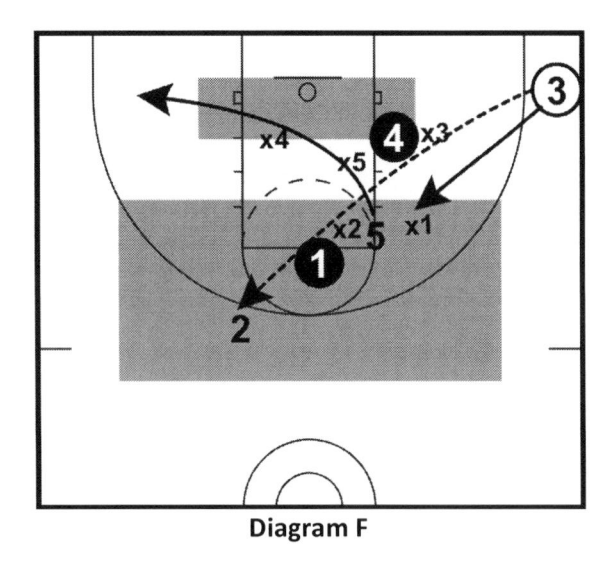

Diagram F

Principles applied in Diagram F:

- Screen the zone – Top Blocker #1 screens X2
- Cut to gaps or open spaces – Mover #5 cuts on the skip pass
- Move the ball from side-to-side – Diagonal skip pass

Putting It All Together

Diagram G

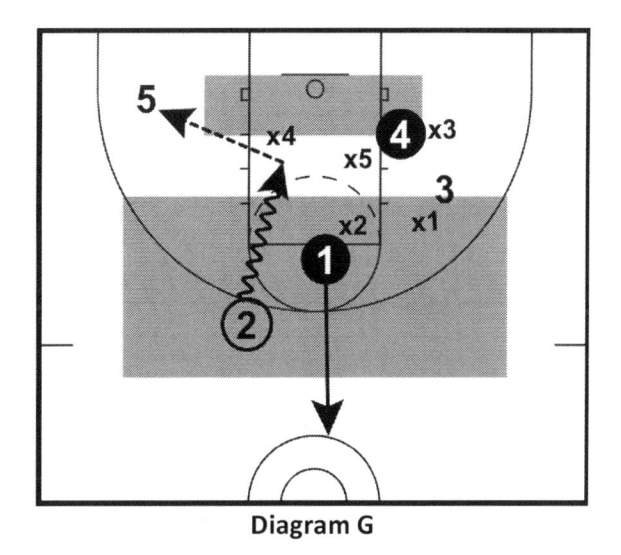

Principles applied in Diagram G:

- Overload the zone – make one defender guard two offensive players
- Dribble use – dribble penetration
- Screen the zone – Top Mover #1 screened X2
- Defensive floor balance

Top-Bottom versus 1-2-2 Zone Defense

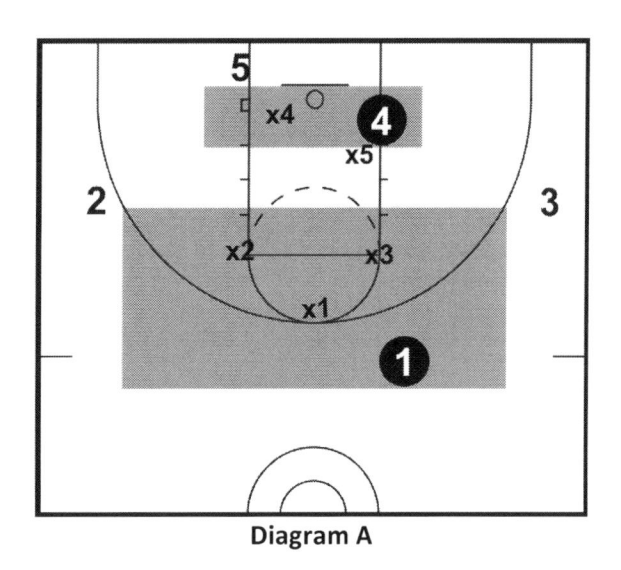

Diagram A

Principles applied in Diagram A:

- Line up in the gaps of the zone
- Distort the zone with the use of an alignment

199

Coaching Basketball's Zone Attack Offense Using Blocker-Mover Motion Offense

Diagram B

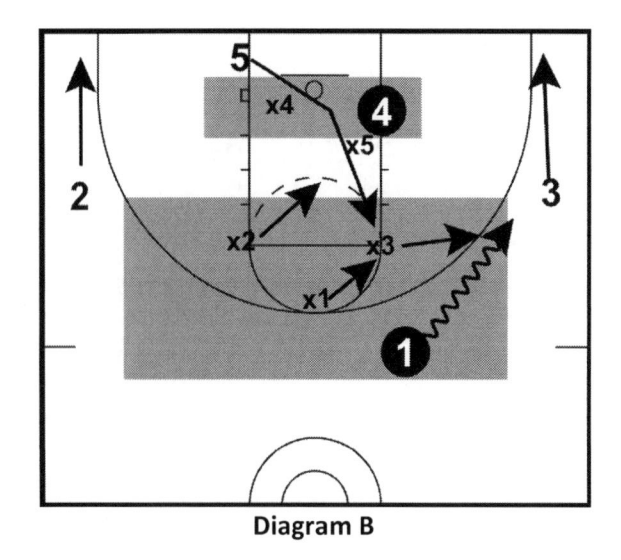

Principles applied in Diagram B:

- Dribble use – dribble push
- Hunters hunt gaps and Blockers – Mover #5 fills the ball side high post

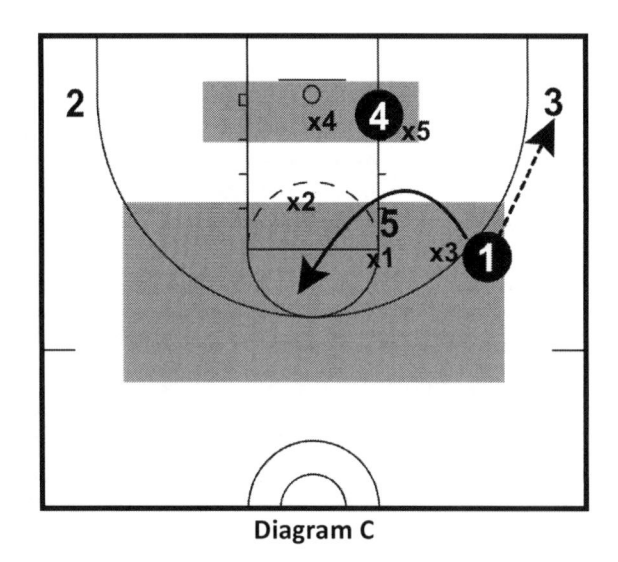

Diagram C

Principles applied in Diagram C:

- Move the ball and move people.
- Fill gaps in the zone – Top Blocker #1 fills the foul line area

Putting It All Together

Diagram D

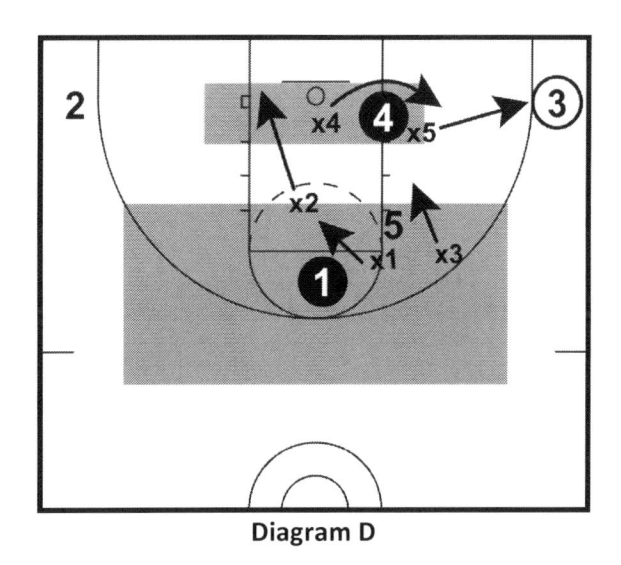

Defense shifts in Diagram D:

All zone defenses become a 2-3 zone defense when the ball is in the corner.

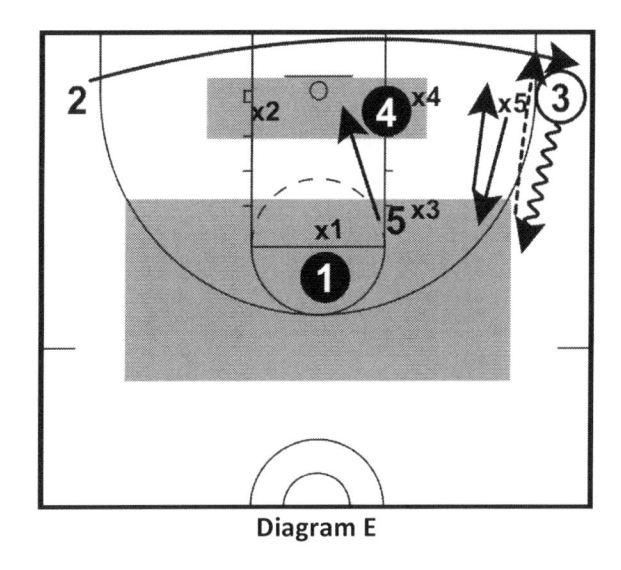

Diagram E

Principles applied in Diagram E:

- Dibble off – distort the zone by moving the defender out of their area
- Dribble follow – Mover #2 follows Mover #3
- Movers hunt gaps and Blockers – Mover #2 fills the ball side corner gap
- Mover #5 moves in the gap in the middle of the lane towards the help side.

Coaching Basketball's Zone Attack Offense Using Blocker-Mover Motion Offense

Diagram F

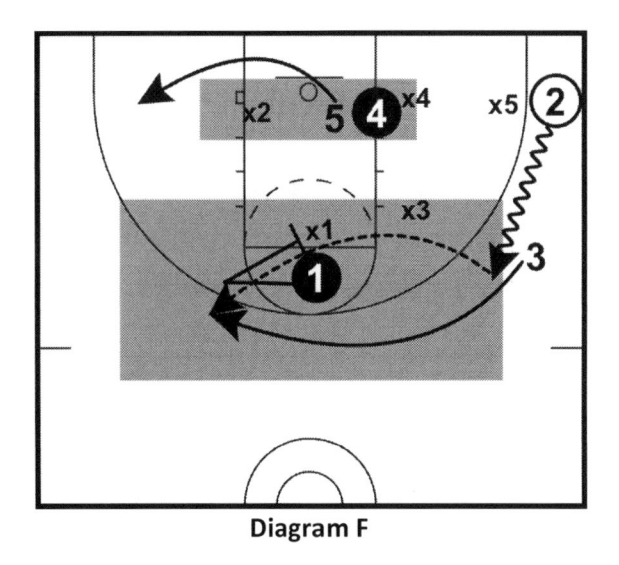

Principles applied in Diagram F:

- Dribble off – dribble push
- Screen the zone – Top Blocker #1 screens the top back defender of the zone
- Fill the gap – Mover #5 fills the short corner

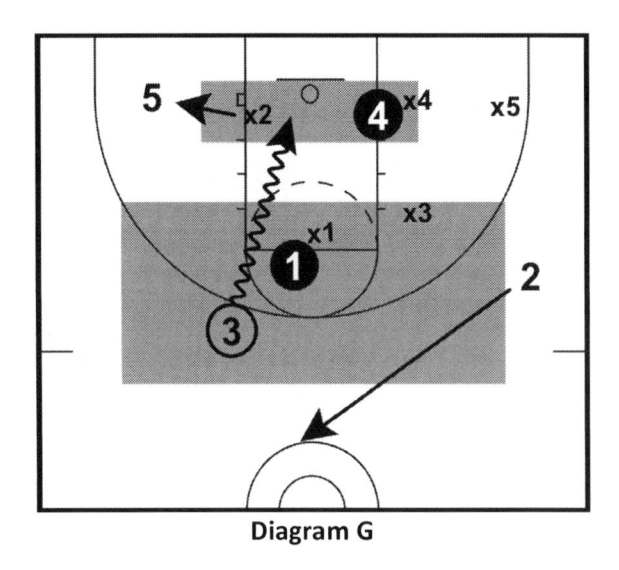

Diagram G

Principles applied in Diagram G:

- Overload the zone
- Make one defender guard two offensive players
- Dribble penetration
- Balance the floor for defensive floor balance

Top-Bottom versus 1-3-1 Zone Defense

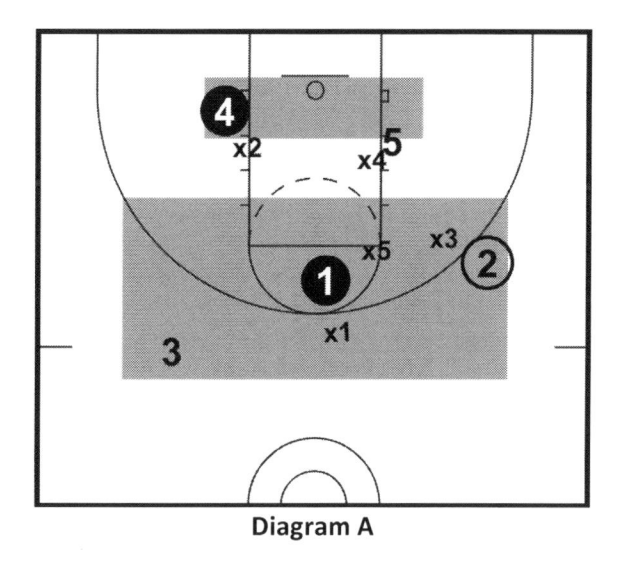

Diagram A

Principles applied in Diagram A:

- Distort the zone – alignment used to distort the zone

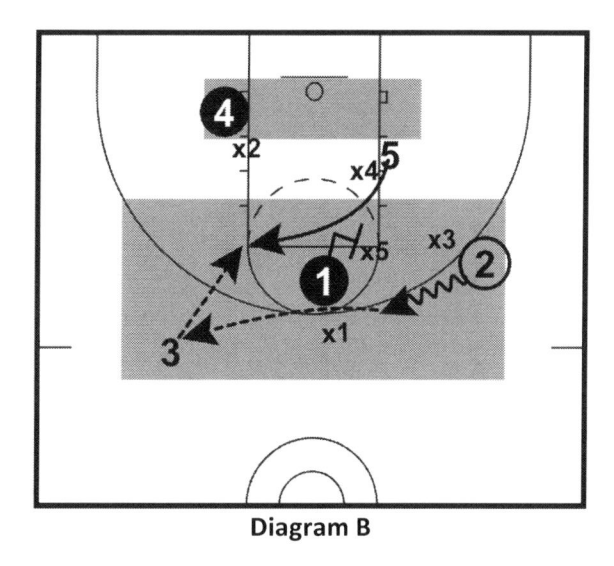

Diagram B

Principles applied in Diagram B:

- Dribble use
- Move the ball side-to-side
- Screen the zone – Top Blocker #1 screens X5
- Mover hunts gaps and Blocker – Mover #5 flashes into new ball side high post

Coaching Basketball's Zone Attack Offense Using Blocker-Mover Motion Offense

Diagram C

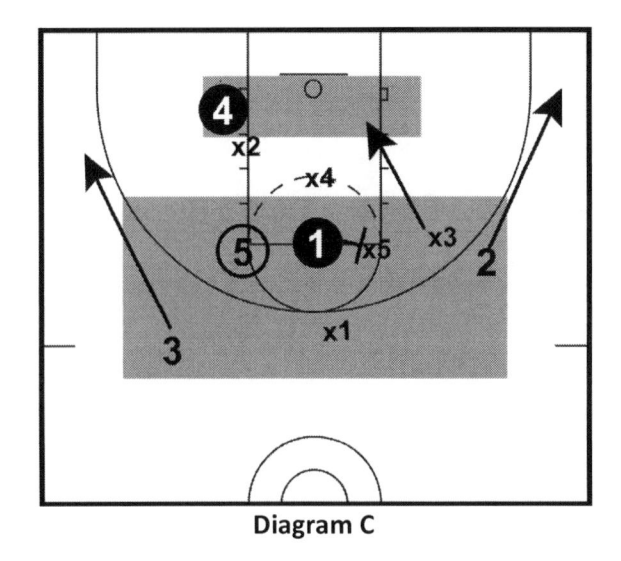

Principles applied in Diagram C:

- Movers hunt gaps and Blockers – Moves #2 and Movers #3 move to gaps
- Mover #5 can shoot the ball or drive

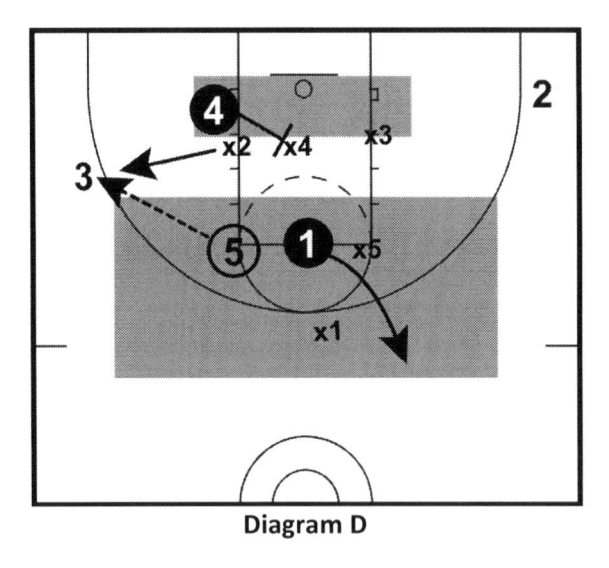

Diagram D

Principles applied in Diagram D:

- Balance the floor for defensive floor balance
- Go to the next defender and seal – Bottom Blocker #4 posts up

Putting It All Together

Diagram E

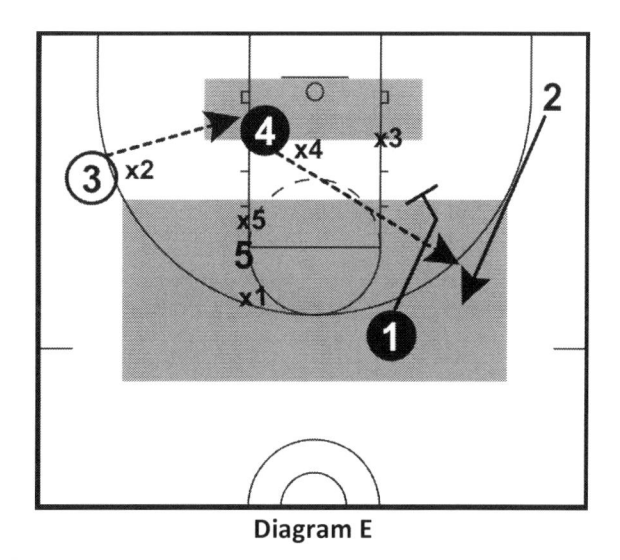

Principles applied in Diagram E:

- Feed the post – Bottom Blocker #4 can score or fan the ball
- Blockers hunt Movers – Top Blocker #1 sets an angled down screen
- Movers hunt gaps and Blockers – Mover #2 moves behind the screen for a 3 pt. shot
- Fan the ball diagonal and opposite – Bottom Blocker #4 fans the ball to Mover #2

Lane-Wide versus 2-3 Zone Defense

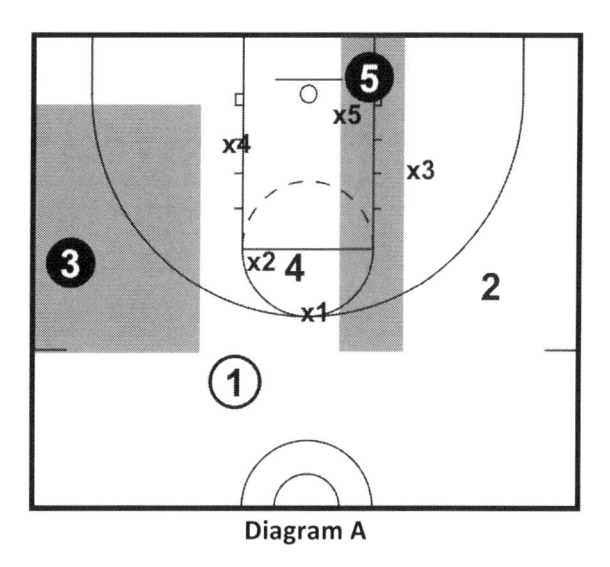

Diagram A

Principles applied in Diagram A:

- Distort the zone – alignment used to distort the zone defense
- Line up in the gaps of the zone defense

205

Coaching Basketball's Zone Attack Offense Using Blocker-Mover Motion Offense

Diagram B

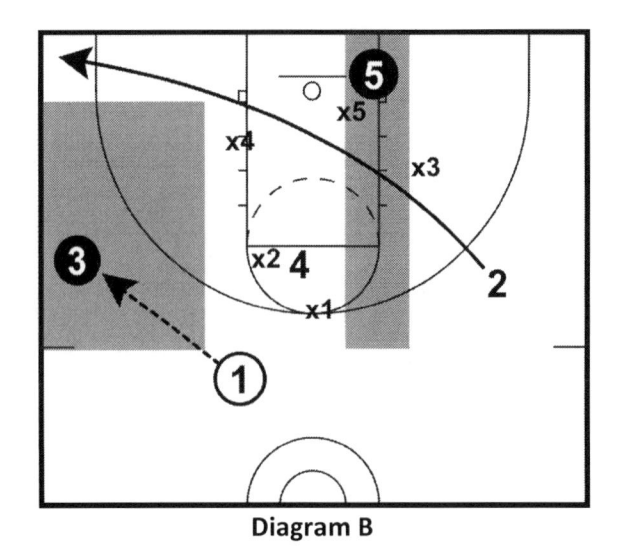

Principles applied in Diagram B:

- Movers hunt gaps and Blockers
- Move the ball and move people

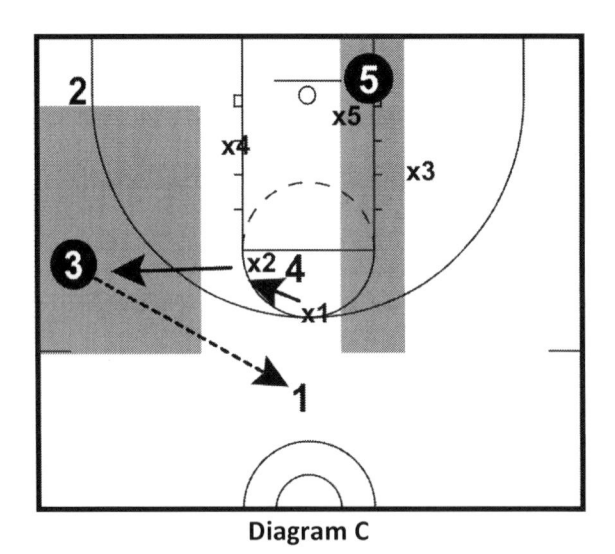

Diagram C

Principles applied in Diagram C:

- Move the ball

Putting It All Together

Diagram D

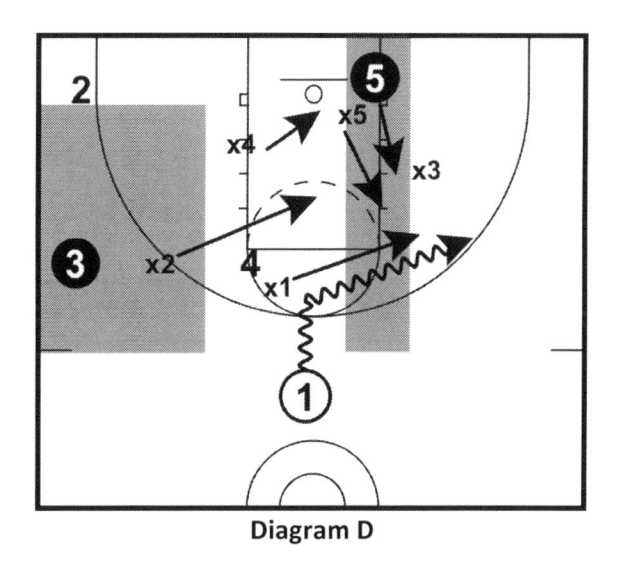

Principles applied in Diagram D:

- Dribble use – drive and freeze (do not pick up dribble unless necessary)

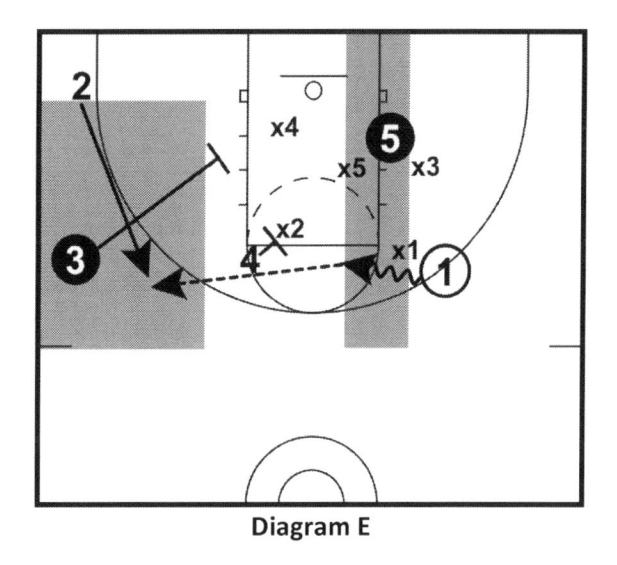

Diagram E

Principles applied in Diagram E:

- Dribble use – reverse the ball
- Dribble use – freeze X2
- Screen the zone
- Blockers hunt Movers – opportunities to screen
- Movers hunt gaps and Blockers

Coaching Basketball's Zone Attack Offense Using Blocker-Mover Motion Offense

Diagram F

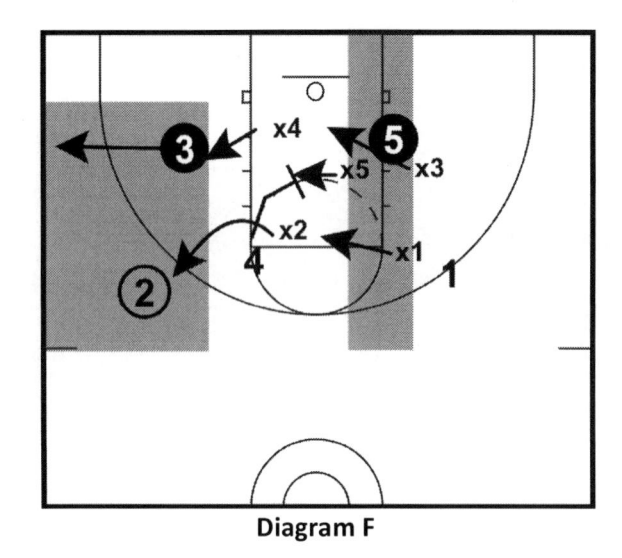

Principles applied in Diagram F:

- Screen the zone
- Mover #4 goes to the next defender and seals
- Maintain proper spacing – Wide Blocker #3 spaces out

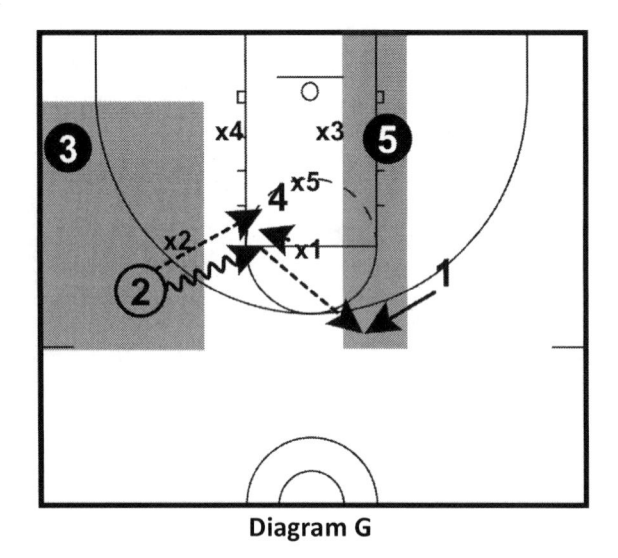

Diagram G

Principles applied in Diagram G:

- Dribble use – middle penetrate
- Dribble use – freeze X1
- Reverse the ball side-to-side

Putting It All Together

Diagram H

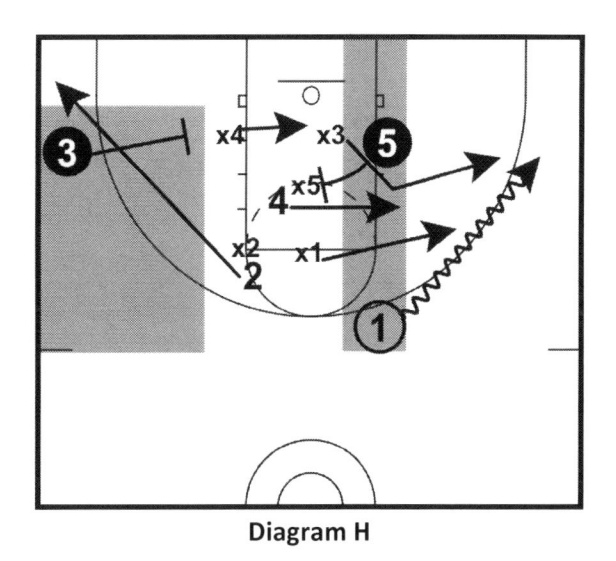

Principles applied in Diagram I:

- Dribble use – dribble down to feed the post
- Screen the zone – Center screen by Lane Blocker #5 for Mover #4
- Screen the zone – Wide Blocker #3 sets a screen in for Mover #2
- Blockers hunt Movers – look for screening opportunities
- Movers hunt gaps and Blockers – Move #2 cuts to corner for 3 pt. shot
- Mover #4 flashes into the ball side mid-post

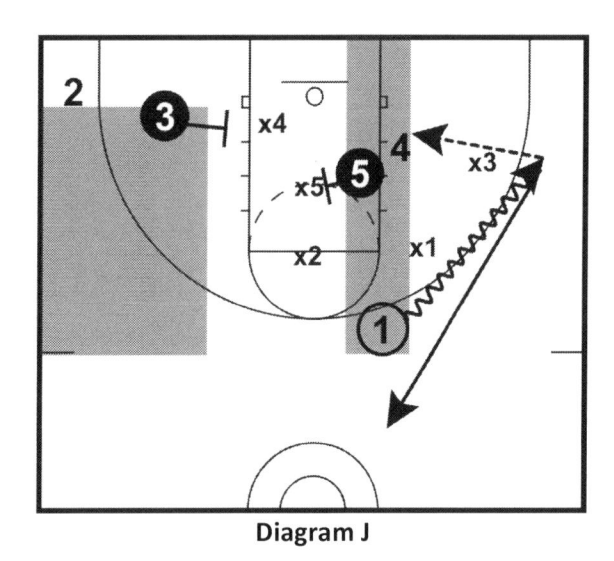

Diagram J

Principles applied in Diagram J:

- Feed the post
- Screen the zone – Wide Blocker #3 screens in for Mover #2
- Defensive floor balance – Mover #1 balances the floor

Lane-Wide versus 1-2-2 Zone Defense

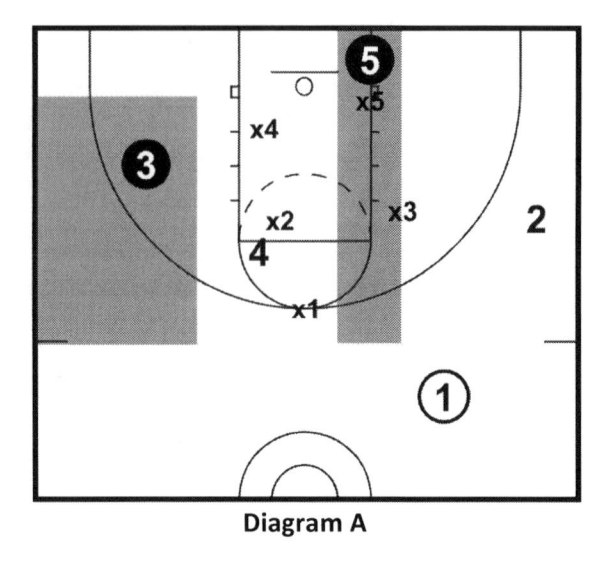

Diagram A

Principles applied in Diagram A:

- Distort the zone defense – use alignment to distort the zone defense
- Line up in the gaps

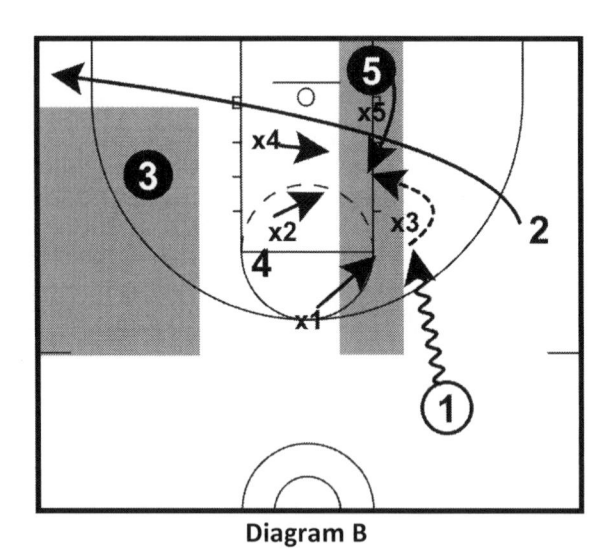

Diagram B

Principles applied in Diagram B:

- Dribble use – dribble push Mover #2 - freeze X3
- Move the ball move players
- Movers hunt gaps and Blockers – Mover #2 fills help side corner
- Feed the post – Lane Blocker #5 posts up hard – collapses defense

Putting It All Together

Diagram C

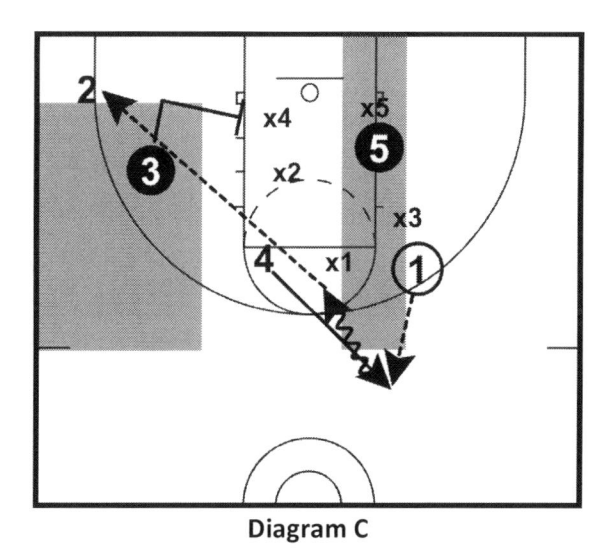

Principles applied in Diagram C:

- Relieve pressure to the high post middle – Mover #4 steps out
- Dribble use – Mover #4 drives to freeze X1
- Screen the zone
- Wide Blocker #3 screens X4 with a screen in
- Blockers hunt Movers – look for opportunities to screen
- Reverse the ball side-to-side

Lane-Wide versus 1-3-1 Zone Defense

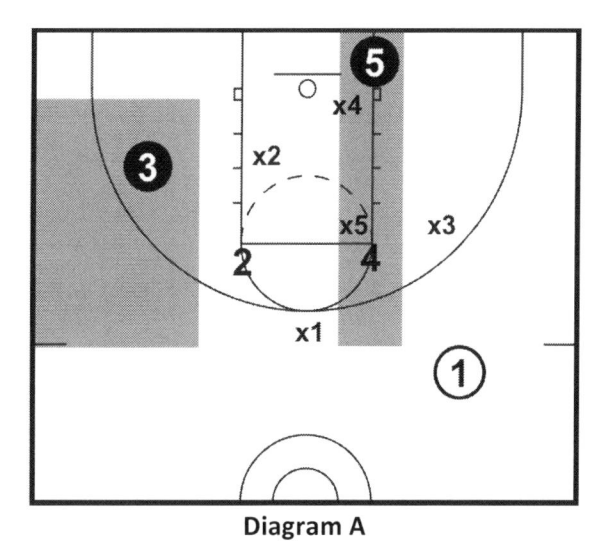

Diagram A

Principles applied in Diagram A:

211

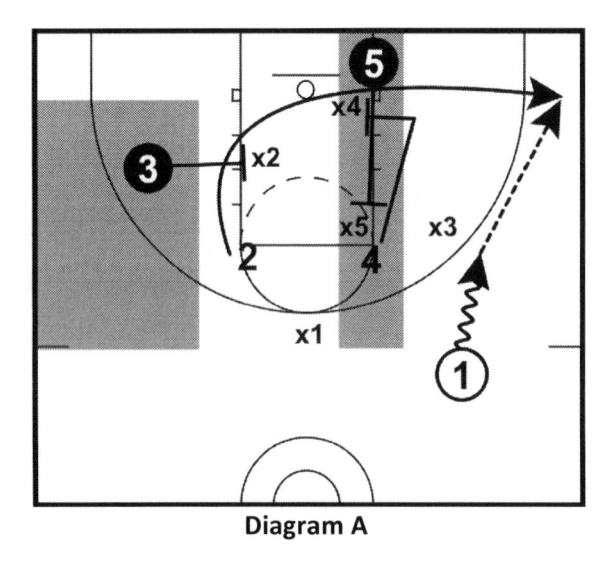

Coaching Basketball's Zone Attack Offense Using Blocker-Mover Motion Offense

Diagram A

Principles applied in Diagram A:

- Distort the zone defense – use alignment to distort the zone defense
- Line up in the gaps

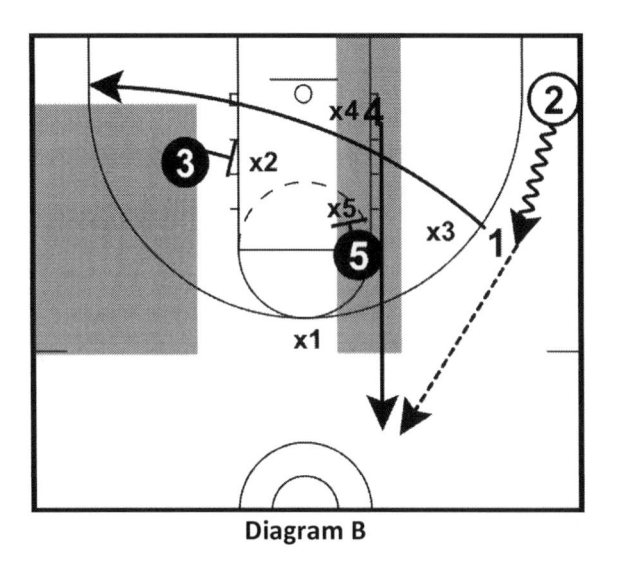

Diagram B

Principles applied in Diagram B:

- Dribble use – dribble off
- Relieve pressure with the high post middle
- Screen the zone – Lane Blocker #5 screens down – Wide Blocker #3 screens in
- One perimeter per perimeter area
- Movers hunt gaps and Blockers – Mover #1 cuts to use Wide Blocker #3's screen in

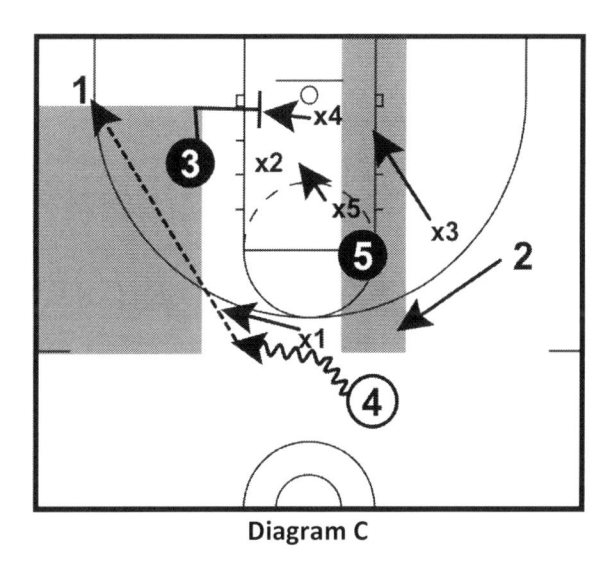

Putting It All Together

Diagram C

Principles applied in Diagram C:

- Dribble use – Freeze and slide X1
- Screen the zone – Wide Blocker 33 screens in X4
- Move the ball side-to-side
- Movers hunt gaps and Blockers – Mover #2 moves diagonal opposite the ball

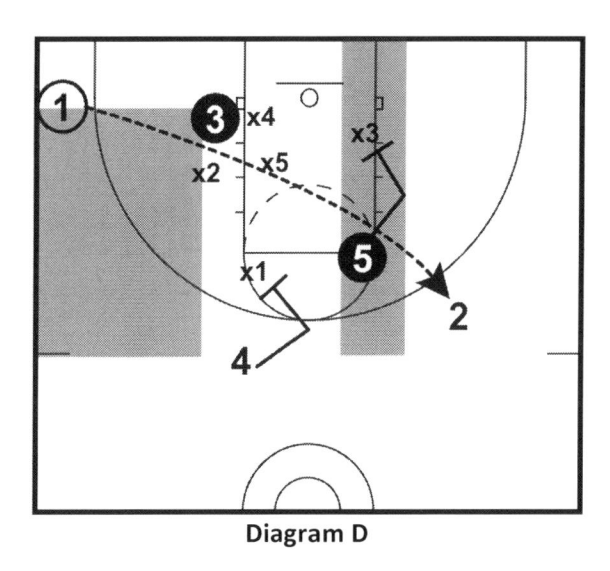

Diagram D

Principles applied in Diagram D:

- Screen the zone – Mover #4 down screens X1
- Blockers hunt Movers – look for opportunities to screen
- Move the ball from side-to-side – diagonal skip pass

Coaching Basketball's Zone Attack Offense Using Blocker-Mover Motion Offense

Diagram E

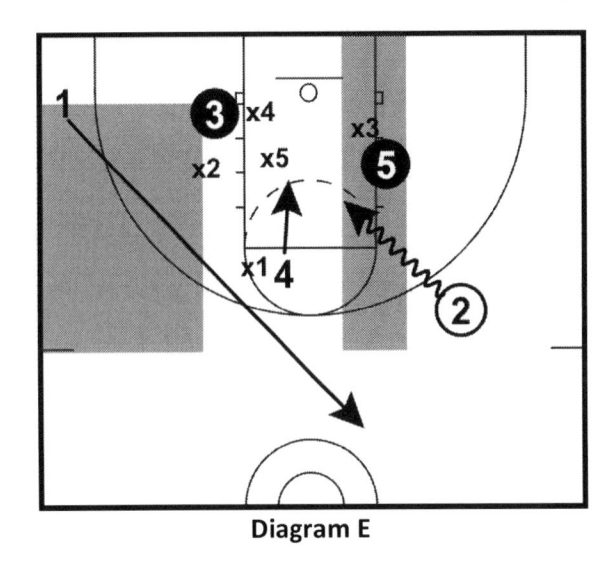

Principles applied in Diagram E:

- Dribble use – shoot the 3 pt. shot or drive middle
- Defensive floor balance – Mover #1 balances the floor defensively

For FREE diagrams of blank alignments (Lane-Lane, Top-Bottom and Lane-Wide) to draw diagrams for your own purposes, please visit my website: www.kcsbasketball.com. Go to the Handouts & Clinic Notes page and click on the Blocker-Mover page.

30

Applying Zone Attack Principles to an Existing Zone Attack Offense

The purpose of this book is to help coaches take zone attack principles and either build their own zone attack offense or improve an existing offense by adding zone attack concepts and principles that fit current personnel.

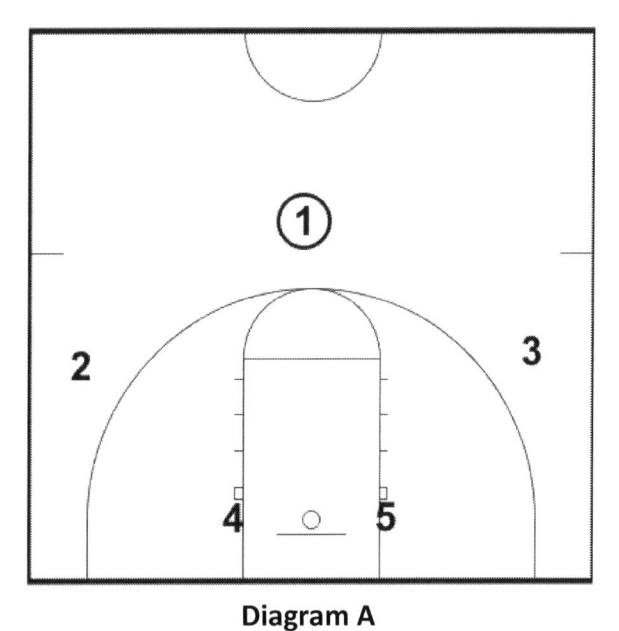

Diagram A

A common alignment for attacking an even front zone defense such as the ever popular 2-3 is shown in **Diagram A** (The zone defense has been omitted for clarity). Note, the two post players are lined up well below where two offensive post players would commonly initiate a zone attack. This principle is designed to stretch the zone defense vertically, creating larger than normal gaps. The wings are space well beyond the three-point line to create horizontal stretch to the zone.

The basic movement of the zone is simple. When the ball is passed to a wing the ball side low post slides up and posts up in the low post. The post opposite the ball flashes into the high post (**Diagram B**).

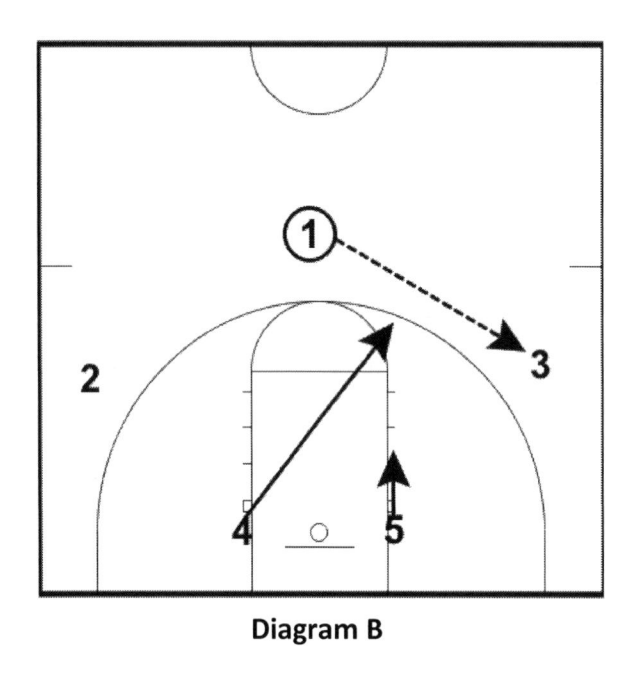

Diagram B

The ball is reversed around the perimeter to the other side of the court. On the pass from the point guard to the help side wing the high post, #4, flashes across the lane to the ball side low post. #5 flashes across the lane to the high post (**Diagram C**). This simple movement is an actual zone offense used by many teams and is often used successfully.

The offense can be improved by adding various zone attack principles to the existing offense. **Diagram D** depicts several concepts being applied. #1 sets a down screen for #3 while #4 moves to the short post area to distort the zone defense.

Applying Zone Attack Principles to an Existing Zone Attack Offense

Diagram C

Diagram D

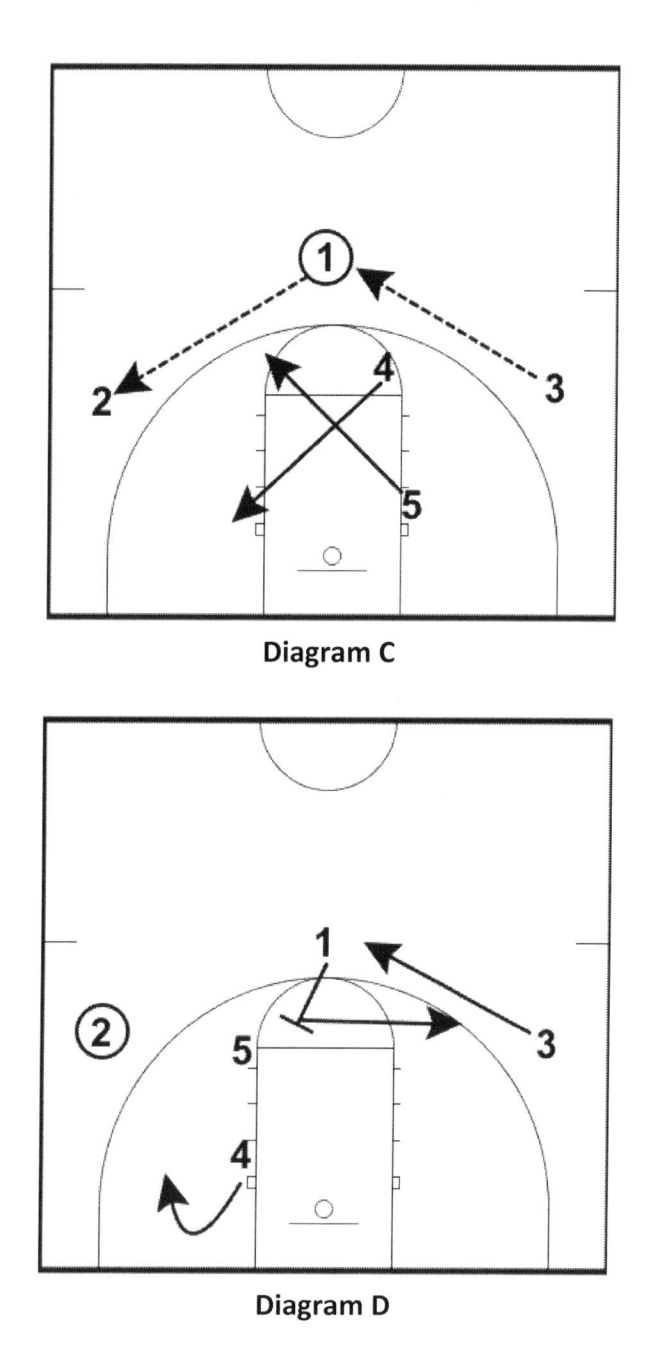

Diagram 20-E depicts the ball being entered to the short post and then skip passed to #1. #5 rolled down the lane looking for a pass from #4 in the space created by the defense being distorted to cover #4 in the short corner. If #5 does not receive the pass from #4, #5 moves to the other side of the lane and posts up on the new ball side.

Diagram E

Diagram F

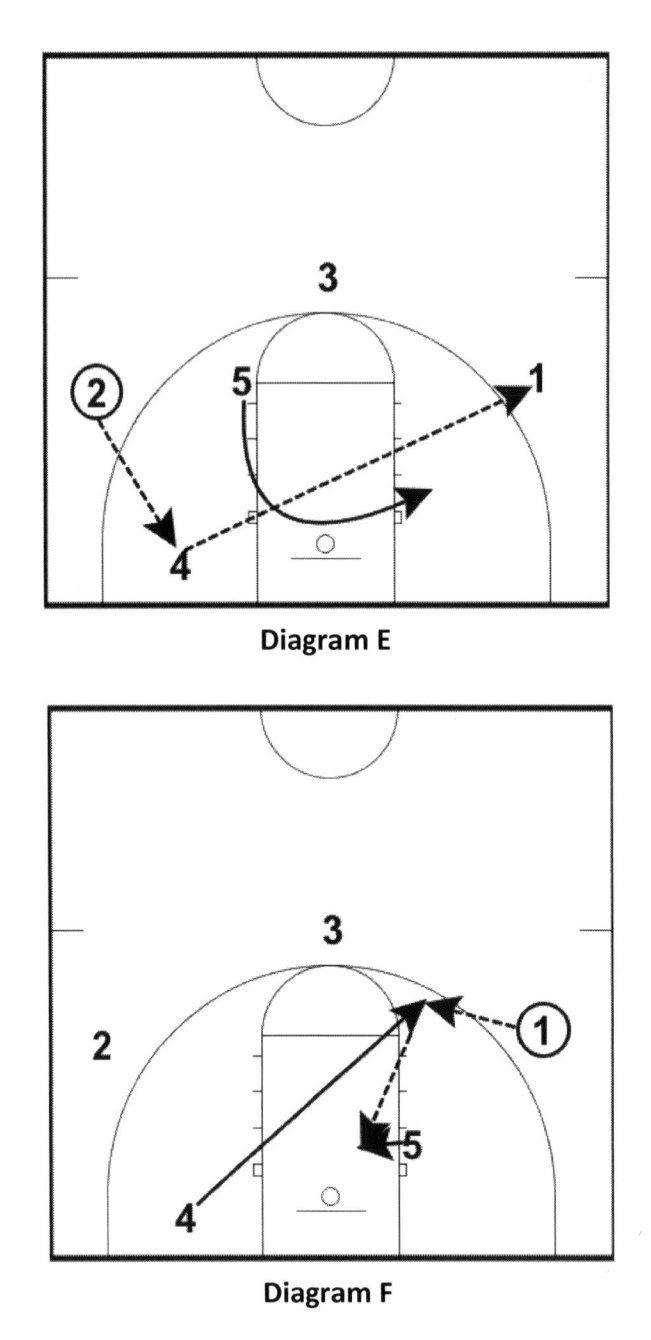

In order to continue running the base offense, #4 flashes into the high post and receives an entry pass from #1 (**Diagram F**). #4 faces-up assertively and #5 steps into the nearest post defender to receive a high low pass for a score.

The offense moves into offensive floor balance to rebound and defend against the fast break. Players #2 and #1 get back for defensive purposes and #3, #4 and #5 form a rebounding triangle (**Diagram G**).

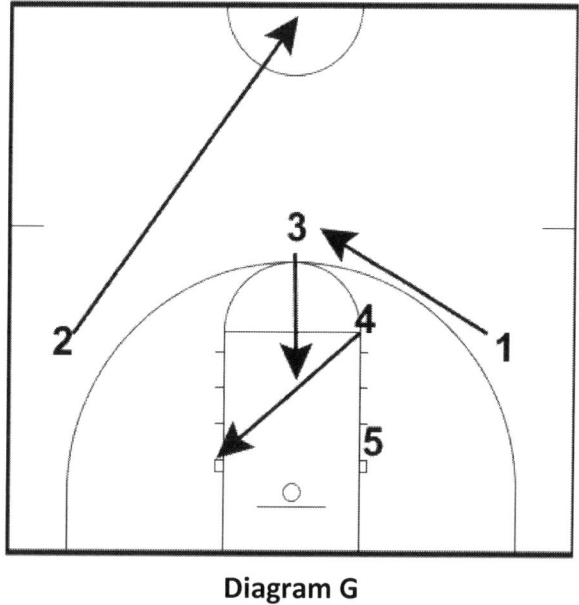

Applying Zone Attack Principles to an Existing Zone Attack Offense

Diagram G

Another example of simple additions to the basic offense is shown in **Diagram 20-H**. #1 executes a dribble loop while #4 and #3 execute a screen-in. #5 posts up on the ball side.

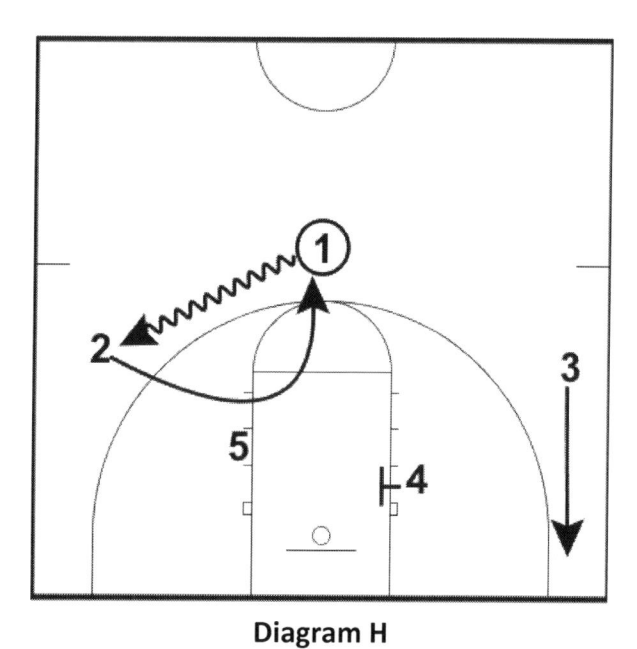

Diagram H

Diagram I

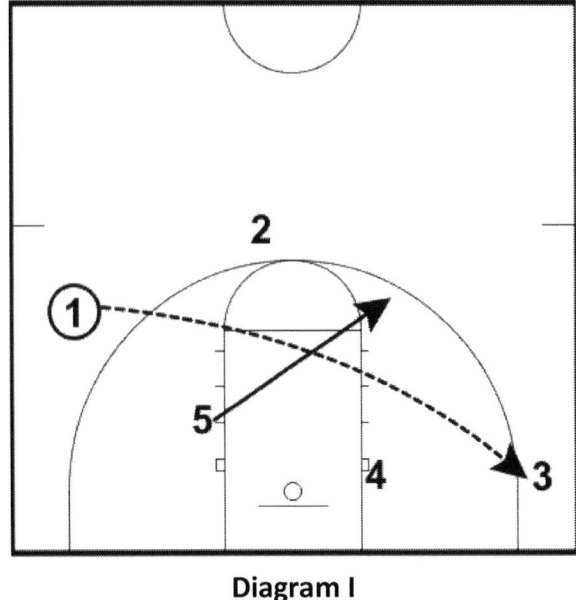

The play continues with a skip pass from #1 to #3. #5 flashes into the ball side high post (**Diagram 20-I**). #3 executes a dribble off while #1 sets a flare screen for #2.

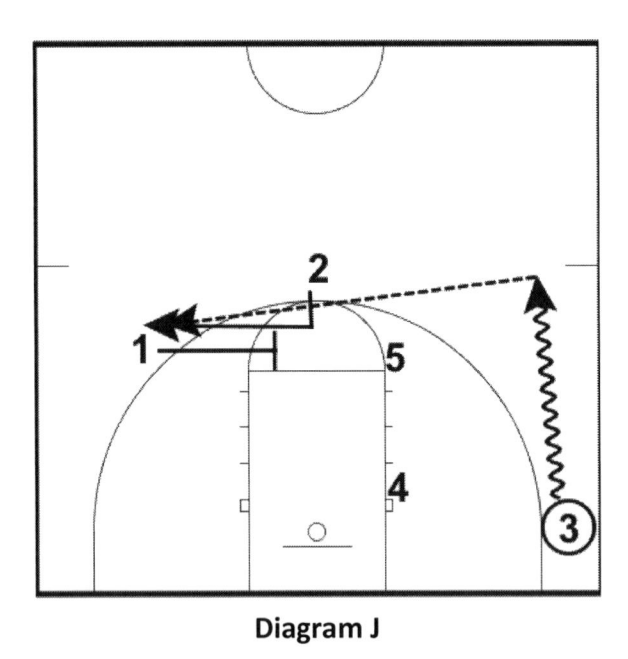

Diagram J

All of the simple additions to the basic offense are combinations of zone attack concepts. By repeating the basic concepts in breakdown form during drill work, players will have little trouble adding these concepts to the basic offense.

31

Thoughts on Teaching and Practicing Zone Attack Offense

Regardless of the offense or defense being used, if the system is sound, the key to the success of the system is the proper execution of the essential fundamental skills at game speed for the benefit of the team. If the system fails, it is not the system, it is the execution of the fundamentals.

Fundamentals might be boring to practice for players and coaches alike but are essential to the success of the offense. Fundamental skills must not only be taught but emphasized. It is not enough to practice fundamentals, the skills must be executed correctly during team concept practice session and games.

Offensive concepts must be broken down into the basic components, taught, mastered and repeated until all players can execute the skills and concepts at game speed for the benefit of the team.

Players need both repetition and variety in practice. A range of drills to teach and practice both individual fundamental skills and team concepts has been provided.

Early in the season use short periods of time for each drill to build intensity and increase the opportunities for large numbers of repetitions in a variety of drills.

Combine drills to create unique situations. The more players are exposed to different situations and allowed to apply the concepts taught to the team, the better the team's problem solving skills will be during games.

Use advantage and disadvantage drills to either allow the offense to have success or have to work harder than normal to succeed. Don't be afraid to create your own drills to teach concepts. Create your own drills by combining or modifying the drills presented here.

If faced with situation of having a weak second string or sub-varsity team to practice against, make practice sessions more challenging by having as many as seven or eight players play defense in a controlled setting. While not exactly game like, this type of practice for brief periods of time does raise the level of challenge required of the first unit to execute properly.

32

Thoughts on Teaching and Practicing Blocker-Mover Zone Attack

Teaching the Blocker-Mover Zone Attack Motion Offense

Learning how Blocker-Mover Offense worked in theory was easier than determining how to teach the offense. For many coaches who are interested in running Motion Offense, the issue of teaching the offense, not simply understanding how the offense should work, is why they do not adopt a motion style of play on offense. With this issue in mind, this chapter might be the most important one in the book.

Considerable planning needs to be done prior to implementing Motion Offense in general and Blocker-Mover in specific. To help develop a plan for teaching Blocker-Mover, the following segments are excellent starting points:

- pre-requisites for teaching a motion system
- Coach Bennett's approach
- my approach
- selecting drills
- thoughts by Coach Don Meyer – also known as Meyerisms

Pre-requisites for Teaching a Motion Offense System

Ask a group of basketball coaches what the most important thing in the game of basketball is and you might get a wide range of answers ranging from rebounding, defense and shooting the ball. All of these are important, but none of these are the correct answer. Possessing a team attitude, a spirit of unity, a willingness to put the welfare and success of the team is the most important thing in the game of basketball. It is also the hardest thing to teach and to instill in players.

Fundamentals are the cornerstone of any sound system of offensive play. This simple fact is magnified where a motion system of play is concerned. Set plays and continuities can generate some success with players who are not fundamentally sound due to the players being forced into areas and positions on the court that will lead to some offensive success.

The same does not hold true with Blocker-Mover. Due to the random, free-lance nature of the movement in Blocker-Mover, the unpredictable nature of movement within the offense, failure to execute fundamentals correctly all the time will result in the offense not working.

Teaching Blocker-Mover offense requires a structured, well thought out plan of teaching players fundamentals, starting with proper footwork and movement skills through developing excellent shooters.

Meyerism: *When the offense fails to work, it is not the fault of the offense, if the system is sound. Rather it is the failure of the players to execute the fundamentals of the game correctly, at game speed and for the benefit of the team that is the problem.*

It should become evident studying Blocker-Mover that motion oriented offense requires a high degree of conditioning. Movers in particular have to be able to move almost constantly and still be able to play with finesse. Blockers, particularly Blockers who play post must have the strength to play a physical style of play for prolonged periods of time. Add a fast break approach to the game and the demands of an assertive, physical defensive style of play, even with a deep substitution pattern, players in this type of system must be in outstanding physical condition.

When selecting an offensive system to run, an important factor to consider is the level of basketball IQ the players involved possess. The more intelligent the group of players, the higher their basketball IQ, the more success the group will have running Blocker-Mover.

If the players have a low basketball IQ, and you as a coach struggle to teach players how to think and understand the game, Blocker-Mover might not be the best offense for you to teach your players.

Teaching Blocker-Mover requires sound teaching skills, a good understanding of sports pedagogy and motor learning, not to mention the ability to provide quality feedback and motivate players to by into the team concept.

Meyerism: *It doesn't matter what you know. It matters what they know.*

Quick Summary of the Pre-requisites to Teach Blocker-Mover:

- Team attitude on the part of all players.
- Sound system of teaching fundamentals of the game combined with mastery of those fundamentals by the players.
- Excellent year round conditioning program.
- Excellent teaching skills on the part of the coach.

Coach Bennett's Approach

Everything Coach Bennett does as a coach is predicated by his five core principles: humility, unity, passion, servanthood and thankfulness. To expand on his philosophy in this book might not be the best venue for coaches. For coaches who are interested in his philosophical approach to coaching, I strongly suggest you obtain two sources of information, one of which is free.

To obtain the free information, simply go to my website, CoachSivils.com, go to the Clinic Notes page of the site, click on the button for Coach Bennett and download the clinic notes labeled LHSCA Coaches Clinic. I personally took these notes and the topics include his five principles, some Blocker-Mover concepts and the genesis of the Pack man-to-man defense. There are some particularly good concepts concerning how to cover screens in these notes.

For a better understanding of his philosophy in action and in practical application, obtain a copy of the book ***A Season With Coach Dick Bennett*** by Eric Ferris. This book is a great look at how the mind of Coach Bennett works as the author Eric Ferris was granted the same kind of access to the Wisconsin Badger program as author John Feinstein was given to the Indiana University program by Coach Bob Knight, the result of which was the infamous book, ***A Season on the Brink***.

Coach Bennett's approach to practice planning centers around his idea that first a coach must prevent his team from losing before the team can win. To Bennett this means two things:

- a team must play great defense.
- the team must take great care of the ball each possession, or as Bennett puts it, "be boss with the ball."

For Bennett the first priority is always defense. Bennett believes 50% of all practice time should be allocated to defense.

On the surface, this may make a lot of coaches scratch their heads. If you spend 50% of your practice time on defense, how do you practice everything else that has to be practiced? Coach John Wooden took the stance that defense needed to have equal emphasis as offense but you spent more time in practice on offense.

Upon closer examination, at least it appeared to me as I learned more about how Coach Bennett went about running practice, Coach Bennett found a way to get his 50% of practice time dedicated to defense and work on everything else that need to be practiced.

Bennett divided practice into thirds, one-third on man-to-man defense, one third to offense and one third to fundamentals. He spent a lot of the fundamental time in practice on individual man-to-man defensive skills and when his players were playing defense during the offense portion of practice, they were still closely scrutinized for the quality of their defense. Bennett found a way to emphasize the importance of defense to his teams.

Meyerism: *Players don't do what you teach them. Players do what you emphasize!*

The first thing coaches comment about after their first encounter with Dick Bennett in person is how humble he is. The second is how intellectual he is in his approach to the game of basketball. In every clinic or coaching school I ever heard Coach Bennett speak at, these three concepts were significant points he always made:

- Dumb the game down.
- If you add something, you have to take something away.
- The more complicated something is, the more you have to teach it piece by piece (part, part, part, part, whole).

Make things as absolutely as simple as possible for your players when you are teaching them. If you have to add something to what you are doing, you must take something out of the system to keep the level of complexity the same. If after all your efforts the system is still complex, then you must teach it to the players one part at a time, building on the foundation you have built.

Blocker-Mover came about as a result of Bennett's desire to simplify things for his players at UW-Green Bay. By creating the Blocker areas and alignments, Bennett simplified the process of who set screens and where the screens would be set. While there may have been five alignments, he never used all five in a season.

Finally, Coach Bennett divided his teaching of offense into two parts. Teaching fundamentals, such as cutting and screening, and teaching whole concept offense. Bennett, like Coach Meyer, believed when the offense did not work it was because the fundamentals of offense, passing, cutting and screening were not being executed. If these were fixed, the offense would work.

The actual practicing and teach of the Blocker-Mover offense was done with a great deal of 5-on-0 work. Bennett believed for players to understand the offense in its entirety, it had to be worked on with a five player unit. Practicing the offense without defense allowed the players to gain familiarity with the process and the options, to learn to work together and to perfect their timing.

If problems developed with a specific part of the offense, Bennett would "repair" the problem during fundamental work. For example, if the Movers were not coming off the screens to his satisfaction, leaving space between the Blockers where defenders could slip screens, then particular attention would be paid to making certain the Blockers and Movers set and used screens to perfection in the next session on fundamental work for offense.

A Quick Summary of Coach Bennett's Approach:

- Bennett centers everything around humility, unity, passion, servanthood and thankfulness.
- Dumb the game down.
- If you add something, you have to take something away (if you add an alignment for a game, you must eliminate, for that game, the use of one of the other alignments).
- The more complicated something is, the more you have to teach it piece by piece (part, part, part, part, whole).
- If something in the offense is not working, correct it during fundamental work.

Thoughts by Coach Don Meyer

Coach Meyer was fascinated by many of the ideas of Coach Bennett and often incorporated parts of Bennett's thinking into what he did with his own system of play.

Meyerism: *You can get all the good ideas. You just can't use them all.*

Coach Meyer would take what he believed would work in his system with his players and "borrow" those parts of Bennett's system that worked for him. Meyer in particular liked the ideas behind the Blocker-Mover system of offense but was not inclined to use the alignments, confining his Blockers to specific areas of the court.

This in part was due to the fact Meyer's team, at this particular time in history the Lipscomb University Bisons, played at an extreme up-tempo pace, something Bennett coached teams were notorious for not doing.

Coach Meyer also referred to his version of Blocker-Mover as "cutters and screeners." His reasoning was "we stole the idea from Bennett, but we have to make it our own."

While Coach Meyer may have not used the alignments with assigned Blocker areas, he did have three concepts he was adamant his players use when attacking a zone:
- Distort the zone

- Screen the zone
- Move the ball and move people

Meyer, like Bennett, was an absolute believer in the concept if the offense was not working or struggling in some way, if the offense was sound in concept, the problems lay not with the offense, but the execution of the fundamentals by the players.

A Quick Summary of Coach Don Meyer's Thoughts on Zone Attack Offense:

- Fix offensive problems by fixing the execution of the necessary fundamentals.
- Distort the zone
- Screen the zone
- Move the ball and move people

My Approach

Team is the most important concept in the game of basketball. As far as I am concerned it is not open for debate. Team concept is integral to Blocker-Mover offense.

Players are willing to accept being Movers without a lot of convincing. Some players are happy to accept the role of being Blockers. Often the players who readily accept the role of being a Blocker would not see much playing time otherwise. The players who see themselves as Movers, not Blockers whose job is to get other players open to score, this can be a bitter pill to swallow for some players, even though Blockers often score a great deal in this system of play.

When players have bought into the team concept and made the individual decision to put the team first and their needs and desires second, it makes the entire process of installing and perfecting Blocker-Mover offense much easier.

I wish there was a step-by-step process to instilling the team concept that worked with each player and each team every season. What I do know is that a constant, daily, heavy emphasis on the team concept, why it is so important and all the different ways it manifests itself is what works for me.

You Get What You Emphasize

Players seldom do what their coach teaches. Players always do what their coach emphasizes. Paying lip service to concepts as important as team attitude, mastery and execution of basic fundamentals, work ethic, sound offensive and defensive play will not produce players or teams who demonstrate these traits.

A coach must emphasize the concepts important to the program, the success of the team and the development of the players. Playing a self-centered, selfish player while verbally stressing the team concept teaches players raw ability is more important than demonstrating a team first attitude.

Playing time is one of the best ways to emphasize what is important. Sitting down a self-centered, selfish player for lack of team play sends a message to every player on the team. If you want playing time, you must demonstrate a team attitude.

Sitting players down for failure to execute team concepts sends a powerful message. Attaching both positive and negative consequences to concepts taught and practiced in daily practice sessions is another way to emphasize essential concepts of any kind.

Consistency is essential. Players watch their coach like a child watches their parents. Players, like children, learn almost as much by observing their coach's attitude, actions and choices as they learn from direct instruction from their coach. *Always be aware, players will do what you emphasize, not what you teach!*

Fundamentals are King

Coaches talk about fundamentals. Coaches often preach fundamentals. But they don't emphasize fundamentals. When asked why the response is almost always the same, "we just don't have the time in practice."

First, let's revisit the earlier concept of the importance of what is emphasized. *Players do not do what their coaches say to do, they do what their coaches emphasize!*

Why do coaches fail to teach fundamentals? Several reasons include:

- The inability to actually teach fundamentals.
- It is difficult to both teach fundamental skills and insist players master the skills and execute them.
- Laziness.
- Teaching X's and O's and running offense and defense is how coaches show their knowledge. Besides, the X's and O's are the fun stuff.
- Some coaches really believe there is not enough time to teach the essential fundamentals.

Yet, what is one of the commonalities of all championship programs in team sports, regardless of the sport? All of these programs, year after year, are fundamentally sound. The coaches who run these programs do not pay lip service to the importance of fundamentals, they emphasize fundamentals.

These successful programs season after season, set screens, make cuts, catch the ball, make their lay-ups and free throws and defend. These teams block and tackle. They field, throw and hit. These teams win because they have mastered the fundamentals and can execute these skills in game settings, at game speed and in game conditions. Their coaches emphasized the importance of mastery of fundamentals!

How did these coaches find the time to teach fundamentals to the point of mastery and the offensive and defensive systems needed to win games? Through careful practice planning, wise selection of drills that taught and reinforced both fundamentals and offense and defense, and last of all, while executing the "fun stuff" the players were required to execute fundamentals.

Another common trait all of these programs have that is directly linked to the emphasis and mastery of fundamental skills. All of these winning programs play with confidence! The confidence that comes from each player
knowing he or she has mastered, and demonstrated that mastery, the essential skills and fundamentals needed for that player to execute his or her portion of the play.

Then there is the wonderful effect of the synergy of all of the individual confidence of each player merged into the group. It is truly a wondrous thing to watch a group of confident individual players who possess a strong team identity and who know that each individual player can, and will, execute successfully their responsibility for the welfare and success of the team, multiply their individual confidence levels by merging their skills for the good of the group!

Have you ever watched a basketball team trailing by one with seconds remaining calmly set up for their last shot, knowing they would not only get their best shooter open for a good shot, but that the ball would arrive at just the right time and the shooter will make the shot? Many an opponent has faced such a team, knowing their best defensive effort won't be good enough. Why? Because the opponent lacked the confidence necessary to disrupt the confident team.

These teams possess this type of confidence because the players have mastered, at the instance of their coaches, the fundamentals of the game.

Use a Hybrid Bennett Approach to Teaching Blocker-Mover

Coach Bennett believes for players to learn and master Blocker-Mover a great deal of 5-on-0 work must be done. To an extent I agree with him. While this approach clearly works for the inventor of the offense, my players struggled with this approach to teaching the system when not combined with a few other specific modifications to the 5-on-0 approach.

The hybrid approach I eventually fell into, thanks to the advice of Coach Meyer, was to work 5-on-0 initially and then to add a limited number of zone defenders. This was a huge benefit for my players.

Working against two, three, four and eventually five zone defenders allowed my players to concentrate on specific skills and offensive building blocks before having to actually attack a full zone defense. Many of the drills included in this book work against a limited number of zone defenders, particularly drills intended to teach and practice specific zone attack concepts.

Use Restrictions to Teach

Perhaps the most famous advocate for using restrictions to teach offense is Coach Bob Knight. Restrictions are a wonderful tool. The offense is instructed it can only be successful by executing the offense in accordance to the restriction or restrictions mandated. Some examples I like to use include:

- designating the player (a specific Mover or Blocker) who is to take the shot.
- establishing a specific number of screens to be set prior to a shot being taken.
- requiring a specific number of side-to-side ball reversals before a shot is taken.
- designating the zone attack tactic or rule to be used to generate the shot.

These are just a few of the nearly infinite number of possible restrictions that can be used to teach. Simply create a set of guidelines, restrictions that will produce the desired type of play.

Use Offensive Building Blocks to Teach and Problem Solve

Habits are essential for basketball players. Habits allow players to play without thinking about each specific movement made, thus slowing them down to the point of being ineffective.

Given the unlimited possible combinations of screens, cuts and penetration opportunities in Blocker-Mover offense, using what I call "offensive building blocks" makes sense.

Screening and cutting situations are created in such a way that the result is typical of what type of action can occur. The same can be done with dribble use rules and Movers hunting gaps and Blockers.

By placing players in the positions where they will repeat the myriad of two and three player combinations that make up all of the potential offensive situations they may use in Blocker-Mover zone attack, they will create habits that allow them to run the offense on autopilot. It is also necessary to work on these tactics against two, three, four and finally five defender zones.

By adding defense to the drills, offensive building blocks can be used to teach players how to problem solve. For example, the opponent's star post player is in foul trouble. The objective is to put another foul on the star post player. To do this, the player the star is guarding needs to obtain possession of the ball in an area likely to draw a foul.

33

Drills to Teach Key Offensive Fundamentals

This chapter includes numerous drills designed to teach essential, basic fundamental skills. Not only are the physical skills included in the drills, but many of the drills require players to combine multiple skills, forcing a higher level of mental processing similar to what a player must be able to do during a game.

By no means are all the drills in this chapter the only way to teach basic skills but they are excellent drills. Please use them as described or feel free to use these drills as a starting point for creation of drills that will fit the exact specific needs of your players, team and program.

A word of warning, never adopt a drill simply because you read it in a book, saw it demonstrated at a coaching clinic or on a DVD. Only use drills that exactly fit your system and teach the fundamentals needed by your players to run your offensive and defensive system.

Basic Movement Drills

UCLA Coach John Wooden thought the skills in these drills were so important he included them in every practice, regardless of the stage of the season.

The skills covered in these drills include change of pace, v-cutting (change of direction), start steps, jump stops, pivots (turns), step lunges and can include defensive skills such as closeouts.

Coaching Basketball's Zone Attack Offense Using Blocker-Mover Motion Offense

Diagram A   Diagram B

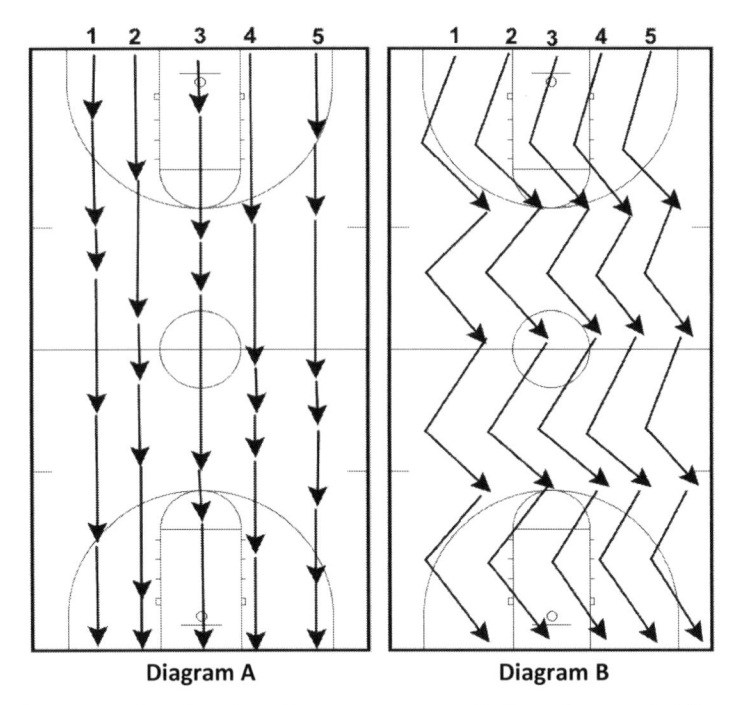

Diagram A depicts the basic alignment used for these drills. Lines of players can be formed across the baseline and the entire court utilized. If space is limited and large numbers of players must be accommodated, the lines can be moved to the sidelines instead. Groups as large as 20 to 25 players can be accommodated on the baseline in most gyms. Each set of skills should be executed twice, meaning the players should make a trip down the court and back. *This is an excellent drill to use immediately at the start of practice to warm the muscles prior to stretching.*

Diagram A also shows players executing "change of pace." Change of pace is a concept that actually requires a good deal of practice. Standing still, jogging, accelerating, decelerating and sprinting are all components of changing pace. Basketball players must master this simple, but not always easy, skill in order to be effective on offense. A key coaching point is to remind players this drill is neither a contest nor a race and standing still is one of the things they must do when executing this drill.

Diagram B depicts the players executing v-cuts en masse. Note, all of the players start by going to their right. This is to prevent injuries due to collision. Players enter the v-cut (change of direction) moving slowly, plant the foot opposite the direction they intend to cut towards, lower their hips, explode in the opposite direction and quickly raise their hands to provide an appropriate hand target for the passer. If players do not master this skill, they will not be able to properly utilize screens to get open in any offense.

Players move on their own, v-cutting as they move down the court. The next line starts when the preceding line is about 15 feet down the court.
Players must "cover distance," meaning moving horizontally at least 15 to 17 feet, and the cut must be at an angle, not a curve. If the player does not cover 15 to 17

feet horizontally, the defense will have an easy time recovering and denying the cutter the ball. Cutting with a curve and not an angle does not produce a sharp, defined change in direction. This poor technique will also allow a defender to make an easy recover and deny a pass to an offensive player.

Diagram C   Diagram D

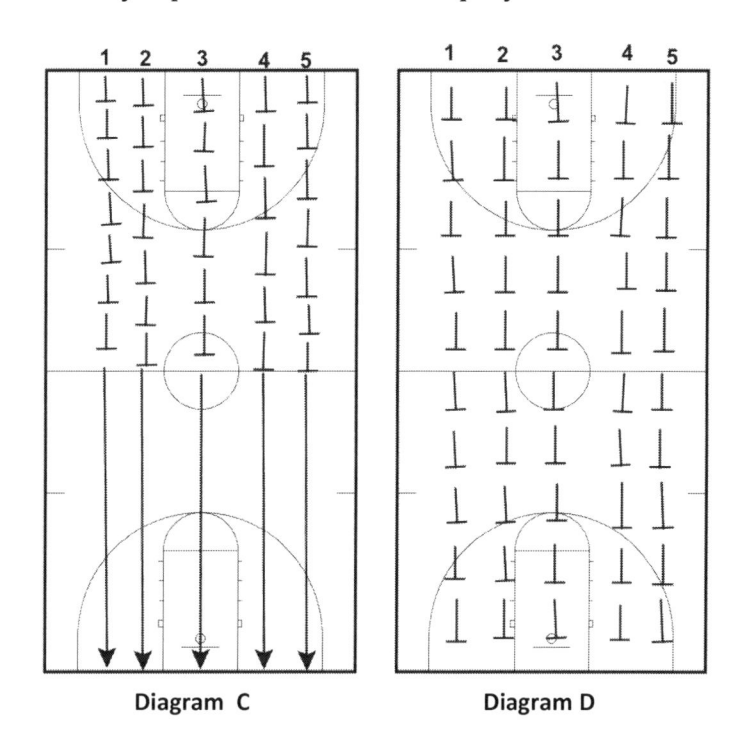

Diagram C depicts players executing step lunges. While not a skill that will be used during a game, step lunges emphasize long, low steps and help players develop balance, flexibility and the long low
and straight step required for either a direct drive or a crossover move. Players must have their hands up, palms out, elbows extensions of their shoulders and the backs of the player's hands should be visible. This further enhances balance and helps to develop the proper hand positioning when a player is posting up. Once the players reach half court they jog to the other end of the court.

Start steps, jump stops (stops) and turns (pivots) are practiced as the last drill in the movement drill series (**Diagram D**). Players execute a long, low start step from a triple threat stance. Players may execute either a direct drive or a crossover step as indicated by the coach or simply decide for themselves which to practice.

Players execute a hop off the foot used to make the long, low start step. Players then execute a jump stop off the hop, making certain the hop is neither overly long or high and both feet come in contact with the court at the same time, allowing for either foot to be used as a pivot foot. Players land softly and in a triple threat stance.

After landing, the player executes a turn or pivot. There are two basic types of turns that can be executed on either foot. A front turn, or pivot, is a turn made towards the front of the player. A rear turn is made towards the rear of the player. Turns can either be left or right footed.

A turn is executed by lifting the heel of the foot to be pivoted on. At the same time the player shifts slightly more weight to the pivot foot and uses the ball of the foot as the pivot point. The opposite leg
is "whipped" around, providing the momentum to complete a 180-degree turn.

The player must stay low through out the entire turn. The key to this is for players to maintain a low, wide base while turning and to keep their head centered between the knees and the chin level. Standing up during a pivot is the worst mistake a player can make in executing a pivot as the player will turn slower and lose balance, requiring more time as the player returns to a good triple threat stance with a wide, low base of body support.

Players move down the court executing long, low start steps, jump stops followed by turns. Of all the movement skills, this series is the most important. Once the preceding group has made two sets of starts, stops and turns the next group may begin.

Fundamental Lines

Fundamental lines is a series of drills designed to practice essential fundamentals, provide a high number of repetitions in a short period of time, build intensity and force players to concentrate on execution. The drills shown in this section can be run from the baseline, the ideal location, or the sideline if space and numbers dictate. Players ideally are in groups of three with a ball but groups of four or five are acceptable.

Diagram A

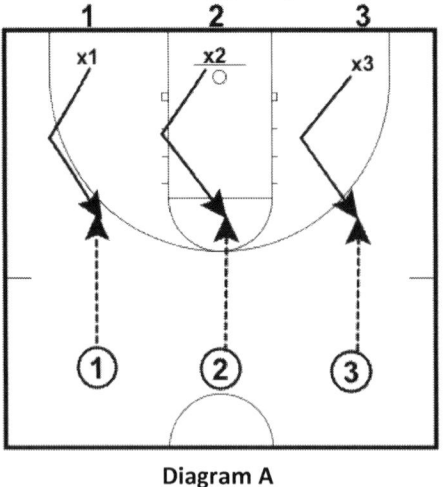

Diagrams A and B depict the drill sequence known as "easy running." This is drill is not meant to be performed at a high rate of speed and is a good warm-up for the more intense drills in this sequence. The first half of the sequence is shown in **Diagram A** as the players on the baseline execute v-cuts. The passers are located near half court and pass to the cutter using their weak hand. Upon catching the pass, the cutter lands in triple threat and executes a weak hand pass back to the passer.

Diagram B

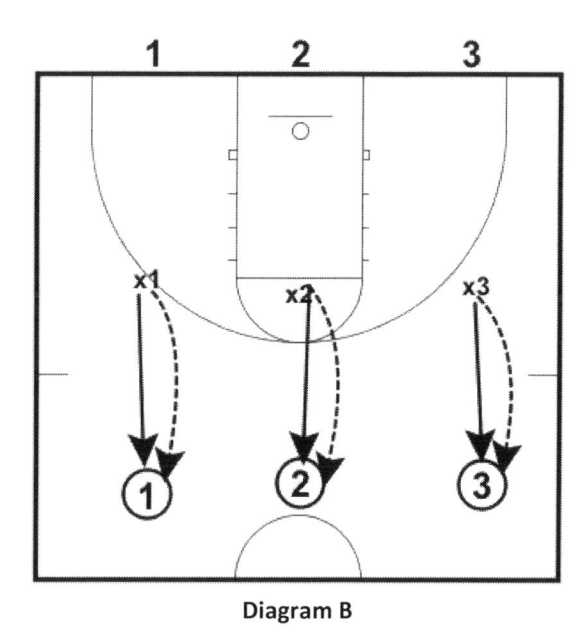

The cutter follows the pass to the passer and executes a jump stop into triple threat and takes an exchange from the passer, who is in triple threat with the ball, by pulling the ball from the grasp of the passer and then executing a rear turn. The passer moves out of bounds and hustles to the end of the cutter line on the baseline.

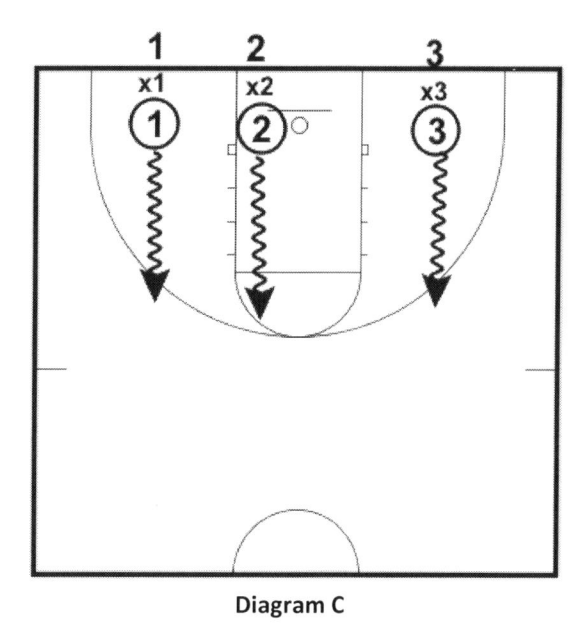

Diagram C

The next sequence in fundamental lines is "live ball." Transition to this second sequence by verbally calling "live ball." The player with the ball in each group, at that time, passes the ball to the first player in line, follows the pass and closes out on the ball.

Diagram C depicts how the live ball series starts. The first player in line executes a two-inch up fake or pass fake and then executes a long, low, straight start step, either a direct drive or a crossover. The player is to travel as far as possible with two dribbles, jump stop and execute a rear turn (pivot) in triple threat position. The player then passes the ball to the next player in line using a weak hand pass.

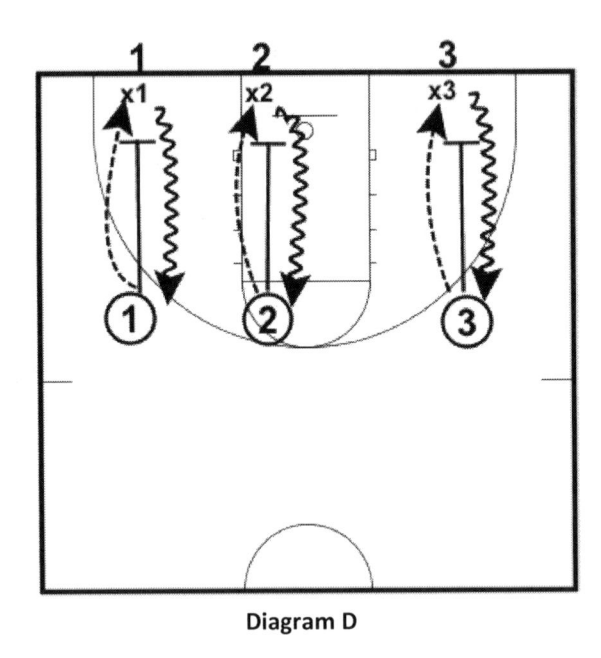

Diagram D

The player receiving the pass steps to the pass to shorten the pass. A good measure for a player or coach to determine if this happens is for the receiving player to be out of bounds when the pass is made and to catch the ball inbounds. The receiver catches the ball in triple threat position with a low, wide, base of balance and support.

The passer follows the pass and executes a defensive closeout. The receiver then executes a live ball move and takes two dribbles, executes a rear turn and makes a weak hand pass back to the next player. The sequence continues until the players are told to progress to the next series (**Diagram D**).

Drills to Teach Key Offensive Fundamentals

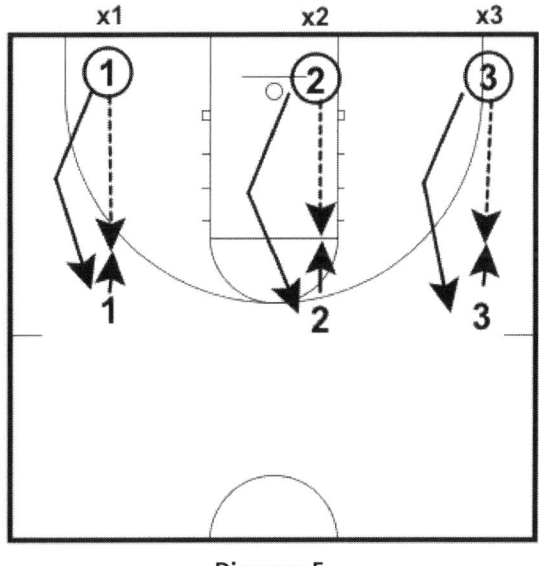

Diagram E

Diagram E depicts the start of the third, and most mentally challenging, phase of the fundamental lines series known as flick passing. Players transition from the live ball series by having a player execute the live ball move followed by two dribbles and pass the ball back to the first player on the baseline. This sequence must always start with the ball in the group of players with at least two players. The player who just executed the live ball move remains 15 to 18 feet away and awaits a return pass to start the sequence.

Following the transition from one drill to the next, the drill starts with the player with the ball on the baseline passing to the single player opposite. In the examples shown in **Diagrams E and F** the players are using a right hand pass to pass away from the defense.

All groups must start with the same pass. The passer follows the pass with a v-cut and a jump stop and rear turn behind the player who just received the ball. By starting the drill with all players using the same hand to pass with, collisions and injuries will be avoided.

The receiver must take a step to meet, or shorten, the pass. The receiver then repeats the procedure of the passer who initiated the drill.

The drill continues until the coach gives the order to change hands being passed with. The drill continues without stopping, players simply change passing hands and the side to which players execute their v-cut. The key rule for players to remember for purposes of safety is to cut to the side of the hand the player passed with.

Coaching Basketball's Zone Attack Offense Using Blocker-Mover Motion Offense

Diagram F

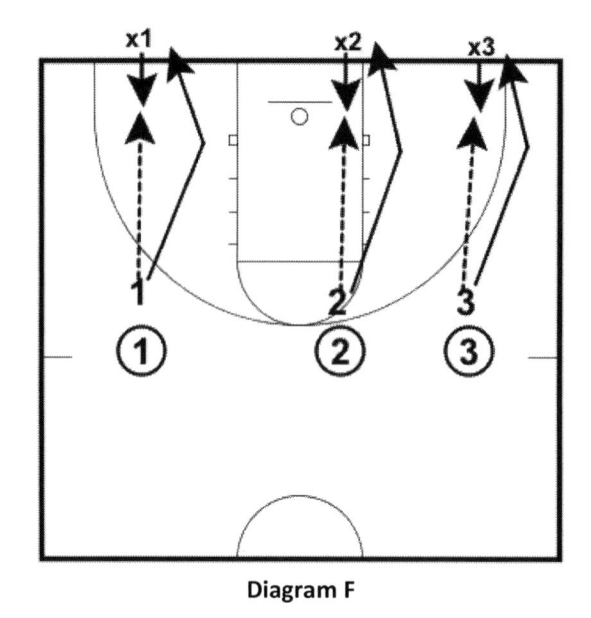

Basic Ball Handling

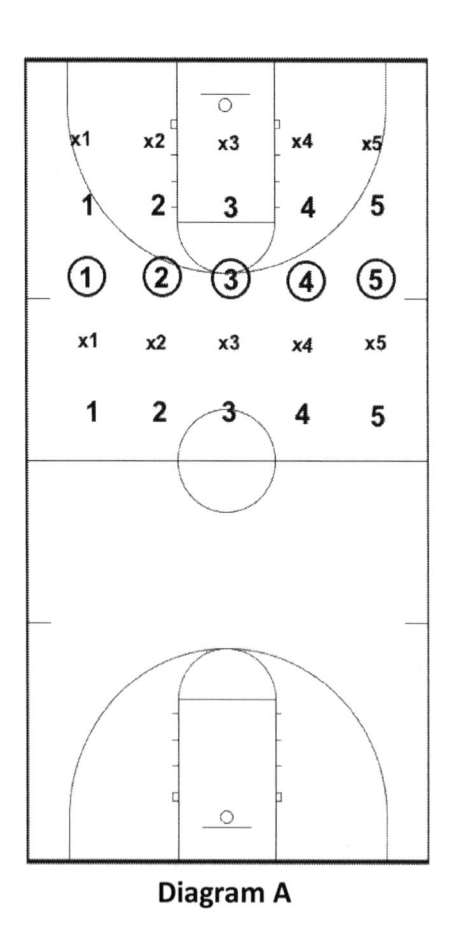

Diagram A

240

The players shown in **Diagram A** depict a formation to use for basic ball handling drills. Each player can have a ball or pairs of players can share a ball. The coach has the players execute on command whatever stationary ball handling drills the coach wants performed.

1-on-0 Face-ups

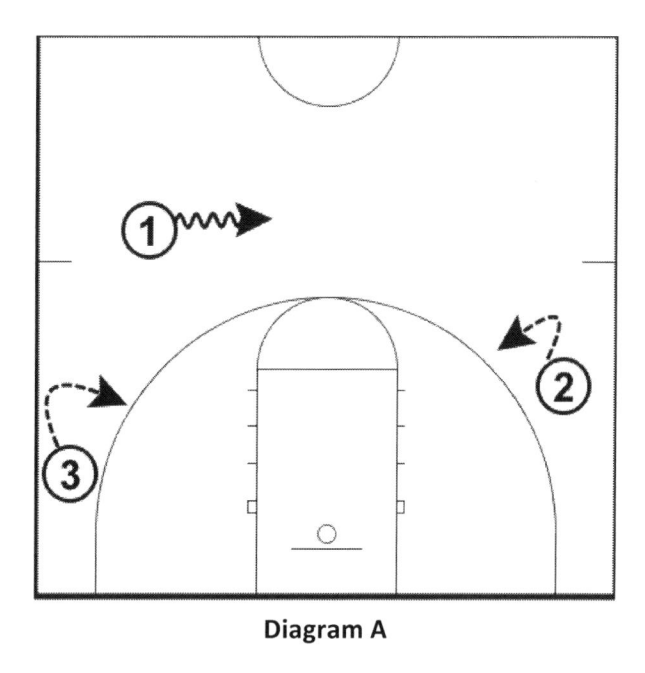

Diagram A

Every player is given a ball and the players quickly spread out over the court and select a goal as their offensive end of the court. Players may take one or two dribbles and then assertively face-up on their inside foot and look under their basket.

Players may pass the ball to themselves by tossing the ball out six to eight feet with considerable backspin and move hard to shorten the pass. After catching the self-pass the player assertively faces-up on the inside foot (**Diagram A**). This drill allows for the entire team to practice face-ups at one time and exercise some creativity in the process.

2-on-0 Face-ups

Players partner up and obtain a ball. The groups of two spread out at the goal in the gym. Players may v-cut to get open, moving a distance of 15-18 feet and receive a pass from the partner with the ball. The receiver then assertively faces-up and looks under the net (**Diagram A**).

Coaching Basketball's Zone Attack Offense Using Blocker-Mover Motion Offense

Diagram A

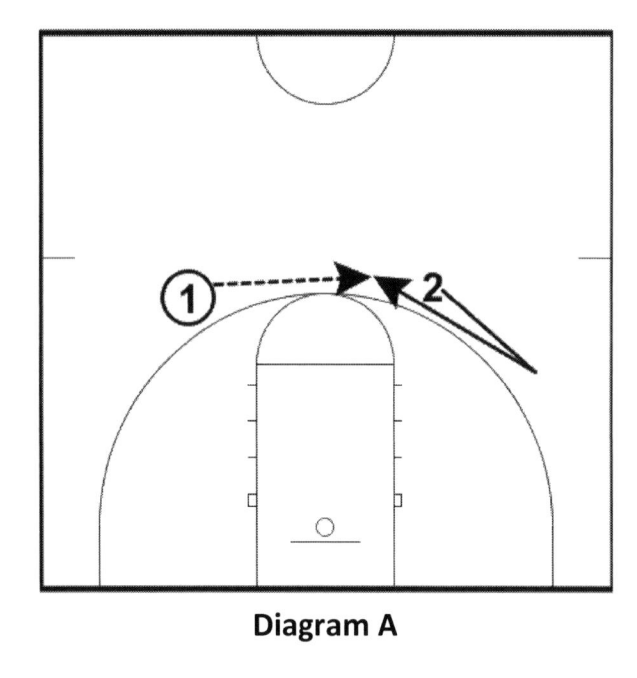

The other method players may practice in this drill is the dribble follow. The ball handler takes one or two dribbles with the partner following. The ball handler picks up the dribble, faces-up, shot or pass fakes and then passes the ball away from the defense to his or her partner (**Diagram B**).

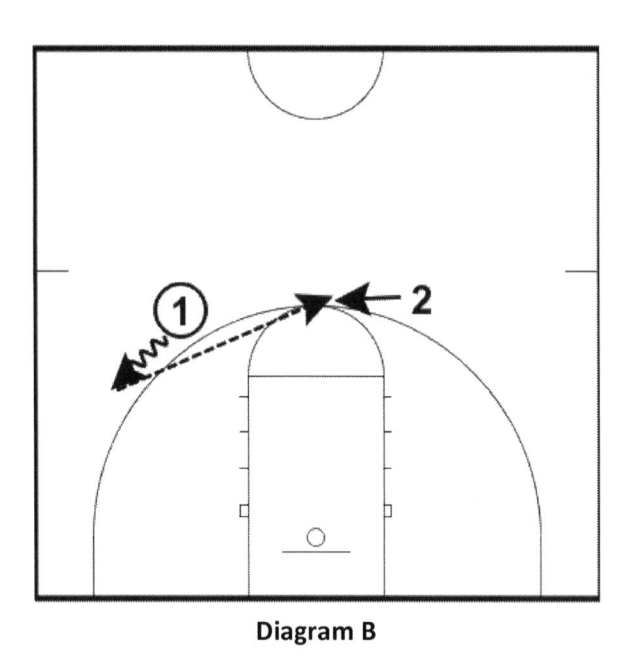

Diagram B

Number 6
Circle Face-ups

Circle face-ups allows for large numbers of players to practice footwork and face-ups at the same time. Players form a circle around a goal. On the whistle or verbal command from the coach, all players move in the same direction. On the second whistle players execute a face-up using correct footwork. Players may face-up off the dribble (**Diagram A**) or off a self-pass (**Diagram B**).

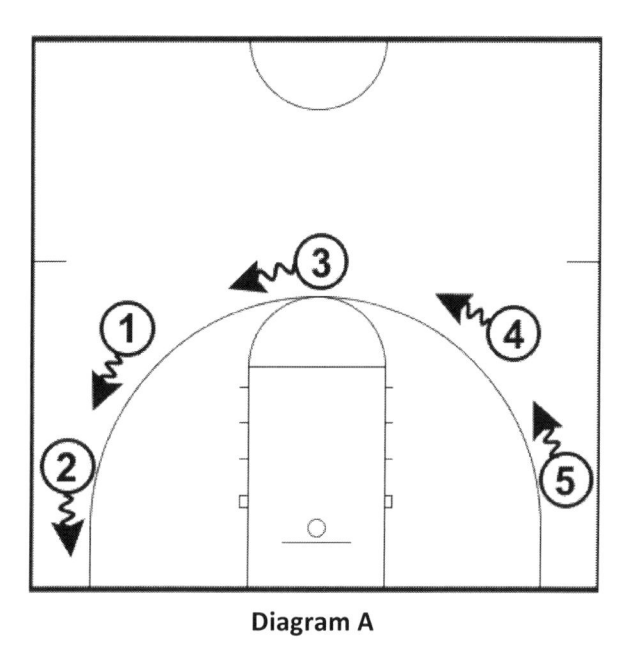

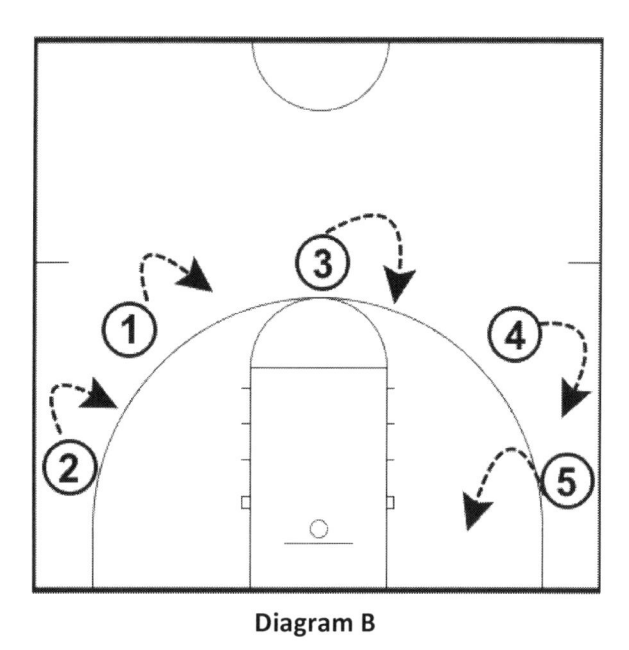

Diagram A

Diagram B

Number 7
One Bounce Lay-ups

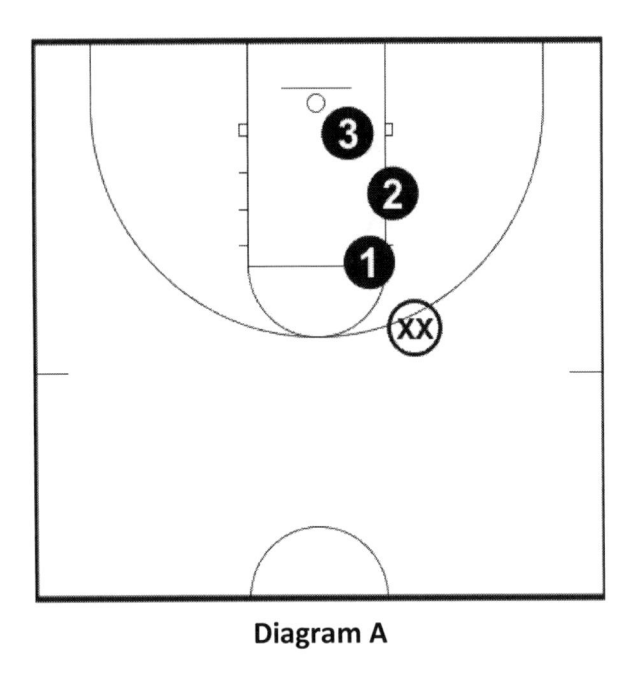

Diagram A

One-bounce lay-ups is an excellent drill to teach players with no basketball experience how to shoot lay-ups correctly. It can also be used to generate a high number of repetitions for players in a short period of time.

Diagram A shows the basic footwork used for the drill. The player starts from the XX location. The play may take three steps with the first step being with the inside foot. The player jumps off the inside foot on the third step. The three steps are indicated with numbered blackened circles. The player dribbles once with the outside hand, chins the ball with elbows out and shoots the ball high soft off the glass.

Diagram B depicts the same footwork from the left side of the goal. Depending on the ability of the player, the distance of the starting point may be varied. Key coaching points include using the terminology of inside and outside to describe the footwork and hand to be used to dribble and shoot with. The players must start in triple threat position and use a long, low start step to begin their approach.

Players can coach themselves when learning how to shoot a lay-up. If the player always takes three steps and the first one is with the inside foot, the player will always execute the footwork correctly.

One-bounce lay-ups can be used to generate a high number of repetitions for a large number of players in a short period of time. By creating groups of four players to a goal with each player having a ball, the players can shoot lay-ups as rapidly as each player can shoot a lay-up, retrieve the ball and hustle to the other side of the court to shoot another lay-up.

Drills to Teach Key Offensive Fundamentals

Diagram B

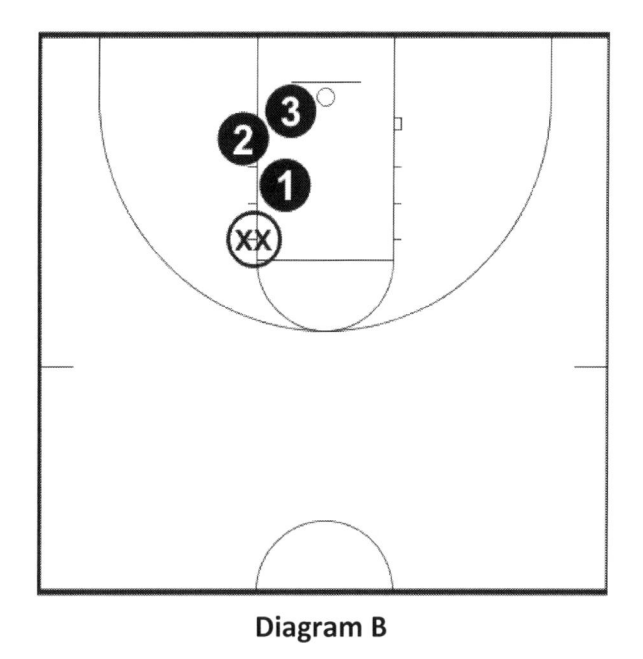

Number 8
Partner Lay-ups

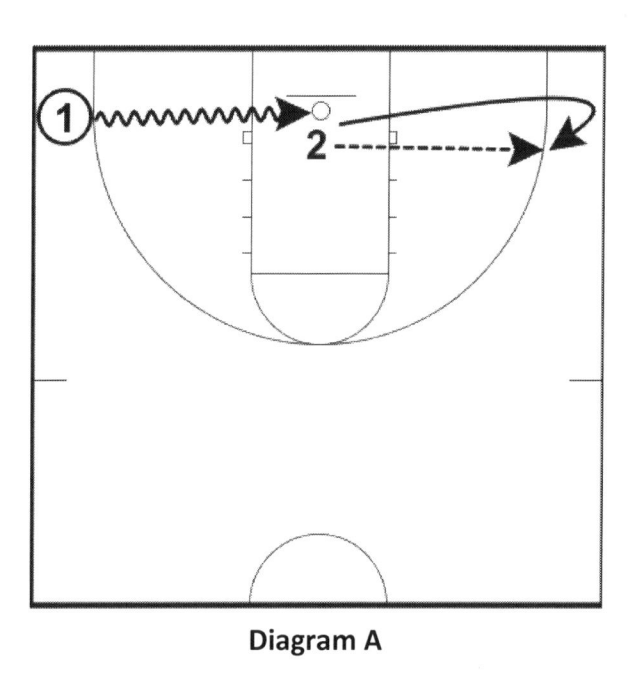

Diagram A

    Diagram A depicts the basic pattern of Partner Lay-ups. The shooter, #1, drives for a lay-up. #2 rebounds the lay-up while #1 cuts hard to the other side of the court. #1 receives the pass by meeting the pass and assuming the triple threat position behind the three-point line. #1 then drives the basket again, repeating the process as depicted in **Diagram B**.

245

Diagram B

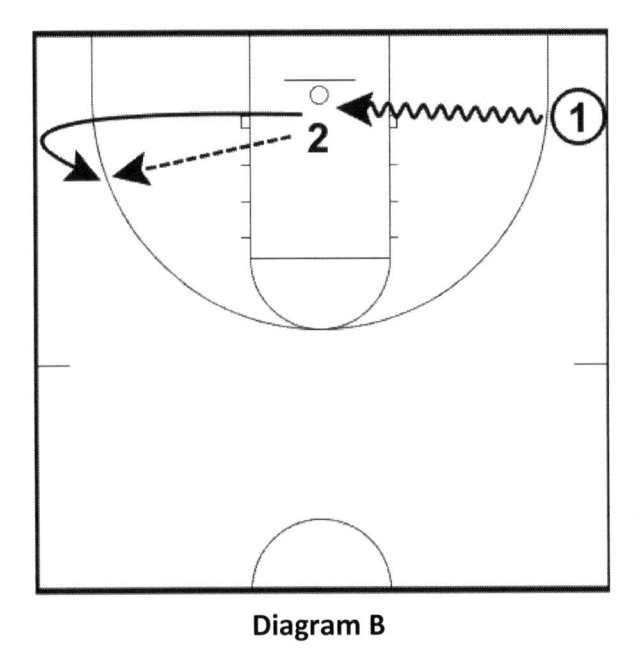

Key coaching points include the following: the shooter tries to execute the drive with traveling with only one dribble, the ball must be shot high soft off the glass and the drive must be initiated from the triple threat position with a long, low start step.

The players work against the clock, starting with one minute and working up to 1.5 minutes. The rebounder keeps track of the number of made lay-ups and missed lay-ups. A target number of lay-ups for the players to make should be set prior to the start of the drill.

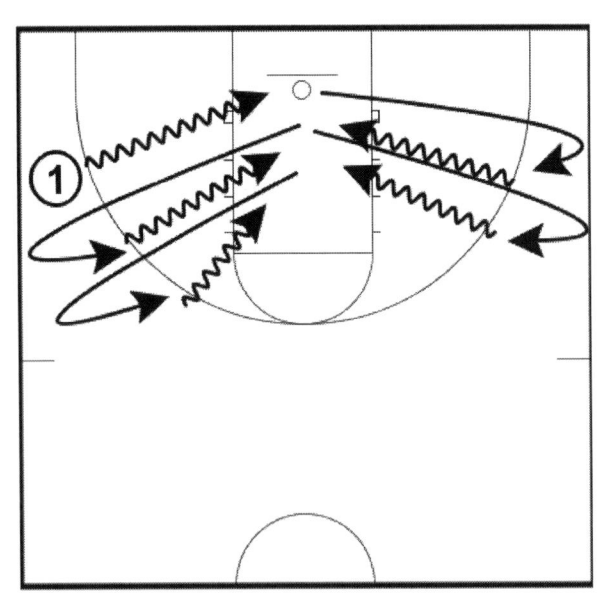

Diagram C

Once the players have mastered the drill, only lay-ups made with perfect technique should be counted as made lay-ups. As the player continues through the drill, the angle of approach moves over slightly for each lay-up attempt as shown in

Diagram C. As the time allotted expires the player will have attacked the goal from 15-20 different approach angles, making the drill extremely game like.

After the first player has gone the partners switch roles with the first shooter rebounding. Two pairs of players can work at the same goal. If six goals are available in a gym a total of 24 players can participate in this drill allowing a large number of lay-ups to be attempted in a three-minute period.

Number 9
Two Line Lay-ups

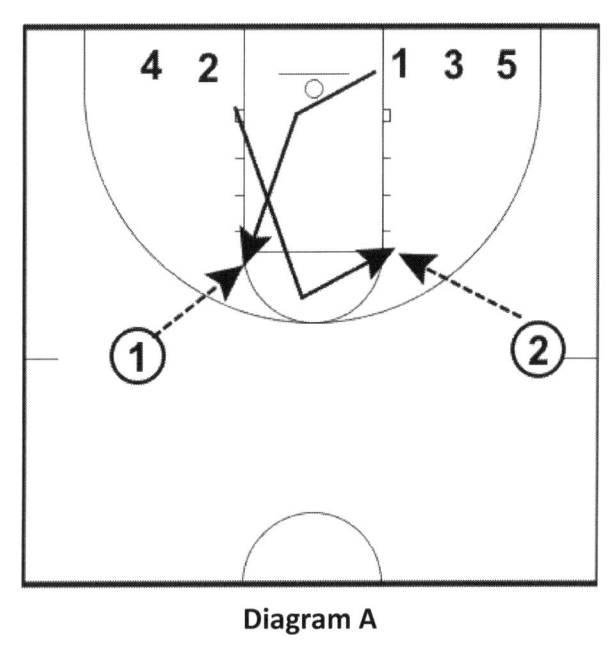

Diagram A

Unlike most versions of two line lay-ups, this drill is highly productive and efficient, working on several skills at the same time. **Diagram A** depicts how the drill is set-up. Coaches or players can act as the two passers.

The cutters make v-cuts to get open in the high post. Notice the different type of v-cut taken by each of the two cutters. It is important for safety reasons to utilize two different v-cuts in order to prevent injuries due to collisions.

NOTE, this is not the primary reason why two different v-cuts are used. The shooters are practicing getting open against a single defender or finding gaps in a zone defense. In a game, if the defender is playing below the line of the ball (the imaginary line between the ball and the offensive player), the cutter must first take the defender down and then v-cut up towards the ball. If the defender is playing above the line of the ball, the cutter must first take the defender up and then cut under the defender.

In **Diagram 9-B** #1 is working against a defender who is playing below the line of the ball and makes a down v-cut. #2 is working against a defender who is defending on or above the line of the ball and makes an up v-cut. The cutter must provide the correct hand target for the passer, call for the ball and meet the pass.

Upon receiving the ball the shooter can either execute a drop step to the goal and shoot a one-bounce lay-up or square up on the inside foot, shot fake, and drive for a lay-up. Be sure to alternate the v-cut used by each of the two lines. Both power lay-ups and running lay-ups can be practiced with this drill.

After making the lay-up the shooter rebounds the ball and passes back to the passer the shooter received the ball from as shown in **Diagram B**. The shooter then moves to the end of the opposite line.

To make the drill as efficient as possible, keep the groups at each goal to no more than 4 to 6 players with two passers if more than one goal is available for practice. Stress technique and execution.

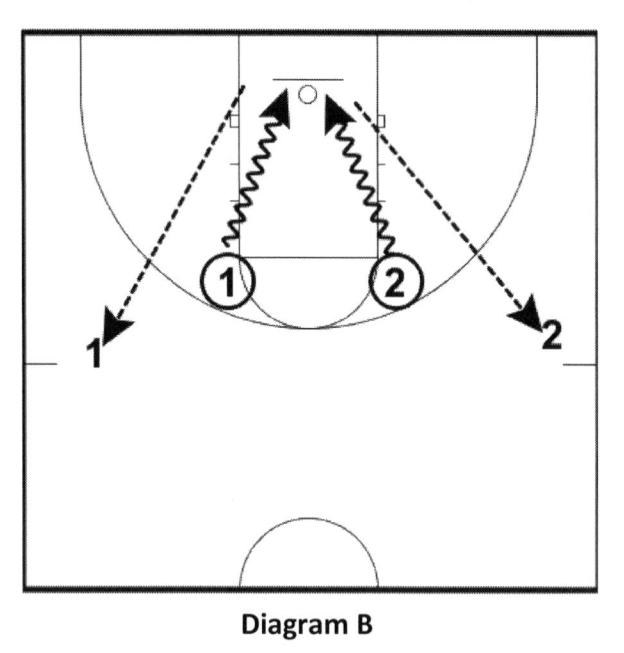

Diagram B

Number 10
Power Shooting

Players form pairs and take a ball and move quickly to a basket. Each player takes power shots close in to the basket while pointing his or her toes at the baseline to learn to shoot the ball with their shoulder protecting the ball from being blocked by a defender.

The shooter must kiss the ball off the glass using a high soft angle to bank the shot. The shooter rebounds all of his, or her, own shots. After ten or twelve shots the player may allow his or her partner to shoot. This is a high intensity drill and is meant to generate a large number of shots in a short period of time.

Number 11
Contested Shooting

After two or three minutes of power shooting, the non-shooting partner contests the shots of the shooting partner. Initially this is done with the defender standing up with arms fully extended (biceps by ears). After ten or twelve shots the partners switch. As the drill progresses the defender begins to make light contact, fouling the shooter. The contact increases until the fouls are reasonably hard.

Number 12
10-2 Post Shooting

10-2 post shooting places an emphasis on post players following their own shot to obtain any missed shots. Perhaps a better name for the drill would be 10-2 put backs count.

The shooter flashes into the high post for a pass from his or her partner (**Diagram A**). The post player faces-up and shoots from the high post. If the shot is made, it counts as one point. If the shooter misses but is able to obtain the offensive rebound before the ball hits the court and score the put back, the put back counts as a point.

The shooter must score ten points before two missed shots hit the court. To make the drill more challenging made shots that hit the court can also count towards the two missed shots.

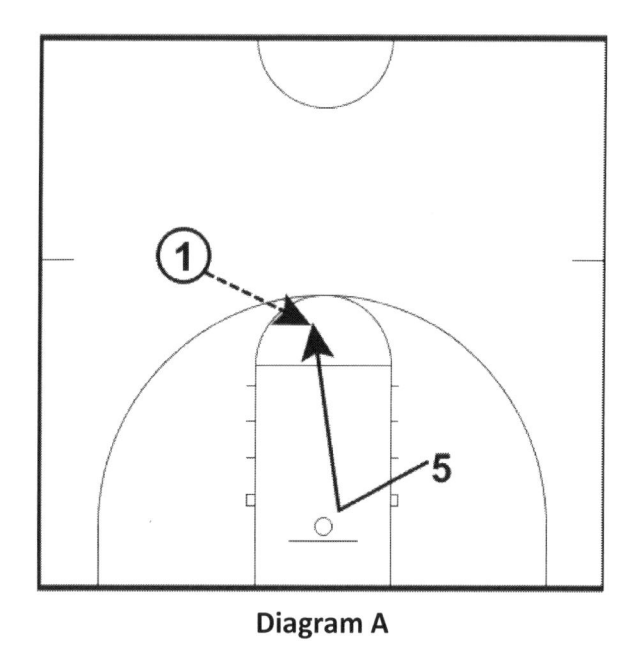

Diagram A

Number 13

2-on-1 Post Shooting

Two-on-one post shooting works on post scoring against live defense. **Diagram 13-A** depicts an entry pass into the low post from the wing. #5 would execute a post move and score after receiving the pass. Initially the defense would be token in nature and work to progressively more difficult to finally fouling the post player on the shot.

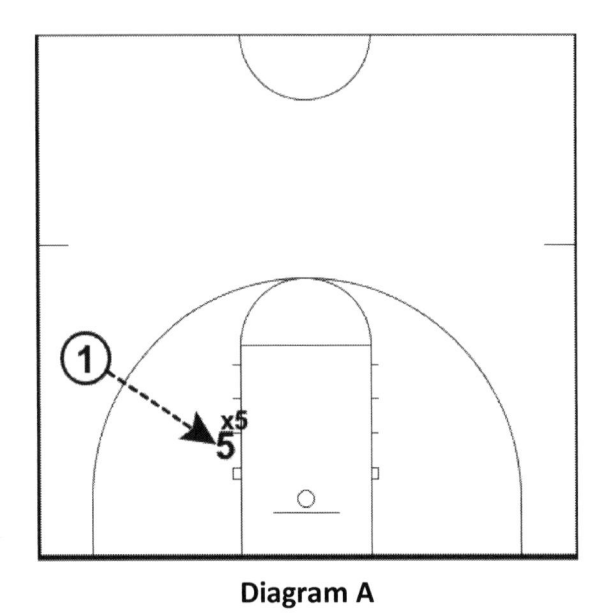

Diagram A

The drill moves to the high low game. The low post player moves to get open with a v-cut and seals the defender. #4 makes the high low pass to #5 who then scores against the defense (**Diagram B**).

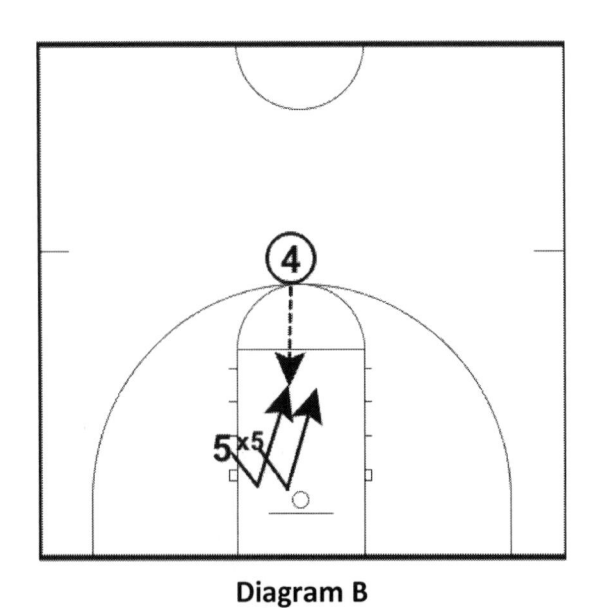

Diagram B

Number 14
2-on-1 Duck Cut Shooting

Two-on-one duck cut shooting combines getting open in the post with passing to cutters moving to open areas of the court against the zone. **Diagram A** shows an entry pass from the wing and #5 hitting the "back half" of a duck cut. Cutters can be the other post player, a perimeter player on the weak side or the perimeter player who made the entry pass to the low post player.

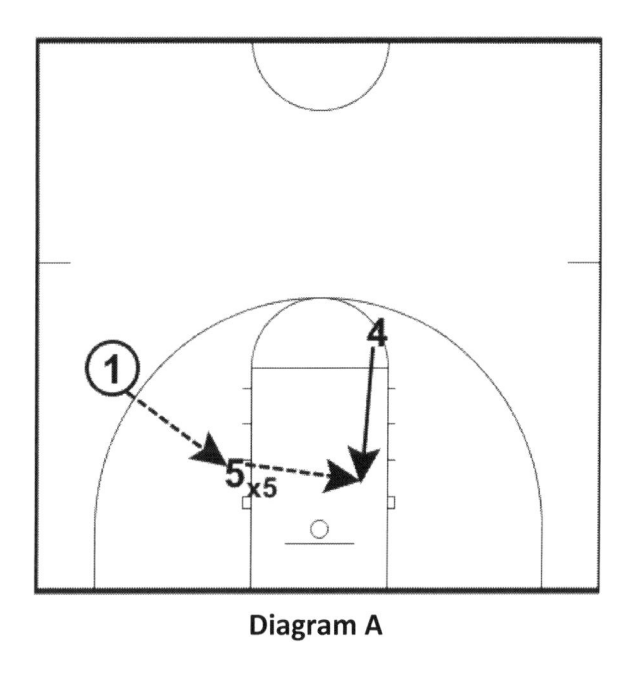

Diagram A

Three Point Shooting Drills

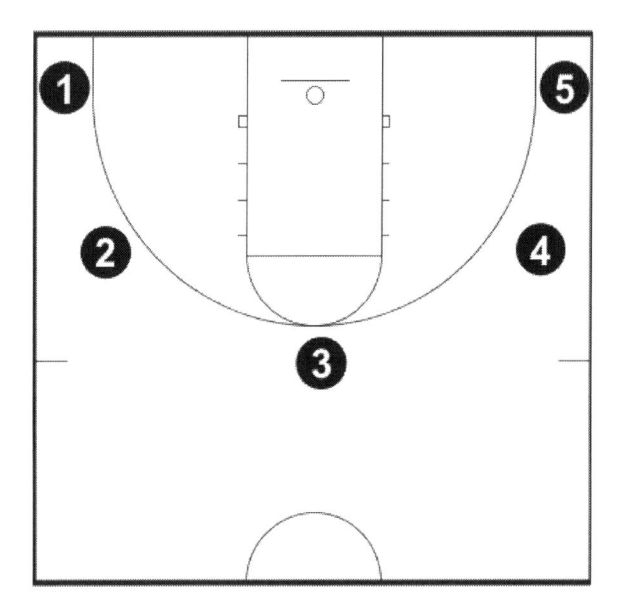

The diagram above depicts the five primary shooting spots perimeter 3-point shooters should practice from. The spots can vary based on the needs of the offense being used. The diagram below shows the area and spots post players who serve as trailers on the fast break should practice from to develop 3-point shooting ability.

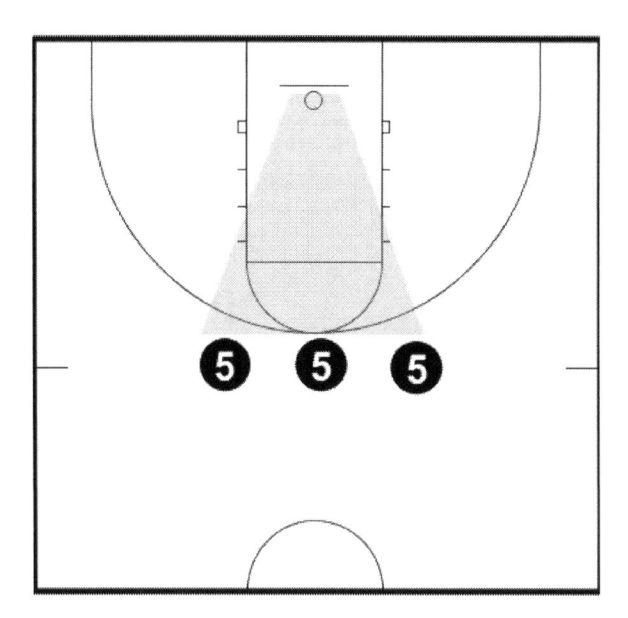

Number 15
Three-point Shootout

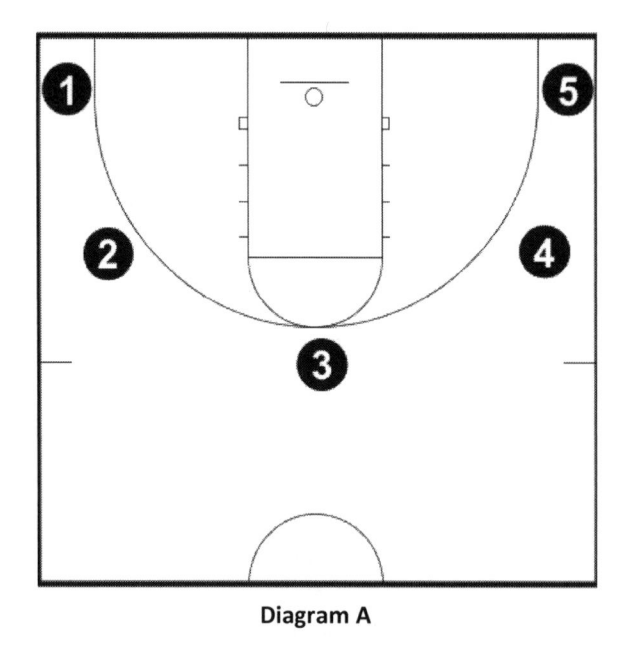

Diagram A

This drill is designed to generate a high volume of three-point shots in a short period of time. One to five shooters can work at a single time with five players rebounding, one designated rebounder for each shooter. Players shoot only from the five three-point shooting spots as indicated in **Diagram A**.

The drill should last for five minutes. Players are allotted one minute per spot after which the shooter rotates to the next spot. The rebounder keeps track of the number of shots made. At the end of the session the number of shots made should be recorded.

Number 16
Forty Point Drill

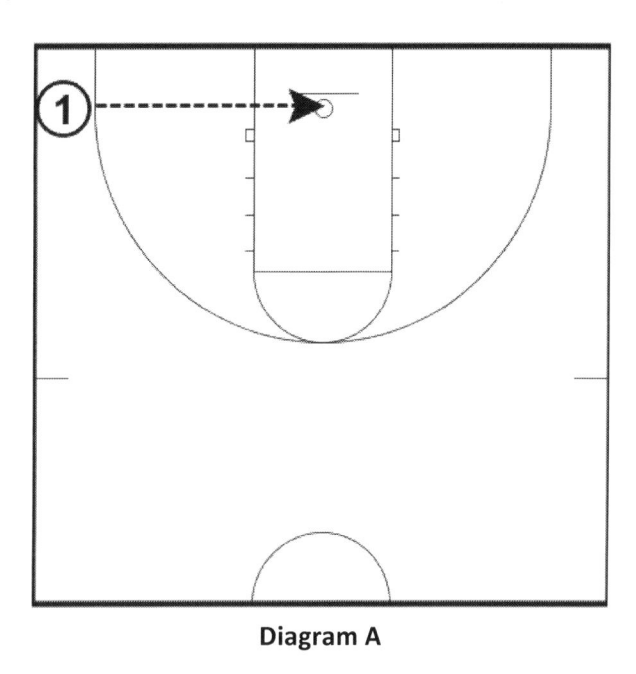

Diagram A

The Forty Point Drill allows players to practice three-point shooting, mid-range jump shots off one dribble, lay-ups and free throws. The drill is so named because players will have scored 40 points when finished (**Diagram A**). The five three-point shooting spots are utilized. The shooter does not move to the next spot until a three-point shot, jump shot and lay-up have been made from the spot being used.

The shooter will score a total of 7 points from each of the five spots for a total of 35 points. The shooter then goes to the free throw line and makes 5 free throws. If a shooter cannot make a three-point shot, the shooter takes a stationary jump shot from 15 feet. The shooter moves behind the three-point line and utilizes a shot fake and one dribble to shoot the pull-up 15-foot jump shot. The final shot is a lay-up. The shooter should attempt to use only one dribble if possible, but certainly no more than two dribbles when driving for the lay-up.

The drill can be used by a player working alone or with a rebounder to speed the process up. This drill can take a fair amount of time so plan accordingly and allot sufficient time in practice for this drill. **Diagram 16-A** shows the shooter taking a three-point shot form the baseline to start the drill.

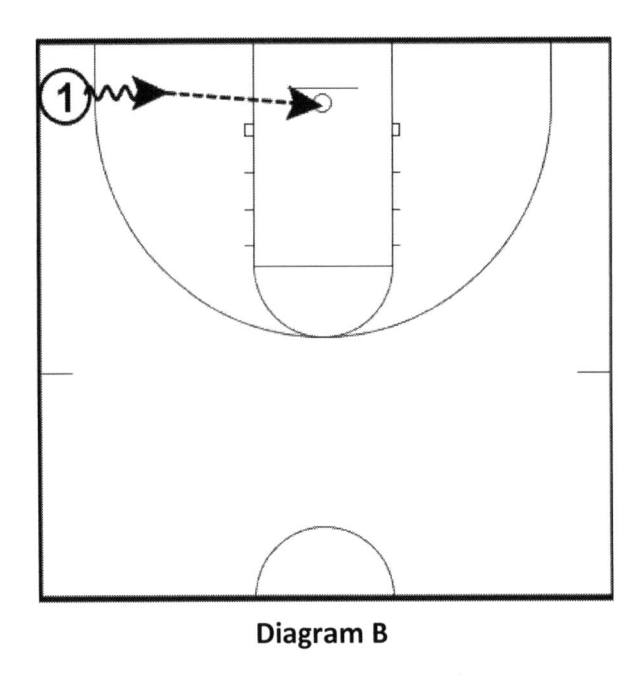

Diagram B

Diagram B depicts the shooter using a shot or pass fake followed by a long, low, direct drive or crossover, one dribble and a 15-foot jump shot.

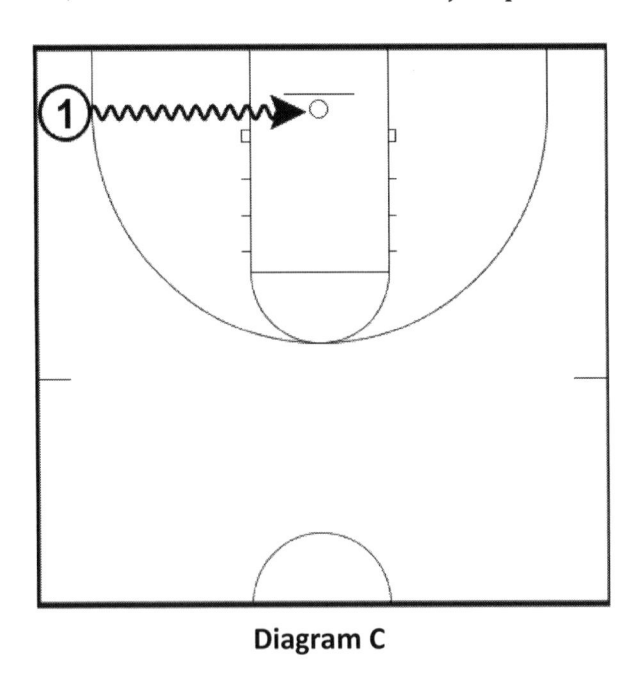

Diagram C

Diagram C depicts the shooter driving from the corner. Because of the angle of the approach for the lay-up, the shooter should not use the outside shooting hand as would be normal, but rather the inside shooting hand (in this example the right instead of the left hand) to allow the shooter to correctly play the ball high and soft off the glass. Using the outside hand to shoot with, which would be the normally

Drills to Teach Key Offensive Fundamentals

correct technique, would create an awkward shooting angle and almost certainly result in a missed lay-up unless a two-foot power lay-up is used instead.

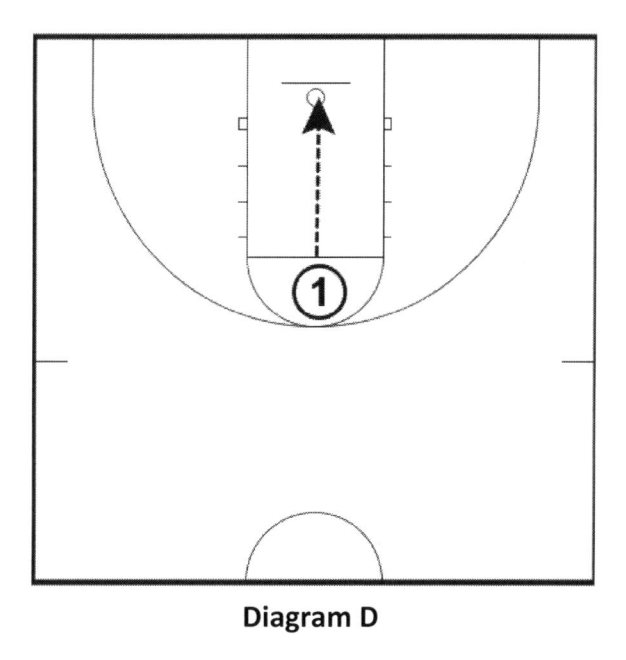

Diagram D

The shooter depicted in **Diagram D** is finishing the drill by making five free throws. The drill can also be done without a rebounder with the shooter working against the clock. This approach adds conditioning to the drill as the shooter must hustle to retrieve the rebound.

Rewards and consequence can be established for a variety of scenarios ranging from a winner who finished first or scored 40 points with the fewest shots. It is up to the coach to be creative.

Number 17
Partner Threes

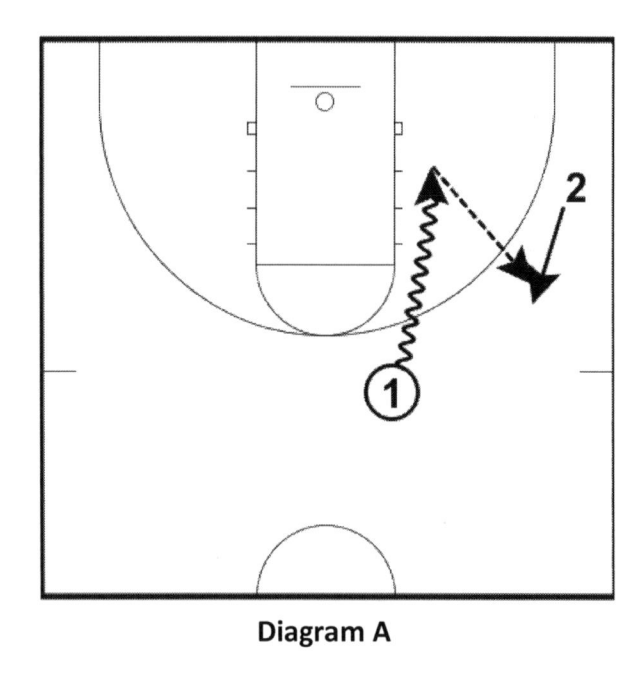

Diagram A

Partner Threes is a simple concept for a drill. Three point shooters are paired together for the duration of the drill and the sequences involved. One player executes the tactic being practiced and passes to the other player who has executed the necessary moves to be open and ready to shoot upon catching the pass. The passer rebounds the shot and passes to the shooter. The two players then switch roles and repeat the process. Players may shoot a preset number before moving on to the next series in the sequence or await the command of the coach.

In **Diagram A** the players are executing a penetrate and pitch. #1 drives the gap to draw #2's
defender. #2 moves up from the baseline to create space and receive the pass from #1. #2 should have feet set, be squared up, hands ready and prepared to shoot upon catching the pass.

The following diagrams demonstrate the various ways two players can create an open three-point shot attempt. The same drill procedure is used for the entire sequence. Please note an important component of the drill is not just the physical repetition of the skills involved and the tactic being practiced but also the ability to recognize the potential to create such a three-point shot in a game by using one of the tactics being practiced.

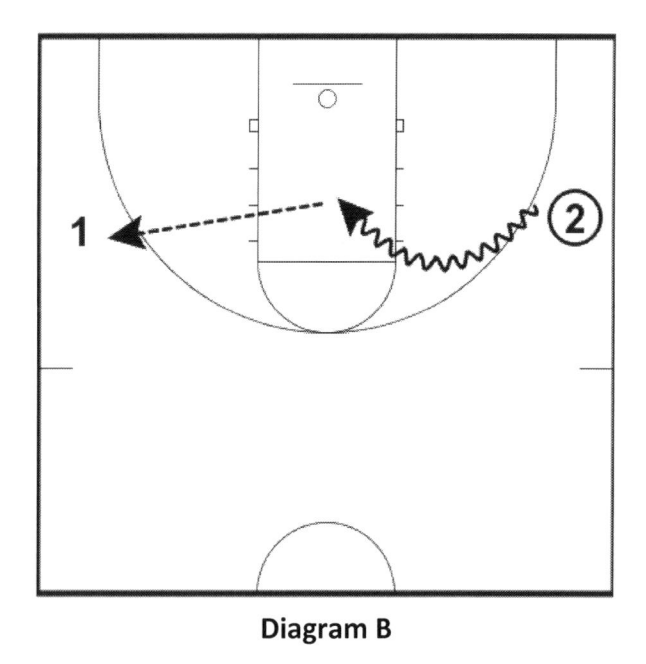

Diagram B

Diagram B depicts a penetrate and skip. #2 drives the middle drawing #1's defender and creating an open three-point attempt.

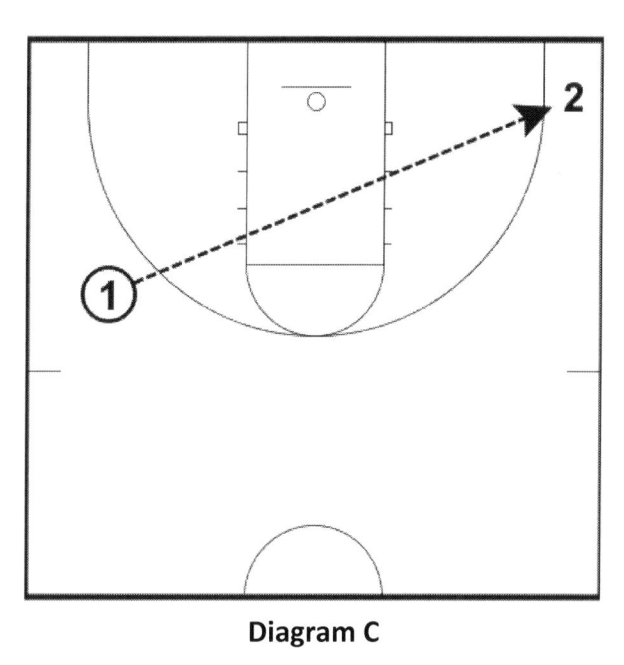

Diagram C

A diagonal skip pass for a three-point attempt is depicted in **Diagram C**. Note the diagonal pass is from the wing to the opposite corner. The same play could be executed with a pass from the corner to the opposite wing with a diagonal pass.

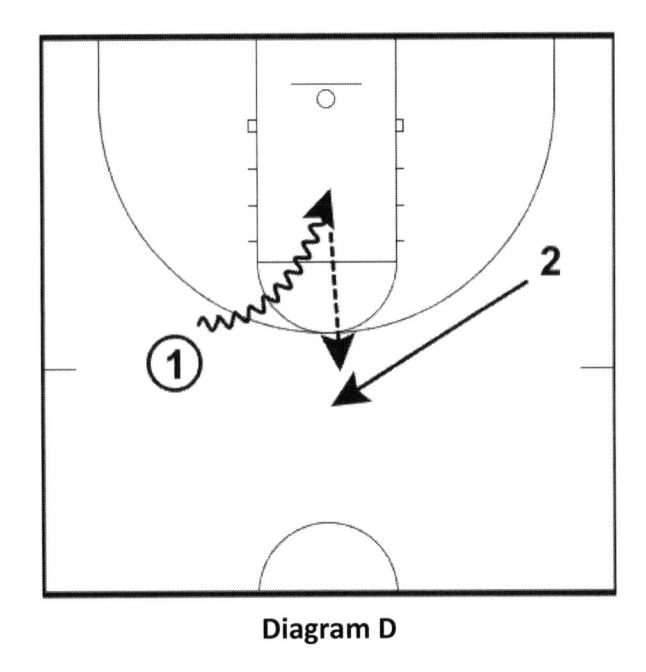

Diagram D

Diagram D depicts what is called a "Euro" because it is a tactic developed in the European leagues. The ball handler #1 drives the middle collapsing the defense and drawing #2's defender. #1 executes a jump stop and rear turn away from the defense while #2 cuts behind #1 for a pass for a three-point shot attempt. #2 must execute proper footwork and be ready to shoot upon catching the pass from #1.

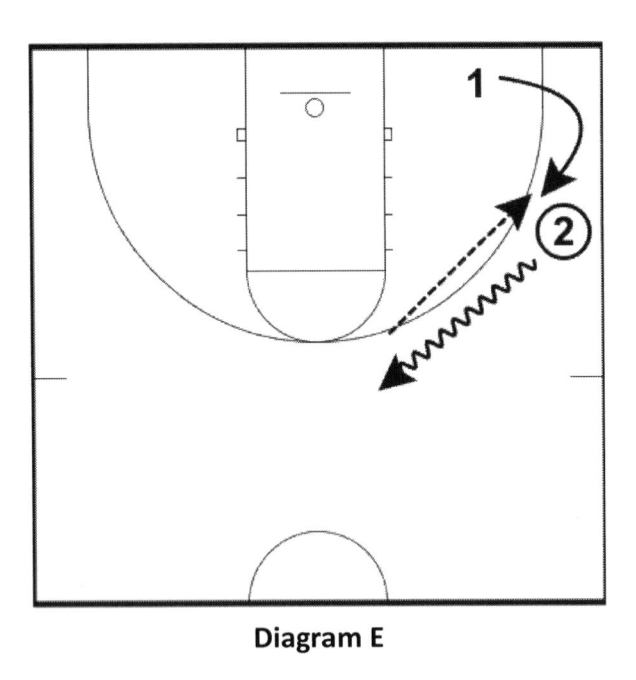

Diagram E

Diagram E depicts a tactic known as a "dribble off" or a "dribble follow." #2 dribbles off the wing towards the top of the key area, "pulling" #1 from the short post area. #1 follows and executes the proper footwork necessary to be ready to shoot a three-point attempt upon receiving a pass. #2 pass fakes to a player on the other side of the court, "rips" the ball and passes to #1 for the three-point attempt. Players can be "dribbled off" for a three from the low post making this a useful tactic for a post player who can shoot three-point shots.

Number 18
Closeout Three's

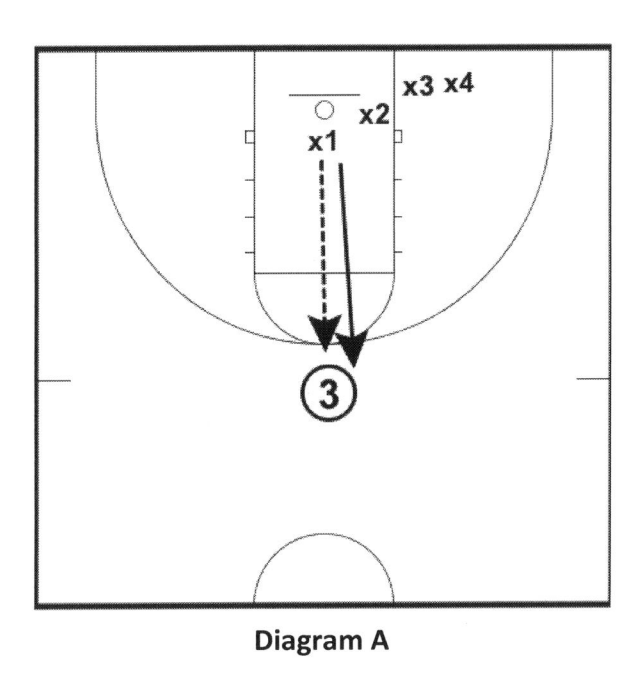

Diagram A

Diagram A depicts a drill designed to help three-point shooters to maintain their concentration as defenders rush them or closeout on the ball. The drill starts with three players under the goal each with a ball. The first player passes to the three-point shooter and then runs at the shooter and attempts to block the shot as he or she flies by. The shot blocker rebounds the shot and returns to the end of the line. The passers each pass and rush the shooter as quickly as possible.

Diagram B

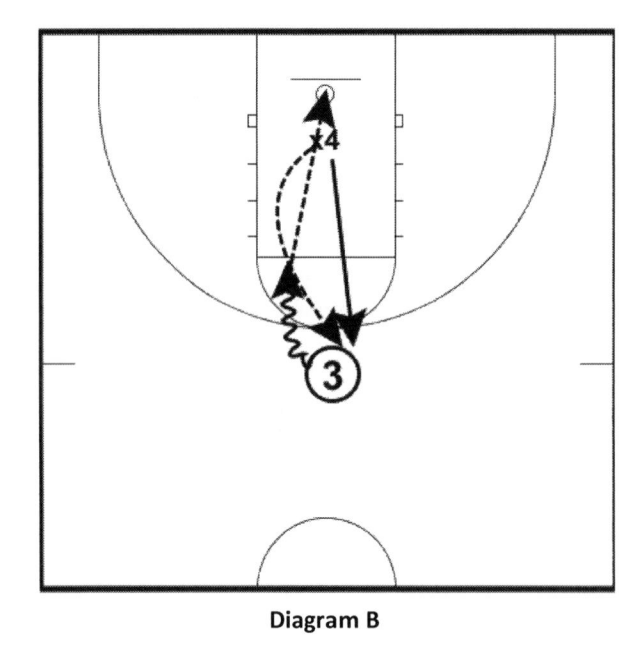

After seven shots the shooter rotates with one of the passer/rebounders. **Diagram B** depicts what happens should the shooter have a shot blocked. Once a passer/rebounder is able to either deflect or block a shot, on the next pass the shooter executes a two-inch shot fake and then dribbles once and shoots a 15-foot jump shot.

Number 19
Feed the Post Sequence

Successful offense requires good offensive post play. Post players, unlike perimeter players, are often at the mercy of the perimeter players. Perimeter players have possession of the ball and can create shots for themselves. Post players are dependent upon perimeter players to deliver the ball into the post.

The ball be passed into the post player and it must be passed away from the defense and in such a way the post player can instinctively know which post move to use to score.

Feed the post sequence teaches perimeter players how to read post defense and determine where to pass the ball from on the perimeter in order to successfully enter the ball into the low post. It also teaches perimeter players how to pass the ball away from the post defense, allowing the offensive post player to simply catch and score. This last skill is known as "keying the shot."

This same sequence of drills also allows for post players to have a high number of repetitions in the key post play skills of posting, sealing, receiving, scoring with a post move and making an outlet pass.

The drill begins with players lined up as shown in **Diagram A**. Large numbers of players can be accommodated in this drill. The perimeter players each have a ball and form two lines as shown. The post players form two lines on the baseline. The drill can be executed from both sides of the goal at the same time.

The drill can start without post defenders and with the offensive post players not making any moves to get open in the low post area. As players improve and learn defense must be added to make the drill more game like.

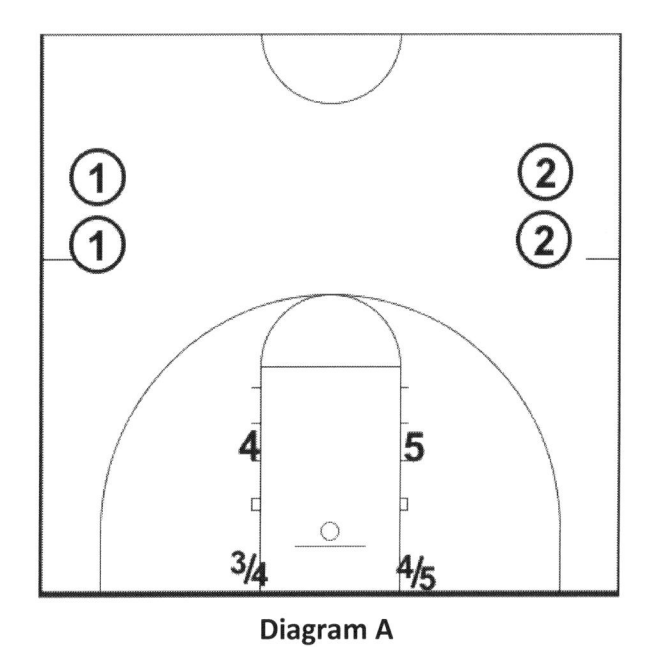

Diagram A

The first entry pass in the sequence is the dribble down. The perimeter player "reads" the defense is playing high, above the low post offensive player, and dribbles down below the post player and makes a pass back to the post. The perimeter player then executes a feed the post and move and moves to receive an outlet pass above the three-point line on the lane line extended. The offensive post player executes a drop step or a catch and score, finishes the play if the initial shot is missed and makes an outlet pass.

The perimeter player assertively turns and faces-up at the goal on the other end of the court and speed dribbles to half court before dribbling to the end of the other line. While waiting in line all perimeter players are maintaining a low control dribble with the ball below their knees while waiting for their next turn. The post player goes to the end of the other post line (**Diagram B**).

When post defense is added the post defender rotates to become the next offensive low post player. Floor clarity only one side of the drill will be shown and only the players involved being depicted.

Diagram B

Diagram C

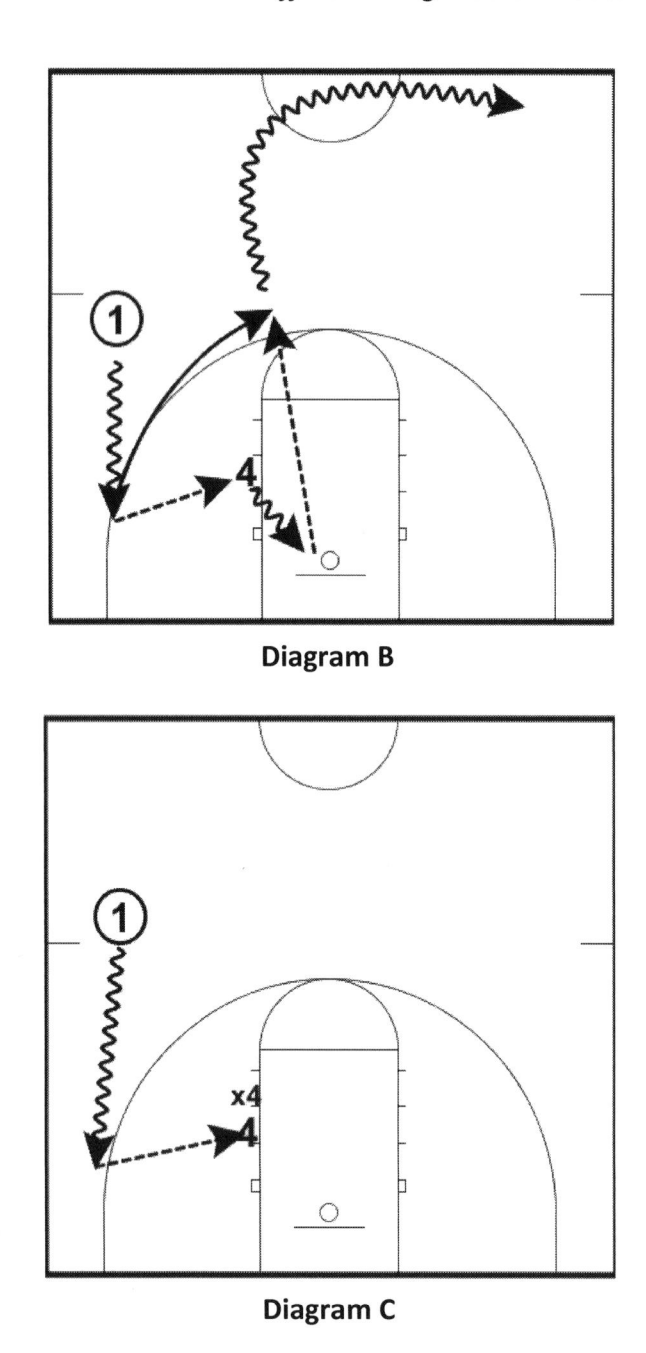

A dribble down is used when the defense plays above the offensive low post (**Diagram C**). If the ball was directly passed to the low post #4 the post defender X4 would have no trouble intercepting or deflecting the pass. The perimeter player #1 must read the defender's location and dribble, or pass, the ball to the appropriate location on the court to make the entry pass. In this example, the ball must be located below the post defender and passed back to the offensive post player.

Any pass thrown on the baseline side of the offensive post player tells that player a drop step or catch and score move to the baseline is available. There are no other defenders to be concerned with. The message of where the best available shot is communicated by the pass from the perimeter player.

Drills to Teach Key Offensive Fundamentals

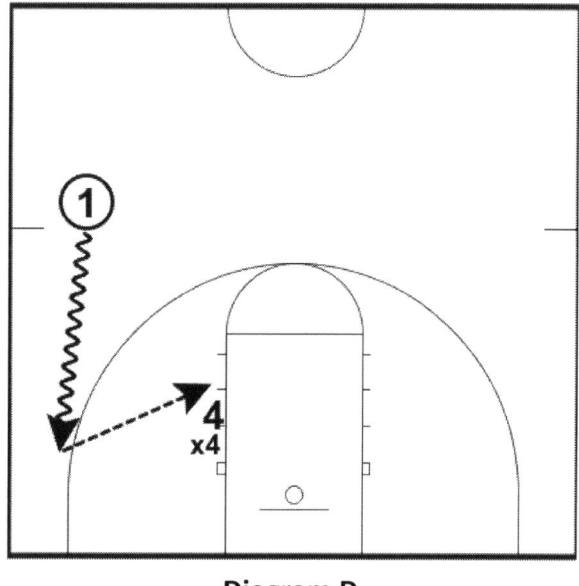

Diagram D

A hard working post defender will react to a dribble down and reposition on the baseline side of the offensive post. The perimeter player again "keys" the shot by passing the ball to the high side of the offensive post player and away from the post defender. The offensive post player knows to turn towards the middle and away from the baseline by virtue of the pass location (**Diagram D**).

Note, the offensive post player must work hard to seal the post defender and show the perimeter player the numbers on his or her chest, creating a defined passing lane and proper post positioning.

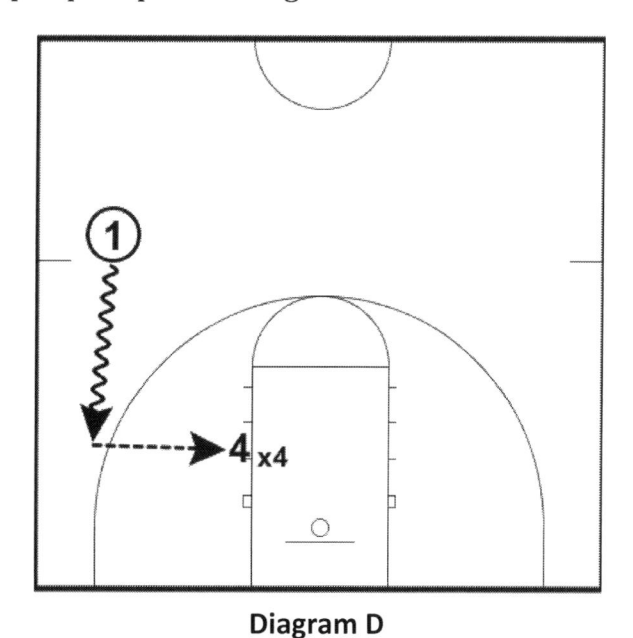

Diagram D

Coaching Basketball's Zone Attack Offense Using Blocker-Mover Motion Offense

If the post defender plays behind the offensive low post the key pass is made directly to the offensive low post player. The message accompanying this pass is "the defense is directly behind you. You must make a post move on your own to score, find a cutter or fan the ball out (**Diagram D**).

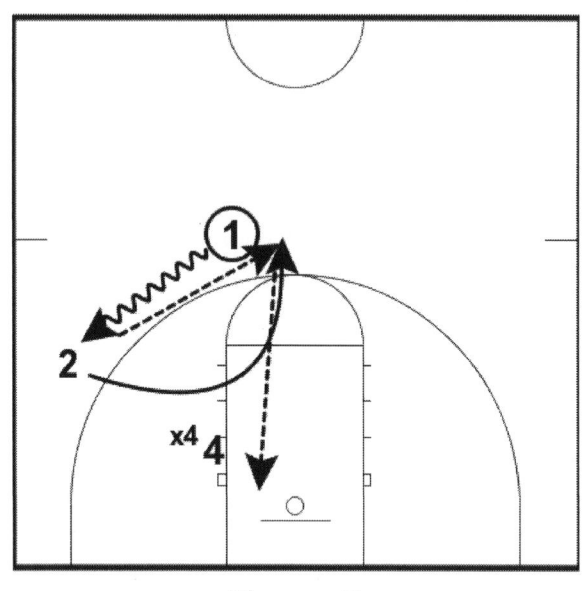

Diagram E

The dribble loop can be used to feed the post effectively when the defense chooses to front the low post. It can also be use when the defense makes a pass from the point to the wing difficult.

The on top ball handler dribbles down and the wing perimeter player makes a loop cut. The ball is passed on top while the offensive post player seals the defender out of the lane.

It is important to note a two hand overhead pass is used to make the entry pass and the pass is not made directly to the low post player. To prevent turnovers and charging fouls, the ball must be thrown directly to the corner of the backboard but low enough for the post player to go up and catch.

By passing the ball to the corner of the backboard, the help defender can be avoided.

Passing the ball where the offensive post must go up to catch the ball keeps hands from touching and deflecting the pass in the traffic of the lane (**Diagram E**).

Number 20
Post Interference Catching

Post players must have the ability to catch the ball in dense defense traffic, with hands grabbing at the ball, bodies being used to push the post out of position and visual distractions impeding a clear view of the ball. Post interference catching is designed to allow the offensive post player to experience these distractions in a controlled setting.

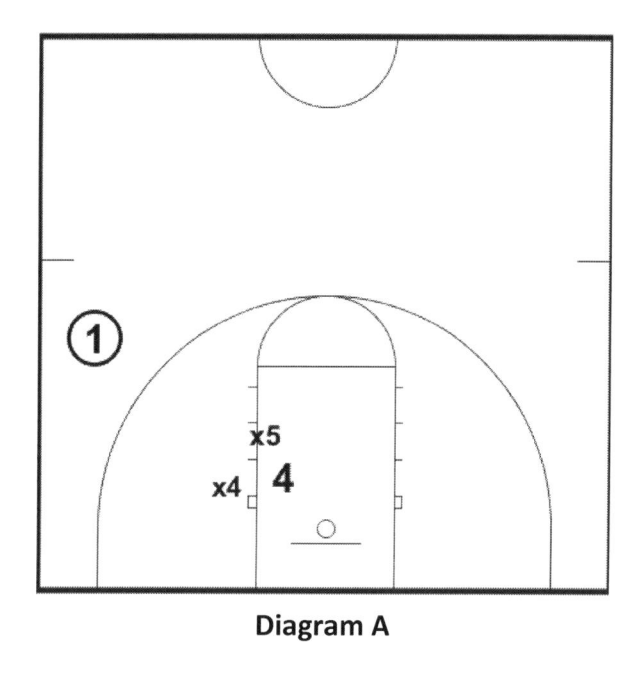

Diagram A

The drill requires four players (or three players and a coach or student assistant). Two defenders line up on either side of the low post posting area. The passer stands in a location used in the team's offense to enter the ball into the low post. The offensive post stands in the lane behind the two defensive players (**Diagram A**).

Diagram B

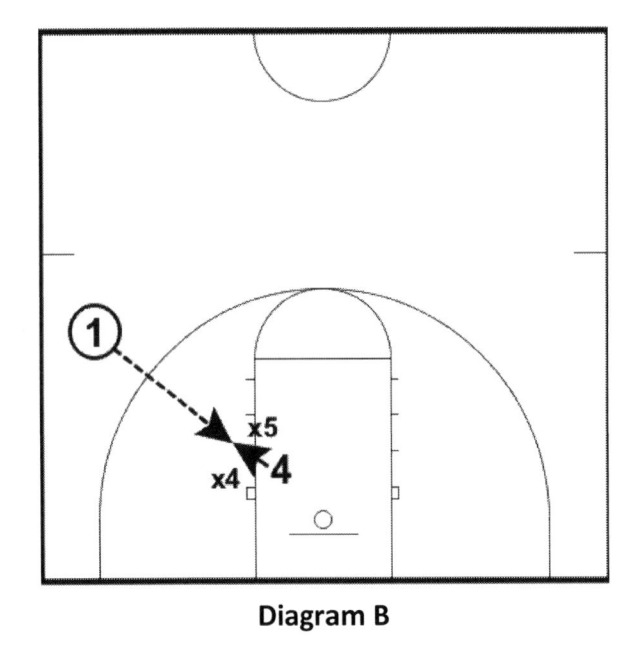

The two defenders wave their arms up and down vigorously in an effort to create a moving physical impediment for the offensive low post as well as a visual distraction (**Diagram B**).

The perimeter ball handler passes the ball to the low post player who must shorten the pass to meet the ball by moving assertively and quickly through the waving arms. The post player must catch the ball in correct posting stance with the ball chinned.

The perimeter ball handler executes a feed the post and move and moves to an "open area" above the three-point line and in line with the lane line extended. The post player executes a drop step move through the two defenders who again attempt to impede the progress of the low post (**Diagram C**). Start with light physical contact and increase the contact as the drill progresses. After four or five repetitions rotate players.

Drills to Teach Key Offensive Fundamentals

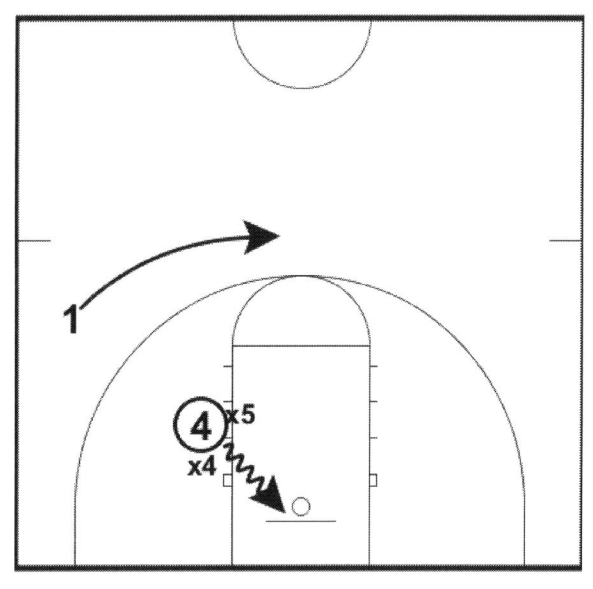

Diagram C

267

34

Drills to Teach Zone Attack Principles and Concepts

Number 1
2-on-2 Freeze and Slide

This simple drill teaches players the basics principles of how to freeze and slide a defensive player as well as cutting to fill an open spot in the zone attack offense. This simple drill involves four total players and can be done for short periods of time to build intensity. After five or six repetitions by the offense, the two groups should switch roles. (**Diagram A** and **Diagram B**).

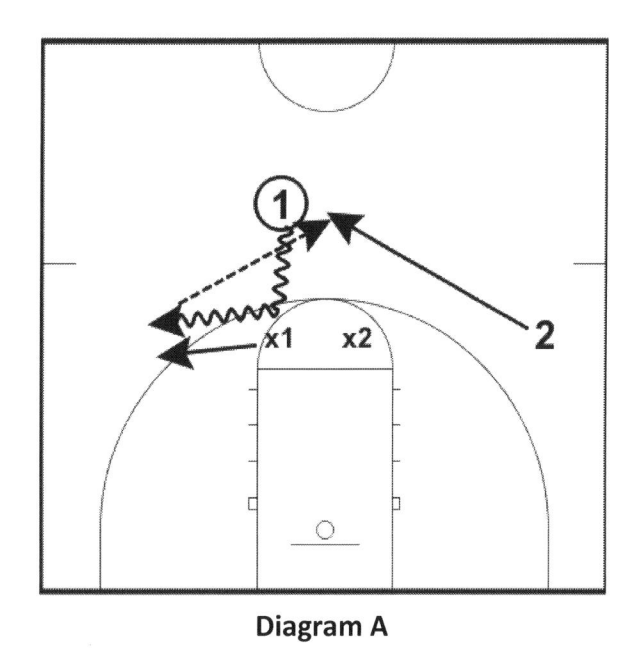

Diagram A

Diagram B

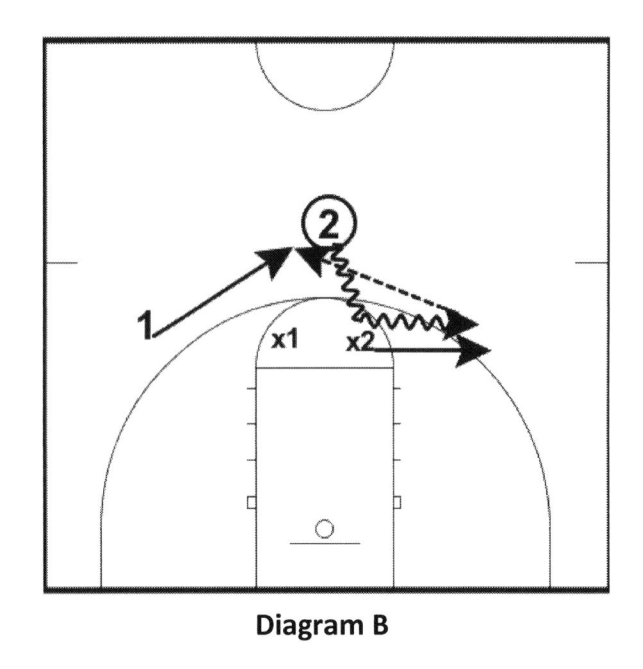

Number 2
3-on-2 Freeze and Slide

3-on-2 freeze and slide combines the dribble attack tactics of freezing and sliding a defender with cutting to fill an open perimeter spot, teaching players to read the defense and how to move to open areas for scoring opportunities or to keep the offense moving (**Diagram A** and **B**).

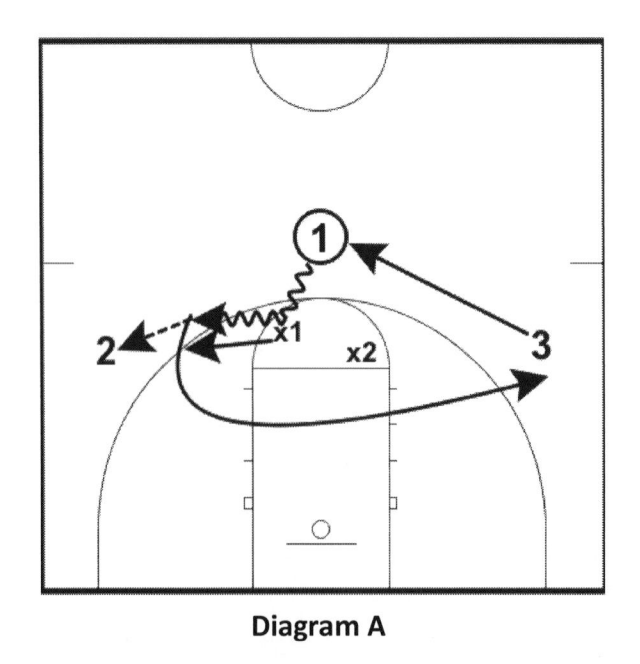

Diagram A

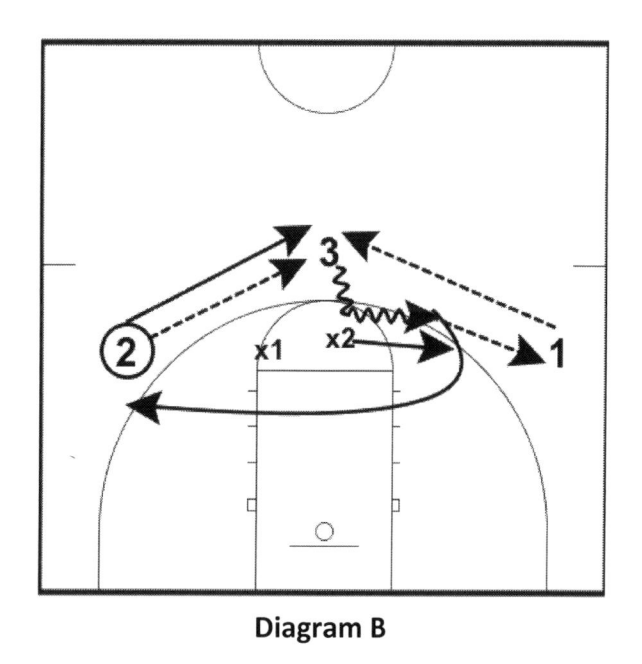

Drills to Teach Zone Attack Principles and Concepts

Diagram B

Number 3
3-on-2 Screen the Zone Series

3-on-2 screen the zone introduces simple screening action for the perimeter players. Down screens and flare screens with the appropriate cuts for these screens are taught with this drill (**Diagram A** and **Diagram B**).

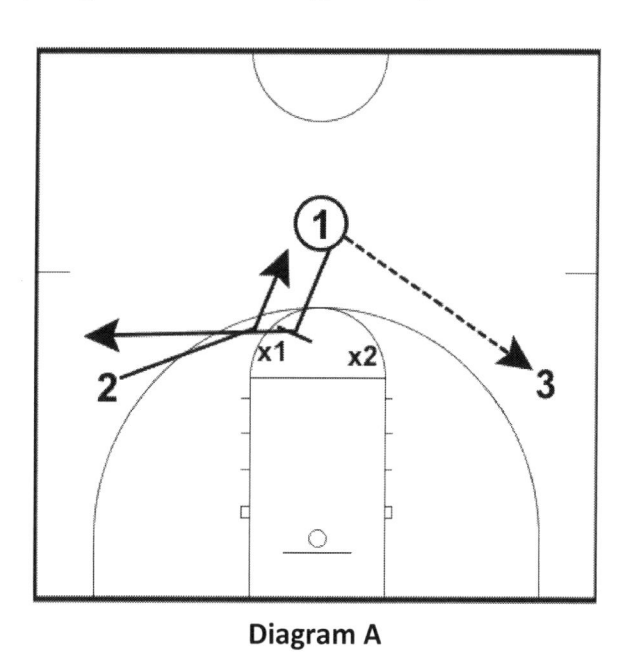

Diagram A

271

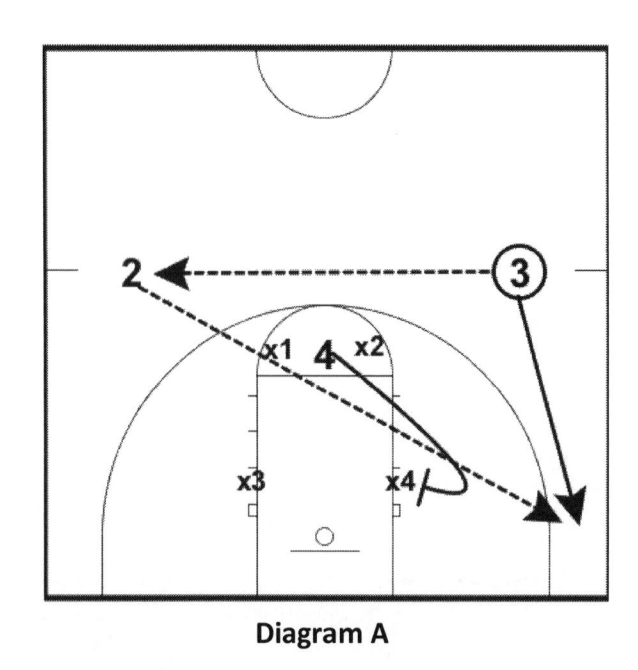

Diagram B

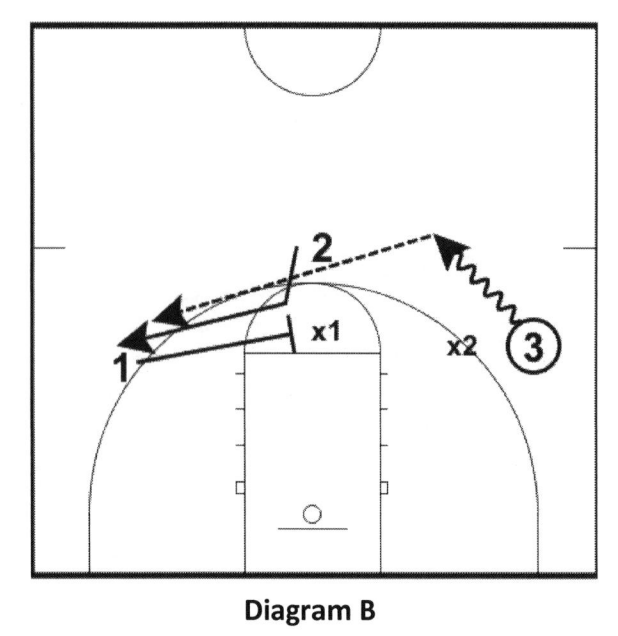

Number 4
3-on-4 Screen the Zone Series

3-on-4 screen the zone introduces a post player in the screening mix. This drill teaches perimeter and post players to work together in attacking the zone defense with screens. Examples of possibilities for screening and cutting action are shown in **Diagrams A** through **D**.

Diagram A

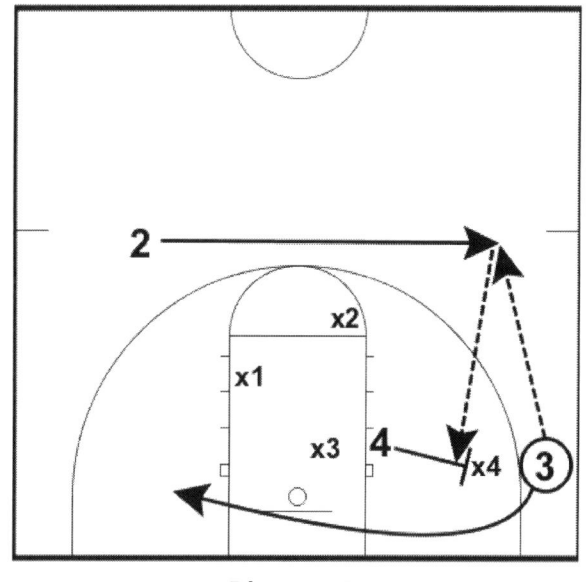

Drills to Teach Zone Attack Principles and Concepts

Diagram B

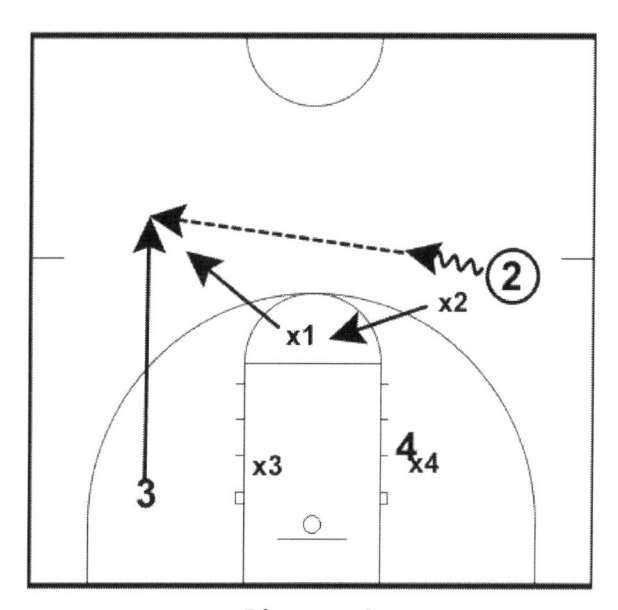

Diagram C

273

Diagram D

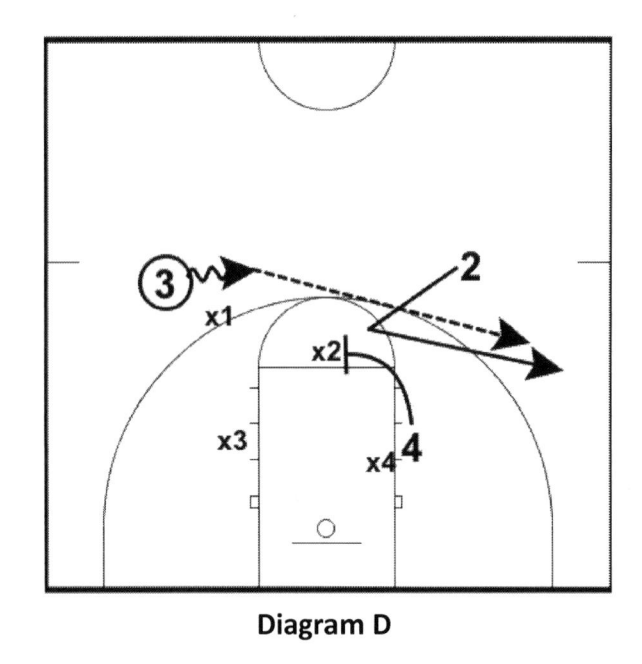

Number 5
5-on-3 Screen the Zone Series

5-on-3 combines perimeter cutting, dribble attack and other concepts with post screening against three backline zone defensive players. This is a great drill to incorporate and perfect the screen-in, screen-out and center screen concepts for post players. It combines the actual screening action with opportunities for the perimeter players to read and recognize what the post players are doing.

Number 6
5-on-4 Screen the Zone Series

5-on-4 screen the zone combines perimeter and post screening concepts. Other concepts such as cutting and dribble attack can be practiced as well in order to perfect timing and for the perimeter and post players to learn to combine the concepts in order to take advantage of the screening action.

Number 7
5-on-2 Post Attack Series

5-on-2 combines perimeter cutting, dribble attack and other concepts with post screening against two backline zone defensive players as would be found in a 1-2-2 or 3-2 zone defense.
 This is a great drill to incorporate and perfect the screen-in, screen-out and center screen concepts for post players. It combines the actual screening action with opportunities for the perimeter players to read and recognize what the post players are doing.

Number 8
5-on-3 Post Attack Series

The 5-on-3 post attack works on timing and recognition of post attack opportunities with both perimeter and post players against the three backline defenders of a 2-3 or 2-1-2 zone. This drill
combines screening, cutting, dribble attack and recognition of post attack concepts and the coordination required between the perimeter and post players.

Number 9
5-on-4 Post Attack Series

The 5-on-4 post attack works on timing and recognition of post attack opportunities with both perimeter and post players against either a box or diamond zone defense simulating 2-3, 1-2-2, 3-2 or 1-3-1 zone defenses. This drill combines screening, cutting, dribble attack and recognition of post attack concepts and the coordination required between the perimeter and post players.

Number 10
5-on-3 Post Screen the Zone

This drill focuses solely on the screening action of post players against the backline of a 2-3 zone defense. Recognition and coordination of movements to take advantage of post screening action is the focus of this drill.

Number 11
5-on-4 Post Screen the Zone

5-on-4 post screen drill focuses on screening opportunities against any type of zone with a focus on post screening action. A box or diamond zone can be used for the five offensive players to attack. Recognition and coordination between the post and perimeter players is taught using this drill.

Number 12
3-on-0 Dribble Attack Series

3-on-0 dribble attack is meant to be a drill where players are forced to use their imagination and creativity in utilizing the various dribble attack concepts. The lack of defenders can be slightly confusing. Visualizing possible defensive scenarios is good for players.

Performing the concepts with no defense also allows the players to focus on the concepts and not avoiding turnovers. It allows the offense to have success no matter what happens so long as the concepts are utilized and executed correctly in terms of cuts, location, handedness of the dribbling, passing to teammates and cutting to fill the appropriate vacant areas.

Number 13
5-on-0 Dribble Attack Series

Like 3-on-0 dribble attack, 5-on-0 dribble attack is meant to accomplish the same goals. This drill adds post players to the mix and allows the posts to work on timing cuts with dribbling. Screening concepts can be utilized as well with the post players reading the dribble attack concepts and setting appropriate screens.

Number 14
3-on-2 Dribble Attack Series

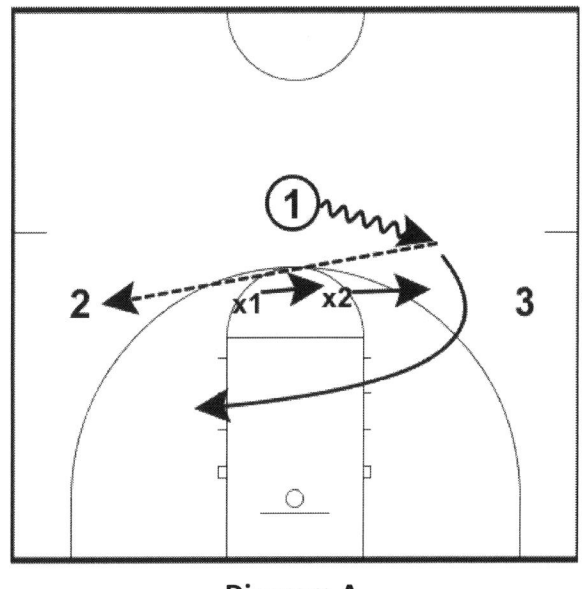

Diagram A

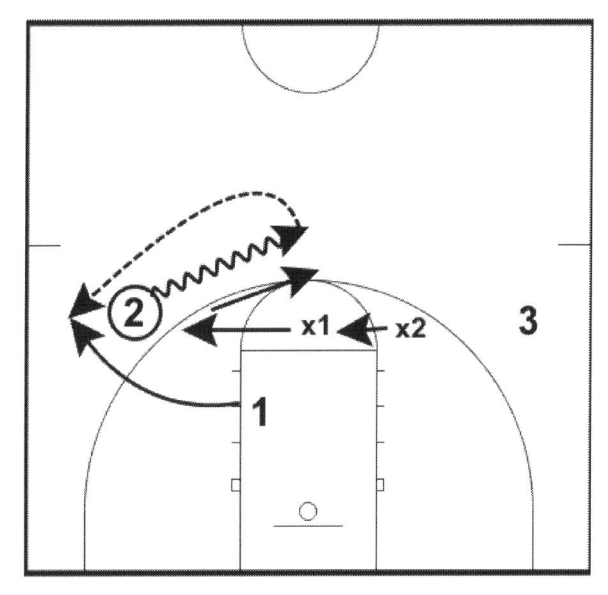

Diagram B

Number 15
3-on-3 Dribble Attack Series

3-o-3 dribble attack is designed to work on dribble attack principles against an odd-front zone defense such as a 1-2-2 or a 1-3-1. A two-guard front is used to attack, making the angles for utilizing dribble attack concepts different, thus requiring specific practice against the odd-front zone defense. **Diagram A** depicts the initial alignment before the players begin to attack the defense.

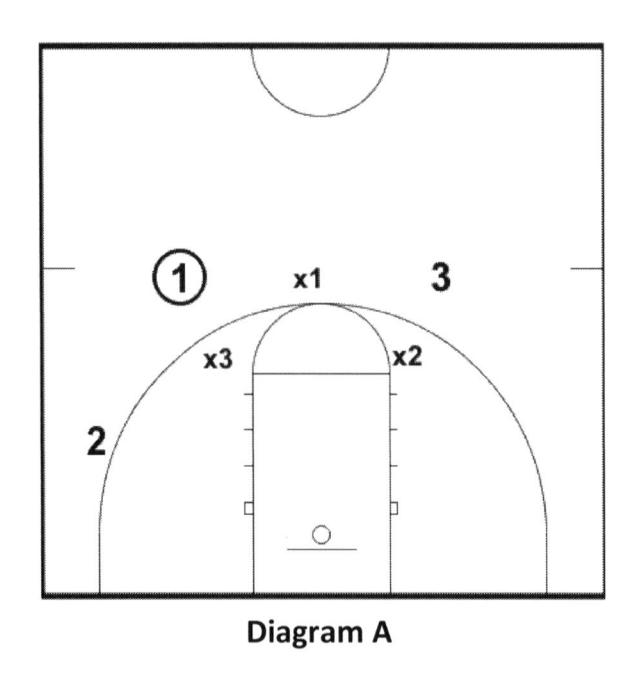

Diagram A

Number 16
3-on-4 Dribble Attack Series

3-on-4 dribble attack expands the area of attack and the skills and concepts being practiced. With the addition of baseline defenders, baseline dribble offs can be added as well as the cuts to set-up the baseline dribble off (**Diagram A** through **Diagram D**).

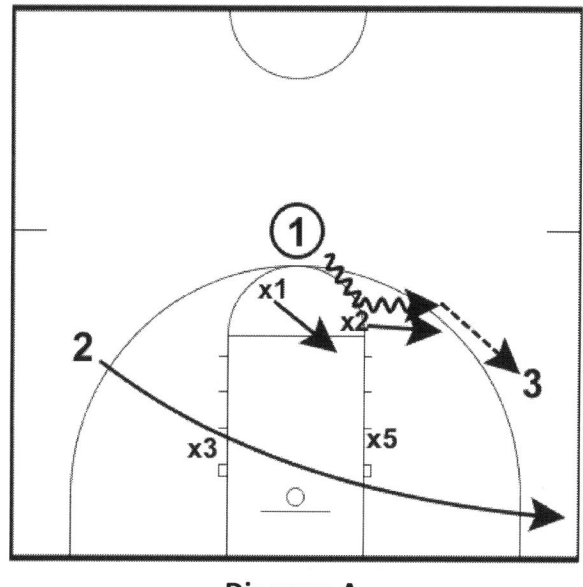

Drills to Teach Zone Attack Principles and Concepts

Diagram A

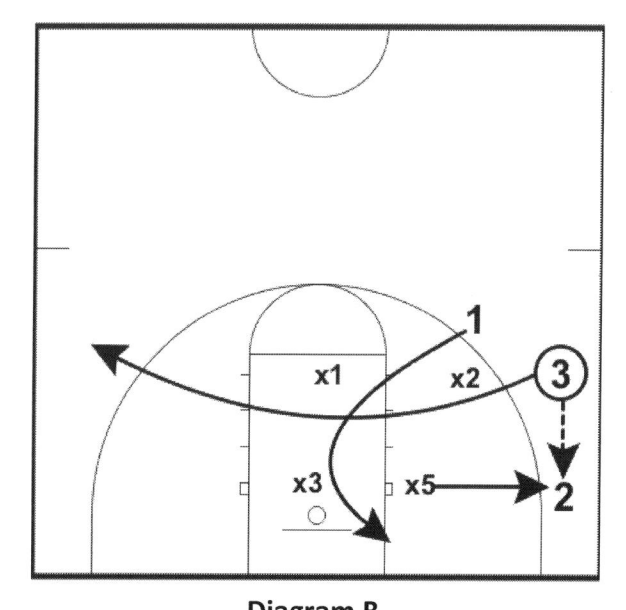

Diagram B

279

Diagram C

Diagram D

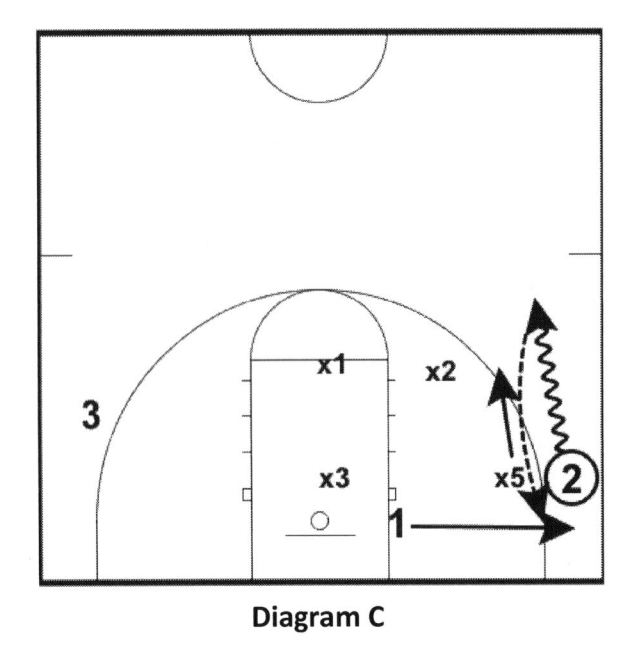

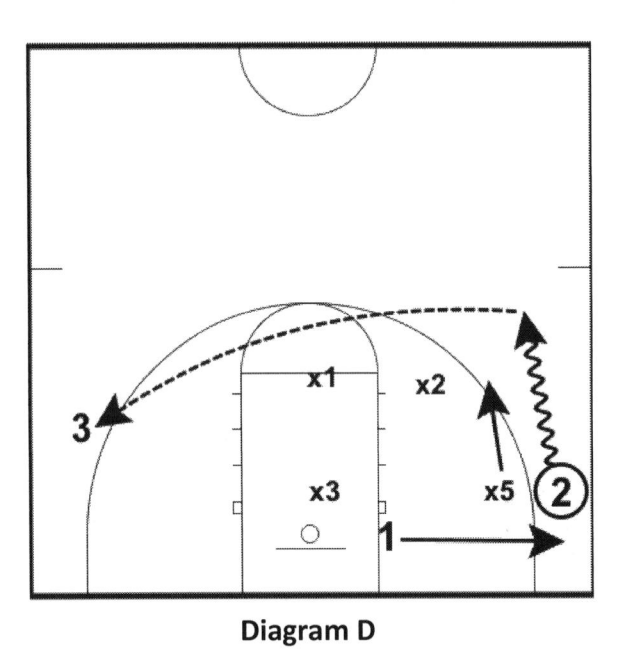

Number 17
5-on-4 Dribble Attack Series

5-on-4 dribble attack adds post players to the mix, allowing every possible dribble attack concept to be utilized. For example, some post players are excellent three-point shooters and using a baseline dribble-off to set up a three-point shot for this player is a sound tactic (**Diagram A and Diagram B**).

Drills to Teach Zone Attack Principles and Concepts

Diagram A

Diagram B

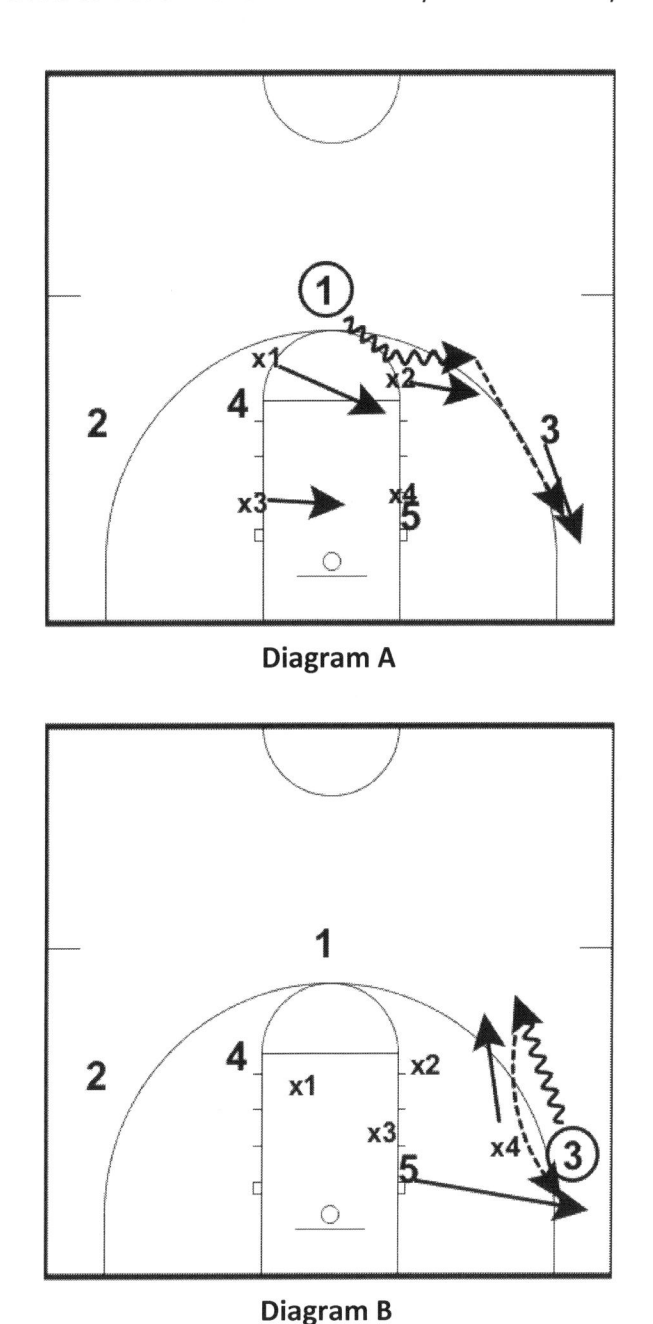

Number 18
3-on-2 Cutter Series

The 3-on-2 cutter series is used to introduce all of the basic zone attack cuts for perimeter players against a two-guard defensive front. This is primarily a teaching drill to introduce and reinforce how to recognize and execute the basic perimeter zone attack cuts.

Number 19
3-on-4 Cutter Series

The 3-on-4 cutter drill teaches cutting against a zone and using as much of the court as possible to spread and move the zone defense. The dribble can be used in this drill to create space or close gaps in the zone offense (**Diagram A** through **Diagram E**).

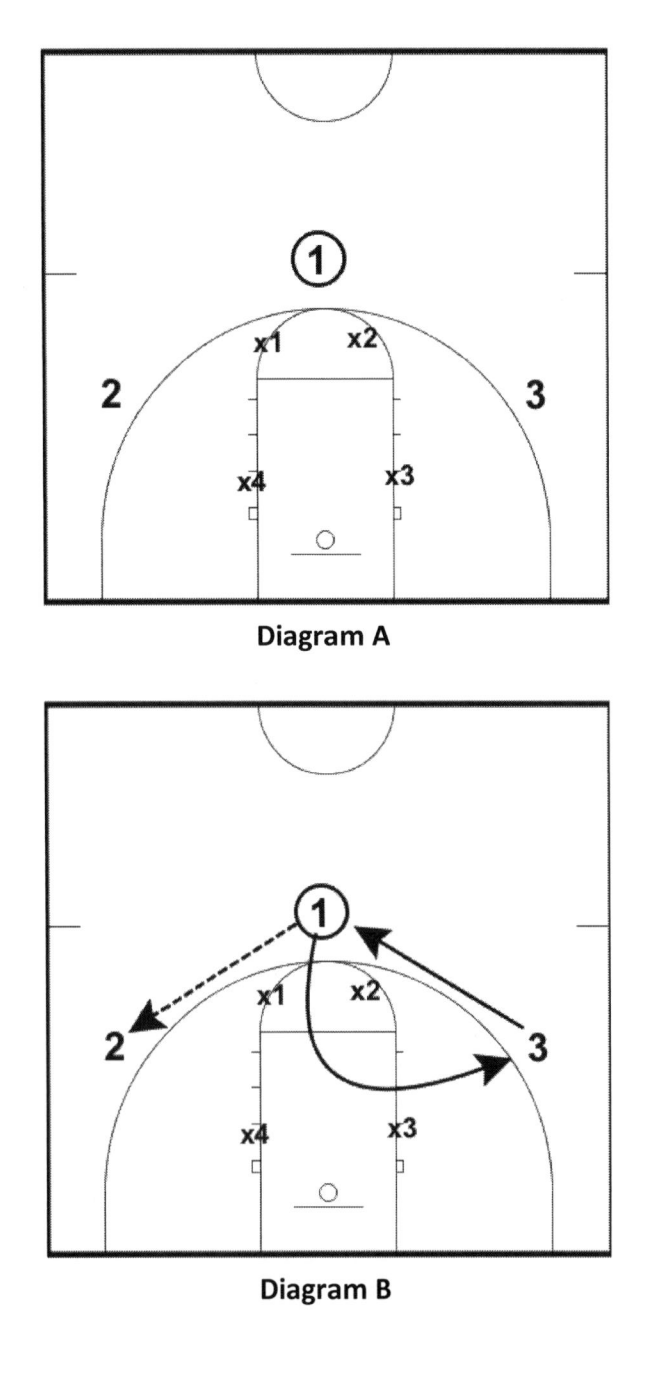

Diagram A

Diagram B

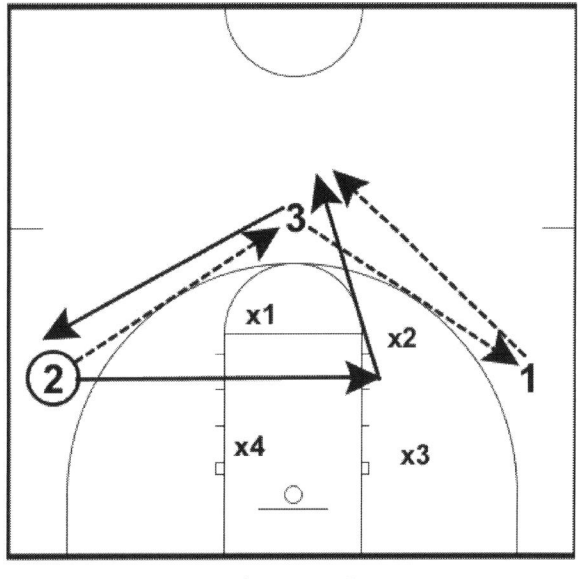

Drills to Teach Zone Attack Principles and Concepts

Diagram C

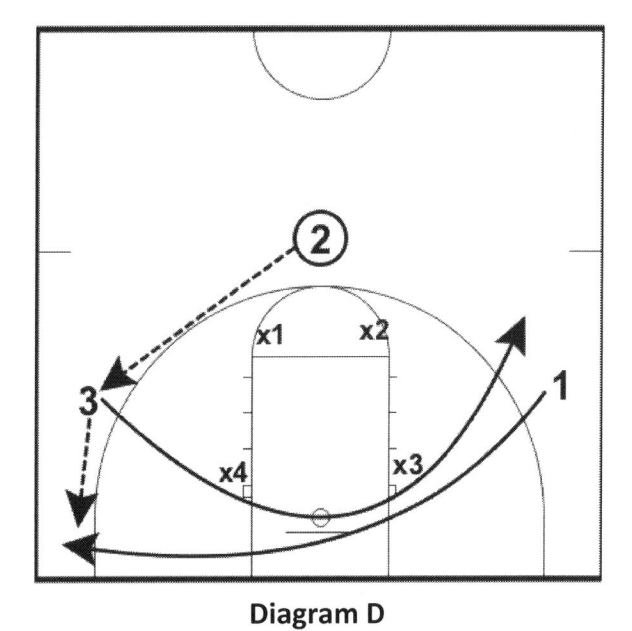

Diagram D

283

Coaching Basketball's Zone Attack Offense Using Blocker-Mover Motion Offense

Diagram E

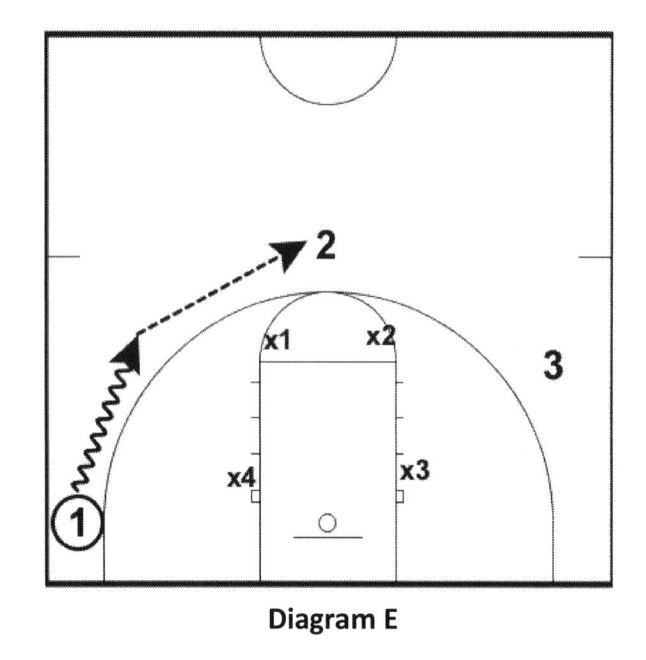

Number 20
5-on-4 Cutter Series

5-on-4 cutter drill places a heavy emphasis on reading the zone defense and using the correct cuts to take advantage of the defense's positioning and alignments. **Diagram A** through **Diagram J** depict a range of cutting movements.

Payers must be encouraged to read the zone defense and to recognize the cutting opportunities available for both themselves and their teammates. A box or diamond zone can be used for this drill.

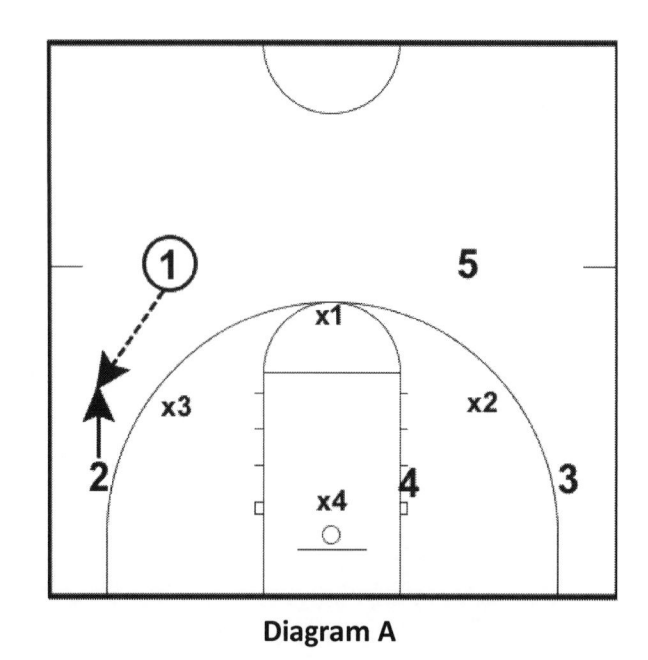

Diagram A

284

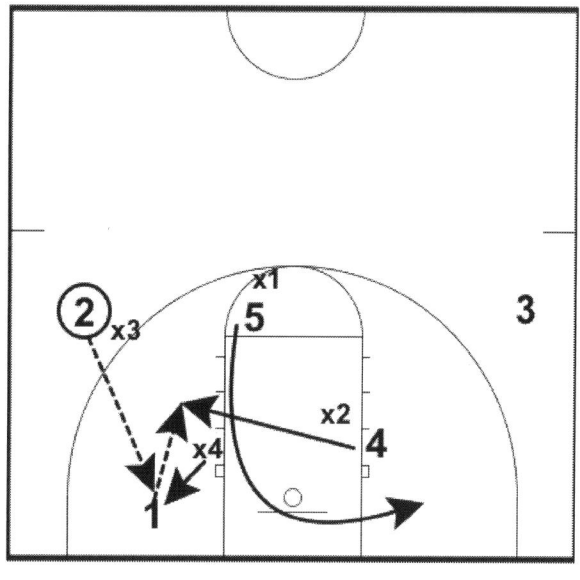

Drills to Teach Zone Attack Principles and Concepts

Diagram B

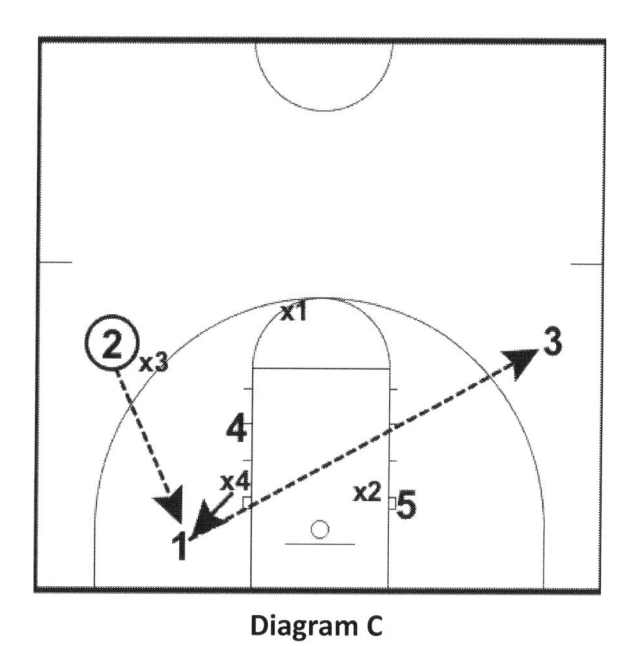

Diagram C

285

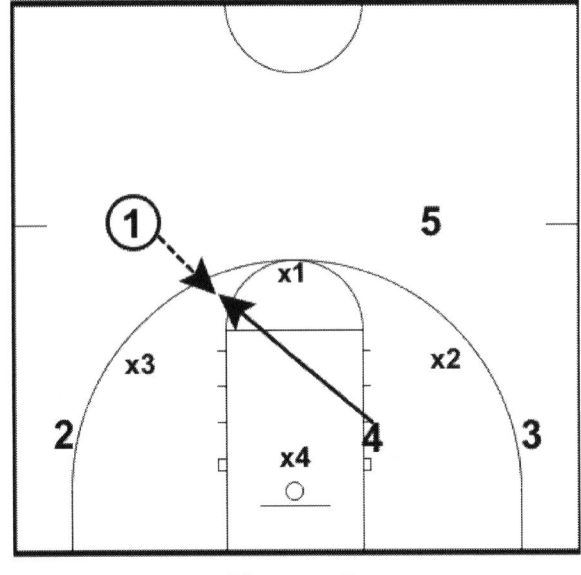

Coaching Basketball's Zone Attack Offense Using Blocker-Mover Motion Offense

Diagram D

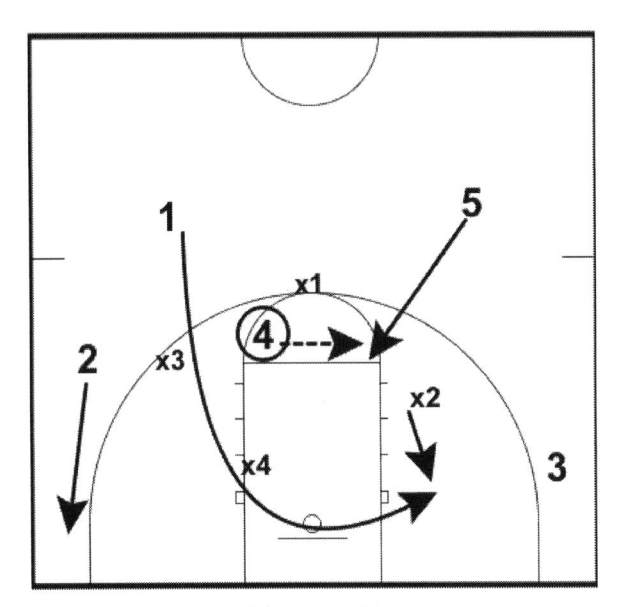

Diagram E

286

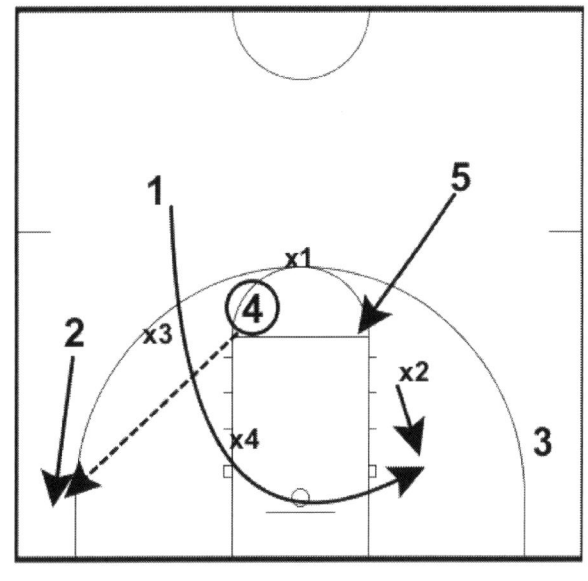

Drills to Teach Zone Attack Principles and Concepts

Diagram F

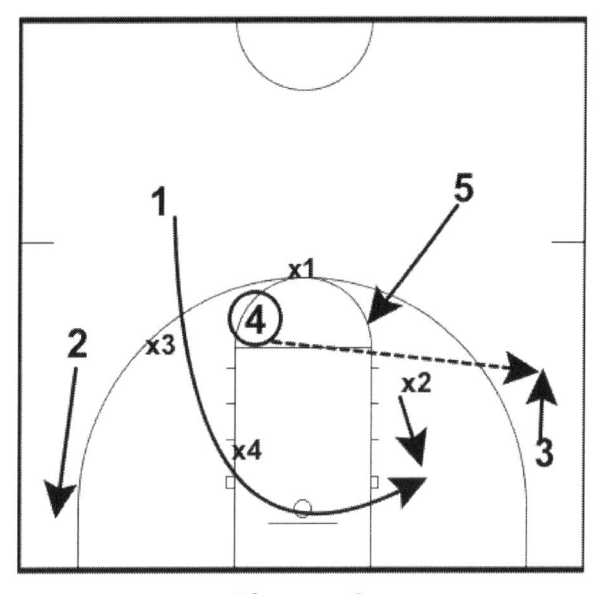

Diagram G

287

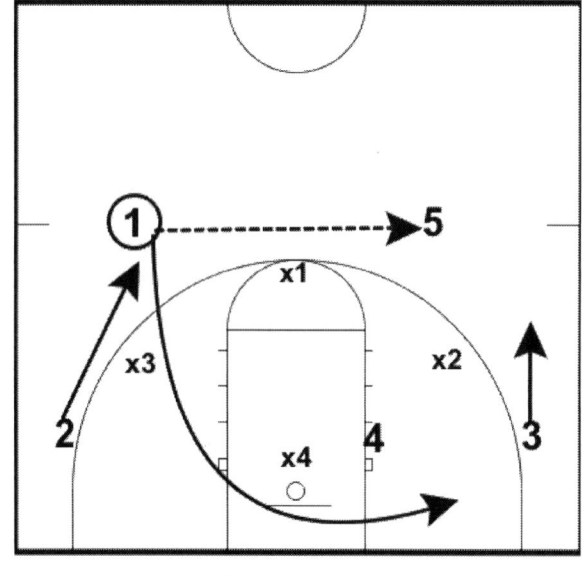

Coaching Basketball's Zone Attack Offense Using Blocker-Mover Motion Offense

Diagram H

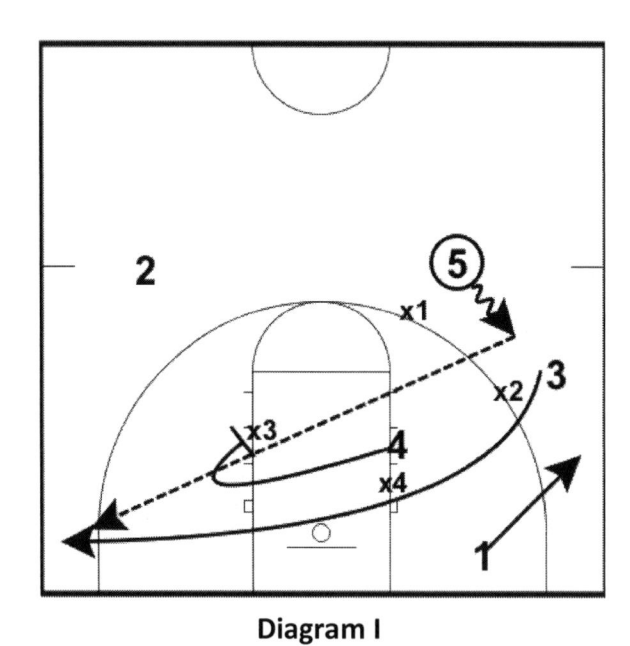

Diagram I

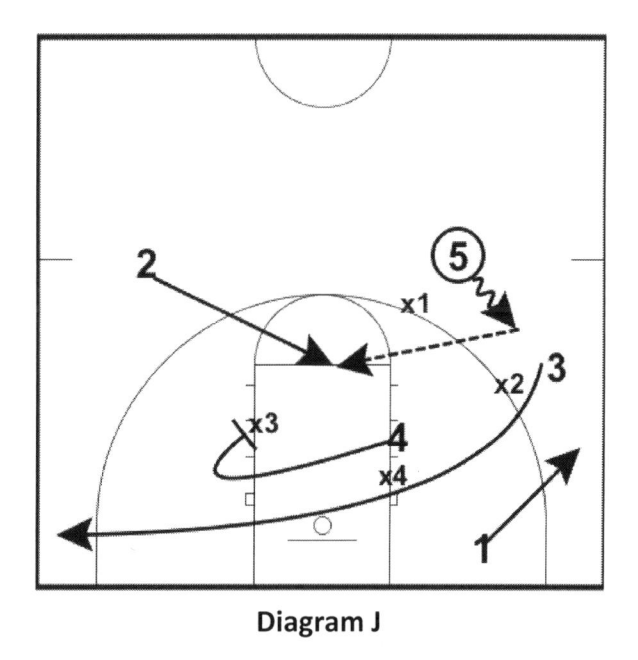

Drills to Teach Zone Attack Principles and Concepts

Diagram J

Number 21
3-on-4 Zone Attack

3-on-4 zone attack focuses on the perimeter concepts of attacking a zone defense. Screening, cutting, dribble attack and penetration concepts are all practiced. If shot attempts are allowed floor balance should be used as well. The defense can be in a 2-2 alignment or a 1-2-1 alignment to allow the offense to work against both a two-guard and one-guard front on defense.

Number 22
5-on-4 Zone Attack

5-on-4 zone attack combines perimeter and post zone attack concepts. Timing of cutting, screening and passing off dribble attack principles is the primary focus of this drill. Floor balance on an offensive shot attempt can be practiced as well.

Number 23
5-on-0 Perfect Attack

Practice does not make perfect, it makes permanent. Perfect practice makes both perfect and permanent.

Players are grouped in units of five players. Each unit must run the zone attack offense perfectly for a designated period of time. Failure to do so must result in a negative consequence. Perfect execution must result in a positive consequence.

The drill should be run 5-on-0. It is a good drill for any time of the season and is perfect right before a water break. This drill should be run only for one or two minutes. Be sure to define very carefully what is deemed perfect execution.

Number 24
Fan the Ball

Fan the ball drill combines feeding the post, posting up and fanning the ball. **Diagram A** depicts the drill sequence. This drill can be done in groups of three if space permits or from lines.

The post player must always look over the shoulder away from the baseline and square the shoulders to the target. After fanning the ball the post should v-cut and re-post to receive another pass. The original passer spots up for a fan pass and the drill continues (**Diagram B**).

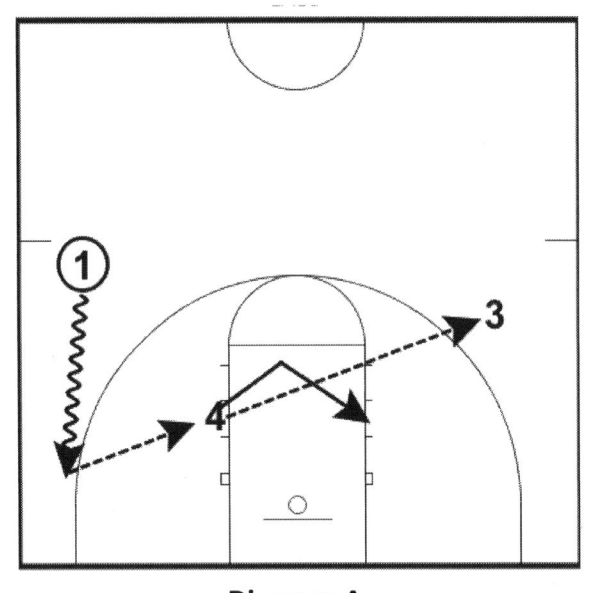

Diagram A

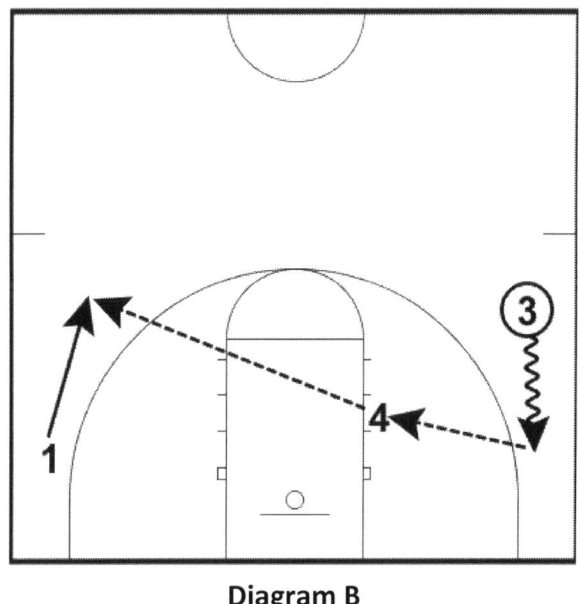

Diagram B

Number 25
Restricted Attack Drill

This drill is run 5-on-5. The offense must execute under specific restrictions. The offense is allowed to score only if the restrictions have been met. Failure to comply with the restrictions can result in a point for the defense or loss of possession.

An example of restrictions could be a minimum number of passes, down screening the zone and having two dribble-offs before a shot can be attempted.

Number 26
Change Drill

This drill places an emphasis on quick thinking. Two groups of five are on the court. One group runs zone attack and the other plays a designated zone defense. After 20 or 30 seconds of zone attack the coach shouts "change." The offense immediately places the ball down on the court and changes to defense. The defensive unit picks up the ball and immediately starts running zone attack.

After the first "change" takes place if the offense taking possession of the ball can score it is allowed to do so. Players like this drill and the intensity level will pick up quickly due to the competitive nature of the drill. Run the drill for 3 to 5 minutes maximum.

Number 27
5-on-0 Triangle Rebounding

This drill is used to teach the concepts involved in offensive floor balance on a shot attempt. Removing defense from the drill allows the players to focus on executing the concepts.

The coach passes the ball to different players to shoot. Shots must be taken from a variety of game shot locations to create game like rebounds. The offense reads the shot and forms the appropriate offensive rebounding triangle while the appropriate players balance the floor for defensive purposes. After several attempts rotate groups.

Number 28
Offensive Rebound Drill

Players will like this drill due to its competitive nature. Two groups of five are on the court. One group is in a zone offense alignment and the other a zone defense. The coach takes a shot and the two teams attempt to rebound the shot, make or miss.

The defense must block out and the offense must execute its floor balance scheme with two defenders back and three offensive players forming an offensive rebounding triangle. It the rebounding scheme calls for four offensive players to go to the glass that is certainly acceptable.

Each rebound counts as one point. The first team to score three points wins. After a consequence and reward have been administered, the teams switch roles and the drill continues.

Number 29
Offensive Rebounding for Threes

This drill is done 5-on-0 initially with defenders being added one at a time. The offense runs its zone attack and after a designated number of passes takes a shot. The offense rebounds the shot, make or miss, executes its floor balance and passes the ball out to the shooter at the top of the key for defensive balance for a three-point attempt.

Number 30
Transition Defense From Floor Balance

Five offensive players are on the court with no defense. The offense runs zone attack for a designated number of passes then takes a shot. The unit executes offensive floor balance and then makes defensive transition down the court. A pre-determined amount of time such as 3 or 4 seconds should be allotted for the entire process after the ball is scored (if the initial shot is missed the offensive rebound must be scored on a put back shot). Consequences and rewards can be attached to the drill. Times can be varied to fit the realistic speed of the group.

This drill is a great conditioning drill and can be substituted for sprints for conditioning. Players always prefer running that involves skills or concepts that will be used in a game over sprints alone.

35

Lagniappe

In my home state of Louisiana there is a concept known as something "lagniappe." It means something extra. The following few pages is an "extra" concept thrown in!

Attacking the Zone Defense With the Fast Break

One of the concepts mentioned earlier in this book is to beat the zone defense down the floor with the fast break and by doing so the offense does not have to face a zone defense, or any defense.

Even the best fast break teams will not always be able to achieve this goal. When this happens an effective way to attack a zone defense is to run a secondary break, also called early offense, to smoothly flow into the zone attack.

The following zone attack secondary break is one of the best I have ever seen in attacking zone defenses and better yet, it incorporates principles and concepts presented in this book. The pattern and spots the secondary break starts from are not written in stone.

This example is meant to demonstrate how to use concepts to create a fast break attack to utilize to flow into a zone attack offense and create scoring opportunities at the same time. By basing the secondary on zone attack principles there is less for the players to learn, freeing the players to be assertive in attacking the zone at the end of the fast break.

Diagram A on the next page shows the starting point for this secondary break. In this example the point guard has initiated the secondary with a 1-5 pass.

Coaching Basketball's Zone Attack Offense Using Blocker-Mover Motion Offense

Diagram A

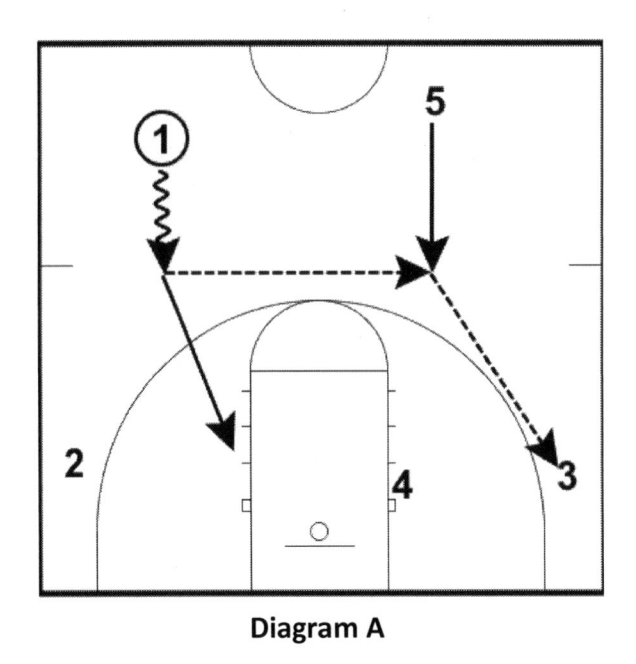

After passing the ball to #5, #1 makes a basket cut. #5 passes the ball to #3 and makes a basket cut to the low post opposite the ball. #3 dribbles off the baseline if a three-point shot or post entry pass is not available. #1 continues cutting all the way to the ball side corner and receives a pass from #3 (**Diagram B**).

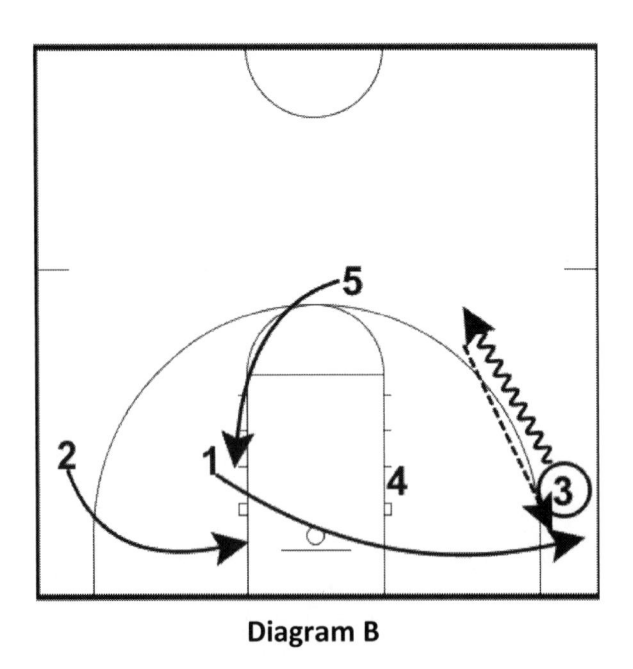

Diagram B

If #1 does not have a three-point shot or a post entry pass available, #1 also dribbles off the baseline. #2 cuts through the lane along the baseline to the ball side

296

corner. #3 makes a long cut to the corner opposite the ball side while #5 sets a screen-in. #1 can choose to pass the ball to #2 in the corner or make a skip pass to #3 to run the screen-in (**Diagram C**).

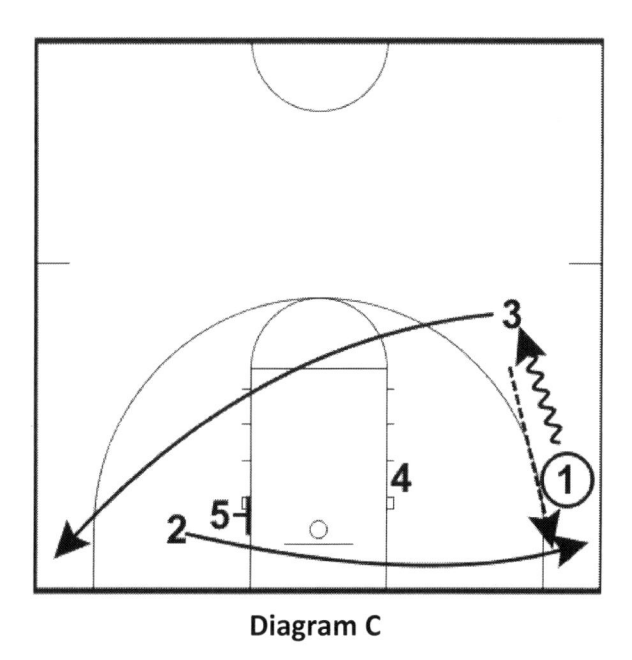

Diagram C

This simple break utilizes good spacing, bringing the ball to the post player, the baseline dribble off and the screen-in concept. The zone defense will be challenged quickly by the combination of concepts in rapid succession following quick defensive transition down the court.

36

About the Author

A 25 year veteran of the coaching profession, with twenty-two of those years spent as a varsity head coach, Coach Kevin Sivils amassed 479 wins and his teams earned berths in the state play-offs 19 out of 22 seasons with his teams advancing to the state semi-finals three times. An eight time Coach of the Year Award winner, Coach Sivils has traveled as far as the Central African Republic to conduct coaching clinics. Coach Sivils first coaching stint was as an assistant coach for his college alma mater, Greenville College, located in Greenville, Illinois.

Coach Sivils holds a BA with a major in physical education and a minor in social studies from Greenville College and a MS in Kinesiology with a specialization in Sport Psychology from Louisiana State University. He also holds a Sport Management certification from the United States Sports Academy.

In addition to being a basketball coach, Coach Sivils is a classroom instructor and has taught U.S. Government, U.S. History, the History of WW II, and Physical Education and has won awards for
excellence in teaching and Teacher of the Year. He has served as an Athletic Director and Assistant Athletic Director and has also been involved in numerous professional athletic organizations.

Sivils is married to the former Lisa Green of Jackson, Michigan, and the happy couple are the proud parents of three children, Danny, Katie, and Emily. Rounding out the Sivils family are three dogs, Angel, Berkeley, and Al. A native of Louisiana, Coach Sivils currently resides in the Great State of Texas.

37

To Contact the Author

By e-mail: kcsbasketball@comcast.net

Follow on Twitter:

http://twitter.com/#!/CoachSivils

Website: kcsbasketball.com

Please sign-up for the FREE e-newsletter, **The Roundball Report** from the link on the website.

While you are visiting, checkout the Hoops Blog and Basketball Store.

For More Blocker-Mover Motion Offense

Available from online book retailers!

Available from online book retailers!

What others are saying about *Game Strategy and Tactics for Basketball: Bench Coaching for Success:*

Game Strategy and Tactics for Basketball is a great compilation of ideas and thoughts that any coach for any sport at any level can benefit from. I have been involved in coaching basketball at the collegiate and scholastic level for 25 years and gained great insight and ideas by reading this book. As a coach, you can never stop learning, regardless of how long you have been in the profession. I have known Coach Sivils since 2002 and he is one of the most knowledgeable coaches I have ever known. He willingly shares his thoughts in this book. His thought provoking approach makes for an easy read and will definitely stimulate thought and, most likely, change the way you go about coaching!

Rusty Rogers - Two time NAIA Division II Women's National Championship Coach and Two time NAIA National Coach of the Year

"Coach Kevin Sivils is a respected coach and administrator who knows what is important in the game of basketball from actual game and practice experience. Split second decisions from the bench are often the defining moment in highly competitive games at any level. The ability to instantly and accurately give your team its best chance to win under pressure with a reasoned and wise "gut decision" cannot be underestimated. Your first step should be to read Kevin's book and then put his principles to use in your coaching career as you plan your strategy and tactics for the season and individual games.

Jack Bennett – Head Coach University of Wisconsin-Stevens Point (retired)
NCAA Men's Division III National Champions 2004 & 2005

"Coach Sivils book is the best I have ever read on the topic of bench coaching. I wish I'd had this information – all in one place – twenty years ago, because Coach Sivils addresses EVERY aspect of getting your team ready to win those close games: from time and score situations, selecting the right defensive or offensive strategy, making substitutions, or maximizing your home court advantage.

If you have been looking for a rigorously thorough handbook on basketball tactics and strategy, you have found it!"

Coach Doug Porter – Head Women's Coach, Olivet Nazarene University
National Scoring leaders: 2005, 2006, 2007, 2008
Chicagoland Collegiate Athletic Conference Champions: 2000, 2005, 2007

"Coach Sivils clearly brings his experience in the game of basketball to his writing. He is a great teacher who acquired great gifts over the years and it's great he wants to share those gifts with other coaches."

Bill Reidy - Long time successful high school and AAU coach

Made in the USA
Middletown, DE
10 December 2017